Ransomware Evolution

Ransomware is a type of malicious software that prevents victims from accessing their computers and the information they have stored. Typically, victims are required to pay a ransom, usually using cryptocurrency, such as Bitcoin, to regain access. Ransomware attacks pose a significant threat to national security, and there has been a substantial increase in such attacks in the post-Covid era. In response to these threats, large enterprises have begun implementing better cybersecurity practices, such as deploying data loss prevention mechanisms and improving backup strategies. However, cybercriminals have developed a hybrid variant called Ransomware 2.0. In this variation, sensitive data is stolen before being encrypted, allowing cybercriminals to publicly release the information if the ransom is not paid. Cybercriminals also take advantage of cryptocurrency's anonymity and untraceability.

Ransomware 3.0 is an emerging threat in which cybercriminals target critical infrastructures and tamper with the data stored on computing devices. Unlike in traditional ransomware attacks, cybercriminals are more interested in the actual data on the victims' devices, particularly from critical enterprises such as government, healthcare, education, defense, and utility providers. State-based cyber actors are more interested in disrupting critical infrastructures rather than seeking financial benefits via cryptocurrency. Additionally, these sophisticated cyber actors are also interested in obtaining trade secrets and gathering confidential information. It is worth noting that the misinformation caused by ransomware attacks can severely impact critical infrastructures and can serve as a primary weapon in information warfare in today's age. In recent events, Russia's invasion of Ukraine led to several countries retaliating against Russia. A ransomware group threatened cyber-attacks on the critical infrastructure of these countries. Experts warned that this could be the most widespread ransomware gang globally and is linked to a trend of Russian hackers supporting the Kremlin's ideology.

Ensuring cyber safety from ransomware attacks has become a national security priority for many nations across the world. The evolving variants of ransomware attacks present a wider and more challenging threat landscape, highlighting the need for collaborative work throughout the entire cyber ecosystem value chain. In response to this evolving threat, a book addressing the challenges associated with ransomware is very timely. This book aims to provide a comprehensive overview of the evolution, trends, techniques, impact on critical infrastructures and national security, countermeasures, and open research directions in this area. It will serve as a valuable source of knowledge on the topic.

Ransomware Evolution

Edited by
Mohiuddin Ahmed

CRC Press
Taylor & Francis Group
Boca Raton London New York

CRC Press is an imprint of the
Taylor & Francis Group, an **informa** business

Designed cover image: © Shutterstock

First edition published 2025
by CRC Press
2385 NW Executive Center Drive, Suite 320, Boca Raton FL 33431

and by CRC Press
4 Park Square, Milton Park, Abingdon, Oxon, OX14 4RN

CRC Press is an imprint of Taylor & Francis Group, LLC

ISBN: 978-1-032-74271-7 (hbk)
ISBN: 978-1-032-74498-8 (pbk)
ISBN: 978-1-003-46950-6 (ebk)

DOI: 10.1201/9781003469506

Typeset in Times LT Std
by Apex CoVantage, LLC

"My niblings: Faizaan, Faiza, Aleena, and Ayesha"

Contents

Preface

Ransomware is a type of malicious software that prevents victims from accessing their computers and the information they have stored. Typically, victims are required to pay a ransom, usually using cryptocurrency, such as Bitcoin, to regain access. Ransomware attacks pose a significant threat to national security, and there has been a substantial increase in such attacks in the post-Covid era. In response to these threats, large enterprises have begun implementing better cybersecurity practices, such as deploying data loss prevention mechanisms and improving backup strategies. However, cybercriminals have developed a hybrid variant called Ransomware 2.0. In this variation, sensitive data is stolen before being encrypted, allowing cybercriminals to publicly release the information if the ransom is not paid. Cybercriminals also take advantage of cryptocurrency's anonymity and untraceability.

Ransomware 3.0 is an emerging threat in which cybercriminals target critical infrastructures and tamper with the data stored on computing devices. Unlike in traditional ransomware attacks, cybercriminals are more interested in the actual data on the victims' devices, particularly from critical enterprises such as government, healthcare, education, defense, and utility providers. State-based cyber actors are more interested in disrupting critical infrastructures rather than seeking financial benefits via cryptocurrency. Additionally, these sophisticated cyber actors are also interested in obtaining trade secrets and gathering confidential information. It is worth noting that the misinformation caused by ransomware attacks can severely impact critical infrastructures and can serve as a primary weapon in information warfare in today's age. In recent events, Russia's invasion of Ukraine led to several countries retaliating against Russia. A ransomware group threatened cyberattacks on the critical infrastructure of these countries. Experts warned that this could be the most widespread ransomware gang globally and is linked to a trend of Russian hackers supporting the Kremlin's ideology.

Ensuring cyber safety from ransomware attacks has become a national security priority for many nations across the world. The evolving variants of ransomware attacks present a wider and more challenging threat landscape, highlighting the need for collaborative work throughout the entire cyber ecosystem value chain. In response to this evolving threat, a book addressing the challenges associated with ransomware is very timely. This book aims to provide a comprehensive overview of the evolution, trends, techniques, impact on critical infrastructures and national security, countermeasures, and open research directions in this area. It will serve as a valuable source of knowledge on the topic.

SECTION I History of Ransomware Groups

Chapter 1: A Brief History of Ransomware
Chapter 2: A Closer Look at the Famous Ransomware Groups

SECTION II Ransomware in Healthcare

Chapter 3: Actor Behaviour, Notable Incidents in Critical Infrastructures, and Risks to the Health Sector
Chapter 4: Ransomware: Impacts in Healthcare Critical Infrastructure
Chapter 5: The Evolution of Ransomware in Healthcare Organizations

SECTION III Ransomware Countermeasures

Chapter 6: Ransomware Threat Mitigation Techniques: Past, Present, and Future

SECTION IV Human Factors and Futuristic Challenges

The book is divided into four sections. The initial section comprises two chapters that delve into the historical aspects of ransomware while highlighting the key features of criminal groups. Moving on, the second section consists of three chapters that offer insights into different aspects of the ransomware ecosystem within the healthcare infrastructure. The third section includes three chapters that provide valuable information about ransomware defense tactics and strategies. Lastly, the fourth section covers the human factors within the ransomware ecosystem and presents a futuristic challenge tied to space systems.

Mohiuddin Ahmed
Editor

About the Editor

Dr. Mohiuddin Ahmed is dedicated to educating the next generation of cyber leaders and conducting research to disrupt the cybercrime ecosystem. His research focuses on ensuring national security and safeguarding critical infrastructures from cyber terrorists. Dr. Ahmed has edited several books and contributed articles to The Conversation. He has secured several external and internal grants totaling more than $1.7 million and has collaborated with academia and industry. Dr. Ahmed is a regular speaker at international conferences and public organizations and is sought after by the media for his expert opinion. Additionally, he is a Fellow of the Higher Education Academy, UK. He is also a Senior Member of IEEE and was an ACM Distinguished Speaker. He is an Associate Editor for the International Journal of Computers and Applications and Journal of Cyber Security Technology.

Contributors

Mohiuddin Ahmed
School of Science
Edith Cowan University
Perth, Australia

Md. Sawkat Ali
Department of Computer Science and Engineering
East West University
Dhaka, Bangladesh

Md. Sadi Arman
Institute of Information Technology
Jahangirnagar University
Bangladesh

Nazim Choudhury
Department of Computer Science
University of Wisconsin Green Bay
Wisconsin, USA

Abdullahi Chowdhury
Department of Computer Science and Engineering
East West University
Dhaka, Bangladesh

Michael Crowley
School of Science, Centre for Securing Digital Futures
Edith Cowan University
Perth, Australia

Martin Dart
School of Science
Edith Cowan University
Perth, Australia

Kellan Dempsey
Department of Computer Science
University of Wisconsin Green Bay
Wisconsin, USA

Abebe Diro
Department of Information Systems and Business Analytics
RMIT University
Melbourne, Australia

David Ekeh
School of Science
Edith Cowan University
Perth, Australia

Md. Hasanul Ferdaus
Department of Computer Science and Engineering
East West University
Dhaka, Bangladesh

Oliver Guidetti
School of Science
Edith Cowan University
Perth, Australia

Mahamudul Hasan
Department of Computer Science and Engineering
East West University
Dhaka, Bangladesh

Maheen Islam
Department of Computer Science and Engineering
East West University
Dhaka, Bangladesh

Mohammad Manzurul Islam
Department of Computer Science and Engineering
East West University
Dhaka, Bangladesh

Muhammad Usama Islam
School of Computing and Informatics
UL Lafayette, USA

Taskeed Jabid
Department of Computer Science and Engineering
East West University
Dhaka, Bangladesh

Nuray Jannat
Department of Computer Science and Engineering
BRAC University
Bangladesh

Michael N. Johnstone
School of Science, Centre for Securing Digital Futures
Edith Cowan University
Perth, Australia

Kassim Kalinaki
Department of Computer Science
Islamic University in Uganda, Mbale, Uganda
Borderline Research Laboratory
Kampala, Uganda

Salman Sayeed Khan
Department of Computer Science and Engineering
BRAC University
Bangladesh

Jiacheng Liu
School of Science, Edith Cowan University
Perth, Australia

Saleh Masum
Department of Information and Communication Engineering
University of Rajshahi
Rajshahi, Bangladesh

Scott Mather
The University of Notre Dame
Australia

Avisen Moonsamy
School of Science, Edith Cowan University
Perth, Australia

Glenn Murray
School of Science, Centre for Securing Digital Futures
Edith Cowan University
Perth, Australia

Bazlur Rashid
School of Science
Edith Cowan University
Perth, Australia

Mohammad Rifat Ahmmad Rashid
Department of Computer Science and Engineering
East West University
Dhaka, Bangladesh

Ulya Saputri
School of Science
Edith Cowan University
Perth, Australia

Rifat Ara Shams
CSIRO's Data61, Melbourne
Australia

Reemar Tan
School of Science
Edith Cowan University
Perth, Australia

Rashedul Amin Tuhin
Department of Computer Science and Engineering
East West University
Dhaka, Bangladesh

Jing Xiao
School of Science
Edith Cowan University
Perth, Australia

Thong Yang
Computer Science
University of Wisconsin Green Bay
Wisconsin, USA

Acknowledgements

I am extremely grateful for the wonderful book editing experience and would like to express my sincerest appreciation to the publisher for their invaluable support throughout the process. This journey has not only honed my editing skills but also strengthened our patience, communication, and perseverance. I extend my heartfelt thanks to all the contributors, reviewers, and the publishing team. Lastly, I owe a debt of gratitude to my family members whose unwavering support and encouragement have been instrumental in completing this book.

Section I

History of Ransomware Groups

1 A Brief History of Ransomware

Taskeed Jabid, Saleh Masum, Rifat Ara Shams, Abdullahi Chowdhury, Mohammad Manzurul Islam, Md. Hasanul Ferdaus, Md. Sawkat Ali, and Maheen Islam

1.1 INTRODUCTION

Ransomware, a type of malware, is designed to restrict access to the user's system or data until a ransom demanded by the attacker is paid [1]. Cybercriminals have enhanced their ransomware attacks by incorporating advanced encryption techniques, anonymous payment methods, and worm-like capabilities. They have also begun to offer ransomware-as-a-service (RaaS) [2], leveraging improvements in technology and lessons learned from past experiences.

In recent years, the number of ransomware incidents has significantly increased, targeting not just regular users but also governments and businesses across all sectors. Affected entities include Fortune 500 companies [3], banks [4], cloud providers [5], chip manufacturers, cruise operators [6], threat monitoring services [7], governments, medical centres [8], schools [9], universities, and police departments [10]. In 2020, the first death due to ransomware occurred in Germany [11]. These incidents reinforce the growing threat of ransomware, making it the top issue in the ongoing battle between governments, industries, academics, and threat actors.

Ransomware first appeared in 1989 and has been developing with more advanced encryption methods and spread capabilities for over three decades. It forces victims to pay ransoms and has become a common type of malware [12]. The global damage caused by ransomware is expected to surpass USD 265 billion by 2031, with an attack happening every 2 seconds [13].

The 2017 WannaCry attack drew attention back to ransomware. It showed how dangerous and profitable ransomware can be. The main goal of the attack was to create chaos and panic, not to make money. Even though the ransom demand was only USD 300, the overall financial damage was estimated at around USD 4 billion. The rise in recent cyber-attacks can largely be blamed on the COVID-19 pandemic. As companies moved to remote working, employees were more vulnerable to phishing emails, creating security weaknesses in the organization's defense against cyber-attacks. But what sets ransomware apart? It is malicious software designed to restrict users' access to their files, operating system, or device, demanding a ransom payment to restore access [14]. While it is widely known for attacking personal computers, it can also target mobile phones. It alters the device's PIN number and demands a ransom for the new PIN [15].

Ransomware is classified into two primary types – crypto ransomware and locker ransomware. Crypto ransomware is more common and focuses on encrypting files and data on the targeted device. On the other hand, locker ransomware incapacitates the device by locking it, but it typically leaves the stored data unharmed. If malware is successfully eradicated, locker ransomware is generally less effective as data can be saved by moving the storage component to another working device. Conversely, crypto ransomware makes data inaccessible, even after malware removal or moving the storage to another device. However, crypto ransomware generally leaves critical system files unharmed, allowing the device to work, which is potentially needed for ransom payment [15].

Before 2005, online payments weren't as widespread. People were told to pay ransom through text or mailing pre-paid cards. Sometimes, they had to call high-cost numbers where the attacker

DOI: 10.1201/9781003469506-2

made money. These payments could often be traced back to the attacker. However, in 2008, Bitcoin started to be used in ransom situations. Bitcoin is a digital currency that's difficult to trace, making it hard to find the attacker by following the payment. However, Bitcoin also has risks such as large exchange rate changes and hacking of major Bitcoin exchanges [15]. Crypto ransomware often prefers Bitcoin for payments, while locker ransomware tends to favor payment voucher systems. This is largely due to the functionality of the infected computer – Bitcoin can easily be purchased on a machine infected by crypto ransomware, but the lock placed on a system by locker ransomware makes this more difficult. Therefore, locker ransomware victims often resort to buying payment vouchers locally. For the cybercriminals, it's essential to convert the acquired ransomware into usable cash. The method depends on the type of ransomware – for example, those using payment vouchers often launder money using online betting services, transferring it to prepaid cards and using individuals to withdraw the cash. Bitcoin, because of its anonymity, can be spent directly, but due to fear of law enforcement, many criminals resort to Bitcoin-laundering or anonymizing services [15].

A growing concern is politically motivated ransomware, in which state-supported hackers target politically sensitive or strategically important organizations or nations. The attacks are often carefully crafted, leading to the loss of important data, financial impacts, or disruption of critical services. Interestingly, these cyber threats can often be linked to specific countries, leaving a traceable geopolitical impact. Currently, politically motivated ransomware poses a serious security concern that requires immediate response [16].

1.2 RANSOMWARE VERSUS MALWARE

Ransomware and malware are two cybersecurity terminologies often misused interchangeably, but they possess distinct differences. The term *malware*, abbreviated from malicious software, serves as an umbrella term that encompasses ransomware. This distinction implies that, while all ransomware falls under the category of malware, not all malware cases are identified as ransomware. Let's explore in greater depth the subtle yet significant differences among these two forms of cyberattacks.

1.2.1 What Is Malware?

Malware, which stands for "malicious software," includes all categories of harmful or intrusive software including viruses, worms, Trojans, ransomware, and spyware. The purpose of this software is to illicitly access and steal data, override access controls, and infiltrate personal computers. Malware does more than just access; it can essentially cause critical damage to the targeted computer's data or applications [17]. Let's delve into the various types of malware.

1.2.1.1 Spyware

Spyware, a specific category of malware, monitors computer activities. Upon infiltrating an operating system, spyware commences surveilling device-related activities. It records critical information such as passwords, browsing history, social media interaction, and even financial data. Some spyware variants possess the ability to hijack certain device functionality like webcams or microphones, enabling them to record audio and video clandestinely. The harvested information is subsequently transmitted to the perpetrator who orchestrated this malicious scheme [18].

1.2.1.2 Keyloggers

Keyloggers exclusively focus on covertly capturing usernames and passwords [19].

1.2.1.3 Trojan Horses

These are harmful codes or software that pretend to be real apps or files, tricking users into unknowingly installing dangerous malware on their devices [20].

1.2.1.4 Cryptojacking

This involves the unauthorized utilization of another individual's computer system to mine cryptocurrency. This can occur through deceptive phishing techniques or by contaminating a website with JavaScript code that automatically executes on a user's computer [21].

1.2.1.5 Viruses

These types of malware are engineered to propagate from one computer system to another, causing widespread damage [22].

1.2.1.6 Rootkits

This form of malware is specifically designed to enable access to unauthorized areas of a computer, posing significant security threats [23].

1.2.1.7 Spam Bots

Essentially, bots are applications engineered to carry out repetitive tasks. They are categorized as malware when they engage in harmful operations, such as directing web traffic as part of a DDoS (distributed denial-of-service) attack or disseminating spam [24].

1.2.1.8 Worms

These are stand-alone malware programs which are capable of self-replication in order to spread to multiple systems [25].

1.2.2 Adware

This type of software consistently displays advertisements while operating, often in intrusive ways [26].

1.2.3 What Is Ransomware?

Ransomware is a type of malicious software that prevents users from accessing their data unless they pay a certain ransom. The name is a portmanteau of "ransom" and "malware." There are two main categories of ransomware: locker ransomware and crypto ransomware. The former denies users the ability to log into their computers, while the latter encrypts the target data, rendering it unreadable. Upon receipt of the demanded ransom, the attacker offers to provide the decryption key [1]. Here are some examples of ransomware.

1.2.3.1 AIDS Trojan

Dr. Joseph Popp, an evolutionary biologist, wrote the AIDS Trojan, one of the first known examples of ransomware. He spread this by sending infected floppy disks, titled "AIDS Information Introductory Diskette," to numerous people.

1.2.3.2 GPCode

GPCode, first seen in 2004, attacked victims using phishing emails and malicious website links [14].

1.2.3.3 Archievus

Archievus, first detected in 2006, marked a turning point in ransomware development as it was the first to use RSA (Rivest–Shamir–Adleman) encryption [14].

1.2.3.4 WinLock

WinLock, a prominent ransomware, would take over the user's screen and display inappropriate images, forcing the user to send a paid SMS to get their computer access back [14].

1.2.3.5 CryptoLocker

CryptoLocker, a well-known ransomware, attacked about 250,000 Windows computers. It wasn't only targeting professionals but also home internet users. The main way it spread in 2013–2014 appeared to be phishing emails with harmful attachments [14].

1.2.3.6 WannaCry

The infamous WannaCry malware from 2017, which targets Windows PCs, is likely the most notorious of all time. Cyber attackers are still actively using it today [14].

1.3 HISTORY OF RANSOMWARE

In today's cyberspace, introduction of ransomware is not new. In this section, we will discuss the chronological evolution of ransomware, beginning from its creation in 1989 until now. An illustration of the evolution and key developments in ransomware can be found in Figure 1.1.

- **1989:** The AIDS Trojan, also called PC Cyborg, created in 1989, is known as the first-ever ransomware [27]. Twenty thousand virus-infected floppy disks were distributed to the participants of the AIDS conference via mail. The software was designed to encrypt file names on the C:\ drive of the infected computer using a novel symmetric encryption algorithm, leading to demands for ransom. Seven years later, analysts elaborated on the shortcomings of the so-called PC Cyborg and introduced a progressive concept in cryptovirology [28]. They crafted a proof-of-concept (PoC) malware, employing public key cryptography to encrypt user data, as a preventive measure to alert the community about potential online extortion crimes in the future [29].
- **2005–2006:** Ransomware, despite early versions such as the AIDS Trojan and the use of cryptovirology, was mostly inactive until 2005. This was likely due to a lack of advanced technology, limited internet access, and the newness of the World Wide Web (WWW). However, with the increased use of the internet and the WWW, and the creation of social media, blogs, and online shopping, the number of internet users grew to one billion by 2005

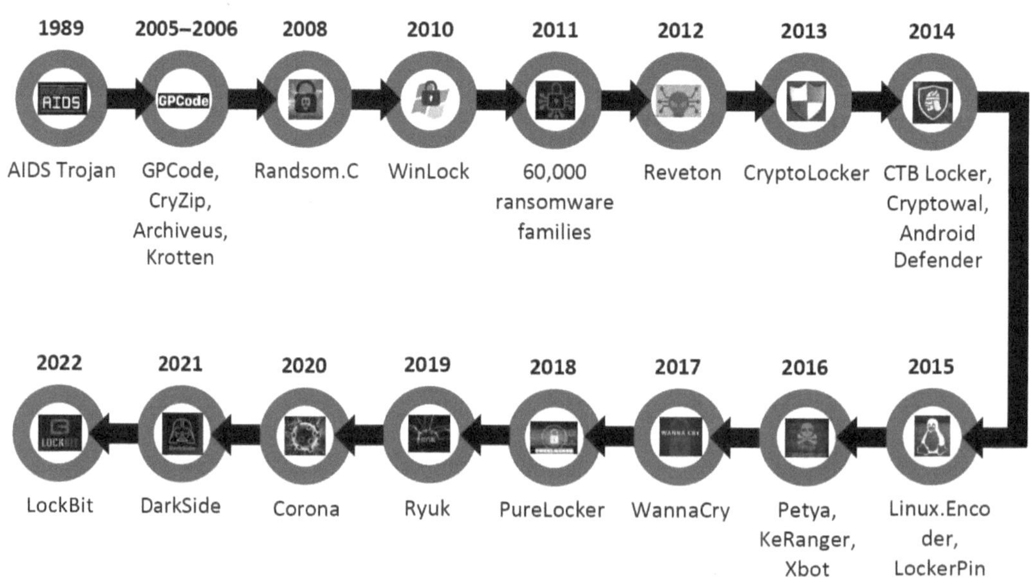

FIGURE 1.1 Evolution of ransomware.

[30]. This resurgence in digital activity led to the return of ransomware, with GPCode as the first modern example. GPCode infected computers via phishing emails and used its own encryption system to lock users' files, storing the encryption key on the affected computer. Despite not being a very effective approach, GPCode set a pattern for future ransomware designs [11]. CryZip, Archiveus, and Krotten were ransomware families that appeared between 2005 and 2006. They were the first to use asymmetric encryption, which involves both public and private keys. This encryption method made it extremely difficult to retrieve data without the attacker's decryption key, representing a significant development in ransomware technology [11].

- **2008:** The first instance of locker ransomware, Randsom.C, emerged in 2008. It locked the user's desktop and showed a ransom message supposedly from Windows Security Center, requesting the user to call a premium-rate phone number to reactivate their license [11]. That same year, Seftad ransomware introduced a new technique of altering the targeted computer's master boot record (MBR) to stop normal booting [31]. It then demanded a ransom payment made through prepaid methods like Paysafecard [11].
- **2010:** WinLock, which appeared around 2010, was a leading type of ransomware. It would take over the user's screen to display explicit images, and the user had to pay a ransom through a paid SMS to regain control of their computer. This unique and aggressive malware caused significant concern among computer users and security experts [14].
- **2011:** Before cryptocurrencies came along, ransomware creators had a significant problem: they struggled to receive ransom payments in a way that didn't restrict them geographically, put them at risk from local law enforcement, and compromised their anonymity. They also needed to be able to transfer large sums of ransom payments. After 2009, cryptocurrencies like Bitcoin became commonplace and solved these challenges for cybercriminals. Because blockchain was believed to maintain the anonymity of these bad actors (though, in reality, blockchain transactions can be traced, making them pseudo-anonymous), ransomware developers were able to bypass their largest operational barrier. This development resulted in a surge of ransomware attacks, with roughly 60,000 new ransomware families being detected in 2011 [11].
- **2012:** In 2012, a significant locker ransomware called Reveton, also known as Police ransomware, emerged with a new approach. Besides locking the victim's computer, it also attempted to extract important information from it [32].
- **2013:** CryptoLocker, first appearing in 2013, was a significant and advanced ransomware that encrypted certain files (like .pdf and .zip) with 2,048-bit RSA and demanded ransom in Bitcoin [11]. It was named the most malicious malware threat of 2013, affecting approximately 250,000 Windows computers by the end of the year. It was found that the criminals behind this were targeting not only professionals but also home internet users. The primary source of infection seemed to be phishing emails with malicious attachments [14]. It initially encrypted 67 file types, including Microsoft Office data files. Victims were given three days to pay about two Bitcoins (equivalent to USD 100 at the time. If the three-day deadline was not met, victims had the option to pay a higher ransom to recover their files. By November, the value of two Bitcoins rose to USD 460, and the penalty for missing the original deadline was increased to ten Bitcoins. By December, the ransomware had infected 250,000 machines and received about 41,928 Bitcoins in ransom payments. A second version called CryptoLocker 2.0 was released later that year by different perpetrators. Throughout 2013, the number of attacks escalated from 100,000 in January to 600,000 in December, with 3% of infected users paying the ransom [15].

Between September 2013 and May 2014, CryptoLocker infected over 500,000 victims, with about 1.3% paying the ransom. In June, a coalition known as Operation Tovar shut down the servers distributing CryptoLocker. Tech companies FireEye and Fox-IT found and released the decryption keys for victims, allowing them to decrypt their files for free.

In February, a weaker ransomware called CryptoDefense was released, and despite its flaws, it generated USD 34,000 in its debut month. An improved version, CryptoWall, was launched in April 2014. It exploited Java vulnerability and spread through malicious ads, earning over USD 1,000,000 in ransom [15].

- **2014:** In 2014, the Curve-Tor-Bitcoin (CTB) Locker emerged, with its label reflecting the key technologies it employed. "Curve" indicated its utilization of Elliptic Curve Cryptography (ECC) for encryption purposes, "TOR" symbolized its reliance on an anonymity-preserving web browsing scheme during ransom payment, and "Bitcoin" denoted the currency used for extortion [33]. In the same year, another cryptographic ransomware called Cryptowall appeared. It used TOR and Bitcoin for operations while deleting volume shadow copies to disable file restoration. This virus infected more than 600,000 systems [11]. The first mobile locker ransomware, Android Defender, emerged in 2014, deceiving users by posing as a legitimate antivirus application [34]. In 2015, Android Defender evolved into the first mobile cryptographic ransomware. Upon infection, it scanned the mobile device's SD card, encrypting files with certain extensions using AES. Decrypting the files was possible by extracting the encryption key hard-coded into the binary [35].
- **2015:** Ransomware began targeting different operating systems from 2015. Linux.Encoder [36] was the first to target GNU/Linux platforms in 2015, encrypting the home directory and website administration directories.

  By the end of 2015, the FBI stated that CryptoLocker attacks had made USD 27 million from ransom payments. CryptoWall overtook CryptoLocker as the main type of ransomware. A study found that ransomware attacks increased by 17.7% between 2014 and 2015, while crypto ransomware attacks surged by 448%. By May, attackers could create ransomware for free using a TOR website, which managed payment and took a 20% cut from each ransom. In September, LockerPin was launched, which infiltrates Android systems, changes the PIN, and charges a ransom of USD 500. In October, it was reported that the total damages from ransomware were USD 325,000,000. A Russian firm named Dr. Web found a new ransomware named Linus.Encoder.1, which targets Linux systems and encrypts files. In November, the fourth version of CryptoWall came about. It uses a new protocol to avoid detection and changes the file names when it encrypts, making it difficult to see what files have been affected [15].
- **2016:** In January, a JavaScript-only RaaS was detected, threatening multiple platforms including Linux and MacOS X. In February, thousands of WordPress sites, a frequently used blogging platform, were infected with ransomware. In April, Petya, a ransomware that locks the entire hard disk until ransom is paid, was discovered. This malware works by overwriting the MBR of the infected computer, hindering its operating system from recovering the unencrypted files [15]. Apple had to issue an update in response to the KeRanger ransomware, the first to target Apple computers [11]. KeRanger activates after three days of installation and encrypts over 300 file types [15]. In February, an Android malware named Xbot was found targeting devices in Australia and Russia, encrypting files and attempting to steal online banking details. In July, Locky ransomware introduced a failsafe to start encrypting files even if a unique encryption key couldn't be requested due to a computer being offline or communication being blocked. Ransomware generated an estimated USD 209 million in the first three months of 2016, putting it on track to a billion-dollar crime. In the same period, 1.2 million ransomware attacks occurred, a 24% increase from the last quarter of 2015. The three main versions are CryptoWall, CTB-Locker, and TorrentLocker. CryptoWall targets both internal and external storage devices, while CTB-Locker and TorrentLocker have affiliate sales programs and harvest email addresses for spamming [15].
- **2017:** In 2017, the WannaCry ransomware emerged and turned out to be the worst cybercrime of the year. It impacted over 250,000 systems across 150 countries by exploiting a

weakness in the Microsoft Windows SMB Server Remote Code Execution Vulnerability [11]. The ransomware used AES encryption on each file with a unique key, which was then further encrypted using a 2048-bit RSA [37].
- **2018:** In 2018, a platform-independent ransomware named PureLocker, written in PureBasic language, emerged. It used hybrid encryption and presented a ransom note, asking victims to contact the attacker through Proton, a secure and untraceable email service [11].
- **2019:** Recently, cybercriminals have begun developing new types of ransomware specifically targeting certain victims. Ryuk, appearing in 2019, targeted only enterprises. Differing from other ransomware, Ryuk primarily infected targets through other malware, particularly TrickBot [11].
- **2020:** In 2020, a very harmful kind of malware called Egregor ransomware was a major threat. This nasty malware is known for its harsh double-extortion methods. Even though it's very destructive, not much is known about it because it uses complex techniques to avoid detection. Egregor is potentially linked to the now non-existent Maze ransomware. Another ransomware, known as Conti, causes a lot of damage with its quick data encryption and spreading abilities. The Conti gang usually uses scam emails to install harmful programs, which lets them control infected computers remotely. After the data is locked, Conti uses a two-step blackmail method [14]. During the 2020 global pandemic, the demand for health centers increased, making them more vulnerable to ransomware attacks. These attacks on health organizations even increased to the point where a new ransomware called Corona was created, which targeted hospitals by encrypting patient health records and displaying a COVID-19-themed ransom message [11].
- **2021:** DarkSide, first seen in mid-2020, carried out the worst cyber-attack of 2021 on the Colonial Pipeline. They only target organizations that can pay large ransoms and avoid governmental, non-profit, and hospital targets [14].
- **2022:** In 2022, the majority of cyber-attacks originated from emerging variants employing duplicitous extortion tactics. In the RaaS arena, the LockBit ransomware quickly built a reputation, attributed primarily to its frequent advancement in attack methods [14].

The evolution of ransomware reveals its origins as a relatively ineffectual threat in 1989, lacking swift, robust encryption methods, various infection vectors, pseudonymous payment methods, and an extensive array of targets. However, as technology advanced, ransomware developers learned from both their failures and technological progress, which has resulted in ransomware ascending to the top of the list of cyber threats. This progression has profound impacts, not only on individual end-users but also on organizations, enterprises, and fundamental infrastructures. Initial ransomware attacks allowed security researchers room to successfully retrieve the files or systems, though this window gradually closed. Nowadays, it's virtually impossible to recover the files or systems without paying the demanded ransom or having a backup available. Successful ransomware attacks inflict significant damage, causing targets to lose not only money and time, but potentially damaging their reputation significantly. The evolution of ransomware continues with transitions from platform-dependent to platform-independent systems and from simple ransomware to a comprehensive RaaS model. All these factors together are contributing to the ever-increasing prevalence of ransomware, making it a pervasive threat to almost all computerized systems.

1.4 NOTABLE RANSOMWARE INCIDENTS

Cybersecurity threats, especially ransomware attacks, have notably escalated, posing significant challenges for organizations around the globe. These malicious operations disrupt essential services, result in substantial data loss and financial burdens, and diminish stakeholder trust. The meticulous examination of several recent ransomware incidents reveals the profound impact of these cyberattacks on various sectors. This analysis not only highlights the tactics and vulnerabilities exploited by attackers but also underscores the pressing need for enhanced cybersecurity measures and greater awareness among potential targets.

In the first half of 2022, there were an estimated 236.1 million ransomware attacks globally, a marked decrease from the 623.3 million attacks recorded in 2021. Despite this decline, ransomware still accounted for approximately 20% of all cybercrimes in 2022. The average cost of a ransomware attack in 2022, as reported by IBM, was $4.54 million, excluding the ransom itself, underscoring the substantial financial impact of these attacks. Chainalysis reports that ransomware attackers extorted at least $456.8 million from victims in 2022, a decrease from the $765.6 million reported the previous year. This reduction is attributed more to the growing unwillingness of victims to pay ransoms rather than a decline in the actual number of attacks. Forbes has issued a warning that by 2025, the world could face a staggering $10 trillion in cybersecurity-related costs if the current approach to cybersecurity remains unchanged [38].

The incidents in 2022 showcased the diverse and evolving threat landscape. High-profile cases included the ransomware attack on Nvidia by the Lapsus$ group, which demanded $1 million and additional fees for the release of sensitive data [39]. Costa Rica faced a national crisis due to attacks by the Conti group, significantly disrupting its economy and government operations [40]. The healthcare sector was also targeted, as seen with CHI Health, a subsidiary of CommonSpirit Health, experiencing disruptions and data breaches [41]. Educational institutions were not spared, with the Los Angeles Unified School District falling victim to the Vice Society group, leading to the exposure of confidential student information [42]. Furthermore, hospitals, including Texas Methodist McKinney Hospital and St. Charles Health System, faced ransomware attacks that had dire consequences on patient care and staff payment processes [41].

The year 2023 saw ransomware attacks become not only more frequent but significantly more sophisticated, with phishing emails remaining the primary attack vector. The REvil ransomware group was responsible for a large portion of these attacks, showcasing the extensive reach and impact of their operations. The increase in ransomware incidents by more than 95% in 2022 affected 72% of businesses globally, highlighting the escalating challenge posed by cybercriminals. The financial impact also grew, with the average cost of a ransomware attack reaching $1.85 million in 2023, and the global average cost of a data breach climbing to $4.45 million, marking a 15% increase over three years [43].

Noteworthy attacks in 2023 further emphasized the persistent threat of ransomware. The Dish Network experienced significant service disruptions, affecting nearly 300,000 individuals. NCR, a financial services firm, was hit by a ransomware attack claimed by the BlackCat/AlphV group, disrupting payment systems. The MOVEit attack demonstrated the vulnerability of software systems, impacting numerous corporations and U.S. federal agencies [44]. Municipal services were also targeted, as seen in the City of Dallas ransomware attack, compromising the personal information of over 30,000 residents. Additionally, suppliers to major corporations like TSMC (Taiwan Semiconductor Manufacturing Company Limited) faced attacks, illustrating the wide-reaching effects of ransomware across different sectors.

These incidents collectively highlight the critical challenges posed by ransomware. They underscore the urgency for robust cybersecurity defenses, proactive measures, and enhanced awareness to mitigate the risks and impacts of these malicious activities. The continuous evolution of ransomware tactics necessitates a vigilant and comprehensive approach to cybersecurity, emphasizing the need for organizations to adapt and strengthen their defenses against these relentless threats.

The increasing risk and impact of ransomware attacks on businesses and organizations highlight a crucial aspect of modern cybersecurity efforts. These attacks, which encrypt a victim's data and demand payment for its release, have become more sophisticated over time, exploiting digital and human vulnerabilities with devastating efficiency. The consequences of ransomware extend beyond the immediate financial cost of the ransom; they can disrupt operations, damage reputations, result in the loss of customer trust, and even lead to legal ramifications associated with data breaches. The operational downtime that follows an attack can lead to significant business losses, including the loss of critical opportunities and, in severe cases, the complete cessation of business activities.

Given the complex and evolving nature of ransomware threats, conducting a thorough analysis to understand and mitigate these risks is imperative. Such an analysis involves examining the tactics, techniques, and procedures used by cybercriminals, identifying potential vulnerabilities within an organization's infrastructure, and keeping abreast of the latest in cybersecurity developments and threat intelligence. This proactive approach enables organizations to tailor their cybersecurity defenses to their specific needs and vulnerabilities, ensuring a more robust protection against potential attacks.

Identifying vulnerabilities within an organization's systems and processes is a critical outcome of this analysis. It allows for the prioritization of security enhancements, software updates, and stronger access control measures to safeguard against intrusion. Moreover, this analysis underpins the development of effective incident response and recovery strategies, equipping organizations with the plans and procedures needed to respond swiftly and efficiently to attacks, thereby minimizing damage and downtime.

A deep understanding of ransomware threats informs strategic decision-making regarding cybersecurity investments. Organizations can allocate their resources more effectively, choosing technologies and training programs that offer the most significant risk reduction. This strategic approach not only enhances an organization's defensive posture but also ensures compliance with regulatory requirements, reducing the risk of legal and compliance issues in the aftermath of an attack.

Thorough analysis and education on ransomware threats are essential for fostering a culture of cybersecurity awareness among all employees. Training and awareness programs are crucial in teaching staff to recognize and appropriately respond to phishing attempts and suspicious activities, significantly reducing the risk of a successful ransomware attack.

As ransomware attacks continue to pose a significant and growing threat to global businesses, the importance of thorough analysis and proactive cybersecurity measures cannot be overstated. By understanding the threat landscape and implementing targeted defenses, organizations can protect themselves against the multifaceted dangers of ransomware, ensuring that their operations remain resilient in the face of this pervasive cyber threat.

1.5 EMERGING THREATS

Ransomware attacks have increased by 80% annually, with more than 37,700 incidents occurring every hour globally. This rate amounts to approximately 578 ransomware attacks each minute. The United States has been the most targeted country, accounting for 47% of all ransomware attacks on organizations. Other significantly affected countries include Italy (8%), Australia (8%), Brazil (6%), and Germany (6%). Phishing remained the most common entry point for ransomware attacks, responsible for 41% of incidents. Moreover, there was a 33% increase in ransomware attacks caused by vulnerability exploitation between 2020 and 2021. June 2021 saw the highest number of ransomware attacks, making up 33% of the total for the year [45].

The manufacturing industry was the most affected by ransomware, with 23% of incidents targeting this sector. In 2021, ransomware attacks cost the US healthcare sector an estimated $7.8 billion in downtime alone, affecting over 19.7 million patient records across 108 individual attacks. Ransom demands ranged from around $250,000 to $5 million.

The top five ransomware strains by quarter from 2022 through 2024, by tracking the relative activity of various strains, are Conti, LockBit, Hive, Royal, BlackBasta, and Play. In 2022 Q1, Conti was the dominant strain but declined sharply following its announced support for the Russian government in February 2022, leading to the emergence of Hive, which saw a large spike in activity as victims became less willing to pay Conti's ransom demands. From 2022 Q2 onward, new strains like Royal, BlackBasta, and Play gained prominence, while LockBit maintained a consistent presence. By 2024, the ransomware landscape appeared more diverse, with multiple strains struggling for dominance and no single strain accounting for more than 25% of activity [45].

The destinations of funds leaving ransomware wallets in 2018–2022 show the diverse destinations of funds. The destinations include sanctions, peer-to-peer (P2P) exchanges, mixing services, mining operations, illicit sources, high-risk jurisdictions and exchanges, gambling platforms, decentralized finance (DeFi) platforms, and centralized exchanges. A consistent presence of funds has been seen across high-risk exchanges and jurisdictions over the years, while the usage of P2P exchanges has slightly decreased. There is an increase in funds channeled to DeFi platforms in 2022, and the proportion dedicated to mixing services, indicative of attempts to obscure the origin of the funds, remains notable [46].

The landscape of ransomware attacks is expected to evolve and intensify, posing even greater challenges for organizations and individuals alike. Several key trends are likely to shape the future of these cyber threats.

- **Increased Sophistication and Targeted Attacks:** Ransomware attackers are becoming more sophisticated in their techniques, leveraging advanced technologies like artificial intelligence and machine learning to enhance their malware's effectiveness. This will lead to more targeted attacks, where cybercriminals meticulously select their victims based on factors such as industry, revenue, and perceived willingness to pay ransoms. These targeted attacks will be more difficult to detect and prevent, requiring organizations to adopt proactive and multi-layered defense strategies [47].
- **Rise of Ransomware-as-a-Service (RaaS):** The emergence of RaaS models will further democratize the cybercrime landscape, enabling even non-technical actors to launch ransomware attacks. RaaS platforms provide ready-made malware, infrastructure, and support, lowering the barrier to entry for cybercriminals. This trend will likely lead to an increase in the overall volume of ransomware attacks, as well as a diversification of the attackers' profiles and motivations [48].
- **Exploitation of Internet of Things (IoT) and Remote Work Vulnerabilities:** The proliferation of IoT devices and the widespread adoption of remote work practices will create new attack vectors for ransomware operators. IoT devices often lack robust security features and can serve as entry points into corporate networks. Similarly, remote work arrangements can expose organizations to risks associated with unsecured home networks and personal devices. Attackers will increasingly target these vulnerabilities to gain access to sensitive data and critical systems [49].
- **Convergence of Ransomware and Data Exfiltration:** Ransomware attacks will increasingly be accompanied by data exfiltration, where attackers not only encrypt the victim's data but also steal it. This trend, known as "double extortion," puts additional pressure on victims to pay the ransom, as the threat of sensitive data being leaked or sold on the dark web looms large. Organizations will need to focus not only on preventing ransomware infections but also on detecting and mitigating data breaches promptly [50].
- **Geopolitical Influences and State-Sponsored Attacks:** Geopolitical tensions and state-sponsored cyber activities will continue to shape the ransomware landscape. Nation-states may employ ransomware as a tool for economic warfare, industrial espionage, or political coercion. The involvement of state actors can make attribution and legal recourse more challenging, as they often operate with impunity. Organizations, especially those in critical infrastructure sectors or with ties to government entities, will need to be vigilant against these politically motivated attacks [51].
- **Regulatory Pressure and Reporting Requirements:** As the impact of ransomware attacks grows, governments and regulatory bodies are likely to impose stricter reporting requirements and penalties for non-compliance. Organizations may be required to disclose ransomware incidents promptly, and failure to do so could result in significant fines and

legal consequences. This increased regulatory pressure will compel companies to invest more in cybersecurity measures, incident response capabilities, and transparency in their dealings with ransomware attacks [52].

1.6 CONCLUSIONS AND FUTURE CHALLENGES

The evolution of ransomware, from its inception in 1989 to the present day, has been marked by a significant increase in sophistication, frequency, and impact. Ransomware attacks have become a pervasive threat to organizations and individuals worldwide, causing substantial financial losses, operational disruptions, and reputational damage. The analysis of notable ransomware incidents has highlighted the tactics employed by attackers, the vulnerabilities exploited, and the pressing need for robust cybersecurity measures.

As technology continues to advance and our reliance on digital systems grows, the ransomware landscape is expected to evolve and intensify, presenting even greater challenges for cybersecurity professionals and organizations alike. The increasing sophistication of attacks, the rise of RaaS models, the exploitation of IoT and remote work vulnerabilities, and the convergence of ransomware with data exfiltration are just a few of the emerging threats that organizations must contend with in the near future.

Geopolitical influences and state-sponsored attacks are likely to further complicate the ransomware landscape, blurring the lines between criminal activities and nation-state objectives. This development will require organizations to adopt a more comprehensive and proactive approach to cybersecurity, taking into account not only technical vulnerabilities but also the broader political and social context in which they operate.

As the impact of ransomware attacks continues to grow, regulatory pressure and reporting requirements are also expected to increase. Organizations will need to invest in robust incident response capabilities, transparency, and compliance measures to meet these evolving regulatory demands and mitigate the legal and financial consequences of a successful attack.

To effectively combat the ransomware threat, organizations must embrace a multi-faceted approach that encompasses technical controls, employee awareness training, and strategic partnerships with cybersecurity experts and law enforcement agencies. Continuous monitoring, threat intelligence sharing, and regular security audits will be essential to staying ahead of the ever-evolving tactics employed by ransomware operators.

The development of advanced technologies such as artificial intelligence and machine learning will play a crucial role in the fight against ransomware. These technologies can help organizations detect and respond to threats more quickly and accurately, reducing the potential impact of an attack. However, as attackers also leverage these technologies to enhance their malware, the cybersecurity community must remain vigilant and proactive in their defense strategies.

The ransomware landscape is set to become increasingly complex and challenging in the years to come. Organizations must adapt and evolve their cybersecurity strategies to keep pace with the growing sophistication and frequency of these attacks. By prioritizing cybersecurity, fostering a culture of awareness, and investing in advanced defense technologies, organizations can build the resilience necessary to withstand the ongoing threat of ransomware and safeguard their critical assets and reputations in the digital age.

REFERENCES

1. C. Barbarin-Renvoise, L. Cizeron, N. Gloux, and J. A. Kinie, "How and why do ransomwares escape the notice of some security tools?," January, 2023.
2. Segun I. Popoola, Ujioghosa B. Iyekekpolo, Samuel O. Ojewande, Faith O. Sweetwilliams, Samuel N. John, and Aderemi A. Atayero, "Ransomware: Current trend, challenges, and research directions," *Proceedings of the World Congress on Engineering and Computer Science*, vol. 1, pp. 169–174, 2017.

3. S. T. H. Team, "Wastedlocker: Symantec identifies wave of attacks against us organizations," https://symantec-enterprise-blogs.security.com/blogs/threat-intelligence/wastedlocker-ransomware-us, 2020.
4. C. Cimpanu, "Chilean bank shuts down all branches following ransomware attack," https://www.zdnet.com/article/chilean-bank-shuts-down-all-branches-following-ransomware-attack/, 2020.
5. Catalin Cimpanu, "Cloud provider stopped ransomware attack but had to pay ransom demand anyway," https://www.zd-net. com/article/cloud-provider-stopped-ransomware-attack-but-had-to-pay-ransom-demand-anyway/, 2020.
6. R. Staff, "Carnival hit by ransomware attack," https://www.reuters.com/article/us-carnival-cyber/carnival-hit-by-ransomware-attack-guest-and-employee-data-accessed-idUSKCN25D2GR, 2020.
7. J. O'Ryan, "Connectwise partners hit by ransomware via automate flaw," https://www.crn.com/news/channel-programs/connectwise-partners-hit-by-ransomware-via-automate-flaw, 2020.
8. K. Collier, "Major hospital system hit with cyberattack, potentially largest in us history," *NBC News*, 2020.
9. L. Abrams, "Suncrypt ransomware shuts down North Carolina school district," https://www.bleepingcomputer.com/news/security/suncrypt-ransomware-shuts-down-north-carolina-school-district/, 2020.
10. B. Fraga, "Swansea police pay $750 ransom after computer virus strikes," *The Herald News*, 2013.
11. H. Oz, A. Aris, A. Levi, and A. S. Uluagac, "A survey on ransomware: Evolution, taxonomy, and defense solutions," *ACM Computing Surveys (CSUR)*, vol. 54, no. 11s, pp. 1–37, 2022.
12. A. Kharraz, W. Robertson, D. Balzarotti, L. Bilge, and E. Kirda, "Cutting the Gordian knot: A look under the hood of ransomware attacks," in *Detection of Intrusions and Malware, and Vulnerability Assessment: 12th International Conference, DIMVA 2015*, Milan, Italy, July 9–10, 2015, Proceedings 12. Springer, 2015, pp. 3–24.
13. D. Braue, "Global ransomware damage costs predicted to exceed $265 billion by 2031," *Cybercrime Magazine (2021). Print*, 2022.
14. S. Razaulla, C. Fachkha, C. Markarian, A. Gawanmeh, W. Mansoor, B. C. Fung, and C. Assi, "The age of ransomware: A survey on the evolution, taxonomy, and research directions," *IEEE Access*, vol. 11, pp. 40698–40723, 2023.
15. R. Richardson and M. M. North, "Ransomware: Evolution, mitigation and prevention," *International Management Review*, vol. 13, no. 1, p. 10, 2017.
16. T. Munk, *The rise of politically motivated cyber attacks: Actors, attacks and cybersecurity*. Routledge, 2022.
17. M. N. Alenezi, H. Alabdulrazzaq, A. A. Alshaher, and M. M. Alkharang, "Evolution of malware threats and techniques: A review," *International Journal of Communication Networks and Information Security*, vol. 12, no. 3, pp. 326–337, 2020.
18. W. Ames, "Understanding spyware: Risk and response," *IT Professional*, vol. 6, no. 5, pp. 25–29, 2004.
19. A. Bhardwaj and S. Goundar, "Keyloggers: Silent cyber security weapons," *Network Security*, vol. 2020, no. 2, pp. 14–19, 2020.
20. S. Kiltz, A. Lang, and J. Dittmann, "Malware: Specialized Trojan horse," in *Cyber Warfare and Cyber Terrorism*. IGI Global, 2007, pp. 154–160.
21. E. Tekiner, A. Acar, A. S. Uluagac, E. Kirda, and A. A. Selcuk, "Sok: Cryptojacking malware," in *2021 IEEE European Symposium on Security and Privacy (EuroS&P)*. IEEE, 2021, pp. 120–139.
22. J. Aycock, *Computer viruses and malware*. Springer Science & Business Media, 2006, vol. 22.
23. M. Davis, S. Bodmer, and A. LeMasters, *Hacking exposed malware and rootkits*. McGraw-Hill, Inc., 2009.
24. J. Song, J. Shimamura, M. Eto, D. Inoue, and K. Nakao, "Correlation analysis between spamming botnets and malware infected hosts," in *2011 IEEE/IPSJ International Symposium on Applications and the Internet*. IEEE, 2011, pp. 372–375.
25. K. Rieck, T. Holz, C. Willems, P. Düssel, and P. Laskov, "Learning and classification of malware behavior," in *International Conference on Detection of Intrusions and Malware, and Vulnerability Assessment*. Springer, 2008, pp. 108–125.
26. B. Uscilowski, "Mobile adware and malware analysis," *Symantec Corporation*, vol. 1, 2013.
27. J. Bates, "Trojan horse: Aids information introductory diskette version 2.0," *Virus Bulletin*, vol. 6, pp. 1143–1148, 1990.
28. A. Young and M. Yung, "Cryptovirology: Extortion-based security threats and countermeasures," in *Proceedings 1996 IEEE Symposium on Security and Privacy*. IEEE, 1996, pp. 129–140.
29. A. L. Young and M. Yung, "On ransomware and envisioning the enemy of tomorrow," *Computer*, vol. 50, no. 11, pp. 82–85, 2017.
30. E. de Argaez, "One billion internet users as of December 2005," 2006.

31. D. Fisher, "New Seftad ransomware attacks master boot record," https://threatpost. com/new-seftad-ransomware-attacks-master- boot-record-113010/74714/, 2010.
32. A. Bacani, "Reveton ransomware spreads with old tactics, new infection method," 2014.
33. J. Wyke and A. Ajjan, "The current state of ransomware," *SOPHOS. A SophosLabs Technical Paper*, 2015.
34. R. Lipovsky', L. Štefanko, and G. Braniša, "The rise of android ransomware," 2016.
35. S. Smith, "The evolution of mobile ransomware," *Avast blog* [Online], https://blog.avast.com/the-evolution-of-mobile-ransomware, 2016, vol. 5, p. 2017.
36. D. Bisson, "Website files encrypted by Linux.Encoder.1 ransomware? There is now a free fix," *Graham Cluley*, 2015.
37. M. Akbanov, V. G. Vassilakis, I. D. Moscholios, and M. D. Logothetis, "Static and dynamic analysis of Wannacry ransomware," in *Proceedings of the IEICE Information and Communication Technology Forum ICTF 2018*. 2018.
38. Chainalysis, "The Chainalysis 2022 crypto crime report" [Online], https://go.chainalysis.com/2022-crypto-crime-report.html, 2022, last accessed: 28 March 2024.
39. N. Singh and S. Tripathy, "It's too late if exfiltrate: Early stage Android ransomware detection," *Computers & Security*, p. 103819, 2024.
40. K. D. Strang and N. R. Vajjhala, "Why cyberattacks disrupt society and how to mitigate risk," in *Cybersecurity for Decision Makers*. CRC Press, 2023, pp. 1–28.
41. M. Ofe, "A qualitative study exploring security practices healthcare providers need to reduce the risk of successful ransomware attacks on electronic health record systems," Ph.D. dissertation, Colorado Technical University, 2023.
42. N. Pattnaik, J. R. Nurse, S. Turner, G. Mott, J. MacColl, P. Huesch, and J. Sullivan, "It's more than just money: The real-world harms from ransomware attacks," in *International Symposium on Human Aspects of Information Security and Assurance*. Springer, 2023, pp. 261–274.
43. Chainalysis, "The chainalysis 2023 crypto crime report" [Online] https://go.chainalysis.com/2023-crypto-crime-report.html, 2023, last accessed: 28 March 2024.
44. W. Davis, "MOVEit cyberattacks: Keeping tabs on the biggest data theft of 2023" [Online], https://www.theverge.com/23892245/moveit-cyberattacks-clop-ransomware-government-business, 2023, last accessed: 28 March 2024.
45. CrowdStrike, "Crowdstrike 2024 global threat report," https://bit. ly/3IZx5Ij, 2024, last accessed: 28 March 2024.
46. J. G. Sekar, A. Chokkalingam, and D. Kesavan, "Evolution of healthcare sector and evolving cyberattacks – a summary," in *Smart Distributed Embedded Systems for Healthcare Applications*. CRC Press, 2023, pp. 155–172.
47. T. McIntosh, A. Kayes, Y.-P. P. Chen, A. Ng, and P. Watters, "Ransomware mitigation in the modern era: A comprehensive review, research challenges, and future directions," *ACM Computing Surveys (CSUR)*, vol. 54, no. 9, pp. 1–36, 2021.
48. G. M. Chiong, "The rise of ransomware: Motivations, contributing factors, and defenses," Ph.D. dissertation, Utica University, 2023.
49. Y. R. Siwakoti, M. Bhurtel, D. B. Rawat, A. Oest, and R. Johnson, "Advances in IoT security: Vulnerabilities, enabled criminal services, attacks and countermeasures," *IEEE Internet of Things Journal*, vol. 10, no. 13, pp. 11224–11239, 2023.
50. K. Takeuchi, T. Kumamoto, Y. Yoshida, and H. Fujima, "Decentralized identity verification system for data access to prevent data exfiltration ransomware," *TechRxiv*, 2023.
51. C. F. Azubuike, "Cyber security and international conflicts: An analysis of state-sponsored cyber attacks," *Nnamdi Azikiwe Journal of Political Science*, vol. 8, no. 3, pp. 101–114, 2023.
52. M. Jeriji and A. Nasfi, "The value relevance of mandatory sustainability reporting assurance," *South African Journal of Accounting Research*, vol. 37, no. 2, pp. 122–138, 2023.

AUTHOR BIOGRAPHY

Taskeed Jabid is an associate professor at East West University. He received PhD in computer vision and image processing from Kyung Hee University, South Korea. He obtained his bachelor's degree in computer science and engineering from East West University (Bangladesh). His researches are in the fields of machine learning, deep learning, image processing, facial image analysis, texture analysis, bioinformatics, computer graphics, and algorithms.

Saleh Masum is a software engineer who has previously held positions at reputable software companies like FatSecret and NowBoarding in Melbourne, Australia. He also worked at Secure Link Services (SELISE) in Bangladesh, expanding his professional skills. He completed his bachelor's degree from the Department of Information and Communication Engineering, University of Rajshahi, Bangladesh. His research interests include software engineering, cybersecurity, and artificial intelligence/machine learning.

Rifat Ara Shams is a postdoctoral fellow at Australia's National Science Agency (CSIRO's Data61). She is working on diversity and inclusion in artificial intelligence and requirements engineering for responsible AI. She completed her PhD from Monash University, Australia, on "Human Values in Software Engineering." Her research interests are artificial intelligence, diversity and inclusion in AI, human and social factors in software engineering and AI, empirical software engineering, and mixed-methods research. To know more about Rifat and her work, explore her homepage: https://sites.google.com/view/rifatarashams.

Abdullahi Chowdhury completed his doctor of philosophy degree from Federation University, Australia, in 2020. He completed his master of information technology degree (2006) from Monash University, Australia, and his bachelor of information technology degree (2004) from Central Queensland University, Australia. Currently, he is working as assistant professor at East West University, Bangladesh. He worked as a postdoctoral researcher at The University of Adelaide under the Modelling, Monitoring and Moderating Human-AI Interactions (M3HAI) project, which is a cross-disciplinary (School of Computer Science and School of Psychology) project involving experts in both AI and human decision-making. He has more than ten years of industrial experience in Telstra, the Australian Taxation Office, and the Australia Post. He also worked as a sessional academic at Monash University, RMIT University, and Federation University. His research interests include cyber security, intelligent transportation system, generative AI, syntactic signal processing, and game theoretic approaches.

Mohammad Manzurul Islam received BSc in computer science and information technology from Islamic University of Technology, Bangladesh, in 2005; MSc in internetworking from the University of Technology Sydney, Australia, in 2013; and PhD in cybersecurity from Federation University, Australia, in 2021. He is an assistant professor at East West University, Bangladesh. He served over 16+ years in many organizations, including universities (Monash University, Australia; Federation University, Australia; Canadian University, Bangladesh; and Stamford University, Bangladesh) and IT industries (ZTE Corporation and Robi-Axiata Limited). His research interests include cybersecurity, machine learning, computer vision, and IoT.

Md. Hasanul Ferdaus is currently working as an assistant professor in the Department of CSE at East West University, Bangladesh, since September 2022. He obtained his PhD degree in computer science from the Faculty of IT at Monash University, Australia, in 2016, his MSc Engg. degree in ICT from KIT, Germany, and Polytechnic University of Turin, Italy, in 2009, and his BSc Engg. degree in CSE from BUET, Bangladesh, in 2004. Dr. Ferdaus has seven years of teaching experience at Australian universities, including Monash University, Central Queensland University, Melbourne Institute of Technology, and VIT. Moreover, he has more than five years of research experience in Australia (CLOUDS Lab, Melbourne University, and Monash University) and Germany (Telematics Institute, KIT, and FZI Research Center for IT). Furthermore, he worked as a system analyst for two years at Robi Axiata, Bangladesh. His current research interests include cloud computing, cybersecurity, IoT, and software engineering.

Sawkat Ali received his BSc in electrical and electronics engineering (EEE) from Ahsanullah University of Science and Technology, Bangladesh. He completed M.Eng. (research) in electrical engineering from the University of New South Wales, Australia, and PhD in electrical engineering from Central Queensland University, Rockhampton, Australia. After the completion of PhD, he worked as a post-doctoral research fellow at Central Queensland University and Deakin University, Australia. He is currently working as an assistant professor in the Department of Computer Science and Engineering, East West University, Bangladesh. His research interests include IoT, machine learning, power electronics, linear and nonlinear control theory and its applications, microgrids, and renewable energy.

Maheen Islam received her B.S. and M.S. degrees from the University of Dhaka, Bangladesh, in 1998 and 1999, respectively. She obtained her PhD degree in wireless mesh networking from the Department of the Computer Science and Engineering, University of Dhaka, Bangladesh, in 2017. She is now working as an associate professor in the Department of Computer Science and Engineering, East West University, Bangladesh. Her areas of research interest include wireless mesh networks, wireless sensor networks, cognitive radio networks, modeling and analysis of network communication protocols, machine learning, and so on. She is a member of GNR (Green Networking Research group) and IEEE.

2 A Closer look at the Famous Ransomware Groups

Reemar Tan, Ulya Saputri, Jing Xiao, Jiacheng Liu, and David Ekeh

2.1 INTRODUCTION

Ransomware represents a significant cyber threat characterized by malicious software that encrypts the victim's data, demanding a ransom for decryption [1]. Ransomware's inception can be traced back to the AIDS Trojan in 1989, which initiated the concept of exchanging a victim's access to their data for payment [2]. Joseph Popp created this malware, distributed via floppy disks, and claimed to raise funds for AIDS research. Once activated, it encrypted file names on the infected systems, demanding payment for recovery instructions. Although it is considered primitive by today's standards, the AIDS Trojan introduced the fundamental ransomware concept of leveraging data accessibility for payment.

Further, the early 2000s saw more sophisticated strains like GpCode and Cryzip [3]. These utilized more robust encryption algorithms, making decryption without a key almost impossible. Notably, GpCode, which appeared in 2004, used RSA (Rivest–Shamir–Adleman) encryption, a marked improvement in complexity and robustness over previous variants, setting a precedent for future ransomware. The transition from isolated actors to organized groups has marked a significant evolution in ransomware deployment. These modern groups often operated with ties to more extensive cybercriminal networks.

Moreover, the mid-2000s to early 2010s saw a proliferation of ransomware facilitated by the anonymizing capabilities of Bitcoin and improvements in digital payment systems [4]. This era marked a significant shift as cybercriminals began to form organized groups to orchestrate ransomware campaigns, maximizing profitability and scale. One of the prominent ransomware families from this period was CryptoLocker, launched in 2013. It was among the first to demand payment in Bitcoin, highlighting the maturation in the operational tactics of ransomware groups. Furthermore, noteworthy groups such as WannaCry, Petya, or NotPetya have demonstrated the destructive capacity of ransomware [5]. For instance, WannaCry affected over 200,000 computers across 150 countries by exploiting the Windows SMB (Server Message Block) protocol. Recent groups like DarkSide and REvil have refined ransomware into a service model, targeting high-revenue organizations through advanced tactics [6]. These ransomware group tactics include spear-phishing, social engineering, exploiting network vulnerabilities, and so on. These groups meticulously select their targets based on potential ransom yields and system vulnerabilities. Due to their critical need for data access and weaker digital infrastructures, they often focus on healthcare, government, and industrial sectors.

The evolution of ransomware reflects broader trends in cybercrime, where attackers leverage technological advancements and socio-economic dynamics to refine their methods. Ransomware attacks can cripple the operational, financial, and reputational aspects of targeted organizations. According to Adorjan and Colaguori, ransomware is estimated to cost victims around $20 billion globally in 2021, a surge from $11.5 billion in 2019. Beyond financial losses, ransomware attacks disrupt services, erode customer trust, and impose psychological stress on stakeholders [7]. Today, ransomware groups like corporate entities operate with a level of sophistication. They employ developers, negotiators, and customer support to manage their operations and maximize profits. These

DOI: 10.1201/9781003469506-3

developments signify a shift from opportunistic malware deployment to strategic, enterprise-level operations prioritizing long-term sustainability and profitability.

2.2 RANSOMWARE GROUPS

2.2.1 LockBit

2.2.1.1 History and Variants

The large number of victims whose data has been claimed on LockBit's leak site has contributed to the group's reputation as one of the most active and notorious ransomware groups in recent years. It operates by maintaining and offering a particular type of ransomware to individuals or groups known as affiliates. These affiliates are provided with access to the ransomware and are supported in deploying it in exchange for upfront fees, ongoing subscription fees, a percentage of the profits, or a combination of these forms of compensation. See Section 1.2.

Due to the presence of multiple affiliates, LockBit ransomware operations display substantial variances in tactics, techniques, and procedures (TTPs). The variations in observed ransomware TTPs pose a significant problem for organizations striving to uphold network security and defend against the ransomware threat. The LockBit ransomware has targeted organizations of different scales in a wide range of vital infrastructure sectors, such as but not limited to government, healthcare, education, transportation, manufacturing, and financial services.

2.2.1.2 Recruitment Process

2.2.1.2.1 Affiliate Program

The LockBit affiliate program grants access to the ransomware and offers support for its deployment in exchange for an initial payment, ongoing membership fees, a share of profits, or a combination of these payment methods. The membership fee costs 1 bitcoin, but it is eligible for a return from the collective ransom profits. The ransom share profit is split into two portions, with 80% allocated to the affiliate and 20% allocated to LockBit [8].

Despite LockBit's claims to have a policy of not targeting hospital data that could potentially lead to patient deaths (refer to Table 2.1), it has been implicated in numerous cyberattacks that have endangered lives for the sake of financial gain. This includes incidents where LockBit forced two major hospitals in upstate New York to redirect ambulances and an attack on Toronto's hospital for sick children just days before Christmas. These attacks resulted in delays in diagnosis and treatment for patients, causing significant distress for affected families. The clinical teams faced difficulties in accessing lab reports and imaging results [9].

2.2.1.2.2 Bug Bounty Program

The LockBit ransomware group had introduced LockBit 3.0, along with a new dark web platform and a bug bounty program that offers rewards of up to $1 million for discovering vulnerabilities in

TABLE 2.1
Businesses and countries that are restricted for attacking and decrypting data [8]

Forbidden to Attack	
Business Type	**Country**
Oil and gas industry Critical infrastructure (e.g., nuclear plant) Institutions where damage to the files could lead to death (e.g., cardiology centers, neurosurgical departments)	Armenia, Belarus, Georgia, Kazakhstan, Kyrgyzstan, Latvia, Lithuania, Moldova, Russia, Tajikistan, Turkmenistan, Uzbekistan, Ukraine, and Estonia

their software and website, proposing exceptional ideas, or effectively revealing the identity of the leader of the organization's affiliate program.

2.2.1.3 LockBit Shutdown

Law enforcement authorities successfully confiscated LockBit's website, infrastructure, and data on February 19, 2024, dealing a significant blow to one of the most active ransomware groups globally. Over the course of the past four years, the LockBit ransomware organization has been consistently and aggressively infiltrating numerous businesses, schools, medical facilities, and governments worldwide. Aside from confiscating technological infrastructure, the law enforcement activities targeting LockBit also involve apprehensions in Poland, Ukraine, and the United States. Furthermore, two suspected members of the group, located in Russia, are facing sanctions. According to the officials, the group's members are located in various parts of the world [10].

2.2.2 CLOP

CLOP stands out among the hundreds of ransomware gangs for its extremely sophisticated attacks. Their activities now not only lead to financial losses but also jeopardize critical data, causing long-term damage to the reputation of the companies involved [11]. The relevance of CLOP's actions goes beyond their direct financial impact. They also reveal major weaknesses in cybersecurity techniques and challenge existing legal frameworks created to address cybercrime.

2.2.2.1 Origin and Early History

Early in 2019, the financially motivated cybercrime group known as FIN11 introduced the CLOP ransomware. This group, known for its expertise in targeting businesses in North America and Europe, primarily engages in cyberextortion for financial gain. Experts consider CLOP a derivative or an advanced version of the previous CryptoMix ransomware, also linked to FIN11 [12]. In addition, CLOP gained a reputation for pioneering the terrifying method of extortion. CLOP ransomware goes beyond typical encryption by also posing a threat to release the encrypted data on the dark web through a dedicated website called CLOP^_-LEAKS, unless the ransom is paid (see Table 2.2). This strategy significantly increases the risks for victims by introducing the additional danger of public exposure to the situation [13].

In addition, the evolution of CLOP has been characterized by a number of prominent incidents. In 2020, the hacking group FIN11 used it to launch an assault against Kiteworks' File Transfer Appliance, resulting in the unauthorized access and theft of data belonging to a pharmaceutical company [14]. CLOP had intensified its activities by 2021, impeding about 600 Windows processes and accumulating more than $500 million in ransom payments. In 2022, the group discovered a significant vulnerability in Accellion FTA devices, impacting more than 9 million individuals and resulting in a substantial payment known as the magnificence-movement settlement [15]. Several sectors, including US federal organizations, the BBC, hospitals, and major firms like Ernst, continued to feel the impact of CLOP in 2023.

2.2.2.2 Evolution of Tactics and Technical Sophistication

The CLOP ransomware has undergone further development by its creators, the FIN11 team, who have continuously improved its system and enhanced the technical complexity of the malware to successfully bypass advanced protection measures. The CLOP developers initially employed advanced persistent tactics (APT) typically utilized by state-sponsored hackers [16]. Living-off-the-land (LotL) employs binaries and scripts that allow attackers to blend in with regular network activity, increasing detection difficulty. It seems that this dual-threat strategy has motivated its targets not only to pay ransoms in order to decrypt their data but also to implement other countermeasures to prevent its public release [17]. These tactics distinguish CLOP as an exceptionally dangerous threat in a digital development environment.

TABLE 2.2
CL0P's brief history

Date	Event
2019	Initially observed in 2019, this ransomware strain emerged as a modification of the CryptoMix malware lineage [20].
2020	The Fin11 group using CL0P ransomware on Kiteworks' File Transfer Appliance [21].
2020	Witnessed a pharmaceutical company's data being compromised by Clop ransomware.
2021	CL0P gained significant recognition in 2021. CL0P not only encrypted files but also obstructed around 600 Windows processes. According to estimates, the total amount of ransom paid as a result of CL0P ransomware attacks reached over $500 million by November 2021 [20].
2022	The CL0P criminal groups successfully exploited a crucial vulnerability in Accellion FTA devices, enabling them to illegally acquire personal data that impacted over 9 million individuals. As a consequence, a class-action settlement of $8.1 million was reached in January 2022 [22].
2023	CL0P ransomware attacks on diverse sectors, including US federal agencies, the BBC, hospitals, and Ernst & Young

Furthermore, CL0P's technological advancements included the integration of modern encryption methods and the implementation of automated frameworks for engaging with victims. These frameworks enabled immediate communication with victims, demanding ransoms and providing instructions on how to make payments, thus simplifying the process of extortion [18]. The group enhances the ability of their ransomware to evade decryption tools by employing complex encryption tactics, hence increasing the difficulty for cybersecurity researchers to understand and overcome the malware [19].

2.2.2.3 The CL0P's Clear Motivation and Process

CL0P explicitly declares that their group is solely driven by financial motives and has no interest in politics. According to the dark web onion site, if the victims are a government, city, or police department, there is no need to fear, as they have completely deleted all their data. There is no need for them to contact CL0P; they have no intention of revealing that information. Furthermore, they explicitly declared that they will publicly disclose all the data gathered from major corporations that refuse to engage in negotiations on the surface web.

2.2.2.4 Evidence of the Collected Data

Smith, Gildea & Schmidt (SGS) is a regional law company that serves numerous clients, including international corporations and individuals with specific legal requirements. This profession includes the majority of the legal jurisdictions in the State of Maryland, as well as the component that deals with complex civil litigation [23]. Evidently, they have fallen victim to the CL0P group. Their sensitive information was uploaded on their leaked website, as described in Section 2.3. The client's sensitive data that has been disclosed includes but is not limited to passport ID, driver's license, Social Security number, and member information. On the dark web, all the data is easily visible and undistorted.

2.2.3 Vice Society

2.2.3.1 History and Variants

Vice Society is a well-known hacking group that is notable for carrying out ransomware attacks specifically aimed at the healthcare, education, and manufacturing industries. This group gained notoriety in the summer of 2021. Vice Society employs a strategy called double extortion, where they force victims to pay for two things: a decryption key to restore access to their whole network, and protection against data disclosure, which is crucial for business recovery. Significantly, Vice

Society deviates from the ransomware-as-a-service (RaaS) framework in its operation. Like other well-known threat actors, Vice Society has a data breach website where they publicly release stolen data from victims who refuse to comply with their extortion demands. Moreover, they distribute specific information about their activities on this website dedicated to leaks.

2.2.3.2 Commodity Tools

Vice Society employs a range of tactics, techniques, and procedures commonly employed by other ransomware participants. These include the use of PowerShell scripts and the use of legitimate tools for malicious purposes. In addition, they gain initial access through publicly available vulnerabilities and elevate privileges after an attack. Vice Society also exploits backdoors, such as SystemBC [24].

PortStarter is a malicious program coded in the Go programming language, designed to create a secret entry point into a computer system. These include the ability to adjust firewall settings and open ports to establish connections with pre-configured command and control (C2) servers.

In addition to these backdoors, Vice Society leverages the remote boot tool Power Admin for deploying ransomware payloads. Power Admin, originally a legitimate tool, offers features such as server and application monitoring, as well as file access auditing. In cases where console security settings are activated within Power Admin, attackers require credentials to execute authorized changes.

2.2.3.3 Attack Methodology

When the Vice Society ransomware organization first appeared, they exploited PrintNightmare's vulnerability in everyday life [25]. Rather than creating their own ransomware, they first made use of HelloKitty, Five Hands, and Zeppelin, among others. By the end of 2022, Vice Society had developed its own ransomware called "PolyVice" (see Figure 2.1).

After encrypting the victim's files, Vice Society would leave a ransom note and attach the contact email and website information of the purchase key to the letter and the desktop background image. If the ransom was not paid within a specified time, the Vice Society would publish the data on the dark web [26].

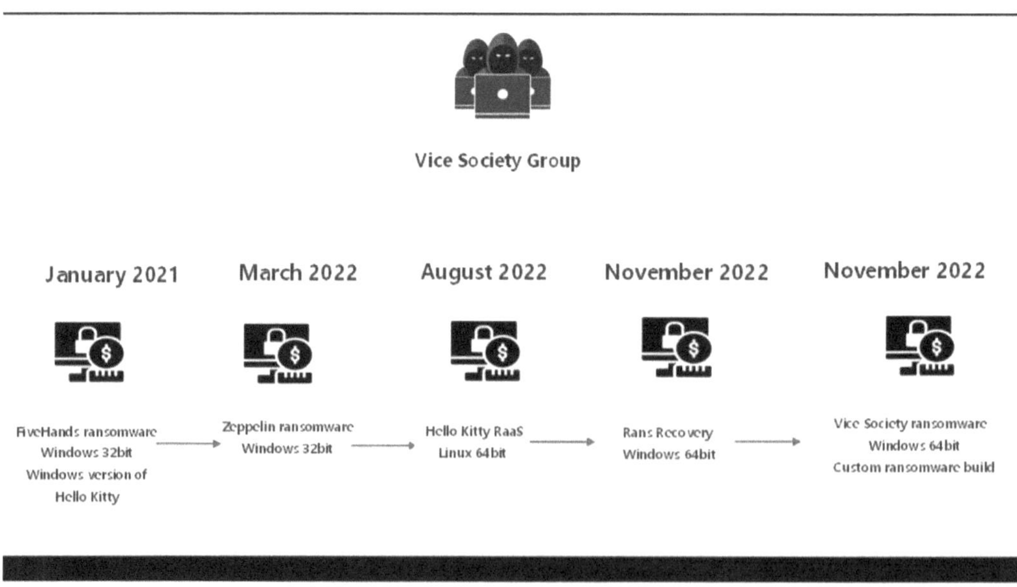

FIGURE 2.1 Vice Society ransomware usage timeline [24].

2.2.4 REvil

2.2.4.1 History and Variants

REvil, also known as Sodinokibi, emerged in 2019 from the remnants of GandCrab ransomware and rapidly gained notoriety for its high-profile and sophisticated attacks. It specialized in double extortion, encrypting victims' data and threatening to publish it unless they paid a ransom. Exploiting critical vulnerabilities, like those in Oracle WebLogic, REvil executed aggressive campaigns against major entities, notably JBS and Kaseya, pushing the envelope in 2020 by introducing new coercive tactics that amplified its threat [27].

In 2021, REvil's increasingly disruptive actions drew intense global law enforcement scrutiny, resulting in arrests and dismantling of their network infrastructure. High-profile breaches attracted political attention, with national leaders actively addressing the cyber threat. The collaborative crackdown, part of Operation GoldDust, highlighted the practical global stance against cybercrime, with significant operational disruption for REvil, arrests, and financial confiscation, marking a potential end to the group's activities under the REvil moniker. This coordinated effort against cyber threats, a testament to the power of global collaboration, highlighted the international dedication to combating ransomware and cybercriminal operations [28, 29].

2.2.4.2 Recruitment Process

However, in the dark realm of cybercrime, REvil's recruitment for their ransomware group operated like a standard job recruitment process. They sought out skilled hackers and groups through channels on the dark web and cybercrime forums. Prospective affiliates would need to demonstrate their capability to breach networks, preferably having a background in exploits, phishing, or other cyberattack methods. The goal was to assemble a network of independent operators who could execute attacks globally, ensuring REvil's malware would proliferate beyond any single entity's distribution capabilities [31].

TABLE 2.3
REvil history

Date	Event
April 2019	REvil ransomware was first discovered, with links to the recently retired GandCrab ransomware [30].
2020	The introduction of double-extortion techniques began bold attacks on public figures and organizations [30].
Early 2021	Attacks on major service providers like JBS and Kaseya caused significant disruptions [30].
Mid-2021	Global law enforcement began coordinated efforts to dismantle REvil operations [31].
July 2021	REvil carried out a large-scale attack on Kaseya, and soon after, their infrastructure went offline [31].
September 2021	A free universal decryptor for REvil's ransomware was released by Bitdefender [32].
October 2021	REvil's servers were hacked and forced offline in a multi-country operation [33].
November 2021	The U.S. Department of Justice revealed indictments against a person associated with REvil [34].
January 2022	The Russian Federal Security Service reported dismantling REvil and charging several of its members [35].
Throughout 2022	Follow-up on dismantled operations and tracking of potential resurgences under different names [36].
2023	Continuous monitoring and defense against ransomware strains that may have evolved from REvil's foundations [31].

2.2.4.2.1 Affiliate Program

REvil's affiliate program was a key component of their operational structure, allowing for decentralized distribution of their ransomware. Affiliates were responsible for initiating attacks and spreading the malware, which meant they needed to be adept at various cyberattack vectors. Successful affiliates had experience penetrating enterprise networks, utilizing security vulnerabilities, and using social engineering tactics. The nature of the work required discretion, technical prowess, and an understanding of the cybercriminal ecosystem. Profits from ransoms were shared, with affiliates receiving a substantial cut for their efforts [31].

2.2.4.2.2 Job Description

For an affiliate in REvil's RaaS, the job description would entail responsibilities that align with cyberattack campaigns. This would include identifying and exploiting network vulnerabilities, deploying ransomware, managing the attack lifecycle, and negotiating with victims for ransom payments. It is expected that an affiliate will manage its operations while adhering to the standards and expectations of REvil's overarching strategy. Expertise in digital forensics evasion, maintaining operational security, and navigating complex digital environments would be critical to the role; additionally, affiliates needed to communicate with REvil's core team for coordination and ransom collection [31].

2.2.4.3 Payment Process

The design of REvil's payment site allows victims to engage with the threat actors. It typically displays a ransom demand in both US dollars and Bitcoin, provides a Bitcoin wallet address for payment, and has a countdown timer that indicates the payment deadline. The site frequently includes a chat support feature for communication, and it may offer a trial decryption for a limited number of files to demonstrate the ability to decrypt. The overall layout is crafted to guide victims through meeting the ransom demands [31].

2.2.4.4 Victims and Transactions

TABLE 2.4
REvil victims

Name	Date	Details
Acer	March 2021	Acer received a $50 million ransom demand, making it one of the largest ransom demands [37].
JBS Foods	May 2021	REvil targeted the world's largest meat processing company, shutting down operations across the United States, Canada, and Australia [38].
Kaseya	July 2021	REvil executed a supply chain ransomware attack through Kaseya's VSA software, affecting numerous businesses globally [39].
Travelex	December 31, 2019	The foreign exchange company suffered a ransomware attack that led to its bankruptcy, with REvil demanding a $6 million ransom [40].
Quanta Computer	April 2021	A ransomware attack targeted Apple's supplier, resulting in the theft of confidential schematics for future Apple products [41].
Grubman Shire Meiselas & Sacks	May 2020	Demands for payment to prevent the leak of sensitive client data compromised this law firm known for its celebrity clients [42].
Invenergy	June 2021	REvil attacked Invenergy, claiming to have exfiltrated four terabytes of sensitive data, including contracts and the CEO's personal details. Operations were not disrupted [43].
The City of Keizer	June 2020	The city paid a $48,000 ransom to regain control of its computer systems after an attack by REvil [44].

2.2.5 NoEscape

NoEscape ransomware operates through a developer who offers a platform to affiliates, enabling them to use the ransomware tool on targeted systems. These affiliates, often third-party contractors, are responsible for installing and executing NoEscape on behalf of the ransomware operators. The ransomware utilizes a shared-profit model, dividing the collected ransom between the operators and the affiliates [45].

NoEscape encrypts data on both Windows and Linux systems, including VMware ESXi environments. NoEscape distinguishes itself from other RaaS groups by being developed entirely from scratch using the C++ programming language. It provides affiliates with customization options through an interface, allowing them to optimize the speed or thoroughness of encryption, prioritize specific file paths, and choose which services to terminate before initiating encryption. The ransomware uses RSA and ChaCha20 encryption algorithms, supports asynchronous LAN scanning, and can encrypt network file shares and local drives. An intriguing feature is shared encryption, which enables the use of a single encryption key across all infected files in a network, streamlining the encryption and decryption processes.

2.2.5.1 Recruitment Process

2.2.5.1.1 Affiliate Program

NoEscape's affiliate program is a cornerstone of its operational strategy, enabling the extensive dissemination of ransomware across diverse networks. Affiliates play a crucial role in executing attacks and spreading malware using sophisticated methods tailored to exploit vulnerabilities. Successful affiliates exhibit expertise in breaching complex networks, leveraging security weaknesses, and employing advanced social engineering tactics to gain unauthorized access.

Participants in the NoEscape affiliate ecosystem receive substantial compensation through ransom payments, highlighting their pivotal role in the ransomware deployment process. This incentivized model motivates affiliates to actively engage in malicious activities, contributing to the widespread proliferation of NoEscape ransomware across various industries and geographical locations.

The affiliate program empowers individuals and groups with diverse technical abilities to participate in cybercrime, expanding the reach and impact of NoEscape within illicit markets. This decentralized approach enhances the ransomware's adaptability and scalability, presenting a significant threat to organizations of all sizes.

Through a network of affiliates, NoEscape strategically decentralizes its distribution efforts, evading detection and attribution while maximizing the ransomware's effectiveness. This ecosystem encourages collaboration and specialization among cybercriminals, further complicating efforts to combat and mitigate the consequences of NoEscape ransomware attacks.

2.2.5.1.2 Job Description

An affiliate within NoEscape's RaaS program assumes a pivotal role in orchestrating cyberattack campaigns with a diverse range of responsibilities. These include identifying and exploiting various network vulnerabilities to gain unauthorized entry into targeted systems. After securing access, affiliates initiate the deployment of NoEscape ransomware and manage the entire attack process from its beginning to its end. In addition to technical execution, affiliates engage in strategic negotiations with victims to facilitate ransom payments, demonstrating adeptness in communication and persuasion techniques. To ensure operational success and avoid detection, affiliates prioritize maintaining robust operational security measures and upholding consistent communication with NoEscape's core team for effective coordination and support.

REFERENCES

1. Al-Rimy, B. A. S., Maarof, M. A., & Shaid, S. Z. M. (2018). Ransomware Threat Success Factors, Taxonomy, and Countermeasures: A Survey and Research Directions. *Computers & Security, 74*, 144–166.

2. Chaurasia, R. (2018). Ransomware: The Cyber Extortionist. In *Handbook of Research on Information and Cyber Security in the Fourth Industrial Revolution* (pp. 64–111). IGI Global.
3. Patel, A., & Tailor, J. (2020). A Malicious Activity Monitoring Mechanism to Detect and Prevent Ransomware. *Computer Fraud & Security*, 2020(1), 14–19.
4. Whyte, C. (2023). Cryptoterrorism: Assessing the Utility of Blockchain Technologies for Terrorist Enterprise. *Studies in Conflict & Terrorism*, *46*(7), 1126–1149.
5. Ryan, M., & Ryan, M. (2021). Ransomware Case Studies. In *Ransomware Revolution: The Rise of a Prodigious Cyber Threat* (pp. 65–91). Springer Nature Switzerland.
6. Butt, U., Dauda, Y., & Shaheer, B. (2023). Ransomware Attack on the Educational Sector. In *AI, Blockchain and Self-Sovereign Identity in Higher Education* (pp. 279–313). Cham: Springer Nature Switzerland.
7. Adorjan, M., & Colaguori, C. (2023). Scams, Fraud, and Cybercrime in a Globalised Society. In *Crime, Deviance, and Social Control in the 21st Century: A Justice and Rights Perspective* (p. 407). Canadian Scholars.
8. LockBit. (2024). LockBit 3.0 Leaked Data. *LockBit*. http://lockbit3753ekiocyo5epmpy6klmejchjtzd-doekjlnt6mu3qh4de2id.onion/
9. Martin, A., & Matishak, M. (2024, May 7). *LockbitSupp Identified as Dmitry Khoroshev and Indicted for Ransomware Crimes*. https://therecord.media/lockbitsupp-suspect-accused-lockbit-ransomware-gang
10. Burgess, M. (2024). *A Global Police Operation Just Took Down the Notorious LockBit Ransomware Gang*. https://www.wired.com/story/lockbit-ransomware-takedown-website-nca-fbi/
11. Korac, S., Maglaras, L., Moradpoor, N., Buchanan, B., & Canberk, B. (2024). Ransomware: Analysis and Evaluation of Live Forensic Techniques and the Impact on Linux based IoT Systems. arXiv preprint arXiv:2403.17571. https://doi.org/10.48550/arXiv.2403.17571
12. Wu, Y., Hao, X., Lin, F., Wang, S., Chen, L., Lin, X., . . . Liu, Y. (2022). Developing a Cerium Lactate Antibacterial Nucleating Agent for Multifunctional Polylactic Acid Packaging Film. *International Journal of Biological Macromolecules*, *220*, 56–66. https://doi.org/10.1016/j.ijbiomac.2022.08.082
13. Nershi, K., & Grossman, S. (2023). *Assessing the Political Motivations Behind Ransomware Attacks*. SSRN 4507111. https://dx.doi.org/10.2139/ssrn.4507111
14. MacColl, J., Hüsch, P., Mott, G., Sullivan, J., Nurse, J. R., Turner, S., & Pattnaik, N. (2024). *Ransomware: Victim Insights on Harms to Individuals, Organisations and Society*. https://kar.kent.ac.uk/id/eprint/104628
15. Mayeke, N. R., Arigbabu, A. T., Olaniyi, O. O., Okunleye, O. J., & Adigwe, C. S. (2024). *Evolving Access Control Paradigms: A Comprehensive Multi-Dimensional Analysis of Security Risks and System Assurance in Cyber Engineering*. SSRN. https://dx.doi.org/10.2139/ssrn.4752902
16. De Fusco, L. (2023). *Advanced C2 Fingerprinting* (Doctoral dissertation, Politecnico di Torino). http://webthesis.biblio.polito.it/id/eprint/27771
17. Frederick, B. A., & Taylor, O. E. (2023). Analysis on Cybersecurity Control and Monitoring Techniques in Industrial IoT: Industrial Control Systems. *Internet of Things and Cloud Computing*, *11*(1), 1–17. https://doi.org/10.11648/j.iotcc.20231101.11
18. Anthony, R. T. (2023). *Barriers to Adoption of Advanced Cybersecurity Tools in Organizations* (Doctoral dissertation, Capitol Technology University). https://www.proquest.com/openview/9f8f71e9bc9a295a2b600e772fa51323/1?pq-origsite=gscholar&cbl=18750&diss=y
19. Winters, A. (2023). *Automated Control Prioritization Based on Generating Sector-Based Threat Profiles* (Master's thesis, University of Twente). https://purl.utwente.nl/essays/96761
20. Easttom, C. (2023). *Network Defense and Countermeasures: Principles and Practices* (4th ed.). Pearson IT Certification.
21. Spiceworks. (2021). *Zero-Day Flaws in Accellion's Legacy Software Impact Nearly 100 Organizations Worldwide*. https://www.spiceworks.com/it-security/data-security/news/zero-day-flaws-in-accellions-legacy-software-impact-nearly-100-organizations-worldwide/
22, Davidoff, S., Durrin, M., & Sprenger, K. (2022). *Ransomware and Cyber Extortion: Response and Prevention*. Addison-Wesley Professional.
23. Law, S. (2024). *20+ Years of Excellence Serving the Legal Community*. Smith, Gildea & Schmidt Law. https://www.sgs-law.com/
24. Research, S. (2022). Dark Web Profile: Vice Society Ransomware Group. *SOCRadar*. Retrieved August 2022 from https://socradar.io/dark-web-profile-vice-society/

25. Gonzalez, L. N., Pajares, P., Cruz, A. D., & Sto. Tomas, W. (2023). *Vice Society Ransomware Group Targets Manufacturing Companies. Trend Micro.* Retrieved January 24, 2023 from https://www.trendmicro.com/en_ca/research/23/a/vice-society-ransomware-group-targets-manufacturing-companies.html
26. Gumarin, J. (2022). Vice Society: Profiling a Persistent Threat to the Education Sector. *Palo Alto Networks.* Retrieved December 6, 2022 from https://unit42.paloaltonetworks.com/vice-society-targets-education-sector/
27. Apps, A. M., Fee, A., Laroche, M., & LLP, M. (2021). *What Companies Need to Know about Modern Ransomware Attacks and How to Respond.* Retrieved July 14, 2021 from https://corpgov.law.harvard.edu/2021/07/14/what-companies-need-to-know-about-modern-ransomware-attacks-and-how-to-respond/
28. Europol. (n.d.). Five Affiliates to Sodinokibi/REvil Unplugged. *Europol.* https://www.europol.europa.eu/media-press/newsroom/news/five-affiliates-to-sodinokibi/revil-unplugged
29. Tonkin, C. (2021, November 11). Police Arrest REvil Ransomware Gang Members. *ACS.* https://ia.acs.org.au/article/2021/police-arrest-revil-ransomware-gang-members.html
30. Constantin, L. (2021, November 12). REvil Ransomware Explained: A Widespread Extortion Operation. *CSO.* https://www.csoonline.com/article/570101/revil-ransomware-explained-a-widespread-extortion-operation.html
31. Martineau, D. S. (2022, June 3). Understanding REvil: REvil Threat Actors May Have Returned (Updated). *Unit 42.* https://unit42.paloaltonetworks.com/revil-threat-actors/
32. Bitdefender. (2021, September 16). Bitdefender Offers Free Universal Decryptor for REvil/Sodinokibi Ransomware. *Bitdefender.* https://www.bitdefender.com.au/blog/labs/bitdefender-offers-free-universal-decryptor-for-revil-sodinokibi-ransomware/
33. Bing, J. M. (2021, October 22). Exclusive Governments Turn Tables on Ransomware Gang REvil by Pushing it Offline. *Reuters.* https://www.reuters.com/technology/exclusive-governments-turn-tables-ransomware-gang-revil-by-pushing-it-offline-2021-10-21/
34. DOJ. (2022, May 18). *Ukrainian Arrested and Charged with Ransomware Attack on Kaseya.* DOJ. https://www.justice.gov/opa/pr/ukrainian-arrested-and-charged-ransomware-attack-kaseya
35. Tsvetkova, T. B. (2022, January 15). Russia Takes Down REvil Hacking Group at U.S. Request – FSB. *Reuters.*
36. CISA. (2021, July 12). *Kaseya Ransomware Attack: Guidance for Affected MSPs and Their Customers.* CISA. https://www.cisa.gov/news-events/news/kaseya-ransomware-attack-guidance-affected-msps-and-their-customers
37. Team, C. (n.d.). Sodinokibi/REvil Ransomware Gang Hit Acer with $50M Ransom Demand. *Cybereason.* https://www.cybereason.com/blog/sodinokibi/revil-ransomware-gang-hit-acer-with-50m-ransom-demand
38. Press, T. A. (2021, June 3). REvil, a Notorious Ransomware Gang, Was Behind JBS Cyberattack, the FBI Says. *NPR.* https://www.npr.org/2021/06/03/1002819883/revil-a-notorious-ransomware-gang-was-behind-jbs-cyberattack-the-fbi-says
39. Sason, D. (2021, October 21). REvil Ransomware Attack on Kaseya VSA: What You Need to Know. *Varonis.* https://www.varonis.com/blog/revil-msp-supply-chain-attack
40. Irwin, L. (2020, August 12). Travelex's Ransomware Ordeal Leads to Forced Administration. *IT Governance.* https://www.itgovernance.co.uk/blog/ransomware-victim-travelex-forced-into-administration
41. Combs, V. (2021, April 21). Apple Supplier Quanta Hit with $50 Million Ransomware Attack from REvil. *TechRepublic.* https://www.techrepublic.com/article/apple-supplier-quanta-hit-with-50-million-ransomware-attack-from-revil/
42. STAHIE, S. (2020, May 13). Law Firm Used by Celebrities Affected by REvil Ransomware and Data Breach. *Bitdefender.* https://www.bitdefender.com.au/blog/hotforsecurity/law-firm-used-by-celebrities-affected-by-revil-ransomware-and-data-breach/
43. Abshire, L. (n.d.). *REvil Ransomware Group: Invenergy Hack, JBS, Sol Oriens and More.* US Cybersecurity. https://www.uscybersecurity.net/cyberNews/revil-ransomware-group/
44. Keizertimes, E. A. (2020, June 22). Keizer Officials Pay $48k Ransom to Regain Control of City Computers. *OregonLive.* https://www.oregonlive.com/news/2020/06/keizer-officials-pay-48k-ransom-to-regain-control-of-city-computers.html
45. Montini, H. (2024, February 9). *NoEscape Ransomware: What You Need to Know.* https://www.provendata.com/blog/noescape-ransomware/

AUTHOR BIOGRAPHY

Reemar Tan is a master degree student specializing in cybersecurity at Edith Cowan University (ECU). He is a systems and cloud engineer responsible for deploying and designing disaster contingency strategies, ensuring data reliability, and configuring IT infrastructure for optimal performance and security. Reemar has a proven track record of accomplishment in the I.T. industry, with over 12 years of experience. He is a Linux expert and has successfully obtained well-known certifications, including VMWare Professional, Microsoft Azure Solution Architect, Azure Network and Security, Azure DevOps Expert and AWS Solution Architect, Red Hat Systems Administrator, and others. Due to his extensive expertise in I.T. infrastructure, cloud computing, networking, security, and application development, he exhibits an in-depth understanding of the overall functionality of I.T. This enables him to design and operate I.T. systems with high efficiency and optimal security.

Jiacheng Liu is pursuing a master's degree in cyber security at Edith Cowan University. His current research focuses on investigating and analyzing software ransomware organizations. Jiacheng is skilled in threat analysis and cyber defense strategies, leveraging his expertise to combat cybercrime effectively. His passion for traveling and fishing provides him with a balanced lifestyle and fresh perspectives, which he brings into his research work. When he's not delving into the intricacies of cyber threats, Jiacheng enjoys exploring new destinations and spending peaceful moments fishing. His diverse interests, combined with his analytical skills and cyber security expertise, contribute to his comprehensive approach to understanding and addressing cyber threats.

Ulya Saputri is pursuing a master's degree in cyber security at Edith Cowan University. She is currently participating in an internship program with a natural gas and electricity provider company, where she works as a SCADA (Supervisory Control and Data Acquisition) security analyst. In this role, Ulya focuses on investigating and mitigating threats to SCADA systems, ensuring the security and integrity of critical infrastructure. Her responsibilities include analyzing potential vulnerabilities, implementing robust security measures, and monitoring SCADA networks for any signs of cyber threats. Throughout her internship, Ulya has gained hands-on experience in real-world scenarios, enhancing her skills and understanding of the complexities involved in securing essential services. Ulya has a 3.5-year-old daughter who shares her interest in science and technology. In their spare time, they enjoy visiting museums, attending science and technology exhibitions, and creating projects together. These activities not only provide quality bonding time but also inspire a love of learning and discovery in her daughter.

David Ekeh is currently pursuing a master's degree in cybersecurity at Edith Cowan University (ECU). David's journey began in a close-knit family as the second of four children from loving and passionate parents. David's hobbies include basketball, research, and solving puzzles. These activities not only balance his rigorous academic schedule but also enhance his analytical and strategic thinking skills. David aspires to significantly impact cybersecurity, particularly in digital forensics and other security aspects. He aims to develop innovative solutions that enhance digital security, ensuring a safe and secure environment for individuals and organizations. Throughout his journey, David has learned the importance of perseverance, curiosity, and integrity. Each challenge has been an opportunity for growth, and each success has been a testament to the support and guidance of his family, friends, and mentors. The values instilled in him from a young age continue to guide his decisions and actions, shaping him into the person he is today.

Jing Xiao is a dedicated cybersecurity professional currently pursuing a master's degree in cybersecurity at Edith Cowan University. With a keen interest in ransomware investigation, Jing Xiao has engaged deeply with complex cybersecurity concepts, employing advanced technical strategies to investigate and synthesize data related to cyber threats and vulnerabilities. When not immersed in study, Jing enjoys traveling, music, and dancing, finding inspiration and relaxation in exploring new cultures and connecting with nature. Before embarking on master's journey, Jing Xiao earned a bachelor's degree in biomedical science (pharmacology) from the University of Western Australia.

Section II

Ransomware in Healthcare

3 Actor Behaviour, Notable Incidents in Critical Infrastructures, and Risks to the Health Sector

Michael N. Johnstone, Michael Crowley, and Glenn Murray

3.1 INTRODUCTION

This chapter examines the state-of-the-art literature on the effect of ransomware in the context of the critical infrastructure space to better understand the motivations of the threat actors and their victims. The definition of critical infrastructure has been broadened recently (at least in Australia), which increases the threat surface and therefore the opportunities for bad actors and the threats to victims. This research aims to provide an overarching analysis of foundational ransomware research, with a focus on how the evolution of the threat actors' motivations has increased the problem for victims via a review of significant incidents within the past 15 years.

Dragos [1, p. 22] reports that the LockBit ransomware was the most-used ransomware variant against industrial organisations in 2023, accounting for 25% of total ransomware incidents (at least those known to, and collected by, Dragos). What is interesting is that LockBit, like many ransomware groups, operates as a ransomware as a service (RaaS) provider, a concept discussed in the next section.

Branquinho [2] notes that current supervisory control and data acquisition (SCADA) systems (also called Operational Technology or OT) that comprise critical infrastructure networks are not the same as their precursors from the 1970s (although that same equipment is possibly still functioning today). SCADA operations were implemented separately, which is a stark contrast to current systems, which have complex functionalities and rely on corporate networks (and allied Information Technology or IT) to be connected to the SCADA environment for provisioning and production control. This melding of OT and IT, whilst appearing attractive, has several drawbacks, as described by Murray et al. [3], particularly that the melding increases the attack surface of a heretofore secure network.

Branquinho [2] presents two cases of ransomware attacks in Brazilian OT systems, one relating to a furniture factory, the other to a power utility. In the former case, a firm lost customer and supplier data and a factory was shut down for 15 days. The criminals demanded a relatively low ransom (~USD$3,000), but the company refused to pay, which generated a loss of ~USD$100,000 due to the production stoppage and subsequent delivery delays. This case is an example of irrational actor behaviour, which will be discussed later in this chapter.

The resurgence of high-profile ransomware attacks in critical sectors such as healthcare has been noted, emphasising the urgent need for effective defences to protect sensitive health data and ensure the continuity of medical services. The U.K. NHS WannaCry ransomware attack partly relied on internal users for initial infection, highlighting the vulnerability of healthcare critical infrastructure to insider threats and the need for robust security measures to mitigate such risks [4]. Specific instances in the health sector are covered shortly in the section "Impact of Cyberattack on Healthcare".

DOI: 10.1201/9781003469506-5

3.2 ACTOR BEHAVIOUR

Johnstone, Crowley and Murray [5] note two properties of Cybercrime as a Service (CaaS) that are particularly relevant to a discussion of the intersection of ransomware and critical infrastructure. First, that CaaS has democratised cybercrime, making advanced hacking tools and expertise accessible to individuals with malicious intent leading to an increase in cyberattack frequency and sophistication. Second, that cybercrime is a business in that it bears all the hallmarks of business, namely, products, consumers and a market-driven approach. A further property, which can be inferred from these two, is the rational actor behaviour that could be predicted about such transactions, given existing theory.

A common misconception is that ransomware is deployed by sophisticated cybercriminals, who are adept at navigating the arcane world of cyberspace. Ransomware is certainly developed by experts, but deployment is often operationalised by means of dashboards. Collier and Clayton [6, p. 13] observe that "the vast majority of people involved in cybercrime never develop any significant technical sophistication, nor is there any particular need for them to do so in order to continue to make money, cause harm, and compromise systems".

Much as conventional business has moved to a service orientation, a recent threat assessment report noted that (at least from a European perspective) "cybercrime services are widely available and have a well-established online presence" [7, p. 6]. Thus, ransomware has moved to a commoditised business orientation where the services can be hired by anyone prepared to pay for them. This movement has lowered the bar to entry and provided a reminder that the motivation for attacks on critical infrastructure can be strictly a profit-motivated business transaction. This idea will be explored in the following pages.

Rational actor behaviour, in the context of ransomware, is an interesting variation of the Prisoner's Dilemma (a risk/reward exercise in game theory where two rational actors can either co-operate for mutual benefit or betray the other actor for individual reward). The Prisoner's Dilemma itself is an example of a Nash equilibrium [8]. A Nash equilibrium is a strategy in game theory where a player's strategy is a best reply to the strategies chosen by the other player. In a Nash equilibrium, no player has an incentive to deviate unilaterally from their strategy. The co-operative aspect of the dilemma involves the victim paying the ransom and the criminal providing access to the locked data (see Table 3.1). Betrayal can be initiated by either party. If the victim betrays (by not paying the ransom), the criminal does not receive the payoff. Advice from law enforcement is that this is what the victim should do under the guise that paying the ransom is aiding criminal activity. The payoff for the victim is that they have kept the ransom money. This is not a rational course of action for the victim for two reasons. First, they still do not have their data, and second, the cost of remediation is likely to be at least the same as if they had paid.

The annual IBM/Ponemon data breach report [9], which collects data worldwide, observes that the cost of a ransomware attack per incident is approximately the same whether or not the ransom was paid (5.14 million USD for ransom not paid vs. 5.06 million USD when the ransom was paid). Therefore, the rational course of action for the victim is to pay the ransom because the victim regains immediate access to the data. Betrayal by the criminal involves taking the ransom without

TABLE 3.1
Payoffs for various outcomes

		Criminal's Choice	
Victim's Choice		Co-operate	Betray
	Co-operate	Pay/Provide key	Pay/No key
	Betray	Don't pay/***	Don't pay/No key

providing the key to unlock the data. An individual criminal could behave in this way, but not for long. Recalling the aforementioned market-driven approach, if a criminal were to not provide their end of the business transaction (the decryption key), then this would alarm other victims and cause them to not pay (which would now be rational behaviour on their part), affecting the profits of other criminals in the same business – thus other criminals would act to self-correct irrational behaviour from a non-rational criminal. Of course, if both parties betray (by not paying and not providing the key), then neither benefit from the transaction.

3.3 ACTOR PROFILES

Prior to the maturation of cybercrime to fit into a service-based economy, the skill, resources and motivation of potential threat actors would fit the profile shown in Table 3.2. Having established the service-oriented nature of cybercrime, along with the rise of the Internet of Things [10], we find that the skill and resources are no longer relevant (as those items are now outsourced) – all that matters is the motivation (assuming that the actor has the wherewithal to pay for the service). Note that both business rivals and organised crime have financial motives. This is not to say that other actors could not be motivated by financial concerns. For example, nation-states could have a superficial financial motivation (to do harm to another nation-state), but their end game would be political.

Having examined actor behaviour from the perspective of game theory (using ransomware as an example) and noted that the service orientation of cybercrime has democratised the "playing field" in terms of ability to conduct attacks, we now profile a range of well-known cyberattacks on critical infrastructure.

3.4 OVERVIEW OF CYBERATTACKS ON CRITICAL INFRASTRUCTURE

> The Australian Government's Critical Infrastructure Resilience Strategy currently defines critical infrastructure as "those physical facilities, supply chains, information technologies and communication networks, which if destroyed, degraded or rendered unavailable for an extended period, would significantly impact the social or economic wellbeing of the nation, or affect Australia's ability to conduct national defence and ensure national security" [12].

Elsewhere, the Centre for European Policy Studies (CEPS) Task Force Report on Protecting Critical Infrastructure in the European Union (EU) defines critical infrastructure as "infrastructure whose failure would result in substantial damage to society and/or the economy" [13].

The European Commission defines critical infrastructures as an asset, system or part thereof located in member states that is essential for the maintenance of vital societal functions, health, safety, security, economic or social well-being of people, and the disruption or destruction of which

TABLE 3.2
Motivations of various threat actors (adapted from [11])

Actor	Skill	Resources	Motivation
Script kiddie	Basic	Low	Annoyance
Business rival	Medium	Medium	Financial
Insider-malicious	Varies	Low	Destruction
Insider-moral	Varies	Low	Ethical
Hactivist	Medium	Medium	Political
Organised crime	High	High	Financial
Nation-state	High	High	Political

would have a significant impact on a member state as a result of the failure to maintain those functions (European Council Directive 2008, cited in [13]).

Furthermore, the European Union – NATO task force on the resilience of critical infrastructure has identified four sectors in its final report in June 2023 [14]. These "four sectors of cross-cutting importance have been identified as providing services that support and enable other sectors: energy, transport, digital infrastructure and space" [14, p. 4]. Significantly, the EU has included the new frontier of space in its consideration of critical infrastructure, recognising the role of satellites as a component of critical infrastructure.

The increase in cyberattacks targeting critical infrastructure sectors such as energy, government and healthcare highlights the cybercriminal's growing sophistication and impact of cyberattacks. These cyberattacks often involve advanced techniques such as malware, ransomware and spear phishing, exploiting vulnerabilities in an increasingly interconnected environment. The impacts are often significant, ranging from disrupted services and financial losses to threats to human safety and national security. The healthcare sector, in particular, faces unique challenges due to the sensitive nature of patient data and the critical role of information technology (IT) and operational technology (OT) systems in patient care. This trend underscores the urgent need for enhanced cybersecurity measures and international cooperation to safeguard these essential services. The escalation of cyberattacks on critical infrastructure reflects a growing concern in our reliance on digital systems.

3.4.1 Notable Incidents

Table 3.3 presents an overview of notable cyberattacks on critical infrastructure, a trend that has increasingly become a global concern. These incidents not only highlight the vulnerabilities in our digital systems but also showcase the diverse methods employed by cyber criminals. From energy to healthcare, the targets of these attacks span various essential sectors, impacting public safety, economic stability and national security. This table encapsulates key details of these cyberattacks, including the year, the specific incident, the targeted sector, and the impact or consequences of each attack. The incidents chosen for this table are representative of the broader challenges faced in securing critical infrastructure against cyber threats.

The cyberattacks listed in Table 3.3 represent a broad spectrum of cyberattacks, including geopolitical impacts, espionage, financial motivated crimes and disruption to critical infrastructure. This highlights the multifaceted nature of cyberattacks. The listed cyberattacks can be grouped into six categories as per Table 3.4. Note that due to the nature of the cyberattacks in Table 3.3, a cyberattack can be listed in multiple categories.

From Table 3.4, we note that the nature of cyber threats is constantly evolving, with cybercriminals using more sophisticated techniques and targeting a wider range of sectors. The complexity and scale of the attacks as per the "Large Scale Data Breaches" category outline the significant impacts on companies and individuals. The broad range of targets, as listed in Table 3.3, signifies that no sector is immune to cyberthreats. The targeting of the healthcare sector reflects not only the financial motivations of cybercriminals but also the potential for significant societal disruption. It raises critical questions about the security preparedness and resilience of healthcare systems in the face of cyber threats.

3.4.2 Impact of Cyberattack on Healthcare

Healthcare, including hospitals are increasingly targeted due to their critical role in public health and the sensitive nature of their data. These attacks exploit weaknesses in security protocols, outdated software, and often underfunded IT and OT infrastructure. The consequences can be significant compromising patient care, risk to patient safety, delays in critical medical procedures, and potential breaches of sensitive patient data. This incident underscores the need for healthcare facilities to prioritise cybersecurity, implement robust data protection measures, and regularly update their IT

TABLE 3.3
Notable cyberattacks on critical infrastructure, 2009–2023, expanded from [3]

Year	Cyberattack	Details	Outcome
2009	GhostNet	GhostNet was discovered by researchers at the University of Toronto. GhostNet was a sophisticated cyber espionage attack that used phishing email and malware to infect networks [15].	Highlighted the interconnectedness of IT and OT systems.
2010	Stuxnet worm	A sophisticated malware was installed via a third-party contractor using a USB drive to an Iran nuclear facility. The malware infected the SCADA system controlling the nuclear centrifuges and changed the values and mechanics to behave abnormally [16].	Nuclear centrifuges and valves were sabotaged/destroyed.
2011	Steel plant infected with Conficker worm	Network and computer systems were infected with the Conficker worm, which spread across the corporate and OT network systems. Communications between the PLCs and field devices were flooded, causing most control system devices in become unresponsive [17].	The malware spread throughout the network and impact the communication of SCADA systems and field devices, which resulted to latency and partial outage on the SCADA network.
2012	Virus targets Saudi Arabian Oil Company	Nation-state hackers attacked Saudi Aramco with the Shamoon virus, which infected 30,000 computers across the network, wiping hard drives [18].	Approximately 30,000 corporate computers systems were wiped clean. The corporate network was down for several days.
2012	Shamoon virus affects computers at Qatari gas firm RasGas	Qatari gas firm RasGas became infected with the Shamoon virus. The attack was believed to be state-sponsored [19].	The website and corporate network of the organisation was impacted for several days.
2012	Canadian software manufacturing company firewall breach	Adversaries compromised the firewall system of Telvent Canada Ltd, stealing critical project SCADA files that were related to the OASyS SCADA project [20].	Theft of critical and sensitive project files related to SCADA systems.
2012	US power plant Infected with malware	The malware was identified on a USB drive used for control system configuration backups in a US nuclear powerplant [21].	Compromised ICS system with an undisclosed impact to the operation.
2014	US Public utility compromise	Adversaries compromised a security system at a US public utility through a brute-force password attack [22].	The system was not directly connected to other OT equipment due to maintenance.
2014	Dragonfly group energy industry reconnaissance campaign	Reported that an adversary group called Dragonfly has been targeting the energy sector in the United States and Europe, using IT-based vectors, such as phishing emails, to pivot into OT networks [23].	Undisclosed, expected loss of critical assets information and business operations process
2014	German Steel Mill attack	A German Steel Mill was breached using social engineering vectors to enter the company network and further compromise the control system network. The compromise resulted in preventing a blast furnace from shutting down when required [24].	Catastrophic damage to the steel mill

(Continued)

TABLE 3.3 ***(Continued)***
Notable cyberattacks on critical infrastructure, 2009–2023, expanded from [3]

Year	Cyberattack	Details	Outcome
2015	Blackenergy3 Ukraine power grid cyberattack	A suspected nation-state adversary group attacked a regional Ukraine power company, compromising the ICS network causing a 3-hour power outage [25].	Around 225,000 customers lost power, deleted files from the master boot records, and shut-down communications.
2015	Kemuri Water Plant	Adversary compromised a water utility online billing system, pivoting into the SCADA network servers and holding the utility company ransom [26].	Modified chlorine and chemical levels on the water used at the treatment plants. Around 2.5 million customer details were stolen.
2017	Triton	An oil and gas plant in Saudi Arabia was compromised through remote access to an engineer workstation. The adversary reprogrammed controller units, causing fail safes to occur shutting down the plant [27].	Failsafe systems worked correctly
2017	NotPetya cyberattack including hospitals globally	NotPetya victims included Maersk, the world's largest ship-building company ($300 million) and FedEx ($400 million) and drug maker Merck ($870 million). NotPetya also attacked a company called Nuance, a patient records company. [28].	Nuance suffered $92 million is losses that effected approx. 70 locations across the globe. The cyberattack impacted hundreds of hospitals and thousands of health clinics around the world.
2017	WannaCry on National Health Service (NHS)	WannaCry in May 2017 globally infected over 300,000 computers across 150 countries. This included 48 UK NHS trusts [29].	Used the "EternalBlue" Microsoft Windows exploit.
2020	Israeli Water	Israeli water systems endured multiple cyberattacks designed to compromise the control systems for pumping stations, sewage systems, wastewater plants, and agriculture pumps. They aimed to spike chlorine and other chemicals to harmful levels into public water, disrupting supply at a critical time for Israel [30].	The attacks were unsuccessful. Had the attack been successful, civilians would further overload hospitals, farmers would unwittingly destroy their crops, and further implications would ravage the country during the pandemic.
2020	SolarWinds supply chain	SolarWinds, a major software company, was the subject of a cyberattack that spread to its clients, which may have started in 2019 but was only discovered in December 2020. Malicious code was added into the company's software system. The system, called Orion, is widely used by companies to manage IT resources. Orion updates, which included the hacked code, were received by as many as 18,000 SolarWinds customers. The code created a backdoor to customer's information technology systems, which hackers then used to install even more malware that helped them spy on companies and organisations [31].	The campaign that infected numerous government agencies and tech companies with malicious SolarWinds software had also infected more than a dozen critical infrastructure companies in the electric power, oil, and manufacturing industries running the same software. The consequence was the penetration of multiple networks.

TABLE 3.3 *(Continued)*
Notable cyberattacks on critical infrastructure, 2009–2023, expanded from [3]

Year	Cyberattack	Details	Outcome
2021	Colonial Pipeline	Colonial Pipeline, the largest pipeline in the United States, was hit with a targeted ransomware attack. The pipeline, which supplied over 45% of the East Coast's gas, diesel, and jet fuel, was forced to shut down its operations entirely. Although the ransomware attack did not directly target the OT, the consequence of the attack was the shutting down of the OT to prevent the risk of the attack and threatening the safety of the OT. This highlights that threats to both human and environmental safety, along with the uncertainty as to the scope of infection, present as risk factors for sensitive industrial environments [32].	It took the pipeline 11 days to partially recover after the company ended up paying $5 million in ransom. By the end of the attack, nearly 11,000 gas stations were still out of gas, and the average cost for fuel per gallon rose nationally, the highest cost in over six years.
2021	Newfoundland and Labrador Healthcare	In October 2021, Canadian healthcare authority Newfoundland and Labrador Healthcare was hit with a significant cyberattack, which impacted patient care and data security [33].	An unauthorised third-party (ransomware gang "Hive") accessed the health care infrastructure causing significant system outages.
2022	DTEK Group (Ukrainian energy company)	DTEK, a Ukrainian energy company owning several coal and thermal powerplants, incurred a cyberattack by Russian hackers to aid Russia's war efforts against Ukraine [34].	DTEK Group said the goal of the attack was to destabilise the technological processes of the distribution and generation processes. DTEK reported that the cyberattack didn't have any negative effect.
2022	Gestore dei Servizi Energetici SpA (GSE) (Italian state-owned energy services)	BlackCat, also known as ALPHV claimed to have downloaded 700 GB of data from GSE, including information on projects, contracts and accounting, and uploaded images of documents from the hack [35].	BlackCat stole 700 GB of files from the Italian energy agency's servers.
2022	CommonSpirit Health	The ransomware attack occurred on 2 October 2022, and forced CommonSpirit Health to take its systems offline, impacting more than 100 CommonSpirit facilities across the United States. During the attack, the personal data of more than 623,700 patients were exposed [36].	The ransomware attack it suffered in October 2022 cost the company US$150 million.
2022	AcidRain wiper malware	In May 2022, Ukraine was attacked by a widespread wiper malware during the war with Russia. AcidRain Wiper used brute-force attacks to wipe files across network systems [37].	Displayed the destructive capacity of cyber warfare
2022	Optus data breach	In September 2022, Australia's second largest telecommunications company Optus suffered a significant data breach. This cyberattack was significant enough to prompt national response to increase cybersecurity measures in Australia [38].	Personal information of millions of Optus customers, including contact details, phone numbers and ID numbers were compromised.

(Continued)

TABLE 3.3 ***(Continued)***

Notable cyberattacks on critical infrastructure, 2009–2023, expanded from [3]

Year	Cyberattack	Details	Outcome
2022–2023	Medibank cyberattack	The Medibank cyberattack started in 2022 and continued into 2023. About 9.7 million current and former customers were compromised. Of note is that Medibank decided not to pay the ransom. Medibank believed that paying the ransom didn't ensure the release of the stolen data. Since the cyberattack, Russian man Aleksandr Ermakov has had sanctions applied, including financial penalties and a travel ban into Australia [39].	The compromised data included health claims data, Medicare numbers, passport numbers and visa details for international customers.
2023	MGM Resorts cyberattack	The MGM Resorts suffered a complex security breach in 2023 by a criminal gang known as Scattered Spider. The attack started though a social engineering tactic that allowed the access into MGM's systems [40].	The substantial financial loss for MGM Resorts was estimated at $8.4 million in revenue per day. This attack highlighted the need for effective password management, implementation of multi-factor authentication (MFA) and threat monitoring.
2023	MOVEit mass cyberattack	A Russian group known as CLOP exploited a vulnerability in the MOVEit file transfer software [41].	The attack impacted approximately 2,667 organisations including high-profile companies IBM, Cognizant, Deloitte, PwC and EY. Also healthcare services through Maximus Federal Services
2023	23andME data breach	The 23andME data breach was a significant cyber incident in the area of genetic and personal data security. The attack was a credential stuffing attack where username and password pairs were obtained from previous data leaks. This exposes the reuse of login credentials across multiple platforms [42].	The cybercriminal collected 5.5 million personal data records, as well as 1.4 million DNA relatives profiles.
2023	Ardent Health Services	The cyberattack targeted Ardent Health Services. Ardent Health Services owns and operates 30 hospitals and 200 care sites across Oklahoma, Texas, New Jersey, New Mexico, Idaho and Kansas. The cyberattack lead to the shutdown of emergency rooms across multiple hospitals [43].	The cyberattack caused hospitals to use handwritten records and resulted in the cancellation of operations. Ardent Health Services restored access two weeks after the ransomware attack.

and OT infrastructure to mitigate such risks. An example of the vulnerabilities in healthcare IT and OT systems is the 2021 ransomware attack on an Illinois hospital, which led to its closure.

In 2022 alone, there was an increase of 74% in weekly cyberattacks on healthcare organisations compared to 2021 [44]. In the United States, healthcare ranked second with an 86% increase from the previous year, totalling 1,410 attacks per week [44]. These statistics reflect a disturbing trend

TABLE 3.4
Synthesis of cyberattacks described in Table 3.3

Serial	Category	Description	Cyberattack Examples
1	State-sponsored	These cyberattacks demonstrate state-sponsored efforts, which are focused at sabotage or espionage with the intent of geopolitical disruption.	GhostNet, Stuxnet, Dragonfly, BlackEnergy3
2	Widespread malware disruption	These cyberattacks have caused widespread disruption and damage across several systems and organisations globally.	Conflicker, Shamoon, BlackEnergy3, AcidRain Wiper Malware
3	Supply chain attacks	Sophisticated attack designed to exploit the vulnerabilities within supply chains. This allows the compromise of multiple organisations through a single-entry point.	SolarWinds, MOVEit, WannaCry
4	Large-scale data breaches	These cyberattacks are data breaches that have affected the privacy and trust of the consumers. They typically target personal and sensitive data.	Uber, Optus, Medibank, MGM Resorts, 23andME, WannaCry
5	Targeting critical infrastructure	These cyberattacks threaten the critical infrastructure. This threatens public safety and national security. The sectors affected include energy, utilities and healthcare.	Triton, GSE, DTEK Group, Colonial Pipeline, NotPetya, Ardent Health Services, CommonSpirit Health, MOVEit, WannaCry
6	Ransomware targeting health sector	Ransomware is continually increasing year on year, causing financial loss and operational disruptions.	CommonSpirit Health, Ardent Health Services, NotPetya, WannaCry

where healthcare facilities are increasingly targeted by cybercriminals due to the valuable and sensitive nature of the data they hold and the higher likelihood of ransom demands being met to prevent the release of such data.

Continuing in 2023, hospitals were impacted by numerous cyberattacks, with ransomware being both increasing and more prevalent [45]. According to an analysis reported in the *HIPAA Journal* (2024), there were 46 ransomware attacks on hospital systems, which impacted 141 hospitals [46]. Alder also noted that the financial impact of these ransomware attacks increased the average cost on healthcare increasing to approximately $11 million [46]. Highlighting the real-world impacts on healthcare, Table 3.3 lists one of the significant cyberattacks that impacted hospitals, which was the Ardent Health Services attack. Brooks [47] reported that this cyberattack caused multiple hospitals to cancel operations, forcing hospital staff to resort to handwritten records.

The MOVEit cyberattack impacted Maximus Federal Services and affected approximately 45 million records [46]. Maximus Federal Services is an American government services provider with global operations across various sectors including healthcare. The services include managing Medicaid, a United States health insurance provider to low-income families, and Medicare, a United States health insurance program for people aged 65 and older.

The human cost of these cyberattacks is also increasingly evident. While quantifying the direct impact on mortality rates is challenging, there have been incidents where disruptions in healthcare services due to cyberattacks have had grave consequences. For instance, in 2020, a ransomware attack on a hospital in Düsseldorf, Germany, forced the closure of its emergency department, resulting in a patient's death while being rerouted to another hospital. Moreover, the increase in cyberattacks during the COVID-19 pandemic has put additional strain on healthcare systems, leading to curtailed emergency services and cancelled operations [48].

Furthermore, vulnerable medical devices are providing access for cybercriminals into the hospital networks. In a 2022 report, Cynerio and the Ponemon Institute highlighted that from the 517 respondents, 56% experienced at least one cyberattack in the past 24 months that involved an Internet of Things (IoT) or Internet of Medical Things (IoMT) device [49]. The report identified medical devices like MRI machines and heart rate monitors as the weakest entry point in hospital cyber defences. The lack of proper cyber defence mechanisms in these devices creates opportunities for cybercriminals to infiltrate hospital networks and initiate cyberattack cycles, leading to increased mortality rates and extended patient stays [49]. This situation underscores the critical need for hospitals to prioritise cybersecurity alongside patient care to safeguard against such vulnerabilities.

It is a common practice to address vulnerabilities within devices and to ensure whether security patches and updates to firmware and operating systems are conducted on a regular basis. Patching and updating Software as a Medical Device (SaMD), IoMT and IoT devices have specific challenges that stem from medical compliance and cost implications. A key issue is the unique challenge in maintaining the security of IoMT devices while adhering to regulatory compliance, such as the Health Insurance Portability and Accountability Act of 1996 (HIPAA) in the United States. These devices, ranging from on-body wearables to in-hospital monitoring equipment, present a varied and complex landscape for cybersecurity [50].

The regulatory landscape for medical devices is evolving to match the pace of technological advancements. Regulators like the Food and Drug Administration (FDA) and the Therapeutic Goods Administration (TGA) constantly update guidelines to address these challenges, emphasising the need for developers to remain informed and engage with regulatory bodies early in the development process [51, 52] However, the dynamic nature of software, which allows for frequent modifications, including security updates, contrasts starkly with the generally more static nature of traditional medical devices.

When software updates are required on medical devices, there is a requirement to determine whether the update significantly alters the device's functionality, performance, or intended use, potentially requiring re-submission for regulatory approval [52]. If the software update does significantly alter the device functionality and/or performance, it may involve the healthcare provider to documentation and possibly report to regulatory body. Guidance from the FDA is that each update must adhere to regulatory standards, which can be complex given the rapid development cycles of software products [51].

This alarming rise in cyberattacks underscores the urgent need for enhanced cybersecurity measures in healthcare systems. Effective strategies include improving data protection, regularly updating IT systems, training staff on cybersecurity best practices, and developing robust incident response plans. The healthcare sector's vulnerability to cyberattacks not only threatens patient data and privacy but also poses a significant risk to patient safety and the overall integrity of healthcare delivery systems. As such, it is critical for healthcare providers and policymakers to prioritise cybersecurity to safeguard against these evolving digital threats.

3.5 PREVENTIVE MEASURES AND RECOMMENDATIONS

The evolution and sophistication of the cyberattacks listed in Table 3.3 necessitate robust and dynamic cybersecurity measures. These include not only technological solutions but also strategic policies, international cooperation, and heightened awareness across all sectors. The integration of cybersecurity into national security strategies, corporate governance, and consumer protection frameworks is crucial. The following is a set of preventive measures and recommendations that organisations can adopt.

- Conduct Regular Audits – Regularly review and assess IT and OT infrastructure and practices to identify vulnerabilities.
- Employee Training – Implement ongoing training programs for employees to recognise and respond to cyber threats, such as phishing attacks.

- Define Cybersecurity Policies – Develop and implement cybersecurity policies, including guidelines for password management, data handling, and response protocols for suspected breaches.
- Update and Patch Systems – Regularly update software and systems to mediate vulnerabilities.
- Access Controls – Implement access controls and implement multi-factor authentication.
- Data Encryption – Encrypt sensitive data both in transit and at rest.
- Incident Response Plan – Develop a clear, actionable incident response plan for potential cyberattacks.
- Information Sharing – Engage in information sharing with other organisations including government agencies for updates on emerging threats.
- Backup data to a storage system that can and is disconnected from the World Wide Web.
- Ensure iCloud storage is covered by a safe political/legal system. That is, confidentiality is not only assured but is subject to international agreements and exists free from regional and domestic political interference.

3.5.1 Remedies – Legal

The Australian Government has enhanced the protection of critical infrastructure with the *Security Legislation Amendment (Critical Infrastructure Protection) Act* (2022) (Cth) (SLACIP Act) coming into effect on 2 April 2022. This legislation amended the *Security of Critical Infrastructure Act* (2018) (Cth) (SOCI Act) to require responsible entities to create and to maintain a risk management plan with those operating systems of national significance complying with a new enhanced cyber security framework. The following factsheets were prepared to assist entities in meeting the requirements of this new legislation:

CISC Factsheet – The Security Amendment (Critical Infrastructure Protection) Act 2022,
CISC Factsheet – Risk Management Program,
CISC Factsheet – Systems of National Significance/Enhanced Cyber Security Obligations, and
CISC Factsheet – Use and Disclosure of Protected Information.

Additionally, the Australian Government has released a Cyber Security Legislative Reforms Consultation Paper as the first step in implementing the 2023–2030 Australian Cyber Security Strategy [53]. The strategy is to issue in "a new era of public-private co-leadership to enhance Australia's cyber security" [54, p. 4]. Governments are also taking the fight to protect critical infrastructure to those who seek to disrupt.

On 23 January 2024 the Australian Government announced that it had "used cyber sanctions powers on a Russian individual for his role in the breach of the Medibank Private network" [55]. The Australian Government has imposed a targeted financial sanction and a travel ban on Aleksandr Ermakov. This sanction makes it a criminal offence, punishable by up to ten years' imprisonment and heavy fines, to provide assets to Aleksandr Ermakov, or to use or deal with his assets, including through cryptocurrency wallets or ransomware payments [55].

Australia has the option to use two types of sanctions, first, as a member of the United Nations pursuant to Article 25 of the *Charter of the United Nations* to implement UN Security Council decisions, and second, under the *Autonomous Sanctions Act* (2011) (Cth) and the *Autonomous Sanctions Regulations* (2011) (Cth). The Australian Sanctions Office within the Department of Foreign Affairs and Trade is responsible for administering these laws [56].

Maintenance of the global economy and overall peace and security depends on the reliable functioning and maintenance of critical infrastructure. The European Union-NATO task force on the resilience of critical infrastructure illustrates a recognition that military preparedness is linked to aspects of what has to date been considered domestic critical infrastructure [14].

In that report, resilience for the EU "encompasses the ability to prevent, protect against, respond to, resist, mitigate, absorb, accommodate and recover from incidents that have the potential to disrupt the provision of essential services" [14, p. 3]. For NATO, "the focus is on critical infrastructure that enables the fulfilment of the organisation's core tasks of deterrence and defence; crisis prevention and management; and cooperative security" [14, p. 3].

The report identified "four sectors of cross-cutting importance have been identified as providing services that support and enable other sectors: energy, transport, digital infrastructure and space" [14, p. 4].

These threats are recognised at the highest levels of the United Nations. The United Nations Security Council holds Arria-formula meetings, and these can cover critical infrastructure, with a 2023 meeting covering the following questions:

What actions can the Security Council take to address cyberattacks against critical infrastructure perpetrated by states?

What role can the Council play to ensure a secure and peaceful cyberspace, build trust between states, and prevent conflicts arising from the malicious use of Information and Communications Technologies (ICTs) by states or non-state actors?

What are the possible venues and mechanisms for a closer partnership between public and private entities for concerted and coherent defense and responses to cyberattacks? [57].

At this meeting the Honourable Mitch Fifield, Australian Ambassador, noted that the "Security Council has a crucial role to play in preventing conflicts arising from the malicious use of ICTs (Information and Communications Technology) by states . . . that All Members of the UN have agreed, by consensus, that existing international law applies in cyberspace". He concluded with the statement that "Cyber and critical technology issues are strategic foreign policy issues – and it is vital that they are treated as such by the international community" [58].

In a clear sign that international entities may be starting to recognise the threat posed by cyberattacks on critical infrastructure like hospitals, the International Committee of the Red Cross/Red Crescent (ICRC) has partnered with research institutions like the Centre for Cyber Trust and Johns Hopkins University Applied Physics Laboratory to explore the technological feasibility of digitalising the Red Cross, Red Crescent and Red Crystal emblems and is seeking the support of states around the world to protect those affected by armed conflicts online. The digital emblem would signal that the marked infrastructure should not be targeted [59].

3.5.2 Remedies – Technical

The aforementioned remedies are legal or policy-based. We now turn to technical remedies, which offer a range of protections, but are concomitant with a range of complexities that make their selection, implementation and maintenance non-trivial. Some simple protection mechanisms were mentioned in the previous section, such as patching systems or regular backup of data. Whilst these mechanisms appear relatively simple to implement, there are associated flow-on risks that need to be evaluated. For example, patching systems or devices is good practice, but in a large or safety-critical system (such as those found in the health sector), the effect of such patching needs to be carefully evaluated prior to deployment to production systems. A security patch may have unforeseen consequences in a specific environment that could not be envisioned by the patch developer. Further, patching may affect maintenance contracts with OEMs of CI devices and may void warranties. Similarly, data backup appears as a simple remedy; however the process of storage and recovery requires careful thought as quality ransomware actively seeks out backups. Questions arise such as Where are the data stored (off-site, in the cloud)? Are the data encrypted (where are the keys stored?)? How/When is the backup tested? Has a restore been tested successfully?

Machine learning-based solutions are attractive, but in general require large training data sets to be effective and are still prone to false positives. Almashhadani et al. [60], for example, conducted a behavioural analysis of crypto ransomware network activities, built a testbed, extracted various network features from benign and ransomware traffic and tested a multi-classifier crypto ransomware detection system.

In the related problem space of spear phishing (as ransomware is sometimes delivered by email), the RAIDER system [61] was able to demonstrate reasonable detection accuracy against a sophisticated "Known Sender" attack, where fake emails greatly resemble those of the impersonated sender. In the case of ransomware, an effective system must exhibit low false positives (must not mis-classify benign [legitimate email, software or traffic] data as ransomware) but also must exhibit low false negatives (must not mis-classify ransomware as benign data). The former leads to user dissatisfaction, the latter leads to a loss of trust – ultimately the result is the same – users don't want to use the system.

The above solutions require the malware to enter the system (or at least enter a DMZ or sandbox) in order to be evaluated. More complex solutions call for hooks into operating systems. One such system, called Redemption, is presented by Kharraz and Kirda [62]. This solution inserts itself into the Windows operating system to provide real-time protection against ransomware. They state that Redemption can ensure zero data loss against current ransomware families and incurs only modest overhead. This is an interesting approach as it uses different types of metrics to detect ransomware, for example, file entropy is measured during reads and writes. As ransomware encrypts files, any large increase in entropy between reads and writes would be indicative of the presence of ransomware.

3.6 CONCLUSION

The increasing frequency of cyberattacks on critical infrastructure necessitates a proactive and robust approach to cybersecurity. It's imperative for these sectors, especially healthcare, to implement stringent security measures, conduct regular audits, and ensure continuous employee training to mitigate these risks effectively. Mitigation is, of course, not the same as being completely safe, therefore, perhaps the answer is to be a hard target (or, at least, harder than anyone else in the sector).

Legal/political remedies give structure, framework and guidance. However, these remedies can only provide an incentive for best practice and post-cyberattack consequences. In contrast, technical remedies can shield users from attack. The universality of the World Wide Web and the resultant connectivity of computer systems require a united approach from individual users through to nation-states for implementing a best practice in cyber usage.

REFERENCES

1. Dragos. "OT Cybersecurity: The 2023 Year in Review". Technical Report. Dragos Inc. 2024.
2. M.A. Branquinho. "Ransomware in Industrial Control Systems. What Comes after WannaCry and Petya Global Attacks". *WIT Transactions on the Built Environment*, 174, 329–334. 2018.
3. G. Murray, M. Johnstone and C. Valli. "The Convergence of IT and OT in Critical Infrastructure". *Proceedings of the 15th Australian Information Security Management Conference*. 2017, 149–155.
4. S. Walker-Roberts, M. Hammoudeh and A. Dehghantanha. "A Systematic Review of the Availability and Efficacy of Countermeasures to Internal Threats in Healthcare Critical Infrastructure". *IEEE Access*, 6, 25167–25177. 2018. https://doi.org/10.1109/ACCESS.2018.2817560
5. M.N. Johnstone, M. Crowley and G. Murray. "The Changing Face of Cyber Crime as a Service: An Australian Perspective". *Journal of Information Warfare*, 23(1), 64–76. 2024.
6. B. Collier and R. Clayton. "A 'Sophisticated Attack'? Innovation, Technical Sophistication, and Creativity in the Cybercrime Ecosystem". *Proceedings of the 21st Annual Workshop on the Economics of Information Security (WEIS 2022)*. 2022.
7. "Europol Internet Organised Crime Threat Assessment (IOCTA) 2023". Report. Publications Office of the European Union, Luxembourg. 2023.
8. J.F. Nash. "Non-Cooperative Games". *Annals of Mathematics*, 54, 286–295. 1951.
9. IBM. "Cost of a Data Breach Report 2023". Report. IBM Corporation, Armonk, NY. 2023.

10. Z. Baig, P. Szewczyk, C. Valli, P. Rabadia, P. Hannay, M. Chernyshev, M. Johnstone, P. Kerai, A. Ibrahim, K. Sansurooah, N. Syed and M. Peacock. "Future Challenges for Smart Cities: Cyber-Security and Digital Forensics". *Digital Investigation*, 22, 3–13. August 2017. https://doi.org/10.1016/j.diin.2017.06.015
11. D. Manuel and M. Warren. "Think Like a Hacker". Presentation, Melbourne. 2017.
12. REM. "Revised Explanatory Memorandum: Security Legislation Amendment (Critical Infrastructure) Bill 2021". Available: https://parlinfo.aph.gov.au/parlInfo/download/legislation/ems/r6657_ems_c345cb8e-87b2-461a-87f953d9aad3afc6/upload_pdf/JC003855_Revised%20Explanatory%20Memorandum.pdf;fileType=application%2Fpdf#search=%22legislation/ems/r6657_ems_c345cb8e-87b2-461a-87f9-53d9aad3afc6%22 page 3
13. "CEPS Report". Centre for European Policy Studies, Brussels. 2010. Available: http://aei.pitt.edu/15445/1/Critical_Infrastructure_Protection_Final_A4.pdf
14. EU-NATO. "EU-NATO Task Force on the Resilience of Critical Infrastructure". Final Assessment Report 0840–23. European Union, Brussels. 2023.
15. B. Schneier. "The Story behind the Stuxnet Virus". *Forbes*. 2010. Available: https://www.forbes.com/2010/10/06/iran-nuclear-computer-technology-security-stuxnet-worm.html–4352814851e8
16. S. Karnouskos. "Stuxnet Worm Impact on Industrial Cyber-Physical System Security". *IECON 2011–37th Annual Conference of the IEEE Industrial Electronics Society*. 2011. https://doi.org/10.1109/iecon.2011.6120048
17. RISI. "RISI Online Incident Database". 2015. Available: https://www.risidata.com/Database
18. C. Bronk and E. Tikk-Ringas. "The Cyber Attack on Saudi Aramco". *Survival*, 55(2), 81–96. 2013. https://doi.org/10.1080/00396338.2013.784468
19. E. Mills. "Virus Knocks Out Computers at Qatari Gas Firm RasGas". *CNET*. 2012. Available: https://www.cnet.com/news/virus-knocks-out-computers-at-qatari-gas-firm-rasgas/
20. B. Krebs. "Chinese Hackers Blamed for Intrusion at Energy Industry Giant Telvent". 2012. Available: https://krebsonsecurity.com/2012/09/chinese-hackers-blamed-for-intrusion-at-energy-industry-giant-telvent/
21. D.E. Sanger. "US Plants Hit by USB Stick Malware Attack". *BBC*. 2013. Available: https://www.bbc.com/news/technology-21042378
22. J. Kirk. "Public Utility Compromised after Brute-Force Attack, DHS Says". *Computer World*. 2014. Available: https://www.computerworld.com.au/article/545681/public_utility_compromised_after_brute-force_attack_dhs_says/
23. M. Braga. "Russia-Linked Hackers Infiltrated US and European Energy Companies, Security Firm Finds". *CBC News*. 2017. Available: https://www.cbc.ca/news/technology/russia-dragonfly-energetic-bear-hacking-energy-us-symantec-1.4276999
24. R.M. Lee, M.J. Assante and T. Conway. "German Steel Mill Cyber Attack". 2014.
25. R.M. Lee, M.J. Assante and T. Conway. "Analysis of the Cyber Attack on the Ukrainian Power Grid". 2016.
26. J. Leyden. "Water Treatment Plant Hacked, Chemical Mix Changed for Tap Supplies". *The Register*. 2016. Available: https://www.theregister.co.uk/2016/03/24/water_utility_hacked/
27. B. Johnson, D. Caban, M. Krotofil, D. Scali, N. Brubaker and C. Glyer. "Attackers Deploy New ICS Attack Framework 'TRITON' and Cause Operational Disruption to Critical Infrastructure". 2017. Available: https://www.fireeye.com/blog/threat-research/2017/12/attackers-deploy-new-ics-attack-framework-triton.html
28. A. Greenberg. "How the Worst Cyberattacks in History Hit American Hospitals". *Slate*. 2019. Available: https://slate.com/technology/2019/11/sandworm-andy-greenberg-excerpt-notpetya-hospitals.html
29. T. Wheeler and J. Alderdice. "Cyber Collateral: WannaCry & the Impact of Cyberattacks on the Mental Health of Critical Infrastructure Defenders". *Changing Character of War Centre*. 2022.
30. K.L. Snider, R. Shandler, S. Zandani and D. Canetti. "Cyberattacks, Cyber Threats, and Attitudes toward Cybersecurity Policies". *Journal of Cybersecurity*, 7(1). 2021. https://doi.org/10.1093/cybsec/tyab019
31. J. Martínez and J.M. Durán. "Software Supply Chain Attacks, a Threat to Global Cybersecurity: SolarWinds' Case Study". *International Journal of Safety and Security Engineering*, 11(5), 537–545. 2021. https://doi.org/10.18280/ijsse.110505
32. J. Beerman, D. Berent, Z. Falter and S. Bhunia. "A Review of Colonial Pipeline Ransomware Attack". 2023 *IEEE/ACM 23rd International Symposium on Cluster, Cloud and Internet Computing Workshops (CCGridW)*. 2023. https://doi.org/10.1109/ccgridw59191.2023.00017
33. A.S. Wilner, H. Luce, E. Ouellet, O. Williams and N. Costa. "From Public Health to Cyber Hygiene: Cybersecurity and Canada's Healthcare Sector". *International Journal*, 76(4), 522–543. 2021.
34. S. Lyngaas. "Russian Hackers Allegedly Target Ukraine's Biggest Private Energy Firm". *CNN*. July 5, 2022.

35. S. Gatlan. "BlackCat Ransomware Claims Attack on Italian Energy Agency". *BleepingComputer*. September 2, 2022. Available: https://www.bleepingcomputer.com/news/security/blackcat-ransomware-claims-attack-on-italian-energy-agency/
36. J. McKeon. "CommonSpirit Health Ransomware Attack Leads to $150M in Losses to Date". *Health IT Security*. February 21, 2023. Available: https://healthitsecurity.com/news/commonspirit-ransomware-attack-leads-to-150m-in-losses-to-date
37. M. Lehto. "Cyber Warfare and War in Ukraine". *Journal of Information Warfare*, 22(1), 61–75. 2023. Available: https://static1.squarespace.com/static/6444894f2a886e74091c9e1b/t/644688e8bdd41523982 16d7c/1682344171937/JIW_22.1+%281%29.pdf#page=69
38. N. Biddle, M. Gray and S. McEachern. "Public Exposure and Responses to Data Breaches in Australia: October 2022". *Centre for Social Research & Methods*. 2022.
39. T. Turnbull. "Medibank Hack: Russian Sanctioned Over Australia's Worst Data Breach". *BBC Breaking News, World News, US News, Sports, Business, Innovation, Climate, Culture, Travel, Video & Audio*. January 23, 2024. Available: https://www.bbc.com/news/world-australia-68064850
40. Z. Siddiqui. "Casino Giant MGM Expects $100 Million Hit from Hack That Led to Data Breach". *Reuters*. October 6, 2023. Available: https://www.reuters.com/business/mgm-expects-cybersecurity-issue-negatively-impact-third-quarter-earnings-2023-10-05/
41. R. Satter and Z. Siddiqui. "Analysis: MOVEit Hack Spawned Over 600 Breaches But Is Not Done Yet -Cyber Analysts". *Reuters*. August 8, 2023. Available: https://www.reuters.com/technology/moveit-hack-spawned-around-600-breaches-isnt-done-yet-cyber-analysts-2023-08-08/
42. L. Newman. "The 23andMe Data Breach Keeps Spiraling". *WIRED*. December 5, 2023. Available: https://www.wired.com/story/23andme-breach-sec-update/
43. H. Landi. "UPDATE: Ardent Health Restores Access to Epic EHR Two Weeks after Ransomware Attack". *Fierce Healthcare*. December 7, 2023. Available: https://www.fiercehealthcare.com/health-tech/ardent-health-struggles-get-systems-back-online-hospitals-reopen-emergency-rooms
44. S. Alder. "Global Healthcare Cyberattacks Increased by 74% in 2022". *The HIPAA Journal*. January 10, 2023. Available: https://www.hipaajournal.com/global-healthcare-cyberattacks-increased-by-74-in-2022/
45. S. Alder. "At Least 141 Were Hospitals Directly Affected by Ransomware Attacks in 2023". *The HIPAA Journal*. January 4, 2024. Available: https://www.hipaajournal.com/2023-healthcare-ransomware-attacks/
46. S. Alder. "December 2023 Healthcare Data Breach Report". *The HIPAA Journal*. January 18, 2024. Available: https://www.hipaajournal.com/december-2023-healthcare-data-breach-report/
47. K.J. Brooks. "Cyberattack Causes Multiple Hospitals to Shut Emergency Rooms and Divert Ambulances". *CBS News* – Breaking news, 24/7 live streaming news & top stories. August 4, 2023. Available: https://www.cbsnews.com/news/prospect-medical-cyberattack-california-pennsylvania-hospital/
48. A.J. Cartwright. "The Elephant in the Room: Cybersecurity in Healthcare." *Journal of Clinical Monitoring and Computing*, 37(5), 1123–1132. 2023. https://doi.org/10.1007/s10877-023-01013-5
49. Cynerio & Ponemon Institute. "The Insecurity of Connected Devices in Healthcare 2022". 2022. Available: https://www.cynerio.com/insecurity-of-connected-devices-in-healthcare-2022?submissionGuid=a 024ca93-c35b-46a4-b682-ccb2d53eb3be
50. R. Agar. "Maintaining Compliance: Data Challenges for IoMT Devices". *Journal of AHIMA*. 2022. Available: https://journal.ahima.org/page/maintaining-compliance-data-challenges-for-iomt-devices
51. Food and Drug Administration (FDA). "Cybersecurity in Medical Devices: Quality System Considerations and Content of Premarket Submissions: Guidance for Industry and Food and Drug Administration Staff". 2023.
52. Therapeutic Goods Administration (TGA). "Changes Affecting TGA-Issued Conformity Assessment Certificates". Australian Government – Department of Health, Canberra. 2021.
53. "CISC Newsflash Edition 14". Australian Government – Department of Home Affairs. January 2024. Available: https://www.cisc.gov.au/news-media/archive/article?itemId=1170
54. "CISC Consultation". Australian Government – Department of Home Affairs. 2023. Available: https://www.homeaffairs.gov.au/cyber-security-subsite/files/cyber-security-strategy-2023-30-consultation-paper.pdf
55. JMR. "Cyber Sanction in Response to Medibank Private Cyber Attack". January 2024. Available: https://www.minister.defence.gov.au/media-releases/2024-01-23/cyber-sanction-response-medibank-private-cyber-attack
56. ASLaw. "Australian Sanctions Law, Parliament of Australia, 2022". Available: https://www.aph.gov.au/About_Parliament/Parliamentary_departments/Parliamentary_Library/pubs/rp/rp2223/Quick_Guides/AustralianSanctionsLaw

57. UNSC. "What's in Blue, Arria-Formula Meeting on 'The Responsibility and Responsiveness of States to Cyberattacks on Critical Infrastructure'". May 25, 2023. Available: https://www.securitycouncilreport.org/whatsinblue/2023/05/arria-formula-meeting-on-the-responsibility-and-responsiveness-of-states-to-cyberattacks-on-critical-infrastructure.php
58. M. Fifield. "Statement Delivered United Nations Security Council Arria-Formula Meeting on Cyber Attacks on Critical Infrastructure". May 25, 2023. Available: https://unny.mission.gov.au/unny/230525_UNSC_Arria_Cyber_Attacks_Critical_Infrastructure.html
59. ICRC. "Newsletter ICRC Law and Policy, Digital Emblem Explained". 2024. Available: https://blogs.icrc.org/law-and-policy/2022/11/03/digital-emblemfive-questions-law-tech-policy/
60. A.O. Almashhadani, M. Kaiiali, S. Sezer and P. O'Kane. "A Multi-Classifier Network-Based Crypto Ransomware Detection System: A Case Study of Locky Ransomware." *IEEE Access*, 7, 47053–47067. 2019. https://doi.org/10.1109/ACCESS.2019.2907485
61. K. Evans, A. Abuadbba, T. Wu, K. Moore, M. Ahmed, G. Pogrebna, S. Nepal and M. Johnstone. "RAIDER: Reinforcement-Aided Spear Phishing Detector". *Lecture Notes in Computer Science*. Springer. 2022, 23–50. https://doi.org/10.1007/978-3-031-23020-2_2
62. A. Kharraz and E. Kirda. "Redemption: Real-Time Protection Against Ransomware at End-Hosts". In: M. Dacier, M. Bailey, M. Polychronakis, M. Antonakakis (eds.) *Research in Attacks, Intrusions, and Defenses*. RAID. 2017. *Lecture Notes in Computer Science*, vol. 10453. Springer, Cham. https://doi.org/10.1007/978-3-319-66332-6_5

AUTHOR BIOGRAPHY

Dr. Michael N. Johnstone is Associate Professor at the School of Science at Edith Cowan University (ECU) in Australia where he teaches network security and mobile app development. As a member of the Centre for Securing Digital Futures at ECU, his work on resilient systems covers secure development methodologies, wireless sensor networks, and the security of IoT devices with a focus on critical infrastructure. With over 30 years of experience in ICT, he provides consultancy services in cyber security for private industry, government, and research organisations and has held various IT roles including programmer, systems analyst, project manager, and network manager before moving to academia. He is a member of the ACM and the ACS.

Dr. Michael Crowley is a barrister, retired law academic, and honorary senior lecturer in the School of Science at Edith Cowan University (ECU) in Australia. Crowley has extensive trial experience, has taught criminal law and procedure for the Law Extension Committee within the University of Sydney, was a revising examiner for the Legal Practice Board of NSW, taught international law and advocacy at Chongqing Technology and Business University, Chongqing, People's Republic of China, and, amongst other units, taught security law, international law, and the law of evidence at ECU. At ECU he was at various times competitions coordinator, course coordinator for law and for forensic investigations. His research interests include terrorism, security law, and international humanitarian law. Crowley has written international humanitarian law mooting problems and continues to sit as a moot judge in international humanitarian law, international commercial arbitration, and negotiation competitions. He is a member of the Board of Management, Health Consumers Council of Western Australia.

Glenn Murray is a former Chief Executive Officer/Managing Director with 20+ years of professional experience, gained in multiple industries. Murray has significant experience as a director focusing on technology-driven innovation projects. This involved building multi-discipline project teams, understanding strategies, embracing innovation, and building technology road maps. Murray has extensive experience in leading multi-million-dollar projects in ASX-listed companies across multiple departments, including innovation projects across the oil and gas industries, mining, heavy vehicle manufacturing, defence (electronic warfare), and telecommunication industries. Murray has built an extensive global network of intelligence, innovation, and technology, and cybersecurity professionals including c-suite level. This, combined with a passion for technology and innovative solutions, allows him to be up to date with the latest technology, as well as with the competitive landscape within the industry. He has a proven history of thought leadership in innovation through presenting at industry events, TEDx, magazine publications, academic publications, news articles, and media interviews. He is in his final stages of completing a Doctor of Philosophy (Ph.D.) in cybersecurity. His work, when combined with a focus on strategic design, digital transformation, innovation, and organisational effectiveness, allows for technology and digitally enabled outcomes. Murray also holds a master's in systems engineering and a bachelor's in electrical engineering with 1st class Honors from the University of New South Wales.

4 Ransomware
Impacts in Healthcare Critical Infrastructure

Martin Dart

4.1 GLOSSARY

APT Advanced Persistent Threat: state-sponsored or sophisticated criminal cyber gangs who can deploy advanced techniques likely to undermine any digital system.

BCC Blind Carbon Copy: an address field for email where multiple recipients can be entered, but when received, each recipient sees only their own email address, protecting the identity of all other recipients.

Brute force A form of cyber-attack that repeatedly attempts to break through security controls (e.g. using a dictionary to automate password guesses).

DoH Department of Health (Ireland)

CI Critical Infrastructure: industries that are essential to the operation of contemporary societies, such as water, sewage, electricity, communications, and healthcare.

Cobalt Strike An attack simulation tool that has been repurposed by attackers to infiltrate and remotely access victim networks.

Conti A form of ransomware used by the Wizard Spider group to conduct double-extortion (Ransomware 2.0)-style attacks.

FTC Federal Trade Commission (United States): independent agency enforcing anti-trust and consumer protection law.

HSE Health Service Executive (Ireland): agency providing multiple social and healthcare services.

HIPAA Health Insurance Portability and Accountability Act (United States): legislation that introduced mandatory data breach reporting for healthcare.

ICO Information Commissioners Office (United Kingdom): independent body established to monitor and enforce information privacy protections.

IoT Internet of Things: digital devices that can monitor environments and report data in real time over digital networks.

IP Intellectual Property: trade secrets that represent the unique value behind a company or process.

Malware Malicious Software: a program or file, often disguised as legitimate, but which ultimately steals or changes data, or allows attackers remote access.

NCSC National Cyber Security Centre (Ireland): government agency protecting public sector and critical infrastructure networks.

NDB National Data Breach scheme: Australia's national data breach reporting program, operated by the Office of the Australian Information Commissioner (OAIC).

NHN National Health Network (Ireland): private digital network connecting health agencies across Ireland, operated by the HSE.

NHS National Health Service: agency delivering healthcare to citizens across the United Kingdom.

DOI: 10.1201/9781003469506-6

NISD	Network and Information Security Directive (European Union): A series of standards introduced to uplift cyber security regulations across the EU.
NSA	National Security Agency (United States): the technical intelligence services agency responsible for managing offensive and defensive cyber capabilities.
OAIC	Office of the Australian Information Commissioner: government entity responsible for monitoring data breaches in multiple industries, including healthcare, via the NDB.
OCR	Office for Civil Rights (United States): the agency monitoring the impact of healthcare data breaches on citizens.
PII	Personally Identifiable Information: sensitive details relating to any individual held in digital systems.
RaaS	Ransomware-as-a-service: An online collection of cyber attackers who will conduct ransomware attacks on a commercial fee-for-service model.
Phishing	Emails crafted to impersonate a person or company but containing malicious links or attachments to facilitate a fraud or cyber-attack.
SMB	Server Message Block: a communication protocol for sharing data and resources across networks. Older versions are highly insecure and have been the vector for high-profile incidents such as the WannaCry cyber-attack.
WannaCry	A 2017 worldwide ransomware attack, attributed to North Korea.
Wizard Spider	Russian cybercrime group suspected of using Conti ransomware to attack the HSE.

4.2 INTRODUCTION

4.2.1 Healthcare's Role in Critical Infrastructure

The first Industrial Revolution that commenced in the late 18th century in the United Kingdom (UK) fundamentally transformed nations across the globe socially and technologically. It fuelled the mass migration of a previously agrarian workforce from the countryside into burgeoning cities built around new manufacturing, distribution, and service industry hubs.

To maintain the flow of wealth reaped by middle-class industrialists and governments from these booming markets, a parallel revolution of "critical infrastructure" (CI) also exploited technological advances to build reliable systems for finance, public and freight transportation, and eventually electricity and communications networks.

The ensuing population explosion in rapidly industrialised cities, where workers crowded into slum housing with no supporting utilities, led to disastrous epidemics of cholera, typhus and tuberculosis, which threatened manufacturing viability. This led to the passing of mandatory public health legislation, and the creation of the first inner-city hospitals intended to maintain the population's health – and their ability to work.

This equilibrium between healthcare, industrial productivity, and social wealth was so effective that in some form it continues to this day in nearly every country on Earth, evolving continually to accommodate the challenges and opportunities new technology presents.

4.2.2 The Emergence of Digital CI Risks

As the success of the Industrial Revolution led to its acceptance as the new normal, subsequent generations have known nothing more than this cycle of technological innovation, newly emerging industries, larger markets, and more wealth. With the self-interests of the industrial and political classes still well served by this model, concerns regarding the stability and security of contemporary public critical infrastructure have evolved throughout the 20th century and into the 21st [1]. Progressing through four major epochs (summarised in Table 4.1) these CI risk concerns have required governments and CI providers to constantly incorporate innovations in

TABLE 4.1
The four critical infrastructure risk epochs

Epoch No.	Epoch Name	Period	Emerging Risks Description
1	The War Years	1914–1944	CI services such as water, communications, power, healthcare, and national security were threatened as a result of the total war waged throughout World Wars I and II. Indiscriminate attacks were undertaken against large civilian populations by newly developed airship, heavy bomber, and ballistic missile technologies.
2	The Cold War	1945–1980	Long-range intercontinental ballistic missiles (ICBMs) threatened CI with their dual threats of kinetic and electromagnetic pulse (EMP) destruction. Public and private transportation CI was also threatened by supply chain disruption throughout the 1970's oil crises and multiple instances of international terrorist bombings and aircraft hijacking.
3	Web 1.0	1980–2004	Government-controlled and nuclear-hardened CI transitioned towards privatised 24×7 digital services, accessible from anywhere on earth. New CI attacks emerged including software viruses that disrupted research and military networks, and "phone-phreaking," which bypassed charges on digital telephone exchanges. An underground "hacker" culture emerged to share the techniques used in such attacks via the new technology of bulletin boards, with members seeking to apply the lessons learned from one attack methodology against other types of networks.
4	Web 2.0	2005–present	The commoditisation of digital services achieved global saturation with the introduction of cheap hardware and always-on high-speed mobile data. Developments in hardware and software (including artificial intelligence) provides CI with the innovations to meet the demands of a global population that has grown by 6 billion since Epoch 1. These same technologies are adopted by military, intelligence, and criminal gangs who develop digital attacks capable of disabling power grids [2], stealing intellectual property (IP), and even destroying components in a heavily fortified uranium enrichment plant [3]. This period also brings the dominance of ransomware as the primary digital CI threat [4].

design, deployment, and governance to ensure that failures of CI do not facilitate a wider social breakdown.

During these first two epochs, manufacturing and transportation CI were considered prime and legitimate targets by malicious attackers, who were normally nation-states conducting military-led wars against each other. The operations of public healthcare were ostensibly protected during these periods by the principles commenced in the 1864 Geneva and 1899 Hague Conventions, whose "rules of war" included protection for hospitals and clinical staff from direct targeting [5]. While terrible destruction was inflicted on them from the indiscriminate bombings of large cities, on the battlefield the impartiality and neutrality of the Red Cross and Red Crescent were largely recognised and respected.

With the arrival of the third epoch of risk a change began to be realised as the nature of healthcare, warfare, and organised crime was transformed by the interconnectivity and availability of powerful and affordable digital systems. Healthcare was certainly a beneficiary of this new wave of ICT innovation, beginning with the introduction of early clinical networks and databases in the 1960s [6], which facilitated greatly improved treatment options for the booming post-war generation. Complete and accurate digital clinical records were now instantly available and sharable, enabling their integration with emerging diagnostic, pharmaceutical, and surgical innovations.

Yet throughout this period an ongoing digital Cold War was also underway. As with every generation of new technology, an accompanying range of fresh vulnerabilities surfaced, capable of negatively impacting CI providers if not effectively managed. The Web 1.0 hacker subculture of technically inquisitive enthusiasts also metastasised, growing into the more cynical and capable Web 2.0-facilitated attackers known as the advanced persistent threat (APT). These APT actors, armed with a pernicious arsenal of weaponised software vulnerabilities, now have the potential to undermine not only the interconnected data assets healthcare CI depends on but ultimately the health of the public the system is designed to protect.

This risk phenomenon was investigated by Choi and Johnson [7], who reviewed the five-year security posture of 588 acute care hospitals across the United States against 971 companies listed on the Fortune 1000 index. They concluded that while there was a narrowing of the security gap between 2014 and 2019, commercial companies outperformed hospitals every year. Of greater concern was that hospitals with the lowest security scores experienced a 38.3%–49.4% probability of a data breach event occurring. While any kind of digital impairment is at best inconvenient, when those systems are used for the treatment of critically ill patients the impacts can be literally life-threatening. Indeed, Choi and Jonson [8] further studied this aspect and discovered that elevated death rates persist for several years after a hospital suffers a serious data breach incident. This is not a theoretical risk, and later in this chapter there is more detail on the story of baby Niko Silar, perhaps the first individual named and identified as dying from the consequences of a hospital ransomware attack.

4.2.3 Government Responses to Digital CI Risk

In May 1998, as the digital threats of the third epoch began to be more fully appreciated, then-US President Bill Clinton issued Presidential Decision Directive 63 (PDD-63) with the stated aim to "maintain the ability to protect our nation's critical infrastructures from intentional acts that would significantly diminish (its) abilities." PDD-63 recognised the growing risk intersect of industrial, military, and cyber systems, and assigned protective responsibilities across national, local government, and private sectors. This was a timely act that many governments around the world have since followed, especially since the risk realities of the fourth epoch have been evidenced in multiple and increasing damaging CI cyber incidents. A selection of these government responses is shown in Table 4.2.

Regarding healthcare CI, the United States again led the way in 1996 with the introduction of the Health Insurance Portability and Accountability Act (HIPAA), which required mandatory reporting of all data breach incidents in healthcare that impacted more than 500 records. Administered by the Department of Health and Human Services (DHHS), over 5,800 qualifying healthcare data breach incidents, which impacted 510 million individual records, have since been recorded. Of these, 703 incidents (12% of the total) were caused by ransomware and are examined in detail later in this chapter.

4.2.4 Healthcare's Strategic Social Role

This drive to strengthen healthcare critical infrastructure has become more urgent since the COVID pandemic, as the post-war "baby-boomer" generation ages and exerts greater demands on healthcare services. The World Health Organization (WHO) reports that the global population of over 60-year-olds has increased 123% in the 30 years to 2024, and over the next 30 years forecasts an additional 91% rise to a projected total of 2.2 billion in 2054 [21]. To meet this growing demand governments are spending ever more to support healthcare at this scale. In 1990 the average gross domestic product (GDP) investment committed to healthcare across 27 industrialised countries was 4.8%. By 2020, 42 countries reported this as 7.29%, with France and Germany exceeding 10% and the United States above 15% [22].

TABLE 4.2
A selection of government responses to CI risk

Country	Year	Action	Note
Australia	2018	Security of Critical Infrastructure Act (Cth) [9]	
	2021	Security Legislation Amendment (Critical Infrastructure) Act (Cth) [10]	Definition extended to include healthcare.
	2022	Security Legislation Amendment (Critical Infrastructure Protection) Act (Cth) [11]	CI assets must be registered, and annual reporting required.
Canada	2021	Action Plan for Critical Infrastructure [11]	
	2022	Critical Cyber Systems Protections Act (CCSPA) [12]	Currently progressing through parliament.
European Union	2006	European Programme for Critical Infrastructure Protection (EPCIP) [13]	Led to the creation of the Critical Infrastructure Warning Information Network (CIWIN) [16].
	2016	Directive 2016/1148 Concerning Measures for a High Common Level of Security of Network and Information Systems Across the Union (NIS1) [14]	Increased operational and reporting standards from NIS1, making them applicable to more industries.
	2023	Directive 2022/2555 On Measures for a High Common Level of Cybersecurity Across the Union (NIS2) [15]	
Singapore	2018	Cybersecurity Act [17]	Introduced the power of the government to designate any computer system "critical infrastructure."
United Kingdom	1999	National Infrastructure Security Co-ordination Centre [18]	Coordinates efforts across government, security services, and academia.
	2007	Centre for the Protection of National Infrastructure [19]	
	2023	National Protective Security Authority [20]	

As these healthcare service and cost demands have increased, emerging digital innovations such as cloud computing, big data analytics, internet-of-things (IoT) devices, artificial intelligence (AI), and telemedicine have become increasingly attractive for their potential to deliver efficient services. Hospitals (and care homes for the aging population) now regularly integrate digital patient systems into the "real world" via cyber-physical systems (CPS), which amalgamate networks of wireless smart sensors and AI with physical control technologies, to autonomously run aspects of patient monitoring and treatments across residential, social, and hospital locations [23, 24].

To appreciate the consequences of cyber risks such as ransomware impacting healthcare CI, we need to look further than the headlines of increasingly frequent events affecting growing volumes of patient records. The digitisation of healthcare at the nation-state level is now a significant economic driver in its own right, and governments use access to the health data of their citizens by industry as a means of subsidising rising costs. As far back as 2006, when the UK government commissioned Sir David Cooksey to report on health research funding in the United Kingdom, he summarised:

> The quality of the health research base, combined with a national health service, creates a major selling point that attracts R&D investment from the pharmaceutical and biotechnology industries, which form a major part of the UK knowledge economy [25].

Subsequent developments in electronic healthcare records and diagnostics have accelerated this *platformisation* of healthcare [26]. In 2019 the UK government announced the creation of NHS-X [27] – a digital transformation unit with a budget of over £1 billion within the National Health Service (NHS) – with a remit to exploit these professional-to-consumer (P2C) opportunities [28].

As we have seen throughout the history of industrialisation, the opportunities on offer from digital transformation come with a downside of increasing risk triggered by complexity, integration, and support issues. This exposes healthcare to vulnerabilities that can be exploited by malicious actors, which may seem an obvious risk in relation to unsupported legacy systems, but can also be the case for cutting-edge solutions deployed in new and unfamiliar circumstances. Examples of this include penetration tests of new healthcare technology demonstrating successful compromises of Bluetooth-enabled insulin pumps [29], pacemakers [30], medical alert pager networks [31], deep brain implants [32], and even AI-supported cancer diagnostic software [33].

Into this volatile mix of low tolerance for service disruption and an increasing cyber-attack surface, the scourge of ransomware finds a perfect environment in which to gain a foothold and create serious problems.

4.2.5 The Birth of Healthcare Ransomware

That healthcare is vulnerable should come as no surprise, as health researchers were victims of the world's first large-scale ransomware attack 35 years ago. The residual first epoch belief that the benevolent mission of healthcare would protect it from deliberate digital attack was disrupted in 1989, with the mass distribution of the first computerised ransomware campaign – the so-called AIDS Trojan, also known as PC Cyborg [34].

This birth of the ransomware threat took an ironic twist when it was revealed that the creator of the malicious software was Dr Joseph L. Popp, an evolutionary biologist with a PhD from Harvard University. Popp developed and deployed his ransomware with all of the tradecraft and characteristics that have marked this category of malware ever since, effectively establishing the six-stage ransomware playbook that has stood the test of time and led to billions of dollars in ransom payments. The phases of Popp's attack were conducted as follows:

i. Breach a third-party list to obtain a list of victims.
Popp sourced his victim list from third parties including mailing lists of attendees at an AIDS research conference in Stockholm in 1988, members of the World Health Organisation (WHO), and subscribers to *PC Business World* magazine. This stymied police efforts to associate the attacker with his targets by any means of direct contact.

ii. Anonymise the means of malware distribution, exploiting jurisdictions with weak legislation.
The means of distribution was designed to obfuscate the source, with Popp posting his malware out on a 5¼-inch floppy disk from London using 20,000 individually addressed and stamped envelopes. Whilst massively time consuming, this avoided the use of an automated franking machine that would have revealed its registered location. At the time the United Kingdom also did not have any computer misuse laws that could be used to prosecute Popp (a citizen of the United States, a country he knew *did* have such legislation and which he therefore avoided posting any disks to). This fact may have further worked to his advantage when he was eventually arrested and extradited to the United Kingdom, which failed to build a prosecution against him using traditional blackmail and criminal damage laws.

iii. Exploit user fears to increase the chance of them engaging with the malware (social engineering).
The subject of the "lure" Popp used to engage users and secure their interaction with the malicious code was also prophetic of more recent health-focused ransomware campaigns, invoking as it did the fear and interest of a global pandemic for which there was at the time no known effective treatment. Popp posted his disks with a sheet of official-looking installation instructions and "benefits" of using the software. This included multiple social engineering prompts including:

- This program provides you with a confidential report on your risk of exposure to AIDS.
- The program provides recommendations to you, based on the life history information you have provided, about the practical steps that you can take to reduce your risk of getting AIDS.

- This program is designed specially to help members of the public who are concerned about AIDS and medical professionals.

iv. Lure users into a false sense of security (and confuse the timeline of the attack).
Popp's software appeared to work as intended at first, providing a questionnaire and feedback regarding HIV-AIDS clinical risk factors. Unknown to the user, however, was that a hidden code had been installed and that was counting the number of reboots of the machine, and once a threshold of 90 was reached an encryption module was activated that made the operating system of the PC inoperative. For some users this number of reboots may have taken several weeks to achieve, by which time any association with the seemingly functional HIV-AIDS survey may have been long forgotten.

v. Deny users any access to their machine in order to motivate their willingness to pay the ransom.
In place of the Windows DOS boot screen at reboot number 91, Popp displayed a bright red prompt (shown in Figure 4.1), which demanded a minimum of US$189 from the user in order to extend a licensing agreement with "PC Cyborg Corporation."
If the user again rebooted their machine, the AIDS Trojan faked an MS-DOS prompt to display the message "The lease for a key software package has expired", and that continuing it may result in the "destruction of all of the files on drive C." If the user tried to reinstall their operating system from a system boot disk, Popp's masking of the legitimate file system only showed one "CYBORG.DOC" file being available, the contents of which only replicated the ransom demand. The user at this stage was faced with only three options: 1) pay up to (hopefully) receive a new recovery disk that would unlock the system, 2) restore their data and operating system from backup onto a fully reformatted hard drive, or 3) accept the loss of their data and start recreating it again from scratch.

vi. Try and obscure the money trail of ransom payments to confuse law enforcement.
Popp sought to establish a money transfer trail that would be impossible to follow. By requiring an international money order payment to a post office box in Panama, Popp felt he could anonymously collect his cheques and leave that country to cash them at will in the future with no resultant trail for law enforcement to follow.
For Popp, the extensive planning and up-front financial investment he made (several thousands of pounds in disk media and postage costs) came to naught, and he is not known to

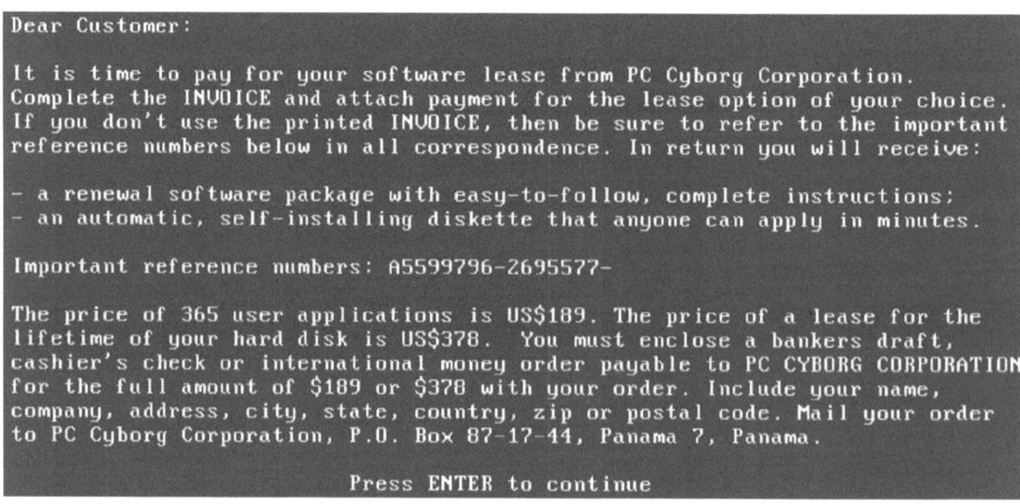

FIGURE 4.1 Ransom demand screen of the AIDS Trojan.

have made any money from the AIDS Trojan. The impact his malware had on users was not so ineffective, with several scientists claiming that machines infected by the AIDS-Trojan actually did contain legitimate HIV-AIDS research data, which was lost once the hard drive was encrypted. This potentially regressed HIV-AIDS research by several years.

4.2.5.1 Increasing Healthcare Data Breaches

In the decades since the AIDS Trojan, it has become increasingly apparent that healthcare is not an industry to be spared the interest of targeted or incidental cyber-attacks. Serious effects from data breach incidents impacting hospitals have been observed throughout the work of Fleury-Charles [35], Kamoun and Nicho [36], Dart and Ahmed [37], and Sen and Borle [38]. Collins [39] investigated 2,219 incidents over six years that impacted the healthcare and education sectors in the United States, while Hendee [40] identified 9,600 worldwide breaches over 14 years and defined the data breach as a "modern epidemic." Posey, in undertaking a longitudinal study, identified a similar trend with categories for "data exposure" and "stolen" outstripping "hacking" as a cause of data breach across 947 incidents [41]. When we accept through such evidence that attackers are not just trying to destroy or disrupt systems, but appear to be exfiltrating data for a financial benefit, we also need to accept that such motivations will cause them to return time and again to seek that benefit – and the bigger a health system is, the greater threat that motivation presents.

In healthcare environments, as with many other industries, ransomware is the cyber criminal's tool of choice to achieve financial reward. This has given rise to many forms of ransomware software families, and even commercially available outsourcing options using online ransomware-as-a-service (RaaS) offerings from criminal gangs. The size and complexity of healthcare also presents highly exploitable environments for the multiple sub-routines ransomware will typically execute. These include systems information gathering and network resource mapping, Application Programming Interface (API) utilisation (for encryption processing), and command-and-control traffic encapsulation for data exfiltration and to report its success back to the attacker [42].

These risks highlight the need to identify specific ransomware threats impacting healthcare for while there is any uncertainty regarding the cause of incidents, or confusion about how to address them, the consequences for staff and patients in medical environments continue. The remainder of this chapter will review the contemporary healthcare ransomware threat, using examples from multiple incidents.

4.3 GLOBAL RANSOMWARE ATTACKS IMPACTING HEALTHCARE

4.3.1 United States

Previous studies of healthcare data breaches have focused heavily on statistics gathered from the United States [41, 43–47], stemming from their 1996 adoption of the Health Insurance Portability and Accountability Act (HIPAA) and US Code of Federal Regulation Title 45 – Public Welfare (45 CFR Part 164 Subpart D). This legislation established mandatory data breach reporting requirements commencing from 2009 and applied to "covered entities" including healthcare delivery, health plans, and health clearinghouse providers – including any third-party "business associates" they contract with. This requirement elevated the issue of breached healthcare records firmly into the public domain, as they require the covered entities to report breaches impacting more than 500 records not only to the individuals impacted but also to local media outlets and the Federal Government.

The central record of these breaches is maintained by the Office for Civil Rights (OCR) at the Department of Health and Human Services (HHS) and has recorded 5,833 incidents over 15 years (2009–2023). Combined, these data breaches represent some form of compromise to the security or privacy of over 510 million patient records [48].

Worthy of note in the HIPPA scheme is the fact that the OCR is also the department responsible for investigating a wide range of civil rights issues including age, race, disability, and national origin discrimination, religious freedoms, and personal conscience. Placing health information privacy in this domain is a strong indication that this issue is seen as central to the American ideal of democracy, especially as the loss of effective healthcare due to such poor handling of medical records is likely to impact marginalised or minority groups especially hard.

For the purposes of this chapter however, the OCR data has a degree of limitation. It does not offer a category of data breach specific to ransomware, requiring instead that reports are assigned to one of the following categories:

i. Hacking/IT incident
ii. Improper disposal
iii. Loss
iv. Theft
v. Unauthorised access/disclosure

What is provided is a free text description field, which 80% of entries do populate. By searching this field for occurrences of the word "ransomware," we can identify a subset of 702 incidents (12%) detailing this form of attack, which have impacted a total of 53.9 million (10%) of all patient records between 2012 and 2023. All of these incidents have been assigned to the "hacking/IT incident" category, and in examining the details of other incidents also assigned to that category, there are many containing descriptions which indicate they may also have been caused by ransomware, even though that word is not specifically used. As such, it is reasonable to assume that the degree of ransomware occurrences this analysis identifies is still likely to represent a significant under-reporting of the true nature of the problem. The occurrences of all confirmed ransomware events impacting all forms of HIPAA-covered entities is shown in Figure 4.2.

A previous attempt to measure the rate of ransomware impacting US healthcare was undertaken by Neprash et al. [49], who examined incidents between 2016 and 2021 and created the Tracking Healthcare Ransomware Events and Traits (THREAT) database. Using multiple correlation techniques, including the HHS data and media reporting, they identified 374 ransomware events. If we filter the data analysis undertaken for this chapter to match the 2016–2021 range, we can now in fact identify 465 ransomware events impacting healthcare providers only, rising to 551 if we include

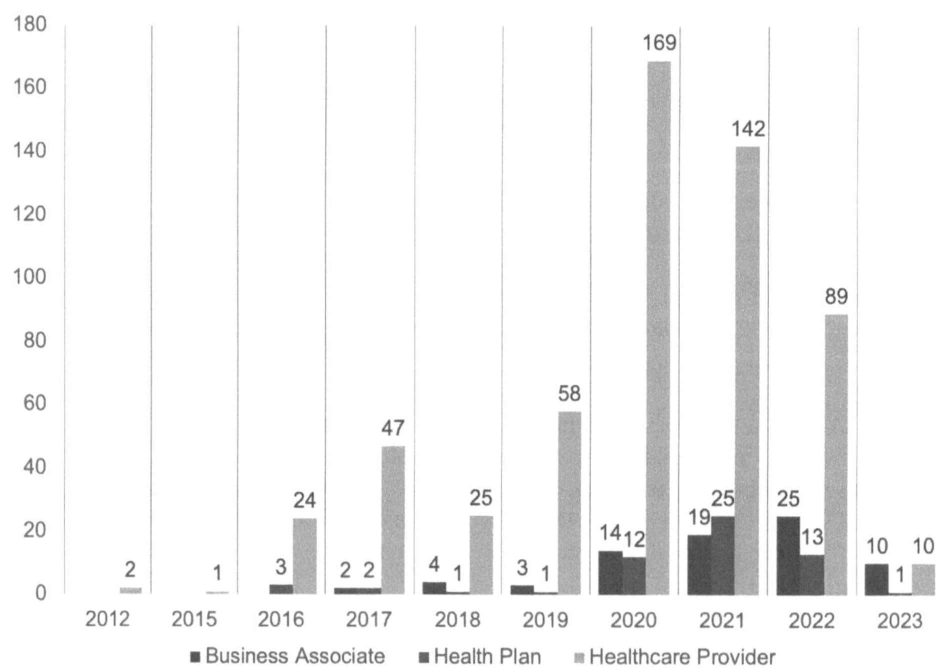

FIGURE 4.2 US healthcare ransomware incidents 2012–2023.

health plans, clearinghouses, and business associates. This discrepancy results from the presentation of data from HSS via two data sets – "archived" (including the full web description field which surfaces the ransomware cause) and "under investigation" – where reports can remain for up to 24 months with no detailed description appended. This long tail of confirmatory investigations means that for two years, occurrences of confirmed ransomware events may remain underestimated by over 47% across the full scope of the US healthcare system.

Returning to the latest full dataset of 702 incidents between 2012 and 2023, we can also observe that the average number of records breached is 76,752 per ransomware incident, versus 89,012 for all other incidents. Figure 4.3 shows a scaled sunburst chart detailing the number of records impacted by ransomware per year in US healthcare, along with the number of incidents per covered entity type per year. This illustrates that while primary healthcare providers are the main locations at which ransomware can strike, there are also a significant number of incidents occurring in health insurance providers, and most concerningly at third-party sub-contracted business associates.

The frequency of business associate ransomware incidents is illustrated further when we filter by those events which impact the largest volume of patient records. Table 4.3 shows the top five such events, revealing that the three largest incidents all occurred at business associates, and breached the privacy of 7.6 million individuals in total.

Figure 4.4 further examines this aspect of the full ransomware data set, revealing that the consequences of ransomware outbreaks at business associates persistently outweighs the impact in other entities. The average number of records involved in each business associate ransomware incident was 202,143, versus 65,487 for healthcare providers and 20,599 for health plans. This shows the

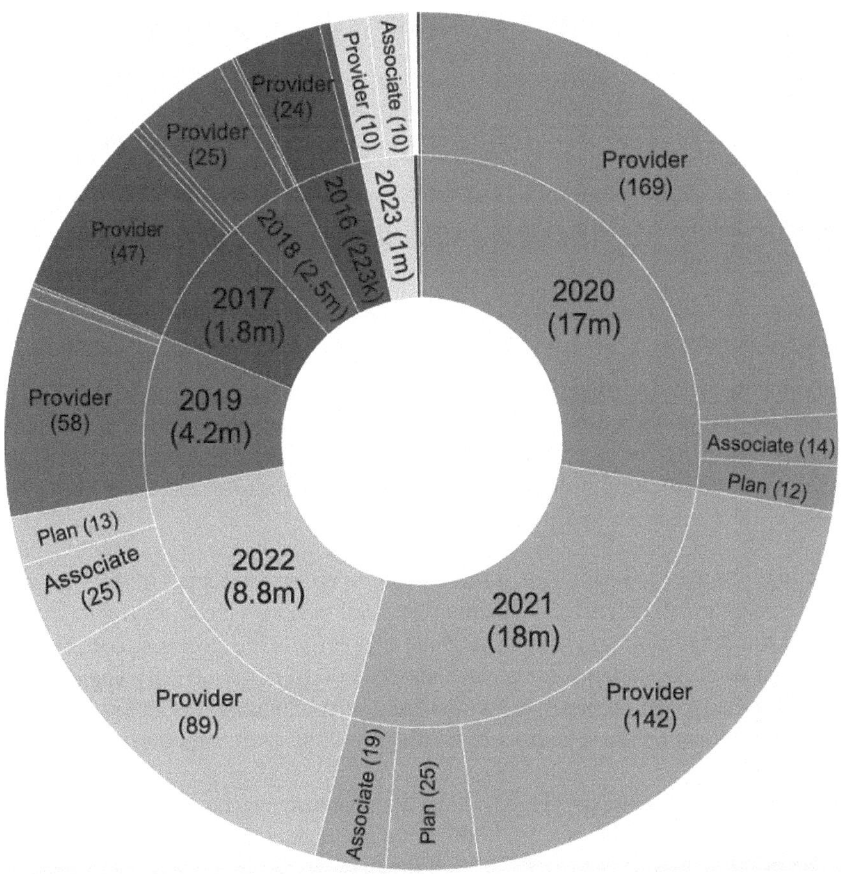

FIGURE 4.3 US ransomware incidents – records breached per year and number of incidents per entity.

TABLE 4.3
Top five largest US healthcare ransomware events

Name of Covered Entity	Covered Entity Type	Individuals Affected	Year
Blackbaud Inc.	Business associate	3,320,726	2020
NEC Networks d/b/a CaptureRx	Business associate	2,600,000	2021
Dental Care Alliance	Business associate	1,723,375	2020
University Medical Center of Southern Nevada	Healthcare provider	1,300,000	2021
Texas Tech University Health Sciences	Healthcare provider	1,290,104	2022

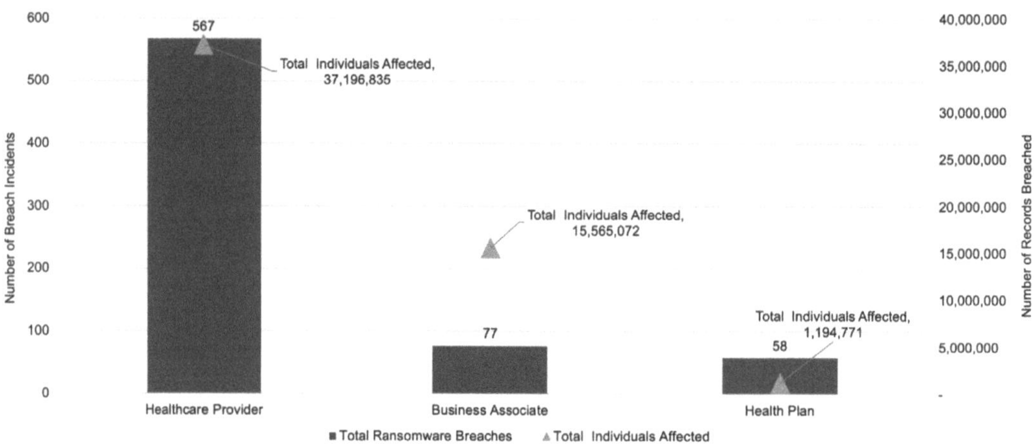

FIGURE 4.4 Total number of US ransomware incidents and records breached per covered entity type.

importance of managing risk from vendors and suppliers when seeking to protect data in large healthcare environments.

4.3.2 United Kingdom

The United Kingdom requires mandatory reporting of data breach incidents, including for healthcare, via the UK Information Commissioners Office (ICO) under controls set out in the *Data Protection Act 2018 (UK)*. This regime has recorded 19,542 breach incidents occurring in healthcare from 2019 to 2023, making it the second most impacted sector in the United Kingdom behind education and childcare (shown in Figure 4.5).

Of all the digitally enabled data breach reasons recorded by healthcare in the United Kingdom, ransomware appears third with 1,174 incidents across all periods (shown in Figure 4.6). When we correlate all of the data breach reasons throughout all periods, the strongest correlation we see is between "ransomware" and "denial of service" attacks ($r = 0.754$, $p < 0.001$), suggesting that there are incidents classified as denial of service which are (understandably) in fact ransomware incidents (it should be noted this is a modest number of incidents – 22 in total, although ten of those occurred in Q3 of 2022 alone).

The United Kingdom's reporting requirements also capture aspects of healthcare data breaches which provide a glimpse into the potential human consequences of ransomware disclosure events. The capturing of "type of data breached" in each incident, summarised in Table 4.4, includes diagnostic and medical procedure information that individuals may not even share with their friends

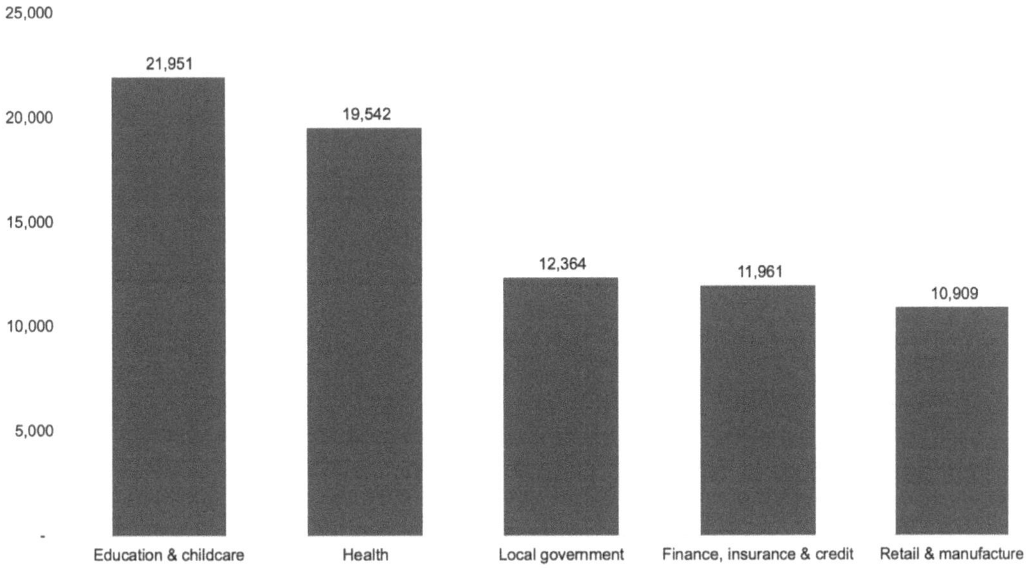

FIGURE 4.5 UK data breach trends, 2019–2023 (by industry).

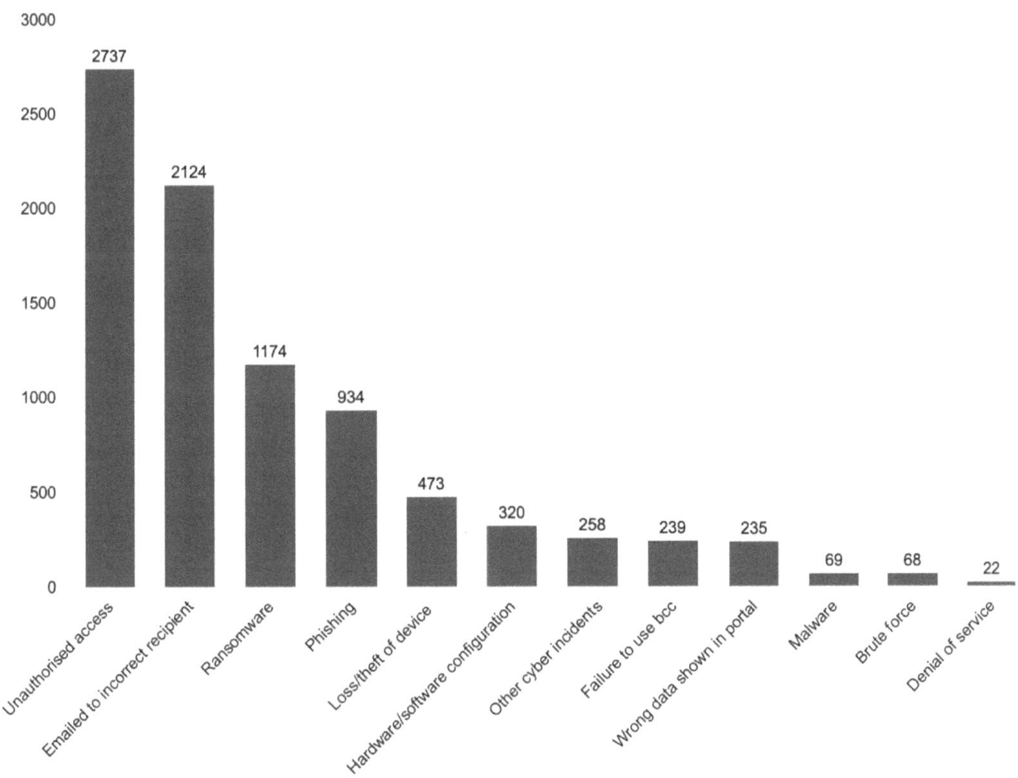

FIGURE 4.6 UK healthcare data breaches – top causes, 2019–2023.

or family, given that it includes sexual orientation, gender reassignment, religious beliefs, genetic conditions, or sex life details. Each one of these categories has been included in healthcare ransomware events in the United Kingdom over a four-year period and represents a persistent threat against those patients impacted, due to the potential for the discovery and sharing of this data for many years to come.

4.3.3 Australia

Since 2018 Australia's National Data Breach (NDB) reporting scheme has been operated by the Office of the Australian Information Commissioner (OAIC), an independent agency within the portfolio of the federal attorney-general. Data or privacy breaches falling within its remit are defined, via the Commonwealth's *Privacy Act 1988*, as "*an act or practice . . . contrary or inconsistent with any of the Australian Privacy Principles* (emphasis added)" [50].

This requirement to report confirmed data breaches applies to all private healthcare providers in Australia, although currently not to all state government agencies delivering public healthcare services (which represent the largest healthcare systems in the country, each treating millions of citizens). This is an important issue to note, as while the NDB scheme was a huge step forwards, there is still no single national scheme that encompasses all critical infrastructure healthcare providers. After reviewing the operation of these legislative controls, Hile [51] identified the shortcomings in the framework, concluding that while the Privacy Act and NDB scheme create an effective attribution framework to identify data breaches, they do little to enable individuals to access legal advice or obtain compensation when providers lose control of medical records. As will be seen later in this chapter in the example of Australia's Medibank Private ransomware incident, the importance of having a framework capable of achieving such functionality is becoming increasingly important.

Throughout the lifetime of the National Data Breach scheme to date healthcare is the Australian industry that has reported the highest volume of data breaches every year – 1,007 incidents in total across 14 reporting periods from 22 February 2018 to 30 June 2023. The annualised trend of these top three industries and the degree of variance by which healthcare exceeds the second-place industry are shown in Figure 4.7. Yet despite the clarity of this trend, it is in stark contrast to the data gathered periodically in the Australian Community Attitudes to Privacy Survey, also run by the OAIC [52]. A question in that survey regarding trust in industry sectors shows the public held a 74% *positive* sentiment in 2023 towards health service providers, considering them as "very" or "somewhat" trustworthy in overseeing patient privacy.

In analysing the cause of data breaches reported by Australian healthcare, Figure 4.8 shows the four main high-level categories identified.[1] This demonstrates that "human error" is by far the biggest cause of reported incidents, accounting for half of all reported data breaches, with "cyber incidents" and "malicious attacks" representing just over one-quarter and one-fifth respectively. "System faults" make up the remaining, very small proportion.

The challenge with this data is that it does not readily identify where ransomware attacks are represented in terms of volume of incidents, which requires an analysis of the further 22 detailed data breach causes reported by the OAIC and shown in Table 4.5 (the first two characters of the code assigned to each line groups each "detailed reason" under a parent "high-level reason" – details of which are shown in the causation map in Figure 4.9).

Using this data we can now see that, classified under the *cyber incident* (CI) category, ransomware attacks are the eighth most common form of cyber incident experienced by Australian healthcare providers – responsible for 61/992 (6.15%) total reported incidents and occurring at least ten times per year.

At this stage of analysis there are two problems to address regarding the Australian data – one of definition and one of correlation.

4.3.3.1 Defining Ransomware

The definition issue stems from the glossary provided at the end of each report from the OAIC, where "ransomware" is defined as:

> Malicious software that makes data or systems unusable until the victim makes a payment [53].

TABLE 4.4
Type of data breached in UK ransomware events

Ref.	Type of Data Breached	Number of Breaches
01	Basic personal identifiers	268
02	Health data	220
03	Data revealing racial or ethnic origin	110
04	Unknown	090
05	Economic and financial data	070
06	Location data	069
07	Sexual orientation data	063
08	Official documents	061
09	Identification data	059
10	Sex life data	044
11	Genetic or biometric data	038
12	Gender reassignment data	027
13	Religious or philosophical beliefs	025
14	Criminal convictions or offences	018
15	Political opinions	010

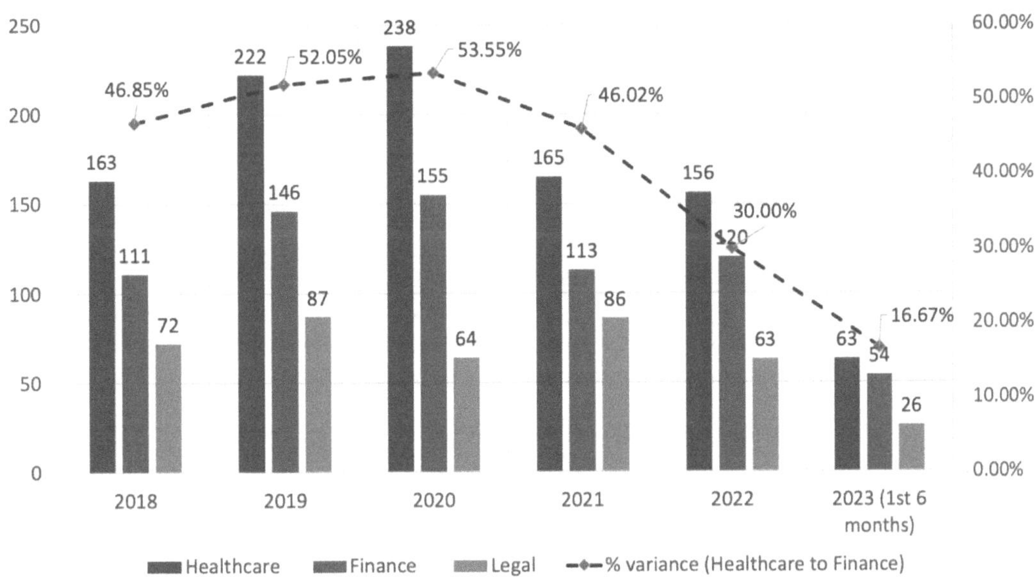

FIGURE 4.7 Australian data breaches, 2018–2023 – top reporting industries.

This is only a partial definition, based on the principles of Ransomware 1.0 established 35 years previously with the AIDS Trojan. It does not take into account the evolution of ransomware attacks in recent years, and does not align to the extended definition of *double extortion* ransomware (also known as Ransomware 2.0 [54, 55]) that was included in the 2021 launch of Australia's National Ransomware Action Plan:

> This trend of data theft, encryption, and public shaming reflects an evolution in ransomware tactics to more effectively extort considerable ransoms from victims. Cybercriminals are now regularly

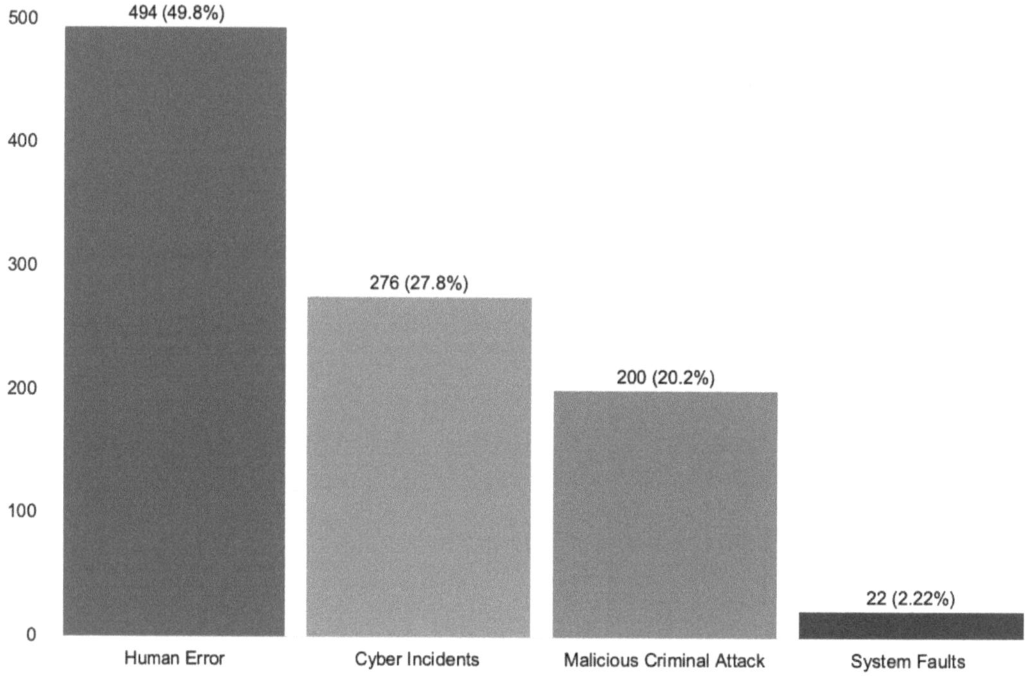

FIGURE 4.8 Australian healthcare data breach causes, 2018–2023.

exfiltrating data, including customer personally identifiable information (PII), prior to encryption and subsequently threatening to release the stolen information publicly unless the ransom is paid. Victims who would have previously been well prepared for, or able to, recover from a ransomware incident are unlikely to be immune to this tactic known as "double extortion" [56].

If a Ransomware 1.0 (encryption only) definition is being applied subjectively to data breach reports as they are received or completed, and the breached system appears still usable (which as we shall see is the case in some Ransomware 2.0 style attacks), there is a reasonable likelihood of these incidents being assigned in error to some classification other than ransomware. As we saw in the US data, this again implies that ransomware incidents may be under reported.

4.3.3.2 Correlating an Australian Ransomware Attack Chain for Healthcare (ARCH)

To appreciate the actual threat that a critical healthcare provider may be facing from all ransomware attack vectors, we should therefore look deeper, to seek otherwise imperceptible correlations between all of the types of data breach incidents being reported and the frequency of their occurrence. The fact that ransomware exploits multiple vectors to breach security controls is not new information and has been illustrated by many researchers [34, 57–59], several of whom have contributed taxonomies to illustrate this issue.

What has not been undertaken previously is to measure real-world examples of these phenomena in action, which the Australian data enables with its record of detailed data breach causes across multiple time periods. By conducting a bivariate Pearson's correlation across these volumetric and temporal characteristics we can evaluate the correlation coefficient (the r value, or presence of a relationship), along with the statistical significance of that relationship (the p value).

The default, or null hypothesis (H_0), for this evaluation is that one type of data breach would not be significantly correlated to any other (with significance established as $p \leq 0.005$). If this were to be the case then, for example, increases in phishing would not show any relationship to increases in physical thefts. If significant relationships could however be evidenced, then the

TABLE 4.5
Detailed Australian data breach causes, 2018–2023

No.		Cause	A: Total (992)	B: Cumulative total	C: μ (Per year)	D: % of all breaches	E: Cumulative %
01	HE03	Email sent to wrong recipient	167	167	27.83	16.83%	16.83%
02	MC03	Theft of paperwork/device	109	276	18.17	10.99%	27.82%
03	CI05	Phishing	091	367	15.17	09.17%	37.00%
04	MC01	Rogue employee/insider threat	078	445	13.00	07.86%	44.86%
05	CI04	Compromised/stolen creds	069	514	11.50	06.96%	51.81%
06	HE02	Loss/insecure disposal	067	581	11.17	06.75%	58.57%
07	HE08	Unauthorised disclosure	066	647	11.00	06.65%	65.22%
08	CI03	Ransomware	061	708	10.17	06.15%	71.37%
09	HE01	Failed to use BCC	050	758	08.33	05.04%	76.41%
10	HE05	PII sent to wrong recipient (mail)	046	804	07.67	04.64%	81.05%
11	HE06	PII sent to wrong recipient (other)	032	836	05.33	03.23%	84.27%
12	HE07	Unauthorised disclosure	024	860	04.00	02.42%	86.69%
13	CI02	Hacking	022	882	03.67	02.22%	88.91%
14	HE09	Unauthorised disclosure (verbal)	019	901	03.17	01.92%	90.83%
15	CI06	Malware	018	919	03.00	01.81%	92.64%
16	HE04	PII sent to wrong recipient (fax)	018	937	03.00	01.81%	94.46%
17	SF02	Unintended release or publication	016	953	02.67	01.61%	96.07%
18	CI01	Brute force	014	967	02.33	01.41%	97.48%
19	MC02	Social engineering/impersonation	013	980	02.17	01.31%	98.79%
20	SF01	Unintended access	006	986	01.00	00.60%	99.40%
21	HE10	Other	005	991	00.83	00.50%	99.90%
22	CI07	Other	001	992	00.17	00.10%	100.00%

alternative hypothesis (*Ha*) would show such interrelated incidents are occurring, and isolating the strongest of these in relation to ransomware can inform our future identification and management of them.

Completing Pearson's analysis across all Australian healthcare breach causes surfaces seven significant correlations that appear to contribute to a ransomware threat ecosystem, which are detailed in Table 4.6. This shows (at line 5) that ransomware incidents appear to be very directly and strongly correlated with phishing incidents throughout the six years of available data, with an r value of 0.748 and a p value of 0.003.

To verify this finding further, Figure 4.10 charts the reporting trends for both of those breach causes across the 13 reporting periods. This shows both causes closely mirroring each other across all periods, and four periods (shaded in the diagram) where a rise in phishing incidents does appear to align closely with a rise of ransomware incidents. This is highly supportive of a conclusion that phishing incidents should receive close attention, as they may frequently be an indicative precursor of impending ransomware events.

Having the depth of data that we do from the OAIC, and the remaining significant correlations shown in Table 4.6, it is also worth considering the other interacting relationships in this threat ecosystem. Figure 4.11 maps each of the strong relationships identified in Table 4.6 onto a basic threat modelling framework comprised of four zones of effect, based on the strength of their r values and the directness of their relationships. This shows how regularly occurring incidents may form a logical *attack chain* of events leading up to ransomware incidents. Beginning with the most directly

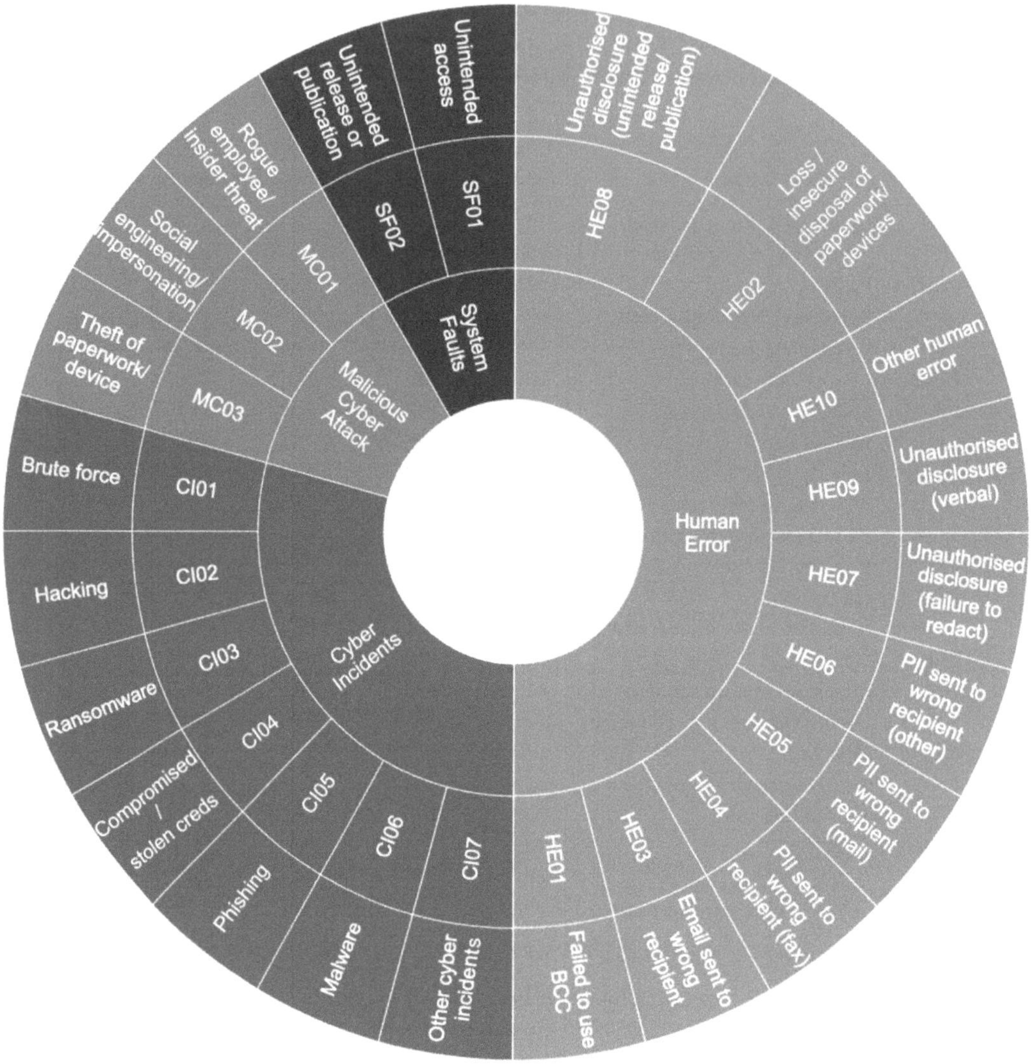

FIGURE 4.9 Mapping high-level to detailed data breach causes and codes.

associated form of incident with ransomware (phishing), we can extend the map to show three subsequent strongly correlated data breach causes:

- SF02: Unintended release or publication
- CI06: Malware
- MC01: Rogue employee/insider threat

Of immediate interest here is that the one human error category in this map (HE06: PII sent to wrong recipient (other)) is in Effects Zone 4, being most directly associated with incidents caused by malware. This is not to suggest that the human element should be discounted, as given its significant prevalence at the higher-level categories (accounting for half of all reported incidents), there is clearly a need to manage this area better. HE06 is also the most obscure of the human error failures, with the others very explicit in their failed methods of controlling PII:

TABLE 4.6
Significant data breach cause correlations

		Correlation Pair	Pearson Correlation (r)†	Sig. (2-tailed) (p) ‡	95% Confidence Interval (2-tailed) Lower	Upper
1	a.	CI05: Phishing	0.879	<0.001	0.635	0.963
	b.	SF02: Unintended release or publication				
2	a.	CI05: Phishing	0.796	0.001	0.437	0.936
	b.	CI06: Malware				
3	a.	HE06: PII sent to wrong recipient (other)	0.789	0.001	0.422	0.934
	b.	CI06: Malware				
4	a.	HE05: PII sent to wrong recipient (mail)	0.758	0.003	0.356	0.923
	b.	HE09: Unauthorised disclosure (verbal)				
5	a.	CI05: Phishing	0.748	0.003	0.335	0.920
	b.	CI03: Ransomware				
6	a.	CI02: Hacking	0.741	0.004	0.322	0.918
	b.	HE09: Unauthorised disclosure (verbal)				
7	a.	CI05: Phishing	0.734	0.004	0.307	0.915
	b.	MC01: Rogue employee/insider threat				

† r values > 0.700 are considered very strongly correlated.
‡ p values < 0.01 are considered of high statistical significance.

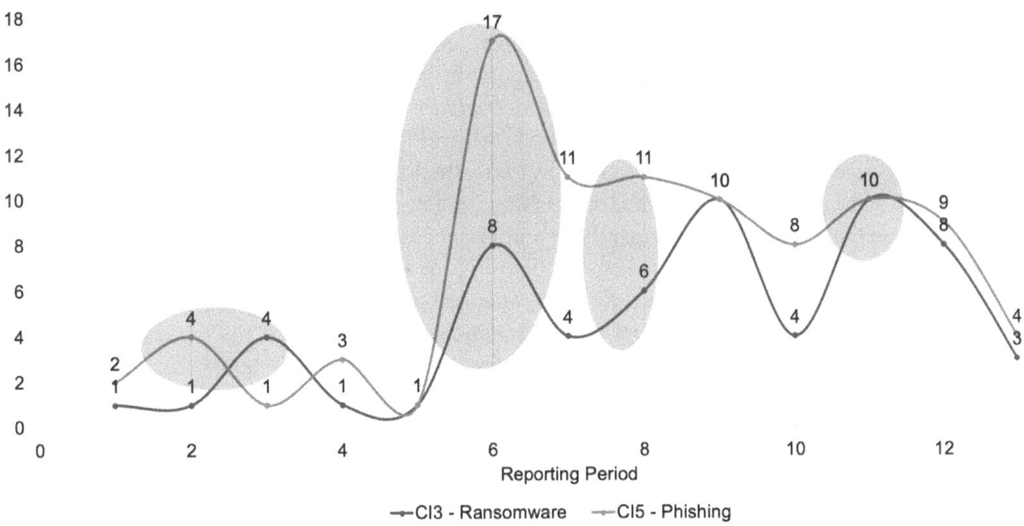

FIGURE 4.10 Temporal correlations of ransomware and phishing incidents, 2018–2023.

- HE05: PII sent to wrong recipient (mail)
- HE04: PII sent to wrong recipient (fax)

HE06, by comparison, is described in the OAIC glossary as:

> Personal information sent to the wrong recipient via channels other than email, fax or mail, for example, delivery by hand or uploading to a web portal.

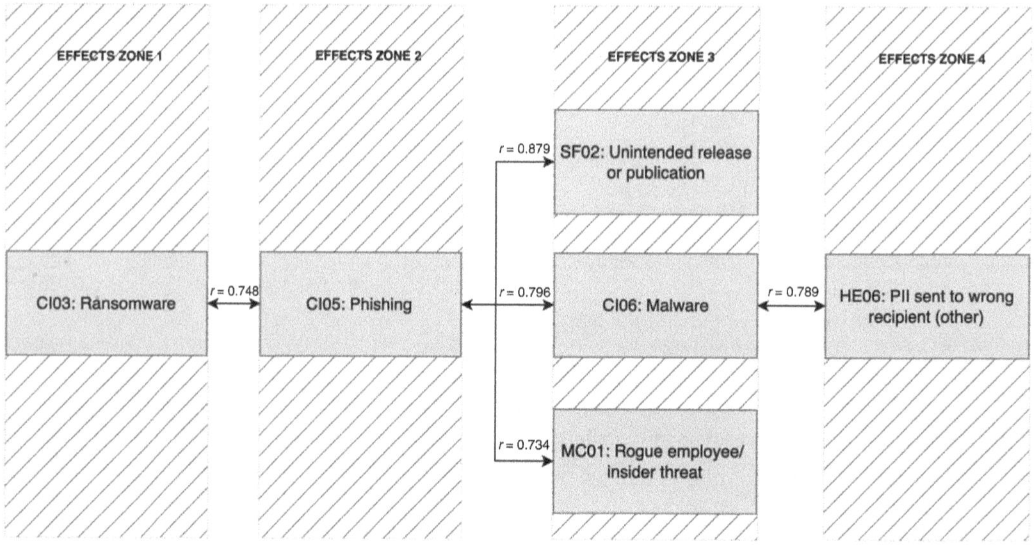

FIGURE 4.11 Map of strongly correlated relationships – the Australian ransomware attack chain for healthcare (ARCH).

The introduction of the web portal explanation raises a high-level alert here, as it is suggestive of an automated process gone wrong, potentially impacting a large number of records at any one time. Web portals are increasingly used in healthcare for referring patients to third-party diagnostic or specialist services, in communications with insurers, in the interface between the provider and Australia's national *My Health Record* digital patient record, or as part of clinical coding requirements needed to confirm government funding for covered procedures.

What Figure 4.11 models therefore is a bespoke Australian ransomware attack chain for healthcare (ARCH), based on evidenced data. It shows how the loss of PII control by any staff member can directly lead to incidents of malware or phishing (targeted against staff or the subject of the lost data), and when that element is successfully executed, incidents of ransomware.

To test this hypothesis via one further iteration, Figure 4.12 charts all of the correlated breach causes included in the ransomware attack chain, mapped across all reporting periods. Here again we can see four distinct peaked clusters of events, where at least three of the breach causes trend upwards together, suggesting that there is indeed a real-world relationship between all of them.

In concluding this analysis of Australian healthcare ransomware risk, we should consider the scale and implication of these identified clusters of ransomware-related breaches. Between them the six categories of the ransomware attack chain account for 357/992 (36%) of all incidents, making them the single most significant and high-risk group of data breaches within the data set. While clearly more work needs to be done in refining cause attribution, this is indicative that the risk of ransomware impacting critical healthcare is persistent, significant, and well concealed – making it all the more dangerous.

4.4 EXAMPLES OF HEALTHCARE CI RANSOMWARE ATTACKS

As revealed before in the figures provided via various government data breach reporting schemes, ransomware is prevalent across the healthcare critical infrastructure industries in many forms and indeed appears to be underreported. In recent years there have been multiple ransomware attacks, leading to devastating consequences for healthcare providers and patients whose medical data has been lost or released into the public domain. This section examines significant examples in more detail to illustrate specific and recurrent themes and consequences.

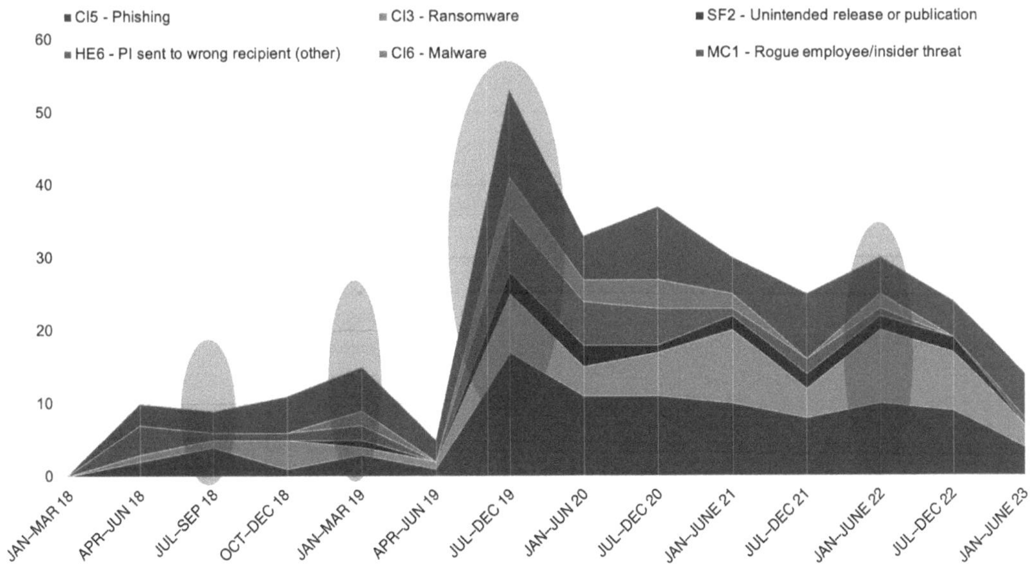

FIGURE 4.12 The healthcare ransomware attack chain charted against OAIC data.

Accepting that healthcare critical infrastructure not only *suffers from* but is an explicit *target of* ransomware is of paramount importance. Aside from the example of its economic value to research companies, the scale of healthcare presents myriad other targeting opportunities based on other actual and perceived attributes. One means of beginning to comprehend the range of motivations attackers might have to target a healthcare provider would be to conduct a Political, Economic, Social and Technological (PEST) analysis [60, 61]. An example of PEST analysis is shown in Table 4.7 using examples of healthcare-specific risks.

These ranges of motivations have emerged across multiple instances of ransomware impacting CI healthcare environments over many years, and examples of some of these are detailed in the remainder of this chapter.

4.4.1 National Health Service (NHS), United Kingdom, 2017

4.4.1.1 Background

On 12 May 2017 the WannaCry global ransomware attack impacted over 230,000 Microsoft Windows machines in 150 countries. WannaCry was designed to exploit weaknesses in the Server Message Block (SMB) v1 protocol, encrypting files via a recently publicised exploit called EternalBlue [62]. However, EternalBlue was not supposed to be in the public domain. It had been developed as a secret cyber weapon by the US government's National Security Agency (NSA) [63] and held as a "zero-day" exploit against which there was initially no publicly available patch. This changed in April 2017 when a hacking group calling themselves the ShadowBrokers obtained a copy of the tool and made it publicly available. Within two weeks it had been conjoined with a second NSA backdoor tool called DoublePulsar and deployed as WannaCry.

After learning that their tools were in the public domain, the NSA knew they could be used at any time to devastating effect. In an attempt to curtail such an attack, the NSA forewarned Microsoft who issued a patch for the vulnerability on 14 March 2017 [64]. Despite this remediation being available for several weeks before WannaCry was let loose on the world, many organisations failed to apply it and so left themselves open to become victims of the software as it automatically replicated itself throughout global networks. As the NSA feared, the release of these military-grade cyber weapons onto public networks subsequently produced extensive and devastating results – in other words, performing exactly as originally intended.

TABLE 4.7
Example of PEST analysis for healthcare ransomware

Category	Attacker Profile	Reason to Use Ransomware
1. Political	a. Criminal gang b. Political/social/religious protester c. State sponsored: government agency or at-arms-length hired hackers	i. Steal medical details of high-profile individuals ii. Publicise/protest sexual health, pregnancy, abortion, vaccination, or assisted suicide services iii. Create public distrust, outrage, or panic against government (possibly as part of a wider political or military conflict)
2. Economic	a. Criminal gang b. Rogue employee c. Individual hackers identity theft (for impersonation fraud) d. Commercial company e. Rogue state	i. Obtain ransom payment from the health provider ii. Obtain ransom payment from patients iii. Commit other fraud against staff iv. Steal research and development data v. Obtain punitive compensation after a contentious HR process
3. Social	a. Disgruntled relationship partner b. Whistle-blower c. Vandal	i. Intimidate, embarrass, and discredit staff due to their identity or role ii. Publicise fraud or corruption iii. Criminal tendencies in the staff population iv. Criminal damage for entertainment or to evidence skills to others
4. Technological	a. Commercial company b. Criminal gang c. State-sponsored – government agency or at-arms-length hired hackers	i. Testing new cyber weapons ii. Hiding an attack against another network iii. Stealing research techniques/intellectual property (IP)

4.4.1.2 Timeline and Impacts on the NHS

By 16:00 GMT on 12 May, approximately five hours into the attack, the United Kingdom's National Health Service (NHS) declared WannaCry a major incident [65]. Around 34 regional healthcare trusts had become directly infected with the malware, and 46 further trusts were reporting disruption due to inter-agency and supply chain communication failures [66]. An estimated 19,494 patient appointments were cancelled, and five hospitals had to divert patients to alternative facilities. About 139 urgent cancer referrals were cancelled, and 1,220 pieces of diagnostic equipment were impacted (not including those that were disconnected from the network to prevent infection).

It was subsequently revealed that NHS Digital (the national unit coordinating NHS cyber security) had issued a *CareCert* advisory on 25 April for all trusts to implement an SMB v1.0 patch, after it had received specific intelligence from British Telecom (BT) on the United States' loss of the EternalBlue exploit. In the "lessons learned" document from the incident it is noteworthy that the authors highlight that this incident occurred not because the vulnerable software was unsupported by the vendor – it was simply left unpatched by the customer [67].

WannaCry was only stopped on the evening of the 12 May after a cybersecurity researcher discovered the "kill switch" which prevented the malware spreading further. Even so, NHS disruptions continued throughout the following week as the recovery effort required many machines to be patched, recovered, or rebuilt. Of note regarding WannaCry is that 68% of the regional health trusts impacted (23/34) employed more than the national median number of staff [66]. This suggests that as larger organisations with more complex networks, they were subsequently slower to process the threat and risk intelligence, which clearly indicated the need for them to update their systems.

The cost implications of WannaCry included an initial £21 million to address vulnerabilities in major trauma centres, and £25 million for organisations to self-assess their non-compliance against other urgent CareCert alerts. A further £150 million was committed between 2018 and 2021 to address other critical cyber vulnerabilities nationwide. Aside from the technology recovery costs, there was also lost revenue from reduced patient activity, which across all trusts has been estimated to be in the region of £35 million. This pushes the known direct costs to the NHS beyond a quarter-of-a-billion pounds.

4.4.1.3 Learning from WannaCry

The WannaCry attack should have been a wakeup call for the healthcare industry, as it showed how ransomware can rapidly escalate service and cost consequences, even when a ransom is not paid. It also illustrates the exposure of a poorly governed healthcare system where, despite warnings being in place and a readily available vendor patch, misalignments between accountability and authority still allowed the attack to be successful.

Regarding the original motivation of the creators behind WannaCry, attribution has been assigned by the US Department of Justice to the North Korean government and their closely associated Lazarus cybercrime group [68]. The Federal Bureau of Investigation (FBI) is also pursuing an arrest warrant against Park Jin Hyok, a North Korean programmer they claim is responsible for launching the original attack [69]. But what links North Korea to the NHS? The uncomfortable answer is most likely "nothing," and this is where the value of the sample PEST analysis shown in Table 4.7 is demonstrated. If we look at the PEST detail, we can see that many of the attacker profiles are unlikely to have a specific interest in the NHS, and the "reasons to use ransomware" column contains many example actions that are nothing to do with healthcare or patients. Yet this is not to claim that WannaCry did not have a *purpose*, and that seems much clearer when we focus more on the macro geopolitical environment of the time rather that the microcosm of the victim experience.

In the four years prior to WannaCry, North Korea had conducted two nuclear weapons tests and multiple satellite launches. In response the United Nations Security Council had imposed increasing sanctions against North Korea, including Resolution 2094 in 2013 which imposed severe banking and financial restrictions [70]. In retaliation North Korea empowered the Lazarus group to conduct international attacks to demonstrate its cyber capabilities and generate an alternative funding stream to mitigate the impact of international sanctions. In 2014 the Lazarus group successfully hacked Sony Pictures, disclosing confidential information publicly before erasing server hard drives. In 2016 Lazarus attempted an even larger theft of US$1 billion from the Bangladesh Bank, undertaking a sophisticated manipulation of the international SWIFT electronic banking system. While only $81 million of the targeted amount was successfully extracted, this demonstrated the motivation and technical capability of the Lazarus group.

Given their growing ambition in a geopolitical context they were highly motivated to influence, the Lazarus group was quick to obtain and exploit the EternalBlue code when the NSA lost control of it in 2017. It is likely therefore that WannaCry aligns with multiple entries in the PEST analysis, including:

- **1/c/iii:** Causing public distrust and outrage against governments around the world (at a time when those governments were sanctioning North Korea).
- **2/e/i:** Generating income to offset the impact of economic sanctions.
- **3/c/iv:** Using this opportunity to show off a capability (potentially to intimidate) and not caring about the collateral damage caused.
- **4/a/i:** This could have been a formal test of a cyber weapon intended for some other purpose that went wrong, with WannaCry spreading in unanticipated ways.
- **4/c/ii:** As WannaCry was so noisy and consumed many hours of news coverage, it could have provided an excellent smoke screen to conduct other attacks while the media and authorities' attention was focused on WannaCry.

Returning to the first epoch examples outlined in the introduction, we saw similar impacts on healthcare when aerial bombing and missile technologies were first used against civilian targets.

Hospital buildings, staff, and patients may not have been the target then, but they were certainly impacted, and the same is true of WannaCry. When Nazi Germany launched V1 rockets against London during World War II they landed across the city randomly as their fuel ran out, but the very capability of Hitler to conceive of, build, and deploy such weaponry was as fear-provoking as the eventual destruction they delivered.

With the interconnectedness of digital technologies, and the capability that many bad actors have to interact with any network in any sector, it is incumbent upon healthcare risk managers to understand these potential impacts from geopolitical tensions. The evidence has repeatedly been seen in cyber incidents between Russia and Ukraine, China and Taiwan, Iran and Israel, and India and Canada. As such incidents can occur at any time, it is important to be prepared for them, and a range of risk mitigations need to be in good order in healthcare networks. This can include vulnerability scanning and rapid patch deployment, good backup and restore practices, regular staff training, tested incident response processes, and full cyber insurance coverage.

4.4.2 Blackbaud Incorporated, United States, 2020

4.4.2.1 Background and Incident Summary

Blackbaud is a software solutions and cloud hosting company delivering training, payment processing, software maintenance, and IT support services. In 2022 they generated revenues of US$1.1 billion from more than 45,000 global non-profit, educational, and healthcare clients. Three years on from the WannaCry attack, a data breach at Blackbaud became the most significant healthcare ransomware incident recorded in the United States throughout the lifetime of the HIPAA data breach scheme, and an example of attack evolution from Ransomware 1.0 to Ransomware 2.0.

On 7 February 2020 attackers gained access to Blackbaud's hosted client databases and spent three months undetected in their systems. Throughout this period the attackers leveraged unpatched software systems and weak local administrator passwords, exfiltrating millions of customer files from thousands of separate client businesses. One of the many healthcare customers impacted was Trinity Health, a faith-based not-for-profit employing 121,000 people in 101 hospitals across 27 states in the United States. Trinity Health was notified of the incident by Blackbaud on 16 July 2020, and it submitted its required reporting under HIPAA to the Office for Civil Rights on 14 September 2020.

The scope of the data stolen from Blackbaud was extensive, including consumers' full name, age, date of birth, social security number, home address, phone numbers, email addresses, financial information, and medical information (including patient and medical record identifiers, treating physicians' names, health insurance information, medical visit dates, and reasons for seeking medical treatment). For Trinity Health, the incident culminated in the loss of 3,320,726 patient records, which the attackers were able to extract as part of their double-extortion (Ransomware 2.0) attack. Blackbaud claimed in their incident response documentation to have removed the hackers from their network before they were able to encrypt any operational systems, but not before the attackers were able to exfiltrate these records [71].

In order to prevent the subsequent disclosure of this data, Blackbaud agreed to meet the ransom demand, paying a fee of 24 Bitcoin (approximately $235,000 at that time). On 29 September 2020 Blackbaud posted to their customer incident update page [71] that they had made this payment:

> with confirmation that the copy they removed had been destroyed . . . we have no reason to believe that any data went beyond the cybercriminal, was or will be misused; or will be disseminated or otherwise made available publicly.

In a 2023 Federal Trade Commission (FTC) filing, however, the secretary of the FTC commented that after they agreed to pay the ransom:

> Blackbaud has not been able to conclusively verify that the attacker deleted the stolen data.

In their Q3 2020 report [72], Blackbaud provided details of the initial impacts and recovery costs relating to this incident, including:

- $3.2 million expenses (legal fees and cyber specialist consultants)
- $2.9 million accrued insurance recoveries
- 160 customer claims from the United States, United Kingdom, and Canada
- 17 federal class action court cases in the United States
- four class action cases in US state courts
- two class action court cases in Canadian courts
- 43 civil investigative demands from US state attorney-generals

4.4.2.2 Regulatory Investigation

The Federal Trade Commission (FTC) of the United States recognised the seriousness of this incident and commenced regulatory proceedings against Blackbaud [73], alleging five counts for violations of the United States' FTC Act, being:

1. **Unfair information security practices:** failing to take reasonable steps to prevent unauthorised access, which likely caused substantive injury to consumers that they could not reasonably avoid themselves.
2. **Unfair data retention:** failure to implement and enforce reasonable data retention practices.
3. **Inaccurate breach notifications:** failure to accurately communicate the scope and severity of the breach to customers.
4. **Deceptive security statements:** misrepresentations that they had used appropriate safeguards to protect consumers' information.
5. **Deceptive initial breach notifications:** failing to admit that consumers' personal information had been subject to the breach.

The FTC case was based on their investigations which they claimed demonstrated that Blackbaud had failed to implement a number of essential security controls, including:

i. Poor password controls, with employees using default, weak, or identical passwords.
ii. A lack of multifactor authentication – including where required by its own policies.
iii. No monitoring for data exfiltration out of its network.
iv. No enforcement of data retention schedules, as required by its own policies – keeping data for many years past its intended use.
v. A lack of timely system patching to mitigate public vulnerabilities.
vi. No regular penetration or security testing of its network and databases.
vii. No firewall controls (allowing the attacker to make unauthorised connection).
viii. Poor network segmentation, allowing the attacker to undertake network enumeration and lateral movement.
ix. No encryption of backup files, which contained complete customer records.
x. No use of data masking – allowing social security and bank data to be stored in unencrypted fields not intended for that purpose.

After a four-year investigation the FTC made its final ruling on this case on 1 February 2024, imposing 13 conditional orders on Blackbaud that will remain in force for 20 years [74], being:

i. Prohibition against misrepresentations about privacy and security.
ii. Mandated data deletion: all non-required customer backup files to be destroyed within 90 days.

iii. Data retention limits: a data retention schedule must be made available on their public website within 90 days.
iv. Mandated information security program: a qualified employee must implement a program, and report on this at least annually.
v. Information security assessments by a third party.
vi. Cooperation with third-party information security assessor.
vii. Annual certification (to the FTC on the status of the security program).
viii. Covered incident reports (reported within ten days to the FTC).
ix. Acknowledgements of these orders must be made by all senior staff in writing.
x. Compliance reports must be made to the FTC for any change in company circumstances.
xi. Recordkeeping, including copies of marketing material relating to privacy and data security practices.
xii. Compliance monitoring – the FTC can request any other reports and interview any employee.

In return for accepting these conditions, Blackbaud was not required to pay any fine or compensation to impacted customers.

4.4.2.3 Learning from Blackbaud

The Blackbaud incident was wide-ranging in its causes and scope implications. As they were a service partner to multiple healthcare providers, as opposed to being a provider themselves, this incident shows that the boundary of control in relation to securing healthcare CI extends far into these third parties and should not be overlooked by those seeking to manage healthcare CI risk. Issues for the consideration of healthcare managers in seeking to avoid ransomware risk should include:

- Third parties delivering essential services must be verified in their security claims.
- Network segmentation (including data isolation within relevant nodes) is essential to prevent attackers from being able to traverse networks at will.
- It is essential to know what "normal looks like on a network – so that the ongoing extractions of gigabytes of data triggers an alert that can be investigated and locked down before millions of records can be stolen in this manner."

In considering the PEST analysis this incident appears to be a much clearer (and successful) example of "2/a/i" – which is targeting by criminal gangs seeking to obtain profit from the payment of ransom demands. Both supporting partners to healthcare and providers themselves should appreciate their attractiveness to ransomware attackers, who work on the assumption that the publicity outrage caused by the release of sensitive medical data can increase the chance of a successful ransom pay-out.

4.4.3 Health Service Executive (HSE), Ireland, 2021

4.4.3.1 Background and Incident Summary

The Health Service Executive (HSE) is the delivery arm of the Irish Department of Health (DoH), responsible for supporting over 70,000 digital devices across 4,000 locations. It is the government's largest single employer with some 130,000 employees, and since 2016 has been classified as "critical infrastructure" under the European Union (EU) Network and Information Security Directive (NISD) [14]. Like all large government health systems, the DoH is unwieldy and bureaucratic and in the 1990s was infamously assigned the synonym "Angola" by former minister for health Brian Cowan – both places, he felt, were littered with unexploded landmines.

Beginning on the 13 May 2021 a devastating sequence of those landmines began to detonate when multiple reports of suspicious activity began to stream into Ireland's National Cyber Security Centre (NCSC), detailing problems occurring across multiple DoH and HSE systems.

By early morning on 14 May 2021 the fully activated malware was causing chaos across the network, impacting 70,000 computers, 4,000 locations, and 54 hospitals which were either non-operational or severely restricted. Approximately 80% of Health Service Executive (HSE) systems were encrypted by the attackers and 700 gigabytes (GB) of data impacted. All healthcare workers lost access to all healthcare diagnostic and medical record information technology (IT) systems. Supporting systems including email, payroll, telephony, finance, and procurement were also inoperable [75]. This was when the attackers revealed their demand to end the attack and get the HSE back online – a $20 million ransom payment, which the Irish government immediately and consistently refused to consider paying.

Unable to recover the network quickly a momentous decision was taken to shut down the entire digital operations of the Irish government's National Healthcare Network (NHN) and commence a process of data recovery from backups, or total system rebuilding. For the first time in history, a nationwide healthcare critical infrastructure service was totally disabled by a ransomware attack.

The cause would turn out to be a variation of the Conti ransomware deployed using the Cobalt Strike security testing platform, by a Russian-linked RaaS gang known as Wizard Spider. The attack vector was linked to a phishing email sent several weeks earlier on 16 March to a single employee, who opened a maliciously crafted Microsoft Excel attachment. This was enough to give the attacker their initial foothold, and in the ensuing weeks they moved throughout the HSE network, obtaining further access via privileged accounts and identifying the data they wanted to target for extraction as part of their Ransomware 2.0 attack. In a further damning revelation, it was discovered that between the initial compromise and the eventual shutdown of the network, there had been multiple reports of suspected malicious activity at several HSE sites, but none had been effectively investigated. These notifications included one from the HSE's own antivirus security provider highlighting these unmanaged threats, which was sent to HSE the day before the full Conti ransomware activation [75]. In 2018 it was also identified that internal audit had been undertaken demonstrating similar vulnerabilities, but these had not been remediated in part due to the subsequent demands of the COVID-19 pandemic response [76].

4.4.3.2 Recovery

A degree of good news arrived for HSE on 20 May when the ransomware attackers provided a link to the decryption key that assisted the incident response team to recover some systems that may otherwise have been locked out forever. There has never been any confirmation of whether this key was provided due to a secret payment being made, if the hacking gang had a sudden bout of guilt, or if a powerful third party brought their influence to bear.

Recovery efforts continued for the next four months, and by 21 September 2021, 100% of servers and 99% of applications were considered to have been recovered. The work needed to build a capable and well-managed cyber security program is ongoing, and likely to take several more years yet to fully roll out.

4.4.3.3 Costs

The HSE ransomware attack was one of the most financially damaging in history, requiring the substantial redesign and rebuilding of most of the IT systems across the national health system of Ireland. Costs were accumulated by multiple impacted stakeholders across the health system, and no single definitive total has ever been agreed on. In its 2022 Report on the Accounts of Public Services, Ireland's Office of the Comptroller and Auditor General reviewed what was known about recovery costs up until that time [77]. A summary of their findings is included in Table 4.8.

4.4.3.4 Learning from HSE

The HSE ransomware attack is illustrative of the consequences caused by a long-term decline in technical currency (so-called technical debt), and a general inability to effectively manage complex environments. The incident is an amplification of what was seen in the NHS WannaCry incident,

TABLE 4.8
Summary of costs from the HSE ransomware attack

Stakeholder	Timeframe	Cost Area	Cost (Euros)
HSE	Immediate	Professional services: investigator, security recovery & consulting	€17m
HSE	Immediate	Hospital cyber costs	€14m
HSE	Immediate	Hardware replacement: replacement of legacy devices and new monitoring platforms	€13m
HSE	Immediate	Cloud migration and software licensing	€7m
HSE	Immediate/short	Additional recurrent funding	€43 m
DoH	Immediate	Direct response costs	€647,700
DoH	Immediate	Interim monitoring and detection services	€305,000
HSE	Long term (est. seven years)	Cyber improvement program	€657 m
Total			€751,953,200

but due to the more centralised nature of Ireland's system, and without adequate procedures and processes in place, the impacts were much more wide-ranging and costly to recover from.

4.4.4 Medibank Private

4.4.4.1 Background

Medibank Private is an Australian health insurance company which in late 2022 suffered a major ransomware attack, resulting in the loss of 9.7 million customer records and a US$10 million ransom demand [78]. The means through which the attackers were able to gain initial entry was by purchasing stolen Medibank user credentials from the dark web, which in turn had been stolen from a third-party IT service provider [79]. These were then used to authenticate against a misconfigured firewall that failed to demand any additional security verification – a failure of readily available two-factor authentication (2FA) controls. Once inside the network the attackers established multiple back door access and commenced a program of lateral exploration into other systems, harvesting further credentials and a significant volume of sensitive customer data [80] which was compressed and extracted.

The total amount of time the attackers spent inside the system is unconfirmed, but the consequences of their actions in the ensuing weeks were dire both for the company and for its customers. For the purpose of studying the consequences of a ransomware attack, the Medibank incident is of particular interest given the massive scale of the data lost, and the fact that Australian share trading rules required the company to continually update the market as the impacts of the incident became apparent. This gives us a very specific insight into ransomware consequences, especially the legal ramification of mishandling those incident update communications.

In the Medibank announcements to market we see many of the typical crisis management themes that emerge from corporate notifications during major cyber-attacks. It should be considered when reviewing these that the purpose of these announcements is for investor, share market, and corporate financial protection – not necessarily understanding or remediating the cyber incident in any practical way. Some of the themes presented in the Medibank communications (and response) include (adapted from Knight and Nurse [81]):

i. Downplaying,
ii. Media spin/admission of responsibility,

iii. Focus on the customer, and
iv. Stock market reaction and corporate impacts

By examining the timeline detailed in Table 4.9, we can see how poor corporate communications can worsen the impact of a ransomware attack, even if this is not realised until legal or regulatory investigations are commenced sometime later. At entries 1–3 we see Medibank claiming repeatedly there is "*no evidence that any sensitive data . . . has been accessed*" and even bizarrely stating (nearly one week after the attack) that although there has been a claim from the attackers that data has been stolen, because systems had not been encrypted this meant "*usual activities for customers continues.*"

Over the next two weeks it is revealed piecemeal in the notifications that 100, then 1,100, then a "substantial number," and finally that in fact 9.7 million customer records were stolen during this hack. That it took 25 days for this major insurer to realise that this quantity of data had been removed from their network (and may have been taken several weeks prior to the known incident with no one realising) is a fact that feeds into the subsequent class actions commencing from entry 17. This initial class action actually justifies its claim for damages across several previous years, stating that Medibank's lack of knowledge regarding its system's security status, and their regular habit of downplaying cyber risk, was a misleading representation "*to investors, about the adequacy of its privacy and information security controls.*" The insinuation is that Medibank had used inappropriately polished cyber security claims to inflate its share price and attract investors, who would not otherwise have considered buying its shares. This action therefore claims that Medibank is liable not only for the immediate consequences of the ransomware incident but also for the longer-term financial losses incurred by those investors.

A summary of the five major stages of the Medibank response to this incident, and the immediate consequences, are shown in Figure 4.13. The reality is that due to the large numbers of participants in the accumulated class actions, the true consequences of this ransomware attack may not be evident for several years yet to come.

4.4.4.2 Consequences on Victims

Given the highly sensitive nature of the data stolen from Medibank, there was always a potential for significant harm should any of that data be publicly disclosed [82]. This nightmare scenario began to be realised for Medibank customers when, after the company refused to consider paying the ransom, the attackers began to release sensitive data as part of their double-extortion approach. From 9 November 2022, the attackers released multiple subsets of the stolen data including:

- A list titled "naughty," which named 100 customers being treated for drug use or mental health issues.
- Details of 303 patients who undertook pregnancy terminations.
- Around 1,500 records of patients diagnosed with cancer, dementia, and mental health conditions.

When this process of trying to ratchet up the pressure to force the ransom payment failed, the attackers declared "case closed" – and released the full 5 gigabytes of remaining data containing all 9.7 million records onto the dark web [83].

4.4.4.3 The Australian Government's Response to Medibank

In the wake of the Medibank ransomware incident, the Australian government implemented a rapid legislative change (within one month) to increase penalties for companies considered to have failed to adequately protect private customer data. The *Privacy Legislation Amendment (Enforcement*

TABLE 4.9
Timeline of Medibank incident

	Date	ASX Announcement/Cybercrime Update from Medibank	Impact
Share price = $3.52			
1	13/10/2022	Medibank announces a pause in trading *"pending a further announcement."* Medibank subsequently confirms it has been the victim of a cyber incident, adding *"there is no evidence that any sensitive data, including customer data, has been accessed."*	Share trading suspended.
2	17/10/2022	*"There remains no evidence customer data has been removed from the network. Normal business operations have resumed . . . (we) do not expect this short disruption to impact the momentum of the business."*	
3	19/10/2022	Medibank requests a trading halt on its shares. *"Today Medibank Group has received messages from a group that wishes to negotiate with the company regarding their alleged removal of customer data. Medibank systems have not been encrypted by ransomware, which means usual activities for customers continue."*	Share trading halted.
4	20/10/2022	*"Medibank has been contacted by a criminal claiming to have stolen 200 GB of data.* • *The criminal has provided a sample of records for 100 policies which we believe has come from our systems.* • *That data includes first names and surnames, addresses, dates of birth, Medicare numbers, policy numbers, phone numbers and some claims data.* • *This claims data includes the location of where a customer received medical services, and codes relating to their diagnosis and procedures.* • *The criminal claims to have stolen other information, including data related to credit card security."*	• 100 medical records confirmed breached and disclosed. • Customers invited to call Medibank and talk to mental health professionals 24/7.
5	21/10/2022	Medibank requests a further voluntary suspension from "official quotation" of its shares for five more days.	Share trading halt extended.
6	25/10/2022	*"It has become clear that the criminal has taken data that now includes Medibank customer data."*	• About 1,100 medical records confirmed breached and disclosed. • Customer insurance product premium increases frozen until 16/1/2023.
7	26/10/2022	Medibank cybercrime, business, and FY23 outlook update: *"We expect that the number of affected customers could grow substantially."*	• Confirms Medibank has no cyber insurance. • A support package for impacted customers was launched. • Estimated six-month remediation costs of between AU$25 million and AU$35 million.
Share trading reinstated. Share price = $2.79 (20-month low)			
8	07/11/2022	Medibank announces they will not pay the cyber ransom demanded.	• Confirms 9.7 million PII records were breaches & disclosed. • In total 485,200 records included diagnostic and treatment codes. • External review commissioned. • Customer support package extended.

TABLE 4.9 ***(Continued)***
Timeline of Medibank incident

	Date	ASX Announcement/Cybercrime Update from Medibank	Impact
9	09/11/2022	Medibank confirms data has begun to be leaked onto the Dark Web.	
10	16/11/2022	Chair and CEO Annual General Meeting update.	• Customer support increased by 300 staff. • Deloitte appointed as external reviewers. • Anticipation announced for future customer and other remediation, regulatory, and litigation costs.
11	28/11/2022	*"Australian Prudential Regulation Authority (APRA) has intensified its supervision of Medibank Private Limited (Medibank) in response to the recent cyber incident."*	Increased regulatory oversight.
12	01/12/2022	*"The Office of the Australian Information Commission (OAIC) has announced it has commenced an investigation into the personal information handling practices of Medibank in relation to the recent cybercrime."* *Maurice Blackburn (lawyers) state they intend to file a representative complaint with the OAIC.*	Increased regulatory oversight. Precursor to potential legal claims against Medibank.
13	14/12/2022	*"Medibank was yesterday notified by Maurice Blackburn that it lodged a representative complaint with the OAIC. The complaint includes allegations that Medibank has breached the Australian Privacy Principles and seeks compensation for individuals whose personal information was exposed as a consequence of the cybercrime."*	Commencement of class action #1 to claim compensation for impacted customers.
14	19/12/2022	*"Medibank has today received a letter from Bannister Law which states that it intends to lodge a representative complaint against Medibank with the OAIC."*	Precursor to potential second legal claims process against Medibank.
15	07/02/2023	*"A class action against Medibank was filed in the Federal Court of Australia today by Baker & McKenzie. The statement of claim includes allegations of breach of contract, contraventions of the Australian Consumer Law, and breach of equitable obligations of confidence."*	Class action #2 claim for compensation begins.
16	23/03/2023	Half-year 2023 financial results.	Full year non-recurrent costs of remediating the cybercrime revised up to AU$40–45 million (not including other, legal, or regulatory costs).
17	29/03/2023	*"A class action against Medibank was filed in the Supreme Court of Victoria and served on Medibank . . . brought on behalf of persons who acquired an interest in Medibank shares 2019 – 2022 and is being brought by Quinn Emanuel."*	Class action #3 begins, seeking compensation for shareholders.
18	21/09/2023	Annual report issued	• AU$46.4 million committed in non-recurring cybercrime costs: o Office & admin $22m o Employee costs $15.6m o IT costs $7.6m o Marketing costs $1.2m • AU$30–35 million further planned for 2024 (not including litigation or regulatory costs). • Bonus payments to ten employees reduced by AU$3.6 million.

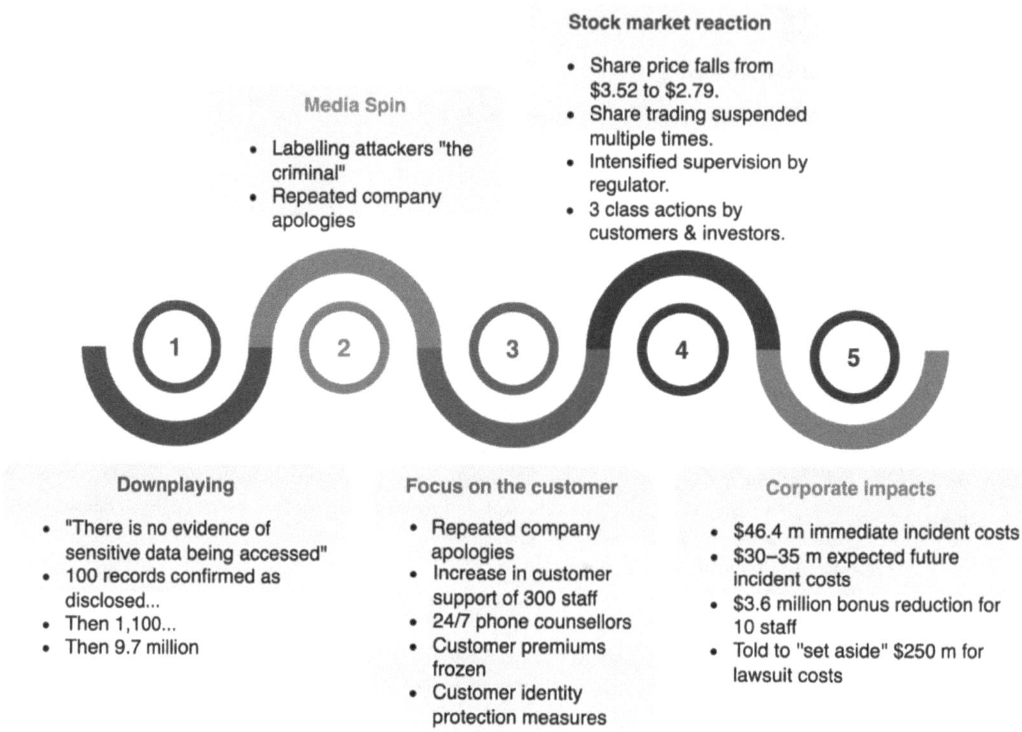

FIGURE 4.13 Medibank ransomware communications responses and summary consequences.

and Other Measures) Bill 2022 (Cth) [84] increased penalties from AU$2.22m to (whichever is the greatest) of:

- AU$50 million.
- Three times the value of any "benefit obtained through the misuse of information."
- About 30% of a company's adjusted turnover.

This legislation followed recent updates to the *Security of Critical Infrastructure Act 2018 (Cth)*, which was amended in 2021 and 2022 to include healthcare as a system of national significance for the first time. Also in 2021 the *Autonomous Sanctions Amendment (Magnitsky-style and Other Thematic Sanctions) Act 2021 (Cth)* [85] was introduced, imposing potential international sanctions for the first time for any individual who engages in "malicious cyber activity."

The tightening of these legislative instruments bore fruit in early 2024 when the Australian government publicly sanctioned Aleksandr Ermakov for this role in the Medibank ransomware attack [86], imposing financial and travel restriction on him in a move also recognised by the US and UK governments [87]. Ermakov had previously been associated with the REvil RaaS group, known for using the double-extortion tactics seen in the Medibank attack.

4.4.4.4 Learning from Medibank

The Medibank incident echoes the findings against Blackbaud, in that any attempt to publicly minimise the impact of an incident immediately following a ransomware attack can have long-term consequences. The fact that companies may not in fact know initially what the impacts are is not a reason to adopt a downplay/say-the-right-thing default. Stating with any perceived confidence that incident impacts are inconsequential and letting customers carry on as normal, and subsequently having to admit to a massive and potentially life-changing data loss for them, can place the organisation in a problematic position regarding culpability and liability.

This example also shows that ransomware incident response should not just rely on technical factors and from the earliest stages needs to include an understanding of the organisation's regulatory and legal obligations. It also highlights the benefits of close relationships with regulators, communications professionals, and cyber insurers – although in this incident it transpired that Medibank had previously cancelled their cyber insurance as the premiums had become unaffordable in their view.

4.4.5 Is Ransomware a Killer?

As these examples illustrate, the impact of ransomware on large healthcare systems has caused billions of dollars in damages and breached the privacy of millions of patients. However, one question remains given the critical nature of the services that many of these impacted hospitals deliver: has ransomware contributed to human deaths?

As noted in the introduction, Choi and Johnson identified a 0.34% to 0.45% increase in deaths in 30 days due to heart attack at hospitals that had recently experienced a data breach event – a trend that appeared to continue for years in some clinics [8]. They hypothesised that this would be the case due to the disruption caused not only by the actual attack but by the long period of subsequent system replacements and remediation during which systems were unavailable, unfamiliar, or just not trusted by staff.

Neprash et al. [49] reviewed the mortality rate at hospitals in the United States that specifically experienced ransomware attacks. They identified a 20.7% relative increase in deaths compared to patients that had been treated in the hospital in the period prior to the attack. Where the ransomware incident was serious enough to demand ambulance diversions and cancellations of scheduled care, this rate increased to between 35.9 and 55.3% compared to the pre-attack mean, or 61.8%–73% for patients from the black community.

While these academic reviews present compelling evidence for the presence of a trend, the public's attention is much more focused when there is an individual name that can be assigned to such tragedies. This came close to first occurring on 11 September 2020, when a ransomware attack against Düsseldorf University Hospital in Germany caused sufficient IT disruption to close their accident and emergency wards. Just a few minutes away an inbound ambulance was transporting a critically ill 78-year-old woman suffering from an aortic aneurysm. When Düsseldorf announced its closure, the ambulance was diverted to Helios University Hospital, Wuppertal – 32 kilometres away. This delayed the patient's treatment by an hour, and she died, leading to prosecutors in Cologne considering a case of negligent homicide against the hackers who unleashed the ransomware [88].

Ultimately the medical consensus was that it could not be proven that the patient's death was decisively caused by the ransomware attack, as she was so critically ill, she may not have survived even with the best of care. While in this instance the investigation did not proceed, on the other side of the world a similarly tragic case would result in a submission that named the first individual who, it is claimed, died as a direct result of a ransomware attack against a hospital.

4.4.5.1 The Springhill Medical Centre Incident

The information for this example is primarily sourced from the plaintiff's submission to a civil court action submitted in April 2020 to the Circuit Court of Mobile County, Alabama, in the United States [89]. As of February 2024, a final verdict in the case has yet to be determined, although a trial by jury has been requested.

On 9 July 2019 a ransomware attack hit the 270 bed Springhill Medical Centre (SMC), an acute care hospital in Mobile, Alabama. Later that day the hospital acknowledged it had experienced a "network event" but that the issue had not affected patient care. By 16 July the incident had increased in severity, leading SMC to shut down its IT systems to contain its spread, while also announcing:

> Our staff has continued to safely care for our patients and will continue to provide the high quality of service that our patients deserve and expect.

On the same day as that announcement, Teiranni Kidd was admitted to SMC for the induction of her pregnancy. However, as a result of the ransomware attack, the output from foetal monitoring undertaken at her bedside was not able to be shared online to other nursing staff, who relied instead on the single-copy paper record accessible in the ward only. The court submission claims that this resulted in a reduced standard of care and an incomplete patient record of the baby's health during the delivery.

Teiranni's baby girl, Nicko Silar, was born just before noon on 17 July and experienced multiple complications. Her umbilical cord was wrapped around her neck, and she had suffered kidney and brain damage.

On 23 July SMC issued a further announcement:

> We'd like to assure our patients and the community that patient safety is always our top priority, and we would never allow our staff to operate in an unsafe environment. . . . We continue to bring our network back-up carefully to ensure our systems are operating normally and securely, and there is no truth to the claim that we have experienced a second incident.

Despite transfer to a neonatal intensive care unit and nine months of subsequent treatment, baby Nicko Silar died on 16 April 2020.

The court deposition submitted by Teiranni Kidd against the hospital administration contains echoes of the class actions filed against Medibank and Blackbaud. All three cases claim that the early downplaying of the ransomware incident ultimately intensified the consequences for customers, attempting to placate them at a time when they needed honest and clear information in order to make appropriate risk-based decisions. In the baby Nicko case, this could have included allowing the mother to seek an alternative hospital at which to give birth [90]. Instead, the detailed allegations against the hospital include claims that SMC took away this option by deliberately concealing information regarding:

- The crippling nature of the cyberattack on hospital operations, including the lack of access to critical services and information.
- The inability of hospital departments and hospital personnel to communicate internally or with other departments and personnel.
- The effect on the hospital's electronic systems and data and the specific electronic systems and data that were compromised.
- The extent to which layers of redundancy and other safeguards were compromised.
- The discomfort and concern expressed by hospital personnel about the dangers to which patients were exposed as a result of these issues.

As a result of these actions Teiranni claims that she and her child were caused to suffer personal injuries, which in the case of Nicko Silar ultimately led to her death.

4.5 SUMMARY AND CONCLUSIONS

This chapter has demonstrated that healthcare has been an indispensable component of societies' wider critical infrastructure demand for two centuries, but in the past two decades has faced increasingly serious impacts from emerging digital risks, and specifically ransomware. These consequences are now not only inconvenient or financially costly but are also increasingly linked to the potential loss of human life. With the pace of healthcare digitisation showing no sign of slowing, and the wave of greater automation and system autonomy in the form of artificial intelligence already breaking, a new security paradigm needs to be rapidly adopted.

Ransomware has proven to be the most persistent and destructive risk against healthcare CI, although evidence presented here when analysing the US and Australian data suggests that its prevalence is likely to be significantly under-reported. Given the clear and present danger from ransomware, it is essential that healthcare agencies and governance bodies appreciate the evolution of ransomware from being solely an encryption-based attack (Ransomware 1.0), to now being a multifaceted threat that includes the theft and public disclosure of huge volumes of patient-sensitive data (Ransomware 2.0).

The main element of this that needs to be appreciated is that the first sign of ransomware is rarely the on-screen demand for payment but is likely to be a log entry weeks or months before showing persistent data exfiltration, unusual user behaviour, or logins from new locations. The pivotal contributors to each of the incidents highlighted in this chapter came from failures in business-as-usual (BAU) operational activities such as vulnerability management, staff training, and vendor risk management. The historical evidence available from these activities shaped the overall narrative regarding each organisation's attitude towards cyber risk governance, and in the case of Medibank and Blackbaud was used to justify class action claims for compensation against them when they were shown to be lacking. With this in mind improving, documenting, and preserving multifaceted evidence from these processes should be considered a foundational aspect of mature ransomware incident response planning.

4.5.1 Remediations

As demonstrated using the *Australian ransomware attack chain for healthcare* (ARCH) diagram, while ransomware is a phenomenon directly executed via technical systems, evidence that it may be an imminent threat should not depend only on searching for ransomware events themselves. The protections required to foil ransomware requires an organisational risk appreciation of the attacker motivations outlined in the PEST analysis shown in Table 4.7. This should then be supplemented with specific intelligence gathered from systems to identify and record trends in cyber-attacks, incidents, data breaches, and data disclosures of all severities – an approach we can refer to using the *cyber-AIDD* mnemonic [91]. The importance of this wider view was demonstrated in the correlations shown in Table 4.6, where the risk of ransomware can be indicated by other precursor events occurring elsewhere in the ARCH ecosystem.

For a healthcare entity seeking a strategic approach to implement ransomware protections, the following definition succinctly captures the technical and governance elements that need consideration: Ransomware protection is achieved via the security risk management processes and actions followed by organisations to protect the confidentiality, integrity, and availability of data and assets used in cyber space from attacks, incidents, data breaches, and data disclosures.

A summary of the cyber-AIDD components contained in this definition is detailed in the following sections.

4.5.1.1 Attacks

Attacks may vary significantly from actual ransomware through a wide range of system denial-of-service (DoS) attacks, website defacement, the introduction of destructive malware, or the theft or alteration of specific data. Identifying and recording different attack types and methods is an important step in removing the healthcare excuse for inaction that such attacks were somehow an accident, unlucky, or "not meant for us." It also shows that while attacks may commonly target legacy or unsupported systems, they can also impact cutting-edge solutions being used in new configurations. Implementing continual monitoring to identify what "normal" looks like and rapidly identifying anomalies that may indicate a compromise is underway enable a healthcare provider to lock down these backdoor accesses that ransomware attackers may subsequently seek to exploit when those specific weaknesses become more widely known [23, 92].

4.5.1.2 Incidents

Several well-developed international standards are available that define what an organisation *should* do to identify and manage security incidents when attacks are identified, including:

- ISO/IEC 27035 "Information Security Incident Management" [93].
- National Institute of Standards and Technology (NIST) "Special Publication 800–61 – Computer Security Incident Handling Guide" [94].
- European Union Agency for Cybersecurity (ENISA) "Good Practice Guide for Incident Management" [95].
- SysAdmin, Audit, Network and Security (SANS) "Incident Handlers Handbook" [96].

Despite these mature standards being available, adoption resistance can initially be high in a healthcare setting due to the considerable scope and resourcing required to commence implementation. This can lead to ineffective outcomes when ransomware strikes and decisions are made in haste, without full awareness or knowledge of the true nature of the incident [97, 98]. A further risk in attempting an established standards approach is that incident management can suffer from scope creep, if it attempts to define the much broader problem of information security management [99]. This creates a problem for healthcare providers who can become mired in incident response "paralysis by analysis" [100] as they seek to define too many systems and processes, and manage too many risk mitigations.

In seeking a simplified and efficient approach that can aid with managing ransomware, there are two high-level incident distinctions that should first be recognised – that of "events" versus "incidents" [101]:

- **Security events:** an occurrence of a system, service, or network state indicating a possible breach of safeguards.
- **Security incidents:** an unwanted, unexpected cyber event, or a series of events that have a significant probability of compromising business operations.

The NIST Special Publication (SP) 800–61 introduces a further element to these definitions, subdividing "events" in a way that is useful for recognising that many events are in fact "noise" that need to be filtered out during incident response processing. This results in an optimum hierarchical definition for cyber incidents that may lead to ransomware, being comprised incrementally of:

1. Events.
2. Adverse events.
3. Computer security incidents.

For a healthcare provider, being able to adopt and implement at least rudimentary incident recording, reporting, and control processes aligned to each these three categories is a foundational requirement for minimising the ransomware threat. This will provide a tangible early warning system to identify otherwise invisible attacks, as well as the detail to understand the impact, scope, and methodology behind them.

4.5.1.3 Data Breaches

The definition of "breach" can relate either to the act of breaking a promise or agreement or to any opening created in a protective structure that allows an attack to take place [102]. When attacks on systems or poor staff procedures result in lost control of sensitive patient data, the healthcare provider is certainly *in breach* of their agreement with the subject of that data. When these attacks bypass effective incident management processes and undermine the protections that should maintain the confidentiality, integrity, or availability of sensitive data, then they have breached the entire healthcare provider's system.

As identified by many other authors [103], there are well-established general technical controls that need to be in place to prevent these breaches from ever becoming exploitable, yet the fact is that each of the ransomware incidents detailed in this chapter is facilitated or amplified by a failure to remediate well-publicised software vulnerabilities. Yes – healthcare networks are complex, but this just reinforces the need to effectively operationalise systems architecture, change management, vulnerability scanning, lifecycle management, backups, and software patching processes.

The Medibank Private and Blackbaud incidents also illustrate the close relationship the public and legal system now assumes between technical and contractual trust controls when breaches occur. To avoid similar legal, publicity, and financial penalty hazards, healthcare organisations must fully investigate and understand all privacy obligations that apply to them, and build the training, operations, and governance processes that deliver against them.

Finally, the data breach statistics evidenced above from Australia, the United Kingdom, and the United States provide sobering evidence that there is clearly some way to go in applying these controls and slowing the rate of healthcare data breach incidents. This gives greater importance to the final consideration of the cyber-AIDD approach – how to manage data disclosure events.

4.5.1.4 Data Disclosures

Unauthorised data disclosure is the ultimate adverse consequence of ransomware – the end state that every healthcare provider is seeking to avoid. The previous stages of 1) attacks, 2) incidents, and 3) breaches may all be realised, yet even then the disclosure of sensitive data does not need to result. It is at this stage that relying on the payment of a ransomware demand becomes a gamble, as there is no guarantee that the attacker won't simply take the money and still release the sensitive data – or see the acceptance as confirmation that other recovery options have failed and further increase the payment demand.

The only mitigation against this is to assume a high likelihood of data breaches occurring, and implement a culture of data minimisation, encryption, and obfuscation by default to reduce the utility of any data that should become the target of ransomware. Such controls should include capturing only essential information in any single system, deleting it once it is no longer needed, using codes in place of sensitive medical diagnosis, and ensuring all data is encrypted when in transit and at rest. If widely applied, the encryption control is especially effective against a Ransomware 2.0 attack, as if a pre-cursor breach is exploited which gives the attacker an opportunity to copy data out, it remains protected from disclosure as the contents will remain in effect unreadable to the attacker and of no value.

Considering these four cyber-AIDD elements holistically helps organisations avoid binary definitions of systems or process as either secure – or not. In reality the concept is a continuum, where security measures are dynamic and dependent upon many unpredictable and interacting elements such as timeliness, user motivations and knowledge, public opinion, legislative requirements, or multiple service-specific aspects. Together these generate a web of trustworthiness, or *cyber resilience*, a term regularly used to also describe a system's capacity to maintain its status of "reliability and dependability in the face of persistent threats" [104]. It is this state of cyber resilience that is the peak measure of protection from ransomware events becoming devastating to the organisation and patients – and one that healthcare critical infrastructure provider should seek to attain.

NOTE

1 The total number of data breaches analysed in Figure 4.7 totals 992, as the 15 healthcare breaches reported in the first period to the OAIC in February 2018 contained no identified cause.

BIBLIOGRAPHY

1. Andrew, L., *The vulnerability of vital systems: How 'critical infrastructure' became a security problem*, in *Securing 'the homeland'*. 2020, Routledge. p. 17–39.
2. Sun, C.-C., A. Hahn, and C.-C. Liu, *Cyber security of a power grid: State-of-the-art.* International Journal of Electrical Power & Energy Systems, 2018. **99**: p. 45–56.
3. Baezner, M. and P. Robin, *Stuxnet*. 2017, Zurich: Cyberdefense Hotspot Analyses (4), Center for Security Studies, Federal Institute of Technology.
4. Lang, M., et al., *The evolving menace of ransomware: A comparative analysis of pre-pandemic and mid-pandemic attacks.* Digital Threats: Research and Practice, 2023. **4**(4): p. 1–22.
5. Corn, G.S., K. Watkin, and J. Williamson, *The law in war: A concise overview*. 2023, Routledge.
6. McLoughlin, I.P., K. Garrety, and R. Wilson, *The digitalization of healthcare: Electronic records and the disruption of moral orders*. 2017, Oxford University Press.
7. Choi, S.J. and M.E. Johnson, *The relationship between cybersecurity ratings and the risk of hospital data breaches.* Journal of the American Medical Informatics Association, 2021. **28**(10): p. 2085–2092.
8. Choi, S.J. and M.E. Johnson, *Do hospital data breaches reduce patient care quality?* arXiv preprint arXiv:1904.02058, 2019.
9. Australian Government, *Security of Critical Infrastructure Act 2018 (Cth)*. 2022, Australia.
10. Australian Government, *Security Legislation Amendment (Critical Infrastructure) Act 2021 (Cth)*. 2021, Australia.
11. Canadian Government, *2021–2023 Action Plan for Critical Infrastructure*. 2021.
12. Canadian Government, *Bill C-26: An Act respecting cyber security, amending the Telecommunications Act and making consequential amendments to other Acts (first reading)*. 2022.
13. European Union, *European programme for critical infrastructure protection (EPCIP)*. 2006.
14. European Union, *Directive 2016/1148 concerning measures for a high common level of security of network and information systems across the union (NIS1)*. 2016.
15. European Union, *Directive 2022/2555 on measures for a high common level of cybersecurity across the union (NIS2)*. 2022.
16. Lindström, M. and S. Olsson, *The European programme for critical infrastructure protection*, in *Crisis management in the European Union: Cooperation in the face of emergencies*, S. Olsson, Editor. 2009, Berlin, Heidelberg: Springer Berlin Heidelberg. p. 37–59.
17. Singapore Government, *Cybersecurity Act*. 2018.
18. The Chartered Institute for IT, *Aligning and sustaining IT infrastructure for business benefit*. 2005. Available from: https://web.archive.org/web/20110521183721/http://www.elite.bcs.org/090605.html.
19. UK Government, *Centre for the protection of national infrastructure*. 2014. Available from: https://webarchive.nationalarchives.gov.uk/ukgwa/20140901165415/http://www.csirtuk.gov.uk/.
20. UK Government, *National protective security authority*. 2024 [24/2/2024]. Available from: https://www.npsa.gov.uk/about-npsa.
21. World Health Organization, *Maternal, newborn, child and adolescent health and ageing: Data portal*. 2024.
22. Esteban Ortiz-Ospin, M.R., *Healthcare spending*. 2024. Available from: https://ourworldindata.org/financing-healthcare.
23. Haque, S.A., S.M. Aziz, and M. Rahman, *Review of cyber-physical system in healthcare.* International Journal of Distributed Sensor Networks, 2014. **10**(4): p. 217415.
24. Paul, S., et al., *On vulnerability and resilience of cyber-physical power systems: A review.* IEEE Systems Journal, 2022. **16**(2): p. 2367–2378.
25. Cooksey, D.S., *A review of UK health research funding*. 2006, London: The Stationary Office.
26. Faulkner-Gurstein, R. and D. Wyatt, *Platform NHS: Reconfiguring a public service in the age of digital capitalism.* Science, Technology, & Human Values, 2021. **48**(4): p. 888–908.
27. Health, D.o. and S. Care, *NHSX: New joint organisation for digital, data and technology.* 2019.
28. Kordzadeh, N. and J. Warren, *Toward a typology of health 2.0 collaboration platforms and websites.* Health and Technology, 2013. **3**: p. 37–50.
29. Bu, L. and M.G. Karpovsky. *A design of secure and reliable wireless transmission channel for implantable medical devices*, in *Proceedings of the 3rd International Conference on Information Systems Security and Privacy (ICISSP)*. 2017. SCITEPRESS.
30. Khera, M., *Think like a hacker: Insights on the latest attack vectors (and security controls) for medical device applications*. Journal of Diabetes Science and Technology, 2017. **11**(2): p. 207–212.

31. Freundlich, R.E., K.L. Freundlich, and B.C. Drolet, *Pagers, smartphones, and HIPAA: Finding the best solution for electronic communication of protected health information.* Journal of Medical Systems, 2018. **42**(1): p. 1–3.
32. Pycroft, L., et al., *Brainjacking: Implant security issues in invasive neuromodulation.* World Neurosurgery, 2016. **92**: p. 454–462.
33. Mirsky, Y., et al., *CT-GAN: Malicious tampering of 3D medical imagery using deep learning.* 2019.
34. O'Kane, P., S. Sezer, and D. Carlin, *Evolution of ransomware.* IET Networks, 2018. **7**(5): p. 321–327.
35. Fleury-Charles, A., M.M. Chowdhury, and N. Rifat. *Data breaches: Vulnerable privacy*, in *2022 IEEE International Conference on Electro Information Technology (eIT).* 2022. Mankato, MN: IEEE.
36. Kamoun, F. and M. Nicho, *Human and organizational factors of healthcare data breaches: The Swiss cheese model of data breach causation and prevention.* International Journal of Healthcare Information Systems and Informatics (IJHISI), 2014. **9**(1): p. 42–60.
37. Dart, M. and M. Ahmed. *Australia's notifiable data breach scheme: An analysis of risk management findings for healthcare*, in *International Conference on Health Information Science.* 2023. Springer.
38. Sen, R. and S. Borle, *Estimating the contextual risk of data breach: An empirical approach.* Journal of Management Information Systems, 2015. **32**(2): p. 314–341.
39. Collins, J.D., V.A. Sainato, and D.N. Khey, *Organizational data breaches 2005–2010: Applying SCP to the healthcare and education sectors.* International Journal of Cyber Criminology, 2011. **5**(1): p. 794–810.
40. Hendee, L.A., *The data breach epidemic: A modern legal analysis.* Journal of Technology Law & Policy, 2021. **24**(1): p. 3.
41. Posey Garrison, C. and M. Ncube, *A longitudinal analysis of data breaches.* Information Management & Computer Security, 2011. **19**(4): p. 216–230.
42. Moreira, C.C., D.C. Moreira, and C. Sales, *A comprehensive analysis combining structural features for detection of new ransomware families.* Journal of Information Security and Applications, 2024. **81**: p. 103716.
43. Seh, A.H., et al., *Healthcare data breaches: Insights and implications.* Healthcare, 2020. **8**(2): p. 133.
44. Raghupathi, W., V. Raghupathi, and A. Saharia, *Analyzing health data breaches: A visual analytics approach.* AppliedMath, 2023. **3**(1): p. 175–199.
45. Kruse, C.S., et al., *Cybersecurity in healthcare: A systematic review of modern threats and trends.* Technology and Health Care, 2017. **25**: p. 1–10.
46. Chernyshev, M., S. Zeadally, and Z. Baig, *Healthcare data breaches: Implications for digital forensic readiness.* Journal of Medical Systems, 2018. **43**(1): p. 7.
47. McLeod, A. and D. Dolezel, *Cyber-analytics: Modeling factors associated with healthcare data breaches.* Decision Support Systems, 2018. **108**: p. 57–68.
48. US Government, *Breach portal: Notice to the secretary of HHS breach of unsecured protected health information.* 2023 [5/8/2023]. Available from: https://ocrportal.hhs.gov/ocr/breach/breach_report.jsf.
49. Neprash, H.T., et al., *Trends in ransomware attacks on US hospitals, clinics, and other health care delivery organizations, 2016–2021*, in *JAMA Health Forum.* 2022. American Medical Association.
50. Australian Government, *Privacy Act 1988 (Cth).* 1988 [14/01/2023]. Available from: https://www.legislation.gov.au/Details/C2022C00361.
51. Hile, J., *Dude, where's my data? The effectiveness of laws governing data breaches in Australia.* Journal of Telecommunications and the Digital Economy, 2021. **9**(2): p. 47–68.
52. Office of the Australian Information Commissioner, *Australian community attitudes to privacy survey 2023.* 2023.
53. Office of the Australian Information Commissioner (OAIC), *Notifiable data breaches publications.* 2023 [14/08/2023]. Available from: https://www.oaic.gov.au/privacy/notifiable-data-breaches/notifiable-data-breaches-publications.
54. Li, Z. and Q. Liao, *Ransomware 2.0: To sell, or not to sell a game-theoretical model of data-selling Ransomware*, in *Proceedings of the 15th International Conference on Availability, Reliability and Security.* 2020, Virtual Event, Ireland: Association for Computing Machinery. p. Article 59.
55. Ahmed, M., et al., *Ransomware 2.0: An emerging threat to national security.* Australian Journal of Defence and Strategic Studies, 2022. **2**: p. 125–132.
56. Australian Government, *Ransomware action plan.* 2021.
57. Richardson, R. and M.M. North, *Ransomware: Evolution, mitigation and prevention.* International Management Review, 2017. **13**(1): p. 10.
58. Oz, H., et al., *A survey on ransomware: Evolution, taxonomy, and defense solutions.* ACM Computing Surveys (CSUR), 2022. **54**(11s): p. 1–37.

59. Beaman, C., et al., *Ransomware: Recent advances, analysis, challenges and future research directions.* Computers & Security, 2021. **111**: p. 102490.
60. Ali, H., *An analysis of identity theft: Motives, related frauds, techniques and prevention.* Journal of Law and Conflict Resolution, 2012. **4**(1): p. 1–12.
61. Nurmi, J. and M.S. Niemelä. *PESTEL analysis of hacktivism campaign motivations*, in *Nordic Conference on Secure IT Systems*. 2018, Springer.
62. Gupta, M. R., et al., *Eternal blue vulnerability.* International Journal for Research in Applied Science & Engineering Technology, 2023. **11**(6).
63. Kettani, H. and P. Wainwright. *On the top threats to cyber systems*, in *2019 IEEE 2nd International Conference on Information and Computer Technologies (ICICT)*. 2019, IEEE.
64. Lily Hay Newman, *The leaked NSA spy tool that hacked the world*, in *Wired*. 2018.
65. Ghafur, S., et al., *A retrospective impact analysis of the WannaCry cyberattack on the NHS.* NPJ Digital Medicine, 2019. **2**(1): p. 98.
66. National Audit Office (UK), *WannaCry cyber attack and the NHS.* 2018.
67. Department of Health and Social Care, *Lessons learned review of the WannaCry ransomware cyber attack.* 2018.
68. US Department of Justice (Press Release), *North Korean regime-backed programmer charged with conspiracy to conduct multiple cyber attacks and intrusions.* 2018 [6/9/2018]. Available from: https://www.justice.gov/opa/pr/north-korean-regime-backed-programmer-charged-conspiracy-conduct-multiple-cyber-attacks-and.
69. Federal Bureau of Investigation (FBI), *Most Wanted: Park Jin Hyok.* 2013. Available from: https://www.fbi.gov/wanted/cyber/park-jin-hyok.
70. United Nations Security Council, *Resolution 2094.* 2013.
71. Blackbaud. *Security incident.* 2020. Available from: https://perma.cc/MB7C-YUAR.
72. Blackbaud, *Form 10-Q: Blackbaud Q3 2020 report.* 2020.
73. Federal Trade Commission (United States), *Blackbaud complaint.* 2023.
74. Blackbaud. *8-K Report of unscheduled material events or corporate event.* 2024. Available from: https://investor.blackbaud.com/static-files/a28d7ebe-7945-46c8-b8db-b6ac5687517f.
75. PWC, *Conti cyber attack on the HSE.* 2021.
76. Cormac McQuinn, J.H.-J., *HSE knew the cyberattack risks but couldn't get ahead of the hackers*, in *Irish Times*. 2021.
77. Irish Government, *Financial impact of cyber security attack.* 2022, Office of the Comptroller & Auditor General. Available from: https://www.audit.gov.ie/en/find-report/publications/2022/12-financial-impact-of-cyber-security-attack.pdf.
78. Prictor, M., *Data breach notification laws – momentum across the Asia-Pacific region.* Journal of Bioethical Inquiry, 2023: p. 1–4.
79. Medibank Private, *2023 Half year results.* 2023.
80. Taylor, J., *Medibank hack started with theft of company credentials, investigation suggests*, in *The Guardian*. 2022.
81. Knight, R. and J.R.C. Nurse, *A framework for effective corporate communication after cyber security incidents.* Computers & Security, 2020. **99**: p. 102036.
82. Ahmed, M. and P. Haskell-Dowland, *Medibank won't pay hackers ransom. Is it the right choice?* in The Conversation, 2022.
83. John Taylor, *Medibank hackers announce 'case closed' and dump huge data file on dark web*, in *The Guardian*. 2022.
84. Attorney-General's Portfolio, *Parliament approves Government's privacy penalty bill.* 2022.
85. Australian Government, *Autonomous Sanctions Amendment (Magnitsky-style and Other Thematic Sanctions) Act* 2021.
86. British Broadcasting Corporation (BBC). *Medibank hack: Russian sanctioned over Australia's worst data breach.* 2024. Available from: https://www.bbc.co.uk/news/world-australia-68064850.
87. UK Government. *UK and allies sanctions Russian cyber hacker.* 2024. Available from: https://www.gov.uk/government/news/uk-and-allies-sanctions-russian-cyber-hacker.
88. William Ralston, *The untold story of a cyberattack, a hospital and a dying woman*, in *Wired*. 2020.
89. *Teiranni Kidd v Springhill Hospitals Inc (Civil Action No. 02-CV-2020-900171).* 2020, Alabama: Circuit Court of Mobile Country.
90. Greg Murphy, *Is malware the new frontier of medical malpractice?* in *Forbes*. 2022.

91. Dart, M. and M. Ahmed, *CYBER-AIDD: A novel approach to implementing improved cyber security resilience for large Australian healthcare providers using a Unified Modelling Language ontology.* Digital Health, 2023. **9**: p. 20552076231191095.
92. Ramu, S.P., et al., *An effective feature engineering for DNN using hybrid PCA-GWO for intrusion detection in IoMT architecture.* Computer Communications, 2020. **160**: p. 139–149.
93. International Organization for Standardization (ISO), *ISO/IEC 27035-2:2016. Information technology – security techniques – information security incident management – Part 2: Guidelines to plan and prepare for incident response.* 2016.
94. Cichonski, P., et al., *Computer security incident handling guide.* NIST Special Publication, 2012. **800**(61): p. 1–147.
95. Miroslav, R. and D. Stikvoort, *Good practice guide for incident management.* European Network and Information Security Agency (ENISA) Miroslav, 2010.
96. Kral, P., *The incident handlers handbook.* SANS Institute, 2011.
97. Tøndel, I.A., M.B. Line, and M.G. Jaatun, *Information security incident management: Current practice as reported in the literature.* Computers & Security, 2014. **45**: p. 42–57.
98. Kossakowski, K.-P., et al., *Responding to intrusions.* 1999, Pittsburgh, PA: Carnegie-Mellon Univ, Software Engineering Inst.
99. Tello-Oquendo, L., et al. *A structured approach to guide the development of incident management capability for security and privacy*, in *ICEIS* (2). 2019.
100. Sharif, A.M., *Paralysis by analysis? The dilemma of choice and the risks of technology evaluation.* Journal of Enterprise Information Management, 2008: p. 11.
101. International Organization for Standardization (ISO), *ISO/IEC 27000 information technology – security techniques – information security management systems – overview and vocabulary.* 2018, Geneva, Switzerland.
102. *Cambridge dictionary.* 2022, Cambridge University Press.
103. McIntosh, T., et al., *Ransomware mitigation in the modern era: A comprehensive review, research challenges, and future directions.* ACM Computing Surveys (CSUR), 2021. **54**(9): p. 1–36.
104. Linkov, I. and A. Kott, *Fundamental concepts of cyber resilience: Introduction and overview*, in *Cyber resilience of systems and networks*, A. Kott and I. Linkov, Editors. 2019, Cham: Springer International Publishing. p. 1–25.

AUTHOR BIOGRAPHY

Dr. Martin Dart has been a cyber security and digital transformation leader for the past 22 years, working internationally across healthcare, government, and private industry sectors. Also holding a BA Honours (double-major) in writing and publishing and ICT, a master's degree in information security and intelligence, and a post graduate certificate in education (PGCE), he is a certified information systems security professional (CISSP) and member of the Australian Information Security Association (AISA). He has presented extensively in Australia and Asia and published several peer-reviewed papers on cyber security issues impacting critical healthcare.

5 The Evolution of Ransomware in Healthcare Organizations

Kellan Dempsey, Thong Yang, and Nazim Choudhury

5.1 INTRODUCTION

Cyberattacks are an integral part of the evolving and dynamic threat landscape undermining and exploiting many organizations and industries. Healthcare delivery organizations (HDOs) are not excluded from this. These HDOs were trailing behind other industries in the adoption and implementation of information technology in their workflow for many decades [1]. However, the Health Information Technology for Economic and Clinical Health (HITECH) Act made them legally obligated to implement digital health records systems [2]. The objectives were to increase the quality, safety, and efficiency of healthcare delivery and transform the industry through the absorption of technology in patient care. As the enterprise workflows of these HDOs were infused with internet-connected health information technology, including computer networks, and medical devices to improve the quality of patient and health care, their exposures to new cybersecurity risks also increased [3]. Among others, protected health information and financial data [4], lack of HDO's interest in any legal actions or responsibilities for the cause of someone's failure to receive treatment [5], and weak and ineffective security protocols turned the HDOs into one of the most vulnerable sectors of cyberattacks [6].

A growing magnitude of these cyberattacks on HDOs and the common cause of healthcare data breaches are due to ransomware [7, 8]. Cybercriminals use ransomware – a type of malicious software (malware), to encrypt digital content to extort money in return for the key/technique to decrypt them by demanding a "ransom" – often via cryptocurrency to maintain anonymity [9]. The healthcare sector is now highly exposed to ransomware attacks due to the rapid adoption of protected healthcare information stored as electronic/online healthcare records. These records are rich in personal information including full names, Social Security numbers, addresses, insurance information, payment/credit card details, driver's licenses, and other health information worth a lot on the Dark Web [10]. Consequently, several high-profile ransomware attacks affected hospitals and disrupted their operations [11]. Variants of the known ransomware such as WannaCry, Petya, and SamSam were found to target approximately 764 healthcare providers [12]. In 2017, the WannaCry ransomware attack on more than 80 hospitals in the United Kingdom's National Health Service caused disruptions in ambulance services, surgical procedures, and critical patient care [13, 14]. However, the HDOs in the United States were the most widely affected by the ransomware attacks, where 44% of the HDOs reported ransomware as their greatest cyber-related concern [15]. In 2016, multiple hospitals were affected by ransomware in the United States that triggered significant data breach incidents to be registered officially [16]. In addition, the frequency of extortion of patients' private information via cyber-attacks increased by 10% compared to the previous year. In 2018, as reported by the "Blackberry Cylance" [17] – a cyber security company, healthcare providers were the fourth most important targets (7%) of ransomware, trailing behind technology (28%), consumer goods (15%), and manufacturing industries (11%). In 2019, the impacts of ransomware attacks on healthcare providers drew public attention to the cybersecurity industry in the United States [18]. Further, the US Department of Health and Human Service Office for Civil Rights' Breach Portal reported over 325,000 healthcare data breaches due to ransomware attacks, where more than 500 people were affected in every individual breach [19].

DOI: 10.1201/9781003469506-7

Since the primary objective of HDOs is to provide life-saving care for people during the most vulnerable moments of their lives, most resources are used on cutting-edge research, machines, and improving the expertise of the physicians and staff. Although this looks like a logical allocation of resources for HDOs, however, this leaves their health information technology under-resourced and under-developed. Being aware of this fact, hackers and malicious actors exploited the system's known vulnerabilities to damage the health information system's integrity, confidentiality, and availability [1]. According to the Federal Bureau of Investigation (FBI) and other US government organizations, cybercriminals exploited the vulnerable situation during the COVID-19 pandemic due to the imposition of the "lockdowns" and "remote work" that allowed people to work from home in unsecured or insufficiently secured networked devices [20]. Consequently, the intruders articulated a variety of stratagems via phishing email campaigns by taking advantage of the intensive public concern of COVID-19 and the demand for legitimate support information (health updates, cures, vaccines, financial packages, and emergency relief, etc.) to distribute ransomware [21]. This triggered a concomitant surge in cyber-attacks to disrupt normal operations and extort private credentials [22].

Although enterprise security received increased focus and awareness from the healthcare community and others concerned, malicious actors yet find it easy to attack HDOs. The requirements for regular electronic health, medicine, care directives, and therapeutic records to provide the necessary patient care and security flaws in health information technology infrastructures are the two main reasons why the HDOs became easy targets for malicious actors. Ransomware attacks cause major disruptions in operations including delivering critical care for patients, encrypting or disabling of electronic health records, forcing clinicians to use the pen-paper method for documenting care, delaying appointments and surgeries, and disrupting ambulance and practice infrastructures [3]. Researchers [23, 24] believe that other than financial costs, ransomware attacks on HDOs are capable of imposing human costs by compromising patient safety and outcomes. Therefore, it poses a real danger to the healthcare business [25]. In this study, we explore what ransomware is, including its categories, why healthcare is a prime target for ransomware attacks, the evolution of ransomware attacks on healthcare, statistical data on the impact of ransomware attacks on HDOs, and finally some mitigation and prevention strategies.

5.2 METHODOLOGY

Using peer-reviewed publications and other reports, we compiled a list of ransomware attacks targeting healthcare organizations. The study addressed the rationality behind healthcare organizations being the prime target of ransomware attacks. We explored and elaborated on information regarding the attacks including the names of the healthcare organizations being targeted, attack methods, the financial impact, and the effects of ransomware attacks on patient care and organizational management. We concluded with a stress on the cybersecurity aspects of the healthcare organizations including the mitigation and prevention strategies found through peer-reviewed publications.

5.3 WHAT IS RANSOMWARE?

Ransomware is a malicious type of software (i.e., malware) designed to infect a network or computer system, encrypt the information (e.g., hard disks, network files, remote drivers), and restrict access to data and functionalities of the system until the demand for a ransom is met [26, 27]. Typically, targeted computers or systems get affected by ransomware via phishing email campaigns destined for individual computer systems. These emails are associated with malicious links or infected texts/files, so malware can infect and/or compromise the computer or a system when the links are accessed or a malicious file(s) are downloaded [28]. The attacker normally possesses the "key" to decrypt the information, which is distributed only when the victim pays the required ransom. The ransom payment is generally made in bitcoins or other cryptocurrencies due to low fees, irreversible, and anonymous transaction types [29]. However, it is not always certain that the user's encrypted files will be returned to the user if a ransom is paid.

5.3.1 Categories of Ransomware

Chesti et al. [26] divided ransomware into two basic categories based on their behavior once inside a computer: (i) locker ransomware and (ii) crypto-ransomware. Locker ransomware locks the victim's system or device not allowing them to use the device; usually, the victim's data are untouched and can be recovered by transferring the storage device to another functioning device. The victim's system or device is blocked by blocking the primary computer function via encrypting files associated with the computer screen and/or keyboard [21]. An example of locker ransomware is "Reveton" [27], which locks the user out of their device by blocking certain operating system features and deceives by giving the user the impression that a local authority locked the user's computer. Crypto-ransomware, on the other hand, encrypts the victim's sensitive files and demands payment for the decryption key. Usually, nothing can be done about the victim's files without the decryption key [26]. Its encryption scheme could be symmetric, asymmetric, or hybrid. Symmetric encryption requires that the encryption key be embedded in the ransomware, therefore if the ransomware is reverse-engineered, the decryption key can be found. Asymmetric encryption does not require that the key be embedded in the ransomware; however, it is slow compared to symmetric encryption and struggles to encrypt large files. Hybrid encryption uses both symmetric and asymmetric encryption. Symmetric encryption encrypts all the files in the victim's system. Once all the files are encrypted using symmetric encryption, then asymmetric encryption is used on the symmetric encryption key [21]. "CryptoWall" and "TorrentLocker" are examples of crypto-ransomware. First occurred in 2014, "CryptoWall" and "TorrentLocker" both used advanced encryption standard (AES), a symmetric block cipher algorithm, to encrypt the victim's data [30].

Matthew Ryan [30] categorized ransomware attacks as targeted or non-targeted attacks. In targeted ransomware attacks, the cyber-attacker creates a ransomware attack for a specific target. This target signifies financial, political, or geographical reasons. The attacker can also target a vulnerability in an individual or organization's particular application or device. Conversely, the non-targeted ransomware attack's objective is to infect as many systems and devices as possible. This ransomware attack generally utilizes a worm or some propagation mechanisms to rapidly spread over any vulnerable system and device.

5.3.2 Ransomware-as-a-Service

Ransomware-as-a-service or RaaS is an emerging business model that has quickly become popular among cybercriminals. RaaS is when expert ransomware developers make their ransomware software available to the public in exchange for a small fee, no fee at all, or a cut of the ransom [31]. Ransomware developers would package all the necessary tools and infrastructure needed to carry out ransomware attacks into what is known as a RaaS kit and sell it through TOR (The Onion Router) websites, websites that provide anonymity and privacy to the user. RaaS kit has helped less tech-savvy cybercriminals be successful in cyber extortion. Due to RaaS, there has been an increase in the frequency of ransomware attacks [32].

5.3.3 Ransomware 2.0

While traditional ransomware centers on encrypting only the victim's data, Ransomware 2.0 employs a double extortion model, where it not only encrypts the victim's data but also takes a copy of that data and threatens to leak that data to the public. Victims of Ransomware 2.0 must now pay a ransom to prevent data loss and data leakage. Ransomware 2.0, however, requires an additional level of skill for the attackers, as the valuable data they are after is not usually going to be found on the first device they get access to. For Ransomware 2.0 to be successful, it must conduct lateral movement techniques, such as credential theft, network discovery, and open-port discovery, and identify vulnerable objects within the network [33].

5.3.4 Ransomware Risk Categories

Spence et al. [19] identified multiple risk categories including medical malpractice, data privacy, property, reputation, and cost and expenses. Medical malpractice can happen if patients are harmed due to impaired patient care. For example, ransomware can bring down the automatic online prescription order and delivery system that can generate erroneous medication for the patients. The Health Insurance Portability and Accountability Act (HIPAA) protects the confidentiality and privacy of patients. This act ensures that businesses take necessary measures to secure the information they may hold. However, ransomware attacks can cause loss of patient data privacy and make businesses violate the HIPAA law. Ben Beitin [34] reported that medical identity frauds increased by 22% in 2015, and 65% of the victims of these frauds paid more than $10,000 on average for the recovery services provided by creditors and legal teams. Regarding reputation loss and harm to future business, Ponemon study [35] reveals that a quarter of the companies under their study expressed dire concerns regarding their reputation losses due to ransomware attacks that can be measured at over three million on average per company. However, the greatest threat is related to losses from the costs and expenses associated with ransomware attacks. In 2016, as reported by Spence et al. [29], the average cost of data breach and associated legal lawsuits was over $3.6 million. Besides, Thamer and Alubady [36] pointed out incident response strategy and information backup plan as risk categories. Incident response strategy is important since an attack by ransomware is not detected until the data is completely encrypted or the system is completely down. The backup plan for the patients' sensitive and confidential information is a risk concern since the same backup plan does not fit all healthcare organizations [6]. Sophisticated ransomware can impact backups and therefore, it is crucial to ensure the security and availability of sensitive data offline.

5.4 WHY HEALTHCARE IS A PRIME TARGET FOR RANSOMWARE?

Healthcare is a very important area of business in the United States, and for many healthcare organizations, ransomware is the leading worry. This is due to multiple reasons, including the amount of private information stored in databases, malicious activity that can be performed with the information, and the ability for cybercriminals to gain access to the information or extort money by using ransomware. The Centers for Medicare & Medicaid Services (2020) estimate that in 2019 the overall share of the U.S. gross domestic product in healthcare sector spending was 17.7%. Despite this, the [37] Cyber Threat Report found an 8% increase in the volume of attacks on healthcare organizations, compared to a large decrease in attacks on government and retail (82% and 50%, respectively), a 41% increase on financial, and a 275% increase on educational organizations.

5.4.1 The Abundance of Electronic Health Records

Under the Health Information Technology for Economic and Clinical Health (HITECH) Act of 2009, healthcare organizations were legally required to convert their physical records to digital, with organizations receiving over $35 billion to help facilitate the switch to electronic, to promote and expand the adoption of health information technology, according to [38]. The rapid creation of electronic health record systems and subsequent moves created a target for cybercriminals, with lots of new, important information stored in electronic mediums, with very little support or supervision given for setting up the security of the electronic health record systems. Another development in recent years is the rise in remote healthcare. The ability to use mobile and other smart devices to manage healthcare leads to much easier and simpler access for customers but also leads to sensitive data being much more accessible, and privacy is affected by the use of smart devices for healthcare [39]. Healthcare systems also did not have the personnel, skill, or financial means to deal with any data breaches and attacks on these new systems. Despite the HITECH Act intending to improve quality and safety, it also caused a large increase in issues regarding sensitive medical information and data theft.

5.4.2 Value of Sensitive Medical Information to Cybercriminals

Ben Beitin [34] found that healthcare data was far more valuable than other data due to the potential uses of it, with the capability for financial or political gain, or the ability to cause damage to others. Medical profiles from an EHR database were found to be selling for $5 per patient, medical insurance cards selling for $1 per card, and full medical credentials were estimated to be selling for over $1,000 each. The Ponemon study [35] released a report in which they found the cost associated per stolen record after a data breach. The estimated costs in the public sector were $71, in retail they were $154, in services they were $223, and finance, the second-highest sector, was at $245 per breached record. The highest data breach costs per record occurred in the healthcare sector at $380 per record.

5.5 History of Ransomware Attacks in Regard to Healthcare Organizations

Ransomware is becoming widely used and has become known to be extremely detrimental to organizations and individuals alike [26]. The group of organizations that has been facing the wrath of ransomware is healthcare organizations. The first ransomware attack was of a healthcare organization. In 1989, Joseph L. Popp distributed approximately 20,000 infected files using a floppy disk through snail mail to a mailing list of people who attended the World Health Organization's international AIDS conference. Named the AIDS Trojan or PC Cyborg ransomware, the ransomware used a simple symmetric cryptographic algorithm, and payment was supposed to be done through snail mail [26]. Over the next couple of decades, cybercriminals began to use more sophisticated encryption algorithms in their ransomware and to lean on email and the internet to spread their ransomware. **Table 5.1** lists different ransomware deployed in different healthcare organizations including the encryption technologies associated with them. The list of encryption algorithm included symmetric encryption methods such as AES (Advanced Encryption Standard) with block cipher mode such as CTR (Counter), ECB (Electronic Book Code), and CBC (Cipher Block Chaining) or asymmetric encryption methods such as RSA (Rivest–Sharmir–Adleman). Attackers would also use a hybrid of the two, where AES is used in the first stage of encryption, and then RSA is used in the second stage of encryption [40]. Some highly publicized ransomware in healthcare organizations are as follows: Locky, SamSam, WannaCry, Ryuk, and Conti ransomware.

5.5.1 Locky Ransomware

The Locky ransomware first appeared in February 2016 when the Hollywood Presbyterian Medical Center in Los Angeles, California, became a hostage of the attack. The Locky ransomware was distributed through the Necurs botnet, a network of over five million computers infected by the Necurs malware. The Necurs botnet can send millions of emails embedded with a malicious Microsoft Office file. According to a security vendor called AppRiver, the range of the email distribution was said to be extensive, with reports that over 23 million phishing emails were sent containing the Locky ransomware over 24 hours. Once the email has been received and the malicious Microsoft Office file attached to the email is downloaded and opened, the user is prompted to enable macros, an automated task feature of Microsoft Office, to decipher an unreadable text in the Microsoft Office file. If the user enables macros, instead of deciphering the unreadable text, the Locky ransomware

TABLE 5.1
A list of ransomwares deployment in different healthcare organizations. The word "deployment" represents how the attacker got the ransomware into the victim's system

Name and Date Appeared	Encryption Algorithms	Deployment	Healthcare Organization Attacked	Sources
AIDS Trojan or PC Cyborg (1989)	Simple symmetric cryptographic algorithm	Mailing a Floppy Disk	Attendees of the World Health Organization's international AIDS conference	[26]
Locky (February 2016)	AES in CTR or ECB mode AES in ECB mode + RSA	Email, Microsoft Office Word document	Hollywood Presbyterian Medical Center in Los Angeles, California, USA	[30] [41]
SamSam (2015-2019)	RSA	Vulnerabilities in servers	Healthcare in the US such as The hospital systems in Baltimore, Buffalo's primary trauma center, clinics and doctors' offices in in Virginia, and a hospital in Greenfield, Indiana	[30] [42]
WannaCry (May 2017)	AES + RSA	Vulnerabilities in Microsoft Windows' Server Message Block (SMB) protocol	National Health Service in UK	[30] [43] [44] [45]
Ryuk (December 2019)	AES in CBC mode + RSA	Phishing email	Benesov Hospital in Benesov, Czech Republic	[30] [46] [47]
Conti (December 2019)	AES in CBC mode + RSA	Phishing email	Health Services Executive in Ireland	[30] [46] [47] [48] [49] [50]
Defray 777 (March 2020)	AES in ECB mode + RSA	Microsoft Windows/IT network	Brno University Hospital in Brno, Czech Republic	[47] [51]
Snake (May 2020)	AES + RSA	Infected email attachments (macros), torrent websites, malicious ads.	Fresenius in Germany	[47] [52] [53] [54] [55]
Maze (March 2020)	ChaCha + RSA	Phishing e-mails, vulnerabilities of remote desktop protocol, and exploit kits	Hammersmith Medical Research in London	[47] [56]
Zeppelin (May 2021)	N/A	Microsoft Windows/ phone lines/payroll systems	Waikato hospitals in New Zealand	[47]

begins to download and encrypt the user's files in the background. Since the attack on the Hollywood Presbyterian Medical Center Newer versions of the Locky ransomware have been created, which can be concealed in other file types such as Excel, Zip, and even voice messages. These newer versions of Locky also have greater strength in deleting and encrypting recovery options [30].

Once the Locky ransomware finishes encrypting and sending the decryption key to the attacker's command and control server, the victims are prompted with a ransom payment and a step-by-step process on how to make the payment. In the instructions, victims were asked to install the Tor browser, a browser used to anonymously browse the internet. Using the Tor browser the victims were supposed to go to a decryption service website to pay for the decryption key. The majority of Locky victims were reported to being asked for a ransom payment between 0.5 and 1 Bitcoin, according to Sophos, a security research company [41]. It is difficult to get the exact ransom amount paid to the attackers of all the Locky ransomware due to the continuous changes of the Locky ransomware; however, Google researchers found that Locky was the first ransomware to generate over $1 million a month, with total ransom payments exceeding $7.8 million [30]. Also, the Hollywood Presbyterian Medical Center in Los Angeles, California, was reported to have paid $17,000 worth of Bitcoin to the attackers to get back their patients' data [57]. The attackers used the Locky ransomware to conduct the attack.

5.5.2 SamSam Ransomware

First discovered in 2016, the SamSam ransomware targeted hospitals, healthcare organizations, and municipal governments in many cities in the United States [26]. This makes SamSam an example of targeted ransomware. Cybersecurity researchers have named the cybercriminal group behind the SamSam ransomware attacks as Gold Lowell. It is believed to be privately developed by Gold Lowell and not available to the public. To prevent antivirus detection, the SamSam ransomware is not sold or given to other cybercriminals on online forums and is updated frequently. This ransomware attacks through vulnerabilities in servers. In 2015 and 2016, this ransomware group looked into the vulnerabilities in Java. The group then later transferred on to target the vulnerabilities in Microsoft's Internet Information Services (IIS), file transfer protocol (FTP), and remote desktop protocol (RDP). The group now mainly works on accessing networks through single-factor external access protocols, such as RDP or virtual private networks. Once the group has gained access to the network, several tools are used to deploy the SamSam ransomware [42].

After the ransomware finishes encrypting, an apologetic message is shown to the victim demanding payment in exchange for the decryption key. The ransom amount that the group charged to decrypt one system is set at around $10,000 while all systems on the network can be decrypted for $50,000. The group were also willing to decrypt a file for free for the victim to show that they have the capabilities to decrypt the victim's system [42]. They made $6 million from the ransom payment paid by the victims of the attack [26].

5.5.3 WannaCry Ransomware

Appeared on May 12, 2017, the WannaCry ransomware affected 150 countries and over 300,000 computers [26]. Of those 150 countries and 300,000 computers, the United Kingdom's National Health Service (NHS) was one of the many victims of the attack. According to Ryan [58], 34 out of the 236 NHS trusts (comprising acute and specialist hospitals, community service providers, and ambulance services) were infected by the ransomware and locked out of their devices. Also, 603 primary care and other NHS organizations were infected by the ransomware, including 8% of GP practices (595 out of 7,454). There were no reported cases of patient data being stolen or compromised as a result of the WannaCry attack on the NHS; however, the NHS identified 6,912 appointments that were canceled as a direct result of the attack and an estimated 19,000 appointments in total that may have been affected [44]. The WannaCry ransomware was able to create such a widespread disruption due to its worm-like functionality. "WannaCry" exploited the "EternalBlue" vulnerability in Microsoft Windows' Server Message Block (SMB) protocol. By exploiting this vulnerability alongside using "DoublePulsar", a backdoor tool that allows attackers to remotely execute code on a compromised computer, the WannaCry ransomware was able to propagate itself to vulnerable computers across the Internet [31].

No NHS organizations paid the ransom to the WannaCry ransomware attackers [59]. However, in other cases of the attack, all known WannaCry ransom demands were sought through Bitcoin. The amount demanded ranged from $300 to $600 worth of Bitcoin [43]. Despite WannaCry being one of the largest cyberattacks in history, the money gained from the attacks only totals between $80,000 and $140,000 worth of Bitcoin [30]. The reason for this could be attributed to the fact that in the afternoon of the attack being discovered, cybersecurity researchers were able to find a kill switch within the WannaCry ransomware source code and stop it from spreading further [45, 58]. Nevertheless, the actual damage of the attack is said to exceed $1 billion due to the widespread disruption of the attack [30].

5.5.4 Conti and Ryuk Ransomware

The Conti ransomware first appeared in December 2019 and is based on an older ransomware called Ryuk, whose first appearance was in August 2017. The Conti ransomware adds to the Ryuk ransomware the exfiltration feature, which takes the victim's files and possibly publishes them on the dark web to embarrass the victim and further incentivize the victim to pay. Both ransomwares are considered as RaaS, and the author or developer is believed to be of the cybercriminal group called "CryptoTech". However, the distributor or attacker that deployed the Conti ransomware on the Health Services Executive (HSE) in Ireland is believed to be of the cybercriminal group called Wizard Spider [46]. Both the Conti and Ryuk ransomware are spread through phishing emails and utilize the "TrickBot" and "BazarLoader" malware to deploy itself onto the victim's computer. The "TrickBot" and "BazarLoader", an extension of "TrickBot", allow the attacker to gain access to various amounts of tools on the victim's computer, which can be used for credential harvesting, sending out new phishing emails to the victim's address book, data exfiltration, and deploying ransomware such as the Conti and Ryuk ransomware [47]. Once the Conti ransomware is deployed onto the victim's computer, it will look for user files on the local computer, servers, network shares or even cloud-based storage and encrypt them using AES 256 encryption and change the extension of the files to ".CONTI". It will also look to compromise the domain controller server and other key services in the network using administrator access. Finally, a CONTI README.txt ransom note will be left on the victim's computer desktop, in which are instructions on how to proceed with decrypting the victim's encrypted files [46]. As a result of the Conti ransomware attack on the HSE, the HSE shut down all of its IT systems nationwide to contain and assess the attack. This of course led to immediate disruption in healthcare services across the country, and many healthcare professionals had to revert to pen and paper to continue patient care. About 80% of the HSE's environment was across corporate IT services, hospitals, community health organizations (CHOs), and electronic health records were later found to be encrypted by the ransomware [49]. According to a lesson-learned report done by The U.S. Department of Health and Human Services (HHS), the private information of thousands of people who received the COVID-19 vaccine was exposed, and 700 GB of unencrypted data including protected health information (PHI) was stolen [50]. HSE refuses to pay any ransom to the attacker, however the recovery effort totals around $600 million, including $120 million in replacing and upgrading the systems affected by the ransomware, and payments to a third-party cybersecurity support team [48].

5.5.5 Recent Ransomware Attacks on Healthcare Organizations

During the COVID-19 pandemic, with the increase in remote IT operations, the number of ransomware attacks increased by 150%–200%. One notable ransomware that targeted a healthcare organization during this time is called the Maze ransomware. The Maze ransomware first appeared in 2019, attacking Hammersmith Medicines Research Ltd. in London. The Maze ransomware used advanced attack techniques and implemented the double-extortion strategy, which is when the ransomware not only encrypts data but also extracts the data to be sold on the dark web. It was reported that patient data from Hammersmith Medicines Research Ltd. were stolen and published on the dark web.

Another publicized ransomware that targeted a healthcare organization during the COVID-19 pandemic is called the Snake ransomware. The Snake ransomware first emerged in 2020 and targeted critical infrastructure such as manufacturing, health care, smart grids, and transport networks. Like that of the Maze ransomware, the Snake ransomware also implemented the double-extortion strategy. A difference in the Snake ransomware is that instead of encrypting and exfiltrating an individual workstation, it was made to target the entire network [47]. Another difference in the Snake ransomware is that it looks to kill processes related to supervisory control and data acquisition (SCADA) systems, industrial control systems (ICS), remote management systems, and operational communications with shop floor equipment, virtual machines, and network-related software. The Snake ransomware also deletes all shadow copies of files, which are files created by an auto-save feature in many applications [54]. An incident of the Snake ransomware that involved a healthcare organization was the attack on Fresenius Healthcare in Germany. Data from Fresenius Healthcare were stolen, and a portion of it was leaked on the dark web. The leaked data is mostly of patient records containing patient's personal information such as first and last names, gender, birth date, nationality of the patient, profession, postal address, and phone number [52, 54]. The ransom amount from the Snake ransomware attack is unknown; however, Fresenius did pay $1.5 million to resolve a previous ransomware attack [55].

5.6 QUANTITATIVE RESULTS OF RANSOMWARE ATTACKS ON HEALTHCARE ORGANIZATIONS

Now this leads our research to what effects these attacks have had on the patients of healthcare organizations, as well as the organizations themselves. There is a variety of information available from reports of private security firms, as well as some information from the departments of the US Government, namely the Department of Health and Human Services, and within it, the Office of Civil Rights.

5.6.1 Effects on Patient Care

Spence et al. [19] found that ransomware could be related to additional risks regarding medical malpractice or data privacy. A ransomware attack could lead to prescription errors if the Computerized Prescription Order Entry system stops functioning. In ascertaining the consequences of ransomware attack on National Health Service in UK, Aljaidi et al. [3] found that 44% (about 166) of total WannaCry ransomware attacks caused some form of disruption to quality of care, and about 8.6% (32) caused disruptions that last longer than two weeks. Types of disruptions included electronic system downtime for 156 (41.7%) of the attacks, delays or cancellations of scheduled care for 38 (10.2%) of the attacks, and ambulance diversion for 16 (4.3%) of the attacks.

5.6.2 Financial Effects for Patients

Ben Beitin [34] found from previous works that healthcare data was far more valuable than other data due to the potential uses for it, with the capability for financial or political gain, or the ability to cause damage to others. McAfee revealed a study in 2017 regarding information about vendors on the dark web, with one seller having the data of around 400,000 patients, and another vendor selling patient lists, providers, emails, Social Security numbers, dates of birth, and medical records.

This information could be used to get services done or get prescription medications by using a fake identity or by using stolen credentials.

Ponemon [60] reported that there were 500,000 victims of medical identity theft in 2014, increasing by 22% in 2015 to around 600,000. Victims of medical identity theft had to pay an average of $13,500 to legal teams and creditors to recover from the fraud. According to the Consumer Financial Protection Bureau, roughly half of all collections actions on credit reports were due to medical debt, with some of those being due to identities being stolen using protected health information. Credit bureaus wait 180 days before adding medical debts to a report, and while entities covered under HIPAA are supposed to report data breaches to the secretary of the U.S. Department of Health and Human Services and the affected individuals of the breaches for any breach affecting over 500 individuals within 60 days of the breach [61], and some organizations do not report data breaches within the 60-day limit, or don't report breaches at all [34]. This leads to victims not knowing that their data has been breached, and not being able to take proper precautions against potential medical fraud or identity theft.

John Jiang and Ge Bai [62] found that 66% of the 1,461 data breaches their study covered from 2009 to 2019 affected sensitive personal information, including birth dates, driver's license numbers, and SSN, with 65% of the breaches compromising medical information.

5.6.3 Financial Effects on Businesses

Ben Beitin [34] also found some of the financial effects on businesses. Companies averaged $3 million in losses due to damage done to their reputation and customers leaving their businesses and investing money into repairing their reputation. Schiereck Bohn [38] found that the market reacts very limitedly to data breaches, but very negatively following data breaches involving confidential data. Reports of data breaches involving financial information, that is, credit card or bank account numbers, were found to have a large market reaction, but the leakage of social security numbers had a very small impact on the market. Ponemon [35] estimated the additional customer turnover after a data breach to be the second highest in the healthcare sector, behind the finance sector, leading to greater financial losses for organizations. Larger than the losses due to reputation damage, healthcare organizations in 2017 had to spend, on average, $3.62 million in recovering from the breach themselves, and offer services related to a breach, such as offering credit monitoring to patients,

TABLE 5.2
The ten countries with the highest volume of ransomware attacks in 2022 [64]

Country	Number of Ransomware Attacks in Millions
United States	217.49
United Kingdom	71.35
Spain	52.68
Brazil	21.81
Germany	20.17
Colombia	15.52
Netherlands	13.64
Italy	12.47
Norway	8.36
Australia	7.62

and legal costs from any lawsuits leveraged against them. This further increased to $6.45 million in 2019, according to Smart [63], with the average cost of a data breach across all sectors being $3.92 million.

5.7 STATISTICS OF CYBER ATTACKS ON HDOs

Moving on from the results of the attacks, it is important to look at how to prevent them. A study from Jama Network by Neprash et al. [3] found that the number of ransomware attacks has been steadily increasing over the years, with big spikes in 2016, following the mass transfer to electronic health records, and in 2019 following the start of the COVID pandemic and the rise in remote healthcare that occurred at the same time.

5.7.1 Trends in Attacks

For data from 2016 to 2021, Aljaidi et al. [3] created a database that documented 374 ransomware attacks on healthcare organizations, exposing the protected health information of 42 million people. The number of annual ransomware attacks for this period went from 43 in 2016 to 91 in 2021. The amount of PHI exposed per year went from 1.3 million in 2016 up to 16.5 million in 2021, an increase of over 1,100%. A total of 84 of these ransomware attacks were not reported, as they appeared in the researcher's database but did not appear in the HHS OCR database. Of the remaining 290 ransomware attacks, 203, or just over half of the total number of attacks, were not reported within the 60-day window required by the HHS OCR. About 52% of the ransomware attacks were found in the affected multiple facilities of one organization.

Ugwu et al. [65] used AI to categorize and analyze numerous data breaches and found a rise in hacking/IT incidents for data breaches in 2020. On the other hand, the 2022 Healthcare Information and Management Systems Society (HIMSS) Cybersecurity Survey found that 78% of healthcare professionals they surveyed did not experience a ransomware attack in 2022, which was a decrease from 2021; however, this percentage is from a fairly small sample size.

The Cyber Threat Report [37] found that ransomware groups were beginning to shift their targets from the United States to Europe and Asia, with the number of attacks on North America dropping by 48%, and the number of attacks on Europe increasing by 83%. As an example of this shift, Spain went from not being in the top ten list in 2021 to being the third most targeted country in 2022. North America still saw 222.6 million ransomware attacks compared to 204.8 million in Europe, but those numbers are reported to be the closest the continents have ever been, in terms of percentage.

5.7.2 Struggles for Organizations within the United States

Between April 2003 and December 2017, the Office of Civil Rights of HHS looked into 37,023 HIPAA violations, with over 68% of the investigations requiring corrective action (U.S. Department of Health and Human Services, 2017). That number has since increased to 45,387 complaints, with 67% requiring corrective action according to a report that is regularly updated by the OCR [66]. Ponemon [60] found that just under half of the healthcare organizations they contacted had little to no confidence that they could detect every instance of a patient's data being stolen from their databases. The 2018 HIMSS Cybersecurity Survey received responses from 239 security professionals of healthcare organizations, and 84% of responses revealed an increase in allocation of resources to deal with cybersecurity concerns within their organization.

The 2022 HIMSS Cybersecurity Survey also found that the top two issues that organizations are struggling with are; (i) finding enough cybersecurity staff and (ii) not having enough budget. Despite the budget increase (i.e., 47%) from 2022 to 2023, 61% organizations failed to employ enough cybersecurity professionals and 50% of organizations reached beyond their budget [67]. The top reasons it is difficult to find cybersecurity staff are partially due to a lack of qualified cybersecurity staff, partially due to lack of budget, and partially due to offering salaries not competitive enough to fill the positions. The budget changes are a slight decrease from the number of organizations that increased their cybersecurity budget from 2021 to 2022, at 51.5%; however, the difference between the two years is the same difference of organizations that kept the same budget for these same years.

The HIMSS survey also focused on the frequency and quality of cybersecurity training, as attacks are regularly evolving, and security professionals need to stay up-to-date on the latest technology. Many of the organizations surveyed had issues preventing proper training on best practices. Among multiple reasons, 67% stated the lack of timing to do training, 42% attributed the budgetary reasons, and 13% pointed out the lack of quality training available as prospective reasons contributing towards poor training. The study from Ponemon [60] found that employee negligence, likely due to this lack of training, was among the top security concerns for healthcare organizations. Another thing to consider is third-party vendors. Swasey [68] found that 273 (28.8%) of the data breaches they studied from 2010 to 2013 were due to third-party vendors. In many organizations, cybersecurity is 6% or less of the total IT budget for an organization, meaning the organization has to choose how they allocate the money for their security carefully.

5.8 MITIGATION AND PREVENTION OF RANSOMWARE

To mitigate and prevent ransomware, cybersecurity researchers have suggested backing up files and systems, avoiding all spam links if unknown, keeping operating systems, browsers, security systems, and third-party plug-ins patched and up-to-date, and if a computer is found infected by a ransomware, then to immediately turn off the computer, and if the computer is on a network, to turn of the network [32]. This section will explore previous surveys on prevention and mitigation tactics against phishing-based ransomware, ransomware that exploits backdoors and vulnerabilities, ransomware that targets the recovery process, and ransomware that targets the network.

5.8.1 Employee Training and Programs

Baig et al. [7] said that the reason for ransomware getting into an individual or organization's system is due to the lack of resources for protecting data and the adoption of poor cybersecurity practices. A report by IBM showed that in 2014, over 95% of all investigated security incidents were due to human error with the most common reason being a user clicking on a malicious attachment or unsafe web link [19]. Maurya et al. [47] recommend having proper employee training processes and programs in place, so that employees will be more aware of the tactics used by ransomware attackers. They continued to say that this would hinder the ransomware attacker's attempts to carry out phishing-based ransomware attacks. Another survey by Aldaraani Begum [27] also recommended developing and executing a plan for an end user awareness program, stating that smarter end users will surely result in fewer ransomware incidents.

5.8.2 Resetting and Backup

According to Baig et al. [7], mitigation tactics for ransomware can include system resets or reformatting to get rid of the ransomware, recovery from the data backups onto uninfected systems, and reporting of the incident to appropriate authorities. The system resets or reformatting is a procedure that would basically put a computer system back to its original factory settings, completely removing all existing data and software installed, including the ransomware. The reason for this is to reinstate the system's integrity by removing unauthorized ransomware privileges and revert any modification made to system configurations. It also aids in the elimination of potential backdoors or vulnerabilities that may have been exploited by the ransomware.

A different survey by Ahmed et al. [1] also recommended backing up networks or systems so that recovery is possible later. By having a backup of network or systems, the hospital will not have to pay the ransom to recover its systems, instead they could recover its systems from the backup. This procedure of backing up should be done daily so that the hospital can restore its systems from the day before the attack. Another recommendation by Ahmed et al. [1] was to review and validate server backup processes. This step is to confirm that the backup is completed and reliable. By reviewing and validating server backup processes, hospitals can be certain that they will have a backup that is reliable in case of a ransomware attack. Furthermore, Spence et al. [19] said that data must also be backed up to a place that is not connected to computers or networks, or else the backup also becomes encrypted and held for ransom. Cylance [19] suggested to physically store the information offline or in a cloud storage solution not attached to the network. Offsite physical storage of backup data is especially crucial to prevent the types of ransomware that seek out and destroy network backups.

5.8.3 Security Patches and System Updates

Outdated systems are also reasons for successful ransomware attacks. One of the most well-known examples of this was the WannaCry attack in 2017, which affected organizations across the globe [36]. The vulnerability, known as "Eternal Blue" was first leaked by a group of hackers called the Shadow Brokers. Truss [69] looked at another ransomware, named "NotPetya" as a variant of Petra, which also used Eternal Blue but used another exploit called "Eternal Romance", which functions similarly to Eternal Blue by using vulnerabilities to allow attacks on any computers with SMB servers, which are used for computers to share files with other computers, or printers. Harkins and Freed [28] noted that Microsoft released patches to prevent SMB exploits eight weeks before the information was leaked, but individuals and companies might not have updated yet due to potential issues regarding security, and the loss of time spent upgrading.

Maniath et al. [70] found that the main way to improve security apart from training staff to resist social engineering was through exploiting vulnerabilities. The majority of web-based ransomware infections were done through vulnerabilities with Flash. They found that 47% of enterprise machines were not updated to the most recent version of Flash. This is due to a combination of not wanting to spend the time and not having the people to maintain the systems, both of these boiling down to a lack of knowledge or the finances to handle them. Keeping software up-to-date is extremely important to ensuring the safety of a device or network, as updates are regularly published, and any devices not being kept up-to-date can lead to a gap in security that has the ability to spread.

5.8.4 Network Segmentation

Network segmentation is the splitting of the network into distinct parts, usually based on crucial importance. In the context of ransomware, network segmentation can help in stopping the types of ransomware that attack and propagate across the network. Network segmentation involves identifying critical and noncritical network assets, defining segmentation goals, and deploying the appropriate access control mechanisms. Due to the division of network assets, network segmentation can prevent ransomware from gaining access to an organization's most valuable assets. Network segmentation's ability to enforce access control mechanisms for each part of the network restricts ransomware from spreading through the network [47].

5.8.5 Zero-Trust Architecture (ZTA)

A zero-trust architecture (ZTA) is a cybersecurity plan that assumes there is no inherent trust toward any user, device, or network, regardless of their location or security boundaries. Like that of network segmentation, ZTA mitigates and prevents ransomware through micro-segmentation of networks, thereby also limiting the types of ransomware that move across the network to encrypt and steal data. ZTA helps minimize the attack surface and reduces the spread of ransomware by implementing strict access control and by promoting the principle of least privilege, allowing the user access to what they absolutely need to perform their responsibilities and nothing more. ZTA also uses multi-factor authentication, two or more proofs of identity. By doing all of these, ZTA can prevent, in the majority of cases, an unauthorized person using compromised or stolen credentials to get into an organization's network [47].

5.9 CONCLUSION

The main goal of this chapter was to compile data from multiple sources to lay out specific ransomware attacks and show the growth of ransomware attacks in healthcare organizations. We looked at a large variety of previous works and government websites, along with reports from cybersecurity groups in an attempt to make the information more digestible. From our research, we found that a part of the vulnerabilities related to the cybersecurity of healthcare organizations is due to the systems used, but a large portion of the reason that ransomware attacks work is due to the people. Having proper training to mitigate phishing or negligence that could lead to ransomware attacks is important to everyone in an organization. Having a proper response plan and regular familiarization with current types of ransomware and how they might get into a system is vital to maintaining the cybersecurity of an organization. More information is always required regarding cybersecurity, as cybercriminals are always evolving their methods. We believe further research could be done into the root of the ransomware attacks mentioned, as well as ways to prevent or mitigate these specific ransomware attacks, which can help in addressing ransomware in healthcare organizations.

REFERENCES

1. Ahmed, M., Bachmann, S.D., Ullah, A.B., Barnett, S., 2022. Ransomware 2.0: An emerging threat to national security. *Australian Journal of Defence and Strategic Studies*, 125–132.
2. Aldaraani, N., Begum, Z., 2018. Understanding the impact of ransomware: A survey on its evolution, mitigation and prevention techniques, in: *2018 21st Saudi Computer Society National Computer Conference (NCC)*, pp. 1–5. doi:10.110 9/NCG.2018.8593029.
3. Aljaidi, M., Alsarhan, A., Samara, G., Alazaidah, R., Almatarneh, S., Khalid, M., Al-Gumaei, Y.A., 2022. NHS WannaCry ransomware attack: Technical explanation of the vulnerability, exploitation, and countermeasures, in: *2022 International Engineering Conference on Electrical, Energy, and Artificial Intelligence (EICEEAI)*, IEEE, pp. 1–6.
4. Almulihi, A.H., Alassery, F., Khan, A.I., Shukla, S., Gupta, B.K., Kumar, R., 2022. Analyzing the implications of healthcare data breaches through computational technique. *Intelligent Automation & Soft Computing* 32.
5. Arntz, P., 2020. Maze: The ransomware that introduced an extra twist.
6. Bai, G., Jiang, J.X., Flasher, R., 2017. Hospital risk of data breaches. *JAMA Internal Medicine* 177, 878–880.
7. Baig, Z., Mekala, S., Zeadally, S., 2023. Ransomware attacks of the COVID-19 pandemic: Novel strains, victims, and threat actors. *IT Professional* 25, 37–44. doi:10.1109/MITP.2023.3297085.
8. Beaman, C., Barkworth, A., Akande, T.D., Hakak, S., Khan, M.K., 2021. Ransomware: Recent advances, analysis, challenges and future research directions. *Computers & Security* 111, 102490.
9. Beitin, B., 2019. A review of ransomware attacks on healthcare organizations and the effectiveness of honeypots and other countermeasures. ProQuest Dissertations and Theses.
10. Bohn, L., Schiereck, D., 2023. Regulation of data breach publication: The case of us healthcare and the hitech act. *Journal of Economics and Finance* 47, 386–399.
11. Branch, L.E., Eller, W.S., Bias, T.K., McCawley, M.A., Myers, D.J., Gerber, B.J., Bassler, J.R., 2019. Trends in malware attacks against United States healthcare organizations, 2016–2017. *Global Biosecurity* 1, 15–28.
12. Bridges, L., 2008. The changing face of malware. *Network Security* 2008, 17–20.

13. Chesti, I.A., Humayun, M., Sama, N.U., Jhanjhi, N., 2020. Evolution, mitigation, and prevention of ransomware, in: *2020 2nd International Conference on Computer and Information Sciences (ICCIS)*, pp. 1–6. doi:10.1109/ICCIS49240.2 020.9257708.
14. CISA, 2020. Ransomware activity targeting the healthcare and public health sector. https://www.cisa.gov/uscert/ncas/alerts/aa20-302a
15. Clarke, R., Youngstein, T., 2017. Cyberattack on Britain's national health service – a wake-up call for modern medicine. *New England Journal of Medicine* 377, 409–411.
16. Cohen, I.G., Hoffman, S., Adashi, E.Y., 2017. Your money or your patient's life? Ransomware and electronic health records. *Annals of Internal Medicine* 167(8):587–588.
17. National Audit Office, 2017. Investigation: WannaCry cyber attack and the NHS. Department of Health, UK. https://www.nao.org.uk/wp-content/uploads/2017/10/Investigation-WannaCry-cyber-attack-and-the-NHS.pdf, accessed on 27 May 2024.
18. Cooper, S., 2023. What is snake ransomware how to protect against it? https://www.comparitech.com/net-admin/snakeransomware/#:~:text=Preventing%20Snake%20ransomware%20attacks,security%20conscious%20than%20office%20systems, accessed on 27 May 2024.
19. Cylance, B., 2019. A devastating assault on healthcare: HITECH, compliance, and the growth of the ransomware economy. Technical Report. Cylance Inc.
20. Dameff, C., Tully, J., Chan, T.C., Castillo, E.M., Savage, S., Maysent, P., Hemmen, T.M., Clay, B.J., Longhurst, C.A., 2023. Ransomware attack associated with disruptions at adjacent emergency departments in the US. *JAMA Network Open* 6, e2312270–e2312270.
21. Davis, J., 2021. Ransomware post-mortem: Ireland HSE cyberattack, recovery dogged by missteps. https://www.scmagazine.com/analysis/ransomware-post-mortem-ireland-hse-cyberattack-recovery-dogged-by-missteps, accessed on 27 May 2024.
22. Dimov, D., 2020. Lessons learned from the Fresenius ransomware cyberattack. https://www.infosecinstitute.com/resources/news/lessons-learned-from-the-fresenius-ransomware-cyberattack/, accessed on 27 May 2024.
23. Ducklin, P., 2016. Ransomware that's 100% pure JavaScript, no download required. https://news.sophos.com/en-us/2016/06/20/ransomware-thats-100-pure-javascript-no-download-required/, accessed on 27 May 2024.
24. Frankoff, E.L.S., 2021. Hypervisor jackpotting, part 1: CARBON SPIDER and SPRITE SPIDER target ESXi servers with ransomware to maximize impact. https://www.crowdstrike.com/blog/carbon-spider-sprite-spider-target-esxi-servers-with-ransomware/, accessed on 27 May 2024.
25. Gagneja, K.K., 2017. Knowing the ransomware and building defense against it-specific to healthcare institutes, in: *2017 Third International Conference on Mobile and Secure Services (MobiSecServ)*, IEEE, pp. 1–5.
26. Ghafur, S., Grass, E., Jennings, N.R., Darzi, A., 2019a. The challenges of cybersecurity in health care: The UK National Health Service as a case study. *The Lancet Digital Health* 1, e10–e12.
27. Ghafur, S., Kristensen, S., Honeyford, K., Martin, G., Darzi, A., Aylin, P., 2019b. A retrospective impact analysis of the WannaCry cyberattack on the NHS. *NPJ Digital Medicine* 2, 98.
28. Harkins, M., Freed, A.M., 2018. The ransomware assault on the healthcare sector. *Journal of Law & Cyber Warfare* 6, 148–164.
29. HHS, 2022. Lessons learned from the HSE cyber attack. https://www.hhs.gov/sites/default/files/lessons-learned-hse-attack.pdf, accessed on 27 May 2024.
30. Jakes, A., 2023. HIMSS healthcare cybersecurity survey report. https://www.himss.org/resources/himss-healthcare-cybersecurity-survey, 2022, accessed on 23 September 2024.
31. HSE, 2021. Conti cyber attack on the HSE: Independent post incident review. *Health Service Executives*. https://www.hse.ie/eng/services/publications/conti-cyber-attack-on-the-hse-full-report.pdf, accessed on 28 May 2024.
32. Ilascu, I., 2020. Snake ransomware leaks patient data from Fresenius Medical Care. https://www.bleepingcomputer.com/news/security/snake-ransomware-leaks-patient-data-from-fresenius-medical-care/, accessed on 27 May 2024.
33. Institute, P., 2016a. Sixth annual benchmark study on privacy security of healthcare data. Technical Report. Ponemon Institute LLC.
34. Institute, P., 2016b. Sixth annual benchmark study on privacy & security of healthcare data. https://ponemon.org/research/ponemon-library/security/sixth-annual-benchmark-study-on-privacy-security-of-healthcare-data.html, accessed on 27 May 2024.
35. Institute, P., 2017. 2017 Cost of data breach study: United States. https://www.ponemon.org/news-updates/blog/security/2017-cost-of-data-breach-study-united-states.html, accessed on 27 May 2024.

36. Thamer, N., Alubady, R., 2021. A survey of ransomware attacks for healthcare systems: Risks, challenges, solutions and opportunity of research, in: *2021 1st Babylon International Conference on Information Technology and Science (BICITS)*, IEEE. pp. 210–216.
37. Jiang, J., Bai, G., 2020. Types of information compromised in breaches of protected health information. *Annals of Internal Medicine* 172, 159–160.
38. Kanter, G.P., Kufahl, J., Cohen, I.G., 2021. Beyond security patches – fundamental incentive problems in health care cybersecurity, in: *JAMA Health Forum*, American Medical Association, pp. e212969–e212969.
39. Kaspersky, 2024. What is WannaCry ransomware? https://usa.kaspersky.com/resource-center/threats/ransomware-wannacry, accessed on 27 May 2024.
40. Kraszewski, K., 2019. SamSam and the silent battle of Atlanta, in: *2019 11th International Conference on Cyber Conflict (CyCon)*, pp. 1–16. doi:10.23919/C YCON.2019.8757090.
41. Krisby, R.M., 2018. Health care held ransom: Modifications to data breach security & the future of health care privacy protection. *Health Matrix* 28, 365.
42. Lab, E.M., 2020. The state of ransomware in the US: Report and statistics 2019. https://www.emsisoft.com/en/blog/34822/the-state-of-ran somware-in-the-us-report-and-statistics-2019/.
43. Liu, V., Musen, M.A., Chou, T., 2015. Data breaches of protected health information in the United States. *JAMA* 313, 1471–1473.
44. MacRae, J., Franqueira, V.N.L., 2018. On locky ransomware, Al Capone and Brexit, in: *Digital Forensics and Cyber Crime*, Springer International Publishing. pp. 33–45.
45. Malenfant, T., 2021. Impact of ransomware attacks on healthcare. Ph.D. thesis. Utica College.
46. Maniath, S., Poornachandran, P., Sujadevi, V., 2019. Survey on prevention, mitigation and containment of ransomware attacks, in: *Security in Computing and Communications: 6th International Symposium, SSCC 2018*, Bangalore, India, September 19–22, 2018, Revised Selected Papers 6, Springer, pp. 39–52.
47. Maurya, A., Kumar, N., Agrawal, A., Khan, P.R., 2018. Ransomware evolution, target and safety measures. *International Journal of Computer Sciences and Engineering* 6, 80–85. doi:10.26438/ijcse/v6i1.8085.
48. McCoy, T.H., Perlis, R.H., 2018. Temporal trends and characteristics of reportable health data breaches, 2010–2017. *JAMA* 320, 1282–1284.
49. Meskauskas, T., 2022. Snake ransomware virus - removal and decryption options.
50. Minnaar, A., Herbig, F.J., 2021. Cyberattacks and the cybercrime threat of ransomware to hospitals and healthcare services during the COVID-19 pandemic. *Acta Criminologica: African Journal of Criminology & Victimology* 34, 155–185.
51. Mohammad, A.H., 2020. Ransomware evolution, growth and recommendation for detection. *Modern Applied Science* 14, 68.
52. Moran Stritch, M., Winterburn, M., Houghton, F., 2021. The Conti ransomware attack on healthcare in Ireland: Exploring the impacts of a cybersecurity breach from a nursing perspective. *Canadian Journal of Nursing Informatics* 16, 3–4.
53. Neprash, H.T., McGlave, C.C., Cross, D.A., Virnig, B.A., Puskarich, M.A., Huling, J.D., Rozenshtein, A.Z., Nikpay, S.S., 2022. Trends in ransomware attacks on US hospitals, clinics, and other health care delivery organizations, 2016–2021. *JAMA Health Forum* 3, e224873–e224873. doi:10.1001/jamahealthforum.2022.4873.
54. (OCR), 2023a. Breach reporting. https://www.hhs.gov/hipaa/for-professionals/breach-notification/breach-reporting/index.html, accessed on 20 December 2023.
55. (OCR), 2023b. Numbers at a glance – current. https://www.hhs.gov/hipaa/for-professionals/compliance-enforcement/data/numbers-glance/2023-july/index.html, accessed on 20 December 2023.
56. Poulsen, K., McMillan, R., Evans, M., 2021. A hospital hit by hackers, a baby in distress: The case of the first alleged ransomware death. https://www.wsj.com/articles/ransomware-hackers-hospital-first-alleged-d eath-11633008116.
57. Ren, A., Liang, C., Hyug, I., Broh, S., Jhanjhi, N., 2020. A three-level ransomware detection and prevention mechanism. *EAI Endorsed Transactions on Energy Web* 7.
58. Ryan, M., 2021. Conclusion, in: *Ransomware Revolution: The Rise of a Prodigious Cyber Threat*, Springer International Publishing. pp. 153–156.
59. Satheesh Kumar, M., Ben-Othman, J., Srinivasagan, K., 2018. An investigation on WannaCry ransomware and its detection, in: *2018 IEEE Symposium on Computers and Communications (ISCC)*, pp. 1–6. doi:10.1109/ISCC.2018.8538 354.
60. Security, I., 2021. Cost of a data breach report 2021. *Risk Quantification* 73.
61. Sittig, D.F., Singh, H., 2016. A socio-technical approach to preventing, mitigating, and recovering from ransomware attacks. *Applied Clinical Informatics* 7, 624–632.

62. Slayton, T.B., 2018. Ransomware: The virus attacking the healthcare industry. *Journal of Legal Medicine* 38, 287–311. doi:10.1080/01947648.2018.1473 186.
63. Smart, W., 2018. Lessons learned review of the WannaCry ransomware cyber attack.
64. Shmuel, G., 2023. Ransomware trends 2023 report. https://cyberint.com/blog/research/ransomware-trends-and-statistics-2023-report, 2023, accessed on 23 September 2024.
65. SonicWall, 2023. 2023 SonicWall cyber threat report.
66. Spence, N., Bhardwaj, N., Paul, D.P., Coustasse, A., 2018. Ransomware in healthcare facilities: A harbinger of the future? *Perspectives in Health Information Management*, 1–22.
67. Spence, N., Paul III, D. P., & Coustasse, A. 2017, September. Ransomware in healthcare facilities: The future is now. Paper presented at *the Academy of Business Research, Fall 2017 Conference*, Atlantic City, NJ.
68. Swasey, K., 2020. Insufficient healthcare cybersecurity invites ransomware attacks and sale of PHI on the dark web. Center for Anticipatory Intelligence Student Research Reports.
69. Truss, C.L., 2017. Examining the risk factors for hospital ransomware attacks: A qualitative study. *MUSC Theses and Dissertations* 346.
70. Ugwu, A.O., Gao, X., Ugwu, J.O., Chang, V., 2022. Ethical implications of AI in healthcare data: A case study using healthcare data breaches from the US Department of Health and Human Services breach portal between 2009–2021, in: *2022 International Conference on Industrial IoT, Big Data and Supply Chain (IIoTBDSC)*, pp. 343–349. doi:10.1109/IIoTBDSC57192.2022.00070.

AUTHOR BIOGRAPHY

Kellan Dempsey was born on January 9th at Andrews Air Force Base but moved around the world throughout his childhood due to his parents' occupations. After spending some of his childhood in Thailand, he graduated from Stuttgart High School half a semester early, in January of 2018, and worked for a brief period. He then moved back to the United States of America and started working on his bachelor's degree in computer science in September of 2019. He graduated as a part of the class of 2024 and intends to continue his education at UW-Green Bay with a Master's in Cybersecurity.

Thong Yang was born in Thailand. He moved to the US in 2005. He lived most of his life in Green Bay, Wisconsin. He attended Green Bay West High School and graduated as a top 10% of his class. Afterward, he attended the University of Wisconsin Green Bay to further his education. At the University of Wisconsin Green Bay, he pursue his love for computers and technology by taking software development and information security courses. He graduated with a bachelor's degree in computer science with a double emphasis in software engineering and information assurance and security. He is a first-generation graduate student.

Nazim Choudhury is Assistant professor in the department of computer science at University of Wisconsin Green Bay. He finished his PhD in computer science from the University of Sydney in 2018. He worked as a postdoctoral fellow in DARPA funded "SocialSim" Project in the department of Computer Science and Engineering at the University of South Florida. While teaching undergraduate students, he conducted his research in cybersecurity and human computer interaction (HCI). His research is also featured in the national conference for undergraduate research (NCUR) in 2023. His research is funded by the University of Wisconsin Green Bay and WiSys Foundation.

Section III

Ransomware Countermeasures

6 Ransomware Threat Mitigation Techniques
Past, Present, and Future

Md. Sadi Arman, Nuray Jannat, Salman Sayeed Khan, and Muhammad Usama Islam

6.1 INTRODUCTION

Ransomware has emerged as a powerful and dangerous threat demanding our attention with the increase of digital technology usage [1]. Furthermore, the cyber threat landscape has obtained a dramatic and unexpected shift, with ransomware leading the case on the frontier of cybersecurity. The chapter will exhibit a comprehensive understanding of ransomware and the utmost need for effective mitigation techniques.

Before exploring the ransomware mitigation domain, it is crucial to have a precise and succinct definition of ransomware and its operational mechanisms. Azad Ali [2] provides a good definition in his research on malware in general and ransomware in some parts where it is one type of malicious software that encrypts or locks a user's file/computer to demand a ransom payment for restoring access. Zimba and his team [3] add to the definition that the characteristics of ransomware involve the attackers' demand for compensation to share the decryption key with the victim to regain their access to the encrypted data. This system typically uses robust encryption algorithms, making it nearly impossible to retrieve data without the decryption key [2, 3].

It uses diverse methods, including email, malicious attachments or links to threat-inclusive websites, and tries to gain unauthorized access to the target's computer or exploit software vulnerabilities [3]. Upon gaining access to the target, malicious software attempts to encrypt files. It presents a ransom message upon succession, notifying the target's predicament and requests a payment in cryptocurrency, usually Bitcoin as Conti's team [4] points out, in exchange for the decryption code.

Ransomware attacks are treacherous because of their prompt nature [3, 4]. Victims often face a tough decision, which includes paying the ransom and possibly getting their data back or refusing to cooperate, risking irreversible loss of sensitive information [4]. To understand this mechanism completely, developing effective strategies to minimize its effects is essential.

6.2 RANSOMWARE EVOLUTION

It is necessary to explore ransomware's historical events to understand its lineage and vicious transformation. The origins of ransomware, as pointed out by Ryan' work [5], can be delineated back to the late 1980s with the emergence of "AIDS Trojan", an early form of ransomware spread by utilizing floppy disks. Yet, it was only in the early 2000s that ransomware accelerated to substantial momentum [5].

The progression of ransomware throughout history has witnessed several significant affairs, including the exposure of the CryptoLocker ransomware in 2013 [6], representing a critical moment in the advancement of ransomware attacks. They used robust encryption algorithms, making data retrieval practically impracticable without the decryption key [6]. With its impeccable threatening capability, ransomware gained popularity, leading to the origination of several impostors, which further contributed to the widespread distribution of this dangerous program.

DOI: 10.1201/9781003469506-9

TABLE 6.1
Evolution of ransomware

Year	Evolution of Ransomware
1980s	First ransomware (AIDS Trojan) emerges as a research project [5].
1990s	Ransomware starts using PGP encryption for stronger security [8].
2006	Archiveus, the first ransomware with online payments, appears [9].
2013	CryptoLocker sets a new standard with advanced encryption [6].
2014	CryptoWall follows with more sophisticated tactics [10].
2017	Ransomware-as-a-service (RaaS) model gains popularity [11].
2017	WannaCry and NotPetya bring widespread disruption [12].
2019	Double extortion strategy emerges, stealing and encrypting data [7].
2020	Ransomware operators start popularizing dark web marketplaces [4].
2021	Professional ransomware negotiators become prominent [13].
2021	Governments worldwide intensify efforts to combat ransomware [5].
2022	Ongoing evolution of tactics and debate over ransom payments [14].

The pinnacle of this evolutionary process is now known as "Ransomware 2.0" [7]. This ransomware combines data encryption with data theft, going beyond conventional ransomware by encrypting the victim's data and extracting sensitive information as pointed out in Li and Qi's work [7]. The combination of the possibility of data exposure and data encryption has significantly increased risks, leaving victims with difficult decisions about whether to pay the ransom. The systematic development of ransomware in general and its historical context are provided in Table 6.1.

This chapter's primary goal is to provide adequate information and strategies to successfully combat ransomware's growing menace. Ransomware attacks have become more common recently, primarily affecting renowned companies and institutions. Episodes like this have sparked worries, attracting enormous media attention. This chapter aims to lay out a thorough knowledge of ransomware evolution, its classifications, historical context, and most importantly strategies for reducing its impact, of which the introductory part and historical evolution have already been discussed earlier.

The upcoming sections will explain the repercussions of ransomware attacks and tactics that can reduce the probability of an attack and minimize its impact on occurrence. Eventually, the future potential of research to combat ransomware and develop adaptable and resilient solutions will be evaluated, given the constantly evolving nature of cyber threats.

It is imperative to comprehend the classification of ransomware and develop appropriate strategies to reduce or avoid disastrous impacts. Malware, including ransomware, has evolved and diversified to meet specific modes and objectives of attacks [2]. This segment focuses on classifying and describing different kinds of ransomware, such as classical file encryption, mobile ransomware, and more advanced Ransomware 2.0 [1–14] as depicted through a pictorial description in Figure 6.1, emphasizing their unique characteristics.

- **Traditional File-Locking Ransomware:** File-locking ransomware is the oldest and most widespread form of this type of malware [6]. This type of malware encrypts files on victims' computers and demands money to release them. A few prominent examples are CryptoLocker, Locky, and so on. It would be correct to say that traditional ransomware focuses more on individuals and organizations, since they encrypt files and demand payment in cryptocurrencies.

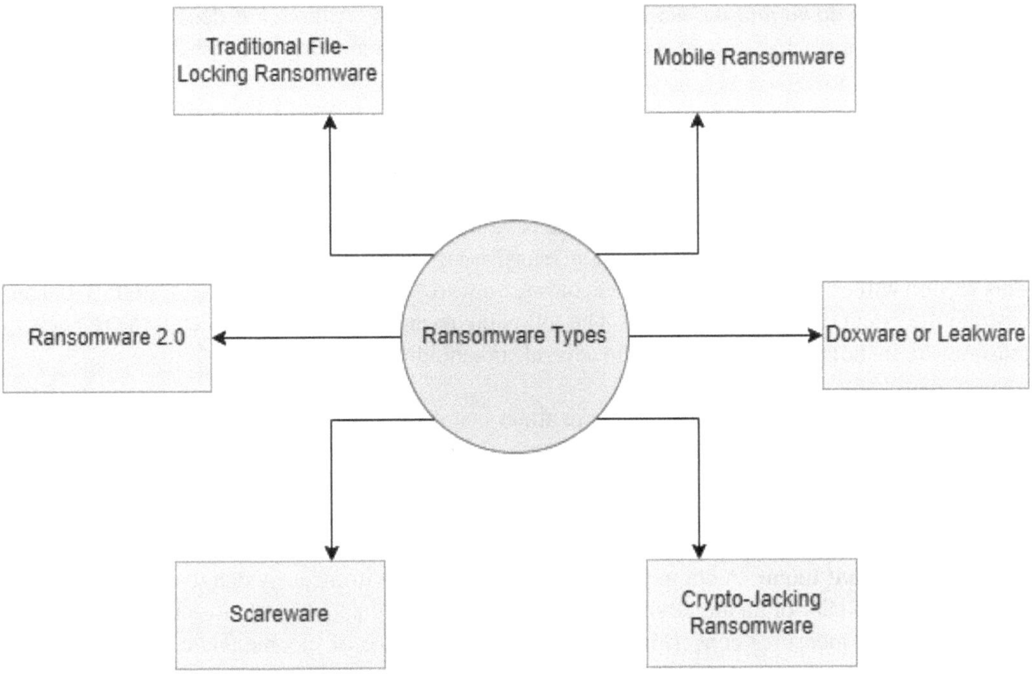

FIGURE 6.1 A pictorial overview of several ransomware and their types.

- **Mobile Ransomware**: Mobile devices have become so popular that criminals modify ransomware for such platforms. As a rule, mobile ransomware explicitly attacks smartphones and tablets, using encryption or device-locking methods to force users into paying a ransom [15]. There have been cases like "Simplocker" and "DoubleLocker" in the Android environment [15]. As a result, these attacks can lead to data loss, block access to the device, or sometimes extortion.
- **Ransomware 2.0:** If the earlier form of this menace was simple enough with only one thing involved, data encryption, then the current version represents an even more sophisticated nature of this threat. It combines data breach with encryption [7]. As an alternative to merely encrypting a target's data, adversaries can also steal sensitive information, creating potential danger if the sum demanded is not paid. The dual approach increases the victim's stress levels and amplifies possible consequences.
- **Doxware or Leakware:** Doxware, also known as Leakware, is a type of malware used to collect and release sensitive data. the Ransomware 2.0 subgroup named this type specifically for data theft and extortion [7]. The adversaries threaten to reveal essential or confidential information unless the ransom is paid. For instance, a dating service named "Ashley Madison" was compromised, and its user records were stolen and held for ransom.
- **Scareware**: They are designed to frighten users into performing specific actions, such as buying unnecessary software applications or submitting personal details [16]. Scareware may be less potent than other ransom-attack forms, but can still cause significant worry. It uses dishonest methods to convince people that their system is affected by a virus or files have been hacked. Consequently, the victims are forced to pay for bogus security tools or services. It plays on fear and spreads lies.
- **Crypto-Jacking Ransomware**: This type of ransomware uses the resources of victims' computers to mine cryptocurrency without their permission [3]. The malware harnesses the victim's computational resources to engage in cryptocurrency mining, resulting in a

system slowdown and increased electricity consumption. Although it does not explicitly request a ransom, it can cause financial harm by raising utility expenses and reducing device efficiency.

6.3 IMPACTS OF RANSOMWARE

Ransomware attacks have significant and extensive consequences, including financial, reputational, and operational impacts. Gaining a comprehensive understanding of the complete range of these repercussions is crucial for constructing a persuasive argument for the alleviation of ransomware. This section will explore the many impacts of ransomware and present specific case studies to demonstrate the extent of damage it may do. The following paragraph discusses in detail the impacts of ransomware in daily lives with respect to several stakeholders.

- **Monetary Implications:** Ransomware attacks can create severe financial problems, causing unwanted and unavoidable expenditures. Victims always face a dilemma – paying the ransom or trying to restore data/system without the involvement of the attacker [1–6]. These undesirable costs include the ransom paid, lost productivity, possible fines, legal implications, recovery, and system reinstatement expenses.
- **Reputational harm:** A company's reputation can suffer immensely due to a ransomware attack. Publicity of an attack may drive customers and stakeholders to lose trust in it [13]. Inadequate measures concerning cybersecurity cause loss of income and clients, leading to long-term effects.
- **Operational disruption:** If ransomware attacks encrypt critical data so that it can't be accessed, it disrupts daily business activities. Consequently, it may cause downtime, slow sales, and hampered customer support [1–14]. It takes much time to bring back systems and data to normal functioning, causing extra operational disruption.
- **Data loss:** Refusal by victims to pay a demanded ransom can lead to catastrophic data loss. Ransomware incidents have seen some organizations lose important or even irreplaceable information. A situation like this can significantly hinder the continuity of corporate operations and impede the organization's capacity to service consumers efficiently [7, 8].
- **Legal and regulatory ramifications:** Legal and regulatory ramifications may materialize due to ransomware attacks. Organizations can incur fines and legal consequences for data breaches and privacy violations, depending on the jurisdiction and the type of data breached [7. 14].

As we start to examine the specific instances, the first good yet worst example is WannaCry [12], which is a ransomware crypto-worm that targets computing devices running the operating system MS Windows by encrypting data and demanding ransom payments in the guise of cryptocurrency. In regard to WannaCry ransomware [12], it is important to note that in 2017, the virus brutally attacked over 200,000 key systems in 150 countries by encrypting the data of susceptible systems and files. The compromised system or file needed to be released, and the attackers requested payment in Bitcoin. These led to significant financial drifts with roughly $4 billion in costs and disrupted healthcare systems, logistics, and manufacturing. Another example is Colonial Pipeline, which experienced a ransomware attack in 2021 [5, 13, 17] through a weak link of password through VPN. The Colonial Pipeline ransomware attack has had far-reaching consequences since it necessitated its closure, causing fuel shortages and an increase in gas prices. They later had to pay a $4.4 m ransom to restore their data and recover that streamlining process they used to have.

These case studies reveal that ransomware causes much more than financial damage; it affects critical infrastructure and hinders the ordinary course of life. Thus, minimizing such after-effects is essential for individuals, companies, and communities.

6.4 STRATEGIES FOR MINIMIZING RANSOMWARE RISKS

The current digital environment necessitates addressing ransomware dangers because they continue to evolve and become more complex. A holistic approach that combines technology defenses with user education and awareness is required to mitigate ransomware properly. This comprehensive analysis will examine several effective methods and strategies to combat ransomware attacks. These plans are essential for individuals, companies, or institutions that wish to protect their information from this everyday menace. In this section we discuss several strategies for mitigating and minimizing such attacks [18–40].

1. User Education and Awareness: User education and awareness are vital in effectively mitigating ransomware. End users ought to be educated on the conceivable dangers of ransomware attacks and the most reliable methods they can use to detect and prevent such attacks [18].
   - Training Programs: Research should be carried out to educate users frequently about the dangers of ransomware, popular techniques used by attackers, and ways of identifying phishing emails or suspicious hyperlinks.
   - Simulated Phishing Campaigns: Use of simulated phishing campaigns is required to evaluate the success of user training programs. These campaigns may help identify those who require more training.
   - User Reporting: Prompt encouragement of users to report any suspicious emails or actions is necessary in tackling such attacks. Development of an intuitive reporting system to guarantee prompt action against possible dangers is one of the keys in battling this menace.
2. Frequent Data Backups and Retrieval: Implementing regular backups and developing a comprehensive data recovery strategy are essential for effectively reducing the impact of ransomware attacks. Maintaining pristine and current backups guarantees the ability to recover data in the case of a cyberattack [19].
   - Automated Backups: Establishment and deployment of automated backup solutions to periodically safeguard essential data should be a requirement. Establishment of numerous redundant backup copies, located both within the premises and outside of it, in order to minimize the risk of data loss would be beneficial practice in case of a major hack.
   - Air-Gapped Backups: Air-gapped backups, which are physically isolated from the network, offer extra safety. Ransomware attackers cannot target information or systems to which they do not have access. This is a possible solution within the domain of data backups to fight ransomware.
   - Data Recovery Testing: Regularly performing tests on data recovery procedures to verify backups' functionality and ability to be swiftly restored would come in handy in times of real need. This reminisce fire drill in organizations but in this case simulations of hack and testing to recover from such hacks.
3. Patch Management: Ransomware frequently capitalizes on established weaknesses in software and operating systems. Timely application of patches is crucial in order to minimize these risks [20].
   - Vulnerability Scanning: Conducting periodic systems scans to identify and assess known vulnerabilities is a good path of recommendation as vulnerability scanning programs aid in the detection of vulnerabilities that necessitate fixing.
   - Patch Management Policies: Establishment and execution of patch management policies to guarantee the quick application of security patches, thereby reducing the period of vulnerability.
   - Priority for Vital Systems: Providing the highest importance to patching vital systems and guarantee prompt application of patches.

4. Solutions for Securing Endpoints: Deploying resilient endpoint security solutions is crucial for detecting and thwarting ransomware infestations [21, 22].
    - Anti-Malware Software: Ensuring the installation and regular upkeep of anti-malware and antivirus software on all devices. These technologies can detect and prevent known ransomware threats.
    - Behavior-Based Detection: Employing behavior-based detection algorithms to recognize anomalous actions on endpoints. Behavior-based technologies can identify ransomware, even if it is a previously unseen version.
    - Frequent Updates: Ensuring that the endpoint security software is regularly updated to enhance its ability to detect the most recent threats efficiently.
5. Protection of Email: Ransomware assaults often utilize malevolent email attachments or links. Robust email security measures are essential to thwart such assaults [23].
    - Spam Filters: Utilizing spam filters to screen and eliminate possible phishing and malicious emails before their delivery to users' inboxes.
    - Email Scanning: Using email scanning programs to examine email attachments and links for potentially harmful content. These tools can obstruct or isolate dubious signals.
    - User Awareness: Consistently informing users of the most effective email security practices, such as refraining from opening attachments or clicking on links from unfamiliar sources.
6. Network Segmentation: *Network segmentation* refers to dividing a network into smaller, isolated segments to enhance security and control access to sensitive information. Network segmentation effectively restricts the propagation of ransomware within an organization. Even if a single segment is compromised, it can be segregated, preventing any impact on the entire network [24].
    - Segmentation Strategy: The approach to dividing a target market into distinct groups based on specific characteristics or criteria and creating a well-defined network segmentation approach that effectively isolates essential systems from less important ones. This method aims to restrict the horizontal mobility of assailants.
    - Access Control: Enforcing stringent access restrictions and regulations to limit communication across different network parts. Only traffic that has been granted explicit authorization should be permitted.
    - Firewalls and Intrusion Detection Systems (IDS): Employing firewalls and IDS based on SOTA ML methods [25] to oversee and regulate data flow across different network sections, identifying and flagging any abnormal activity.
7. Plans for Responding to Incidents: Creating and honing an incident response plan is essential for promptly and efficiently addressing a ransomware assault [26].
    - Precise methods: Establishing unambiguous methods for identifying and containing ransomware threats, reporting instances, and contacting law enforcement if necessary.
    - Communication Strategy: Establishing communication strategies to inform pertinent stakeholders, such as impacted users, executives, and law enforcement, about the situation.
    - Recovery Procedures: Providing a detailed overview of the protocols for retrieving lost data and restoring the system to its previous state. Ensure that backup files are easily accessible.
8. Enhancements in Security and Intelligence against Threats: Remaining knowledgeable regarding the most recent hazards and security patches is crucial for a proactive approach to defending against ransomware [27].

- Threat Intelligence Services: Enrolling in threat intelligence services to receive updates on evolving ransomware threats and strategies.
- Applying Patches and upgrades: Consistently implementing security upgrades for software, operating systems, and network devices to resolve identified weaknesses.
- Surveillance and Aberration Detection: Establishing surveillance and aberration detection systems to detect and pinpoint questionable network activity and behaviors.

Addressing ransomware threats requires a comprehensive strategy integrating technology, user consciousness, and efficient response protocols. By employing these strategies and consistently adjusting to the changing threat environment, people and organizations can effectively mitigate the likelihood of becoming targets of ransomware attacks.

6.5 POTENTIAL FOR FUTURE EXPANSION

Ransomware, a persistent threat that constantly evolves, has seen a range of new responses designed to limit its effects. New possibilities of ransomware amelioration in future include:

1. Artificial Intelligence (AI): AI is broadly applicable to the development of intellectual processes-based projects, such as the ability to augment, conceive, investigate, enthusiastically process knowledge, think, organize, be creative, and problem-solve in a variety of fields, including business analytics, big data, security, and many more, including ransomware threat mitigation. Systems for the identification and avoidance of ransomware can become more complex with the use of AI and machine learning (ML) [28]. AI algorithms are able to identify intricate trends in ransomware attacks that human analysts might miss, which eventually will lead to effective ransomware mitigation and minimization.
2. Zero-trust security: A zero-trust security framework is one in which neither an individual nor a device is automatically trusted by the security ecosystem [29]. Strict authentication and authorization procedures are put into effect in conjunction with the framework in order to regulate individual access to the information and systems. Before acquiring access to any resources, clients must verify their identities and authorize themselves. This is done for security reasons in order to ensure that no unapproved and unauthorized attempts are carried out, thus refusing hackers the possibility of opportunity to exploit it and making it more challenging for ransomware to spread and encrypt data using zero-trust security.
3. Blockchain: The future of blockchain ransomware mitigation entails using blockchain technology's unique security features to increase resistance [30]. An explanation is given in the following:
   - Decentralized Architecture: Blockchain's decentralized network of nodes reduces its single point of failure. Distributing data over the network makes system penetration harder for ransomware attackers.
   - Immutable Ledger: Blockchain's ledger is unchangeable. Data stored in a block cannot be changed later. This feature protects vital data against ransomware manipulation and encryption.
   - Smart Contracts: Self-executing contracts with coded terms. Intelligent contracts can automatically enforce security and access control criteria, decreasing the danger of unauthorized access or harmful activity.
   - Cryptographic Security: Blockchain uses robust cryptography to secure transactions and data. Blockchain-based systems may be secured by adding more assertive cryptographic techniques to ransomware mitigation tactics.

- Permissioned Blockchains: Restricting network access to authorized organizations reduces the attack surface and makes it harder for bad actors to enter the system.
- Blockchain Auditing and Monitoring Tools: Developing tools to monitor and audit blockchain transactions may help spot suspicious ransomware activity early and enable quick response and containment.
- Secure Wallet Management: Blockchain commonly uses digital wallets; thus, strong authentication and encryption can safeguard digital assets from ransomware assaults.
- Education and understanding: Raising users' and organizations' understanding of blockchain security may make the blockchain ecosystem safer. Users must learn to secure their digital assets and ensure blockchain network integrity.

4. Quantum computing: Quantum computing may reduce ransomware threats. Ransomware demands payment to decrypt data. Quantum computing can change this landscape with its processing power [31].
   - Enhanced Cryptography: RSA (Rivest–Shamir–Adleman) algorithm and elliptic curve cryptography (ECC) have the difficulty of factoring huge integers for security [31]. Using Shor's method, quantum computers factor huge numbers exponentially faster than classical computers. Cryptographic protocols used to secure data may become susceptible. To resist quantum computer attacks, post-quantum cryptography techniques are being developed. Transitioning to these algorithms helps protect organizations' data from quantum assaults, including ransomware attempts that leverage classical cryptography flaws.
   - Secure Key Distribution: Quantum key distribution (QKD) secures communication channels using quantum features [31]. QKD lets two parties generate a shared random secret key for message encryption and decryption. The fundamental concept of quantum physics makes eavesdropping detectable.
   - QKD could make it harder for ransomware attackers to intercept or modify encryption keys in critical exchange operations.
   - Classical computers cannot create truly random numbers like quantum computers. Random numbers are essential for cryptography, including key generation. Quantum-generated random numbers make cryptographic systems more secure and more complex to guess encryption keys.
   - Simulation and Analysis: Quantum computers can model complicated systems faster than traditional computers. Using this capability, we can model and analyze cybersecurity threats, including ransomware. Understanding ransomware techniques and vulnerabilities helps cybersecurity specialists create more effective countermeasures and proactive defenses.
   - Advanced Threat Detection: Quantum computing can improve machine learning techniques. These algorithms can uncover malware patterns and anomalies in massive data sets. Quantum computing can improve threat detection and minimize ransomware threats before they do significant damage.
   - Quantum computing may improve cybersecurity, but it is still in its infancy and will take years to implement. In order to mitigate ransomware and other cybersecurity risks, organizations should monitor quantum-safe cryptography advancements and consider adding quantum-resistant algorithms to their security plans.

Furthermore, it is crucial to consider the human element while mitigating ransomware alongside these technological advancements, including disseminating knowledge to users regarding the risks of ransomware and implementing improved security awareness training programs.

The landscape of ransomware threats is ever-changing, with attackers continuously devising novel methods and tools to avoid being detected. Defenders face several obstacles in this situation. An obstacle is that ransomware assaults are progressively evolving in complexity and specificity. Adversaries frequently focus their attacks on particular institutions and take advantage of well-known weaknesses, increasing the complexity of detecting and thwarting attacks for defenders.

Another obstacle is that ransomware assaults are progressively becoming more expensive. In 2022, the mean ransom payment amounted to $812,360, a significant increase from the $312,416 recorded in 2020 [32]. The rise in extortion payments is motivating attackers to persist in the development and execution of ransomware assaults.

Although there are difficulties, there are also several prospects to enhance ransomware mitigation. An opportunity exists to enhance collaboration between the public and commercial sectors. Collaboration between governments, organizations, and security researchers is essential for exchanging knowledge regarding ransomware threats and establishing effective strategies for minimizing their impact.

Another option is to allocate funds toward research and development. Additional resources should be allocated toward advancing novel technology for detecting, preventing, and recovering from ransomware attacks.

6.6 CONCLUSION

The ransomware threat is persistently evolving, and it is becoming a noteworthy risk to all. The chapter has scrutinized various facets of ransomware, including its definition, historical background, the increasing complexity of attacks with the emergence of Ransomware 2.0., and so on. Furthermore, the repercussions of ransomware attacks and strategies to mitigate the associated risks were also elaborately explained.

To combat the ransomware threat effectively, engaging in collaborative efforts and implementing coordinated measures are of utmost priority. In addition, the defense mechanisms must remain constantly watchful, visionary, and adaptable to cope with the dynamic landscape of ransomware attacks. The growing use of the ransomware-as-a-service (RaaS) model and artificial intelligence (AI) by actors and defenders in cybersecurity is crucial in foreseeing the breakout of novel ransomware variants.

As the chapter ends, it is compulsory to spotlight the significance of mitigating the risk presented by ransomware. The possible ramifications might be severe, encompassing financial losses and considerable harm to one's reputation. The significance of international coordination in effectively combating this ever-evolving threat cannot be overstated, and together, a robust defense system to combat ransomware and safeguard the digital future can be developed.

REFERENCES

1. Yaqoob, Ibrar, et al. "The rise of ransomware and emerging security challenges in the Internet of Things." *Computer Networks* 129 (2017): 444–458.
2. Ali, Azad. "Ransomware: A research and a personal case study of dealing with this nasty malware." *Issues in Informing Science and Information Technology* 14 (2017): 087–099.
3. Zimba, Aaron, and Mumbi Chishimba. "Understanding the evolution of ransomware: paradigm shifts in attack structures." *International Journal of Computer Network and Information Security* 11.1 (2019): 26.
4. Conti, Mauro, Ankit Gangwal, and Sushmita Ruj. "On the economic significance of ransomware campaigns: A Bitcoin transactions perspective." *Computers & Security* 79 (2018): 162–189.
5. Ryan, Matthew. *Ransomware Revolution: The Rise of a Prodigious Cyber Threat.* Berlin/Heidelberg, Germany: Springer, 2021.
6. Dargahi, Tooska, et al. "A Cyber-Kill-Chain based taxonomy of crypto-ransomware features." *Journal of Computer Virology and Hacking Techniques* 15 (2019): 277–305.
7. Li, Zhen, and Qi Liao. "Ransomware 2.0: To sell, or not to sell a game-theoretical model of data-selling ransomware." *Proceedings of the 15th International Conference on Availability, Reliability and Security.* 2020.
8. Mansfield-Devine, Steve. "Ransomware: Taking businesses hostage." *Network Security* 2016.10 (2016): 8–17.

9. Drake, Veronica. "The history and evolution of ransomware attacks." *Flashpoint*, 14 July 2023, www.flashpoint.io/blog/the-history-and-evolution-of-ransomware-attacks.
10. Cabaj, Krzysztof, and Wojciech Mazurczyk. "Using software-defined networking for ransomware mitigation: The case of cryptowall." *IEEE Network* 30.6 (2016): 14–20.
11. Alwashali, Ali Ahmed Mohammed Ali, Nor Azlina Abd Rahman, and Noris Ismail. "A survey of ransomware as a service (RaaS) and methods to mitigate the attack." *2021 14th International Conference on Developments in eSystems Engineering (DeSE)*. IEEE, 2021.
12. Watson, F. Charlene, C. CISM, and A+ ECSA. "Petya/NotPetya why it is nastier than WannaCry and why we should care." *ISACA* 6 (2017): 1–6.
13. Wade, Megan. "Digital hostages: Leveraging ransomware attacks in cyberspace." *Business Horizons* 64.6 (2021): 787–797.
14. Kara, Ilker, and Murat Aydos. "The rise of ransomware: Forensic analysis for windows based ransomware attacks." *Expert Systems with Applications* 190 (2022): 116198.
15. Ko, Min-Hyuck, and Dohyun Kim. "Trends in mobile ransomware and incident response from a digital forensics perspective." *Journal of Information & Communication Convergence Engineering* 20.4 (2022).
16. Bagui, Sikha, and Hunter Brock. "Machine learning for Android scareware detection." *Journal of Information Technology Research (JITR)* 15.1 (2022): 1–15.
17. Tsvetanov, Tsvetan, and Srishti Slaria. "The effect of the Colonial Pipeline shutdown on gasoline prices." *Economics Letters* 209 (2021): 110122.
18. Bello, Abubakar, and Alana Maurushat. "Technical and behavioural training and awareness solutions for mitigating ransomware attacks." *Applied Informatics and Cybernetics in Intelligent Systems: Proceedings of the 9th Computer Science On-line Conference 2020, Volume 3 9*. Springer International Publishing, 2020.
19. Thomas, Jason, and Gordon Galligher. "Improving backup system evaluations in information security risk assessments to combat ransomware." *Computer and Information Science* 11.1 (2018).
20. Garuba, Moses, Chunmei Liu, and Nicki Washington. "A comparative analysis of anti-malware software, patch management, and host-based firewalls in preventing malware infections on client computers." *Fifth International Conference on Information Technology: New Generations (ITNG 2008)*. IEEE, 2008.
21. Kharraz, Amin, and Engin Kirda. "Redemption: Real-time protection against ransomware at end-hosts." *Research in Attacks, Intrusions, and Defenses: 20th International Symposium, RAID 2017, Atlanta, GA, September 18–20, 2017, Proceedings*. Springer International Publishing, 2017.
22. Tan, Mark Khai Shean, Sigi Goode, and Alex Richardson. "Understanding negotiated anti-malware interruption effects on user decision quality in endpoint security." *Behaviour & Information Technology* 40.9 (2021): 903–932.
23. Pagán, Alexander, and Khaled Elleithy. "A multi-layered defense approach to safeguard against ransomware." *2021 IEEE 11th Annual Computing and Communication Workshop and Conference (CCWC)*. IEEE, 2021.
24. Baig, Zubair, Sri Harsha Mekala, and Sherali Zeadally. "Ransomware attacks of the COVID-19 pandemic: Novel strains, victims, and threat actors." *IT Professional* 25.5 (2023): 37–44.
25. Cen, Mingcan, et al. "Ransomware early detection: A survey." *Computer Networks* 239 (2024): 110138.
26. Chen, Po-Hao, Robert Bodak, and Namita S. Gandhi. "Ransomware recovery and imaging operations: Lessons learned and planning considerations." *Journal of Digital Imaging* 34.3 (2021): 731–740.
27. Alnajim, Abdullah M., et al. "A comprehensive survey of cybersecurity threats, attacks, and effective countermeasures in industrial Internet of Things." *Technologies* 11.6 (2023): 161.
28. Alraizza, Amjad, and Abdulmohsen Algarni. "Ransomware detection using machine learning: A survey." *Big Data and Cognitive Computing* 7.3 (2023): 143.
29. Muhammad, Tayyab, et al. "Integrative cybersecurity: Merging zero trust, layered defense, and global standards for a resilient digital future." *International Journal of Computer Science and Technology* 6.4 (2022): 99–135.
30. Gu, Jingjing, et al. "Consortium blockchain-based malware detection in mobile devices." *IEEE Access* 6 (2018): 12118–12128.
31. Ciaramella, Giovanni, et al. "Introducing quantum computing in mobile malware detection." *Proceedings of the 17th International Conference on Availability, Reliability and Security*. 2022.
32. Sophos. "Cybersecurity as a service delivered." *SOPHOS*, 27 April 2022, www.sophos.com/en-us/press/press-releases/2022/04/ransomware-hit-66-percent-of-organizations-surveyed-for-sophos-annual-state-of-ransomware-2022.
33. Cichonski, Paul, et al. "Computer security incident handling guide." *NIST Special Publication* 800.61 (2012): 1–147.

34. Baker, Yolanda S., Rajeev Agrawal, and Sambit Bhattacharya. "Analyzing security threats as reported by the United States Computer Emergency Readiness Team (US-CERT)." *2013 IEEE International Conference on Intelligence and Security Informatics*. IEEE, 2013.
35. Pinckard, Jeffrey, Michael Rattigan, and Robert Vrtis. "Mapping of the Federal Financial Institutions Examination Council (FFIEC) cybersecurity assessment tool (CAT) to the cyber resilience review (CRR)." 2016.
36. Pomerleau, Pierre-Luc, and David L. Lowery. "Conclusions and implications for practice and future studies on public–private partnerships." *Countering Cyber Threats to Financial Institutions: A Private and Public Partnership Approach to Critical Infrastructure Protection*. Springer, 2020. 157–195.
37. Möller, Dietmar PF. "NIST cybersecurity framework and MITRE cybersecurity criteria." *Guide to Cybersecurity in Digital Transformation: Trends, Methods, Technologies, Applications and Best Practices*. Cham: Springer Nature Switzerland, 2023. 231–271.
38. Brown, Jason. *Executive's Cybersecurity Program Handbook: A Comprehensive Guide to Building and Operationalizing a Complete Cybersecurity Program*. Packt Publishing Ltd., 2023.
39. Romanosky, Sasha, Karen Schwindt, and Ryan Johnson. "Comparison of Public and Private Sector Cybersecurity and IT Workforces." 2023: 32.
40. Nurthen II, John Michael. *Cybersecurity Risk Assessment Matrix (CRAM): A System-Theoretic Approach to Balancing Operational and Cybersecurity Risk in the Management of Transient Cyber Assets (TCA) in the Maintenance of Operational Technology (OT)*. Diss. Massachusetts Institute of Technology, 2023.

AUTHOR BIOGRAPHY

Md. Sadi Arman, a project manager at Generation Next Technologies, earned a BSc in computer science and engineering from Eastern University with 3.71 CGPA. Further enriching his expertise, he earned an MSc in IT from Jahangirnagar University, with 3.58 CGPA. With a profound interest in cybersecurity and blockchain technology, Sadi is dedicated to steering innovation and security in the digital realm, marking himself as a dynamic force in the tech industry.

Nuray Jannat, a software engineer at UD Platforms Inc., holds a BSc in computer science and engineering from the University of Asia Pacific, achieving 3.96 CGPA. Currently pursuing an MSc in CSE at BRAC University, her passion lies in the realms of image processing, LVM, and signal processing, showcasing a commitment to advancing technology. With a keen eye for innovation, Nuray is poised to make significant contributions to the field of computer science.

Salman Sayeed Khan completed his BSc in computer science and engineering from the Islamic University of Technology, Bangladesh. Currently, he is working as a lecturer at the CSE Department of Brac University. Prior to that, he held position as a software engineer at Samsung R&D Institute, Bangladesh. His research interests revolve around security, trustworthy AI, and human–computer interaction (HCI).

Muhammad Usama Islam received the BSc degree in computer science from the Islamic University of Technology, Bangladesh, and MSc degree in computer science from the University of Louisiana at Lafayette, USA. He is currently pursuing the PhD degree in computer science with the School of Computing and Informatics, University of Louisiana at Lafayette, USA. He worked as a lecturer at the Asian University of Bangladesh. His research interests include human–computer interaction, affective computing, and UI/UX research.

7 Ransomware Threat Mitigation Strategies for Protecting Critical Infrastructure Assets

Kassim Kalinaki

7.1 INTRODUCTION

Ransomware attacks have emerged as one of the most significant cybersecurity threats facing organizations across all sectors, but their implications for critical infrastructure present uniquely alarming risks [1]. As ransomware incidents continue to climb exponentially, critical infrastructure sectors like energy, water, transportation, and healthcare have become prime targets for cybercriminals seeking to extort hefty payouts [2]. Critical infrastructure systems' inherent complexity and interconnection exacerbate an already challenging threat landscape. Networks have grown exponentially in size and complexity over time through digitization efforts to improve operational efficiency and resiliency. However, this growth has also introduced new potential attack vectors that malicious actors are actively probing for weaknesses to exploit [3]. For instance, legacy technology components lacking modern security features are prevalent across critical infrastructure, enabling more entry points for adversaries [2]. Most concerning is that individual attacks may have cascading impacts across multiple entities due to the deeply intertwined nature of critical infrastructure sectors. Hence, the interdependency of these sectors and the essential services they provide mean that ransomware incidents threatening their operational capacity and data integrity jeopardize national security, public health and safety, and economic stability.

The potential impacts of successful ransomware attacks on critical infrastructure assets highlight the alarming vulnerabilities plaguing these vital systems. For instance, recent high-profile attacks like the 2021 ransomware attack on the Colonial Pipeline demonstrate the extensive disruptions ransomware can inflict within critical infrastructure. The pipeline, which supplies nearly half the diesel and gasoline consumed on the U.S. East Coast, was forced to shut down operations for several days due to the attack. The disruption led to fuel shortages across the Southeastern United States, highlighting the far-reaching impacts ransomware can have [4]. Moreover, hospitals may be unable to access patient records or care coordination systems during ransomware incidents, which may severely obstruct urgent care administration [5, 6, 7, 8]. Intelligent transportation networks like railways could have operations and signaling capabilities blocked for prolonged periods [9]. Water treatment facilities and pipelines face risks of dangerous chemicals or contaminants affecting drinking water supplies if cyber intrusions corrupt purification and monitoring tools [10]. As ransomware variants evolve in sophistication, critical infrastructure organizations require urgent strategies for detection, response, and recovery when incidents occur. However, these environments' unique operational demands and legacy systems pose complex challenges for mitigating ransomware threats [2].

Unfortunately, ransomware tactics and capabilities continue advancing at breakneck speeds while defense strategies struggle to keep pace [11, 12]. Attackers have access to sophisticated hacking tools and vulnerabilities circulated in online criminal forums, requiring minimal

DOI: 10.1201/9781003469506-10

technical skills for exploitation. Phishing, brute force, and vulnerability exploitation comprise ransomware's primary initial access vectors [13]. Threat actors have shifted toward "big game hunting" for high-value targets like critical infrastructure that can yield larger payouts, with ransom demands reaching millions of dollars [2, 14]. Attackers often patiently infiltrate networks for endpoint access and perform extensive reconnaissance before deploying ransomware payloads across domains. The monetization process has also matured through the emergence of Ransomware-as-a-Service offerings that significantly lower entry barriers [15]. The malware has grown remarkably more destructive through innovations like auto-propagating worm functionalities. For instance, modern ransomware strains like Conti, WannaCry, and NotPetya can self-spread across entire networks, encrypting vast numbers of systems simultaneously while avoiding detection [16, 17]. Attackers also threaten to publicly leak sensitive data stolen during intrusions if ransom demands are not promptly met, further coercing victims into payment. Even if paid, recovery is complex, costly, and not guaranteed to restore systems fully [18, 19]. Many victims lacking adequate backups have ultimately paid ransoms, incentivizing follow-on attacks. These trends exemplify why enhanced mitigation strategies are urgently required for protecting critical infrastructure entities already in the crosshairs of motivated threat groups. All organizations face cyber risks, but potential life and safety consequences magnify the importance of resilience for hospitals, transit agencies, power plants, and others [2, 4, 5, 9, 10, 20, 21]. Although challenges remain in balancing improved security with operational needs, critical infrastructure sectors must prioritize tackling ransomware exposure through risk-based cybersecurity programs centered on defense-in-depth.

Protecting critical infrastructure from ransomware necessitates a multidimensional approach addressing people, processes, and technology. Human error and lack of cybersecurity awareness frequently precipitate ransomware incidents through simple acts like clicking malicious links [12, 22]. Workforce education, authentication protocols, and reduced user permissions can minimize this common attack vector significantly. Procedural countermeasures like offline data backups, incident response planning, and enabling multi-factor authentication also markedly bolster ransomware resilience. However, technological controls offer the most advanced threat detection and prevention capabilities. Artificial intelligence (AI) that detects behavioral anomalies [23], network segmentation to prevent lateral movement, and tools providing end-to-end visibility of information technology (IT) and operational technology (OT) environments allow rapid identification and response to mitigate ransomware risks [24]. Focusing on basic, high-impact controls offers a pragmatic path to enhanced cybersecurity for under-resourced critical infrastructure organizations struggling to fund enterprise-scale upgrades.

The systemic lack of cyber readiness across critical infrastructure leaves glaring vulnerabilities for ransomware actors to exploit. Constructing robust, multilayered defenses is essential to avoid paying ransoms and ensure uninterrupted delivery of vital services communities depend upon. Ransomware mitigation within critical infrastructure requires framing cybersecurity as a patient safety, energy reliability, and national security imperative, warranting substantial investment and support. Through enhanced governance, information sharing, and public-private partnerships, collective ransomware resilience can be strengthened across interlinked critical infrastructure organizations. By implementing essential technical and procedural safeguards outlined in this chapter, those responsible for critical infrastructure security can close conspicuous gaps and combat escalating ransomware risks. Only by recognizing the interconnectedness of critical infrastructure environments can holistic, impactful threat mitigation strategies be developed to match the scale of the ransomware epidemic. Accordingly, this chapter comprehensively reviews ransomware's growing danger within critical infrastructure sectors, framing the implications and challenges. Moreover, it evaluates the current state of threats, analyzes attacker motivations and tactics, and scrutinizes attack patterns. Furthermore, the chapter delineates diverse mitigation strategies reinforced by real-world examples.

7.1.1 Chapter Contributions

- A comprehensive review of ransomware's growing danger within critical infrastructure sectors.
- A discussion of cybercriminals' motivations, tactics, and patterns in ransomware attacks on critical infrastructure.
- A presentation of different ransomware threat mitigation strategies that can be adopted to prevent the menace of a ransomware attack on critical infrastructure.
- A highlight of real-world cases of ransomware attacks on critical infrastructure and lessons learned.

7.1.2 Chapter Roadmap

After the introduction in section 7.1, the remainder of this chapter is structured as follows. Section 7.2 discusses the ransomware threat landscape, highlighting the current threats targeting critical infrastructure. Section 7.3 discusses cybercriminals' motivations, tactics, and patterns in ransomware attacks on critical infrastructure. Section 7.4 extensively discusses the different ransomware threat mitigation strategies that can be adopted to prevent the menace of a ransomware attack on critical infrastructure. Section 7.5 highlights real-world cases of ransomware attacks on critical infrastructure, exploring the tactics employed by cybercriminals and the profound impact on the affected organizations and the communities they serve. The conclusion is presented in Section 7.6.

7.2 RANSOMWARE THREAT LANDSCAPE

In recent years, ransomware groups have shifted their focus toward critical infrastructure sectors like healthcare, energy, and government entities. The disruption and data exfiltration potential makes infrastructure organizations lucrative targets. Analysis of the current state of ransomware threats targeting critical infrastructure is crucial for organizations to defend themselves against the threats.

7.2.1 Analysis of the Current State of Ransomware Threats Targeting Critical Infrastructure

The overall ransomware landscape saw an explosion of activity in 2021, with a total of 623.3 million ransomware attacks reported.[1] Statista reports that a staggering 236.1 million ransomware attacks occurred globally in the first six months of 2022.[2] Moreover, ransomware attacks surged 18% between the first and second quarters of 2022. The number of incidents escalated from about 130 million globally in Q1 to roughly 106 million in Q2.[3] This rampant growth is fueled by the emergence of ransomware-as-a-service (RaaS) operations that allow cybercriminals with limited technical skills to execute attacks [15]. These trends show no sign of slowing down heading into 2024. Attackers continue to innovate rapidly, utilizing multi-stage extortion tactics, public shaming of victims, and cryptocurrency to hide payments.

One would reasonably assume that the healthcare industry, vital and life-impacting, would be spared from cybercriminal attacks. However, Sophos' new sectoral survey report revealed a shocking 94% spike in ransomware assaults on healthcare.[4] Prominent examples include the shutting down of Ireland's national healthcare IT systems[5] and the New Jersey hospital chain.[6] These shutdowns directly endanger patient health and safety. Moreover, St. Charles Health System overpaid $2 million in salaries to 2,358 employees. This occurred after a cyberattack in December 2021 blocked the hospital's access to timecard data for months.[7] The FBI also warned of an uptick in attacks on agricultural facilities that could impact food production processes.[8] Energy companies saw intrusions into generator supplier networks that power grid operators rely on [25]. If left unchecked, these threats could undermine public health and safety protections.

Ransomware groups are also expanding their extortion and disruption-based objectives beyond just encrypting files. Attackers can now exfiltrate sensitive data prior to triggering ransomware and threaten to release it if the ransom goes unpaid publicly. For example, the prolific Conti crew claims to have stolen over 1.7 terabytes (TB) of data from JVCKenwood company in Japan.[9] Attackers also utilize distributed denial-of-service (DDoS) attacks that flood infrastructure networks and systems with traffic, disrupting operations. These tactics create additional leverage over victims and incentives to meet ransom demands.

Another emerging trend is the narrowing sophistication gap between nation-state Advanced Persistent Threat (APT) groups and cybercriminals. Experts assess with moderate confidence that ransomware developers are increasingly selling malware variants and access to infrastructure operators in underground forums that state-sponsored groups frequent as buyers [26]. The operational cooperation between actors makes it difficult for victims to know attribution. These blurred lines could enable governments to launch disruptive attacks while maintaining plausible deniability around clear attribution. Such a scenario threatens even greater systemic risk from now on.

Defending critical infrastructure requires organizations to take ransomware seriously as a complex business continuity and resilience planning issue. Simply relying on isolated IT security controls is insufficient, given the multifaceted nature of the threat. Organizations should rigorously identify and safeguard critical backup systems, data stores, and recovery processes that keep operations running if primary networks fail. This includes regularly updating "gold images" of critical servers and quickly patching vulnerable internet-facing assets. Performing cyber resilience assessments via "Red Team" simulations of realistic attacks can also help evaluate organizational readiness [27, 28].

In summary, the ransomware environment will remain highly dynamic for infrastructure organizations over the next several years. Attackers will continue evolving techniques faster than most defenses can catch up [12]. However, infrastructure operators can mitigate the impacts of inevitable intrusions by focusing on resilience, backup security, and understanding the actual organizational cost of disruption. Ransomware defense requires a holistic approach, bridging cybersecurity and business continuity best practices. Building processes to limit data exfiltration, restoring critical services rapidly, and coordinating incident response with partners will pay dividends in managing ransomware risk.

7.3 CYBERCRIMINALS' MOTIVATIONS, TACTICS, AND PATTERNS IN RANSOMWARE ATTACKS ON CRITICAL INFRASTRUCTURE

This section's investigation elaborates on the multifaceted nature of ransomware attacks on critical infrastructure, dissecting the driving forces behind cybercriminal motivations, analyzing the sophisticated tactics they deploy, and discerning the discernible patterns that emerge from these nefarious activities.

7.3.1 Motivations Driving Ransomware Threats

This section navigates the various motivations propelling threat actors to deploy ransomware. Understanding the root causes and drivers allows stakeholders to develop more effective strategies to prevent, detect, and respond to ransomware threats against critical infrastructure.

7.3.1.1 Financial Profit Motive

Ransomware offers cybercriminals an easy way to quickly generate direct profits through extorting victims. The rise of cryptocurrencies like Bitcoin has enabled secure, anonymous payments at scale, dramatically lowering the risks of physically collecting ransom payments that existed previously [1, 29, 30]. This has opened up massive money-making potential. Critical infrastructure organizations like hospitals, transportation networks, water purification facilities, and energy providers are extremely lucrative targets for ransomware groups. These organizations provide essential services for societal functioning, and they are perceived as more likely to pay higher ransom amounts to restore systems faster and minimize disruption impacts. The financial allure of ransomware distinguishes it from other cybercrime models, making it an attractive choice for criminals seeking substantial, untraceable income streams. The potential for high payouts contributes to the persistence and prevalence of ransomware attacks in the digital landscape.

7.3.1.2 Strategic Disruption of Adversaries

Some evidence suggests that certain nation-state intelligence services use ransomware to strategically disrupt critical infrastructure in foreign adversary countries [31]. By broadly directing criminal ransomware efforts toward vital industrial sectors, they can inflict significant damage on an opponent's economy and societal cohesion while maintaining distance and plausible deniability regarding the criminal proxies executing the attacks [32, 33]. For example, the Russia-linked Conti ransomware gang notably pledged to refrain from targeting any member countries of the Commonwealth of Independent States (CIS) – former Soviet states closely aligned with Russia.[10] This hinted at Conti potentially coordinating with Russian strategic interests abroad [34]. By crippling critical sectors in Western nations, Conti could advance Russian geopolitical agendas while avoiding direct state attribution behind the attacks. Utilizing the ransomware criminal ecosystem as a mechanism for state-sponsored disruption of adversaries provides significant asymmetric warfare advantages for nation-states [31]. If exposed, it offers flexibility for calibrating chaos while retaining distance from provable intelligence agency involvement.

7.3.1.3 Relative Ease and Low Risk

The accessibility of ransomware tools, either as kits or as services in underground cybercrime markets, has lowered the entry barriers for individuals with limited technical expertise. This democratization of cybercrime tools facilitates the broad dissemination of ransomware attacks. Additionally, using cryptocurrencies enhances perpetrators' anonymity, reducing the perceived risk of detection and prosecution [12]. The combination of user-friendly ransomware resources and cryptocurrency as a transaction medium diminishes the technical and legal barriers to entry. This ease of access and lower perceived risk incentivizes a broader range of actors to engage in ransomware activities.

7.3.1.4 Target Availability

Specific organizations and infrastructure sectors, such as small businesses, healthcare facilities, schools, and state/local government agencies, often exhibit vulnerabilities that make them attractive targets for ransomware attacks [35, 36]. Cybercriminals are opportunistic in selecting victims they perceive as more likely to swiftly pay the ransom to regain access to their critical data and systems. The strategic selection of vulnerable targets increases the likelihood of successful ransom collections. Criminals exploit certain entities' perceived inability or reluctance to invest adequately in cybersecurity measures, maximizing their chances of extorting payments.

7.3.1.5 Increasing Sophistication

The evolution of ransomware variants toward greater sophistication, incorporating features like multilayer encryption, makes decryption challenging without the requisite keys. Victims often face a dilemma where paying the ransom becomes the only viable option for restoring normal business operations, propelling more significant and disruptive attacks [29]. The escalation in ransomware sophistication enhances its effectiveness and exacerbates the impact on victims. The increased difficulty in finding alternative solutions compels targeted entities to comply with ransom demands, contributing to the growth and scale of ransomware attacks.

7.3.1.6 Indirect Revenue Sources

Ransomware threats extend beyond direct ransom payments. Victim data becomes a valuable commodity on dark web marketplaces, allowing cybercriminals to monetize stolen information. Additionally, a RaaS affiliate structure incentivizes collaboration with developers sharing profits with affiliates who distribute the malware [30]. The diversification of revenue streams through indirect methods ensures that cybercriminals can extract value even if direct ransom payments are not received. This multifaceted approach contributes to the resilience and adaptability of ransomware operations.

In conclusion, the motivations driving ransomware threats against critical infrastructure are rooted in a combination of financial incentives, accessibility of tools, strategic target selection, technological advancements, and alternative revenue streams. Understanding and addressing these motivations are crucial for developing effective strategies to mitigate the impact of ransomware on critical systems and infrastructure.

7.3.2 Tactical Tradecraft in Ransomware Campaigns

This section presents the tactics attackers deploy against critical infrastructure in ransomware campaigns.

7.3.2.1 Ransomware-as-a-Service Model

Ransomware is now offered as a turnkey service model to enable broader adoption by less technically sophisticated threat actors. RaaS frameworks provide user-friendly tools and infrastructure to custom-build ransomware attacks [15]. They handle critical functions like data encryption, ransom collection sites, negotiations, and money laundering of cryptocurrency payments. This significantly lowers barriers to launching disruptive campaigns. Many RaaS offerings have affiliate programs that pay partners a cut of ransom payments driven through their toolkits. This creates full-fledged criminal affiliate ecosystems with profit incentives, further fueling global ransomware attacks [34].

7.3.2.2 Extended Recon and Dwell Times Pre-Encryption

Advanced ransomware groups increasingly utilize extended reconnaissance inside compromised networks before deploying ransomware payloads. Rather than quickly encrypting data after an initial breach, attackers stealthily move laterally to gather credentials, map trusted networks, and identify high-value data stores for maximum impact [35, 37]. Delaying the deployment phase also allows bad actors to exfiltrate sensitive data prior to triggering the ransomware. This data theft serves as additional leverage to pressure victims for higher payments during negotiations [30].

7.3.2.3 "Triple Extortion" Bombardment Model

Highly skilled ransomware cartels now pressure victims through encryption disruption, data theft, and DDoS flood attacks. Stealing data before deploying ransomware means additional extortion threats if the initial ransom goes unpaid after encryption activates [14, 29, 38]. Post-encryption DDoS attacks create further urgency around restoring operational capabilities by paying ransoms quickly. The combined threat vectors coerce organizations to meet hefty ransom demands out of fear. This "triple extortion" approach reflects the advanced criminal business models and technical innovations shaping modern ransomware. Defending against it requires matching sophistication in deterrence capabilities across organizations.

7.3.3 Patterns and Stages of Ransomware Attack Progression Based on the Cyber Kill Chain

Ransomware attacks typically follow a well-defined progression, marked by distinct stages adversaries leverage to infiltrate, propagate, and execute their malicious objectives. This section details the patterns and stages of the progression of ransomware attacks against critical infrastructure using the cyber kill chain.

7.3.3.1 Reconnaissance

In reconnaissance, the attacker meticulously researches the target critical infrastructure, mapping out its network topology, identifying potential vulnerabilities, and pinpointing systems handling critical operations. This information-gathering process may involve open-source intelligence, social engineering tactics, or network scanning techniques.

7.3.3.2 Weaponization

The weaponization phase involves developing or acquiring the ransomware payload, often leveraging existing malware families or crafting new variants. The attacker may also prepare additional tools, such as remote access Trojans, backdoors, or exploits, to facilitate the attack and maintain persistence within the compromised systems.

7.3.3.3 Delivery

The ransomware payload and associated tools are introduced into the target infrastructure during the delivery phase. Common delivery vectors include phishing emails with malicious attachments or links, exploiting vulnerabilities in exposed systems or applications, or leveraging compromised supply chain components. In some instances, physical access or insider threats may provide direct entry into the network.

7.3.3.4 Exploitation

In the exploitation phase, the attacker uses identified vulnerabilities or stolen credentials to gain initial access to the target systems. They may leverage the delivered payload or additional tools to escalate privileges, move laterally across the network, and compromise critical systems that handle essential operations.

7.3.3.5 Installation

Once a foothold is established, the installation phase commences, with the attacker deploying the ransomware payload on the compromised systems. The payload may be configured to spread automatically across the network, infecting as many systems as possible while establishing mechanisms for persistence and maintaining control over the infected systems.

7.3.3.6 Command and Control

The command and control phase involves setting up an infrastructure for the attacker to communicate with the infected systems. This allows them to monitor the attack progress, issue commands, and potentially exfiltrate sensitive data or intellectual property. The communication channels may be encrypted or obfuscated to evade detection.

7.3.3.7 Actions on Objectives

Finally, in the actions on objectives phase, after widespread encryption of critical data and systems, the attacker demands a ransom payment, typically in cryptocurrency, to provide the decryption keys. They may set deadlines, increase ransom amounts over time, or threaten to release or delete the encrypted data if it is unpaid. The ultimate goal is to disrupt operations, cause financial loss, and extract payment from the targeted critical infrastructure organization.

Figure 7.1 shows the Cyber Kill Chain of ransomware attacks for the victim organization. Table 7.1 summarizes the cybercriminals' motivations, tactics, and patterns in ransomware attacks on critical infrastructure.

In summary, the main incentives and outcomes powering the growth of ransomware menacing critical infrastructure operators are clear – money and disruption. However, the complexity of the

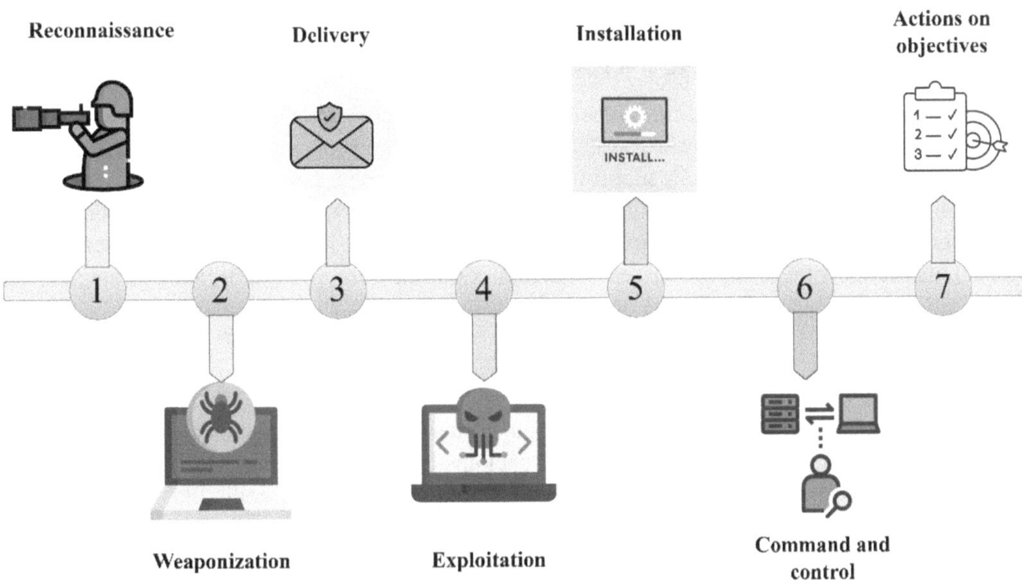

FIGURE 7.1 Cyber kill chain of ransomware attack.

TABLE 7.1
Summary of cybercriminals' motivations, tactics, and patterns in ransomware attacks on critical infrastructure

Category	Summary
Motivations	• Financial gain – Direct ransom payments and monetizing stolen data. • Disruption of adversaries' critical sectors during conflict. • Nation-state interests delegating attacks to cybercriminals as proxies. • Indirect revenue sources • Relative ease and low risk • Target availability • Increasing sophistication
Tactics	• The RaaS model lowers the barrier to extensive attacks. • Initial access brokers constantly finding soft targets. • Long threat dwell times pre-encryption for reconnaissance and data theft. • Triple extortion: encryption, data theft, and DDoS flood attacks
Attack patterns	Cyber Kill chain • Reconnaissance • Weaponization • Delivery • Exploitation • Installation • Command and control • Actions on objectives

underlying ecosystem with multiple motivated actors makes prediction far from straightforward. Tracking financial developments across cryptocurrencies, ransomware investments/partnerships, and shifts in nation-state cyber policies will provide invaluable signals on where threats are headed across the interconnected landscape. What is certain is that ransomware groups will continue evolving attacks to maximize profits from infrastructure targets left unprepared for their evolving extortion models.

7.4 RANSOMWARE THREAT MITIGATION STRATEGIES FOR PROTECTING CRITICAL INFRASTRUCTURE

As technological advancements continue to drive the interconnectedness of critical infrastructure systems, the risk of ransomware attacks has become more pronounced. Cybercriminals have become increasingly sophisticated, adapting their tactics to exploit legacy and modern infrastructure vulnerabilities. Consequently, organizations must proactively develop and implement robust mitigation strategies to safeguard their critical systems and maintain the resilience of essential services. This section extensively discusses the different ransomware threat mitigation strategies that can be adopted to prevent the menace of a ransomware attack on critical infrastructure.

7.4.1 Prioritize Cybersecurity Basics

Implementing robust offline backups should be the cornerstone of any ransomware resilience strategy. Backup schedules need daily incremental backups combined with weekly full system backups of all critical infrastructure and restore points stored on air-gapped media like external drives rotated to secure safes [39]. At least one month of versioned backup history should be maintained to account for possible corruption right before an attack. These backup stores require testing through monthly recovery drills to validate completeness and identify gaps for correction. Detailed restoration procedures need documentation for a streamlined response. In parallel, multi-factor authentication becomes mandatory for all privileged accounts and those associated with remote access while assessing the cost-benefit of applying protections universally across critical systems login [14, 31, 40, 41]. Cataloging systems with corresponding credential inventories allows ongoing confirmation of active authentication enforcement through account tests and access log audits refreshed quarterly. However, prevention mechanisms eventually fail without an educated workforce on the frontlines. Administrators must develop and mandate continuous education on the latest social engineering tactics to correctly identify threats [42]. These lessons are reinforced through periodic simulated phishing and attachment attacks that benchmark employee susceptibility over time. Personnel also need accessible reporting mechanisms to quickly sound alarms on suspicious activity so incident response plans can be activated [43, 44].

In summary, this three-pronged approach blending resilient backups facilitating denial of service, access controls confirming identity, and user awareness providing the perception of abnormalities designs a robust infrastructure posture ready to withstand ransomware strikes as cybersecurity basics prove foundational yet essential in readiness. Neglecting any one aspect leaves exposure for threat actors to cultivate disruption and leverage extortion.

7.4.2 Network Segmentation

Network segmentation serves as a critical ransomware containment strategy by compartmentalizing connectivity and preventing threat actors from achieving whole-system visibility or traversal in attacks [24]. Properly positioned and configured network firewalls divide larger networks into smaller subnets based on system roles, functions, applications, or sensitivity levels. This strict partitioning frustrates lateral attacker movement as compromised access on one subnet has limited visibility of assets on other segments without additional exploitation. Micro-segmentation through software-defined networking takes this concept to finer-grained divisions separating workloads, users, devices, and even singular processes across systems [45, 46]. Robust network segmentation or industrial control system environments require physically dividing IT networks from operations technology by denying any routes across subnets. Keeping business information systems compartmentalized from industrial control loops prevents initial intrusion vectors like phishing or malware from reaching crucial uptime-sensitive operational processes [35]. Any connections enabling telemetry, monitoring, or file exchanges across zones should funnel through unidirectional data diodes, permitting only outbound information flows. Moreover, comprehensive logging and focused intrusion detection systems are vital for segmented environments to provide visibility and alerting on anomalous subnet activity, indicating potential beachhead access or lateral movement attempts across the network [47]. Suspected compromise of any one area through early warnings prompts rapid isolation and investigation, minimizing relationships of trust threat actors can exploit deeper into infrastructure.

Overall, combined with solid backups not exposed beyond segmented environments and access controls preventing unfettered credential theft, network segmentation through firewall divisions and micro-compartmentalization lets defenders maintain ransomware within limited attack planes. This frustrates adversary objectives, contains blast radii, and protects the availability of high-value industrial control process integrity vital for critical infrastructure uptime.

7.4.3 Enable Early Threat Detection

Rapid threat detection proves essential for ransomware mitigation by recognizing the early stages of an attack while still establishing footholds rather than only finding wide-scale encryption later in the kill chain. Detailed security analytics solutions profile normal baseline behaviors across infrastructure systems, leveraging full-packet capture and endpoint data collection to perform behavioral analysis identifying minute anomalies [48, 49]. Predictive analytics can detect ransomware indicators like attempts to stop or tamper with antivirus services, providing a last line of defense against malware installation. Detecting deletion of backup files or disabling functionality preserving previous Windows restore points signals adversary efforts to limit recovery options before main encryption activities. When analytics spots unusual child processes spawning from typical applications linked to ransomware droppers, early discovery prompts quicker action. Any flags for disabling applications that allow listing protections that limit unauthorized executable code from running should trigger alarms [50]. Centralizing feeds from endpoint detections, intrusion prevention systems, firewall activity logs, and cloud application alerts provides necessary correlated insight to recognize distributed ransomware stages unfolding across the network environment faster [14, 51]. Security operations center (SOC) analysts can quickly pinpoint anomalies aligning with ransomware playbooks to speed appropriate urgent response protocols containing the attack's blast radius through credential revocation, affected system isolation, and eradication of the adversary's installed anchor footholds.

Investing in security analytics and monitoring platforms tuned to detect ransomware behaviors at the earliest infiltration phases buys precious time to halt progress before impact expands to demand a ransom payment. When encryption or destruction has already achieved wide reach across networks, options become vastly more limited for critical infrastructure owners.

7.4.4 Secure Communications Channels

Email often serves as the initial infection vector for ransomware attacks when users click phishing links or enable malicious attachments hosting malware droppers. Fortifying the email channel, therefore, cuts off the typical path for entry [52]. Modern tools integrate abilities to scrutinize emails for early signs of malicious indicators based on structural anomalies detected from image and document attachments or irregular and domain-dissimilar links not matching legitimate traffic patterns [53]. Email protection should encompass all links in delivery and reception chains, as threats aim to spoof legitimate corporate domains for social engineering manipulation. Setting up Domain-based

Message Authentication, Reporting, and Conformance (DMARC) across owned disciplines uncovers attempts at impersonation, while reputation filters block high-risk originating addresses [54, 55]. Archiving email communications aids prompt investigations even post-infection to uncover patient zero and attack the root causes for correction. Some services like Microsoft 365 integrate data loss prevention and encryption to prevent the exfiltration of sensitive communications.

However, no prevention provides complete security against ransomware communications infiltrating infrastructure networks through lower-security remote workstations. Analyzing user behavior to uncover atypical activity and prioritized patching schedules helps shore defenses [50, 56, 57]. But securing email channels strikes at the first action of cyber kill chains, directly halting the injection of over 90% of ransomware attacks – crucially stopping most progress before data can be encrypted or destroyed.[11]

7.4.5 Test Incident Response Plans

Even organizations with hardened defenses sometimes experience incidents requiring urgent coordinated containment, eradication, and recovery protocols ready for smooth execution. Comprehensive incident response playbooks should outline decision-making authorities, internal and public communications, technical capabilities, and explicit response procedures [29, 58]. Playbooks require constant updates integrating threat intelligence on the latest adversary tactics, techniques, and strategies to ensure measures align with realistic ransomware behaviors. Simply possessing documented plans proves insufficient without intensely training critical employees on individual responsibilities during various breach scenarios to prevent confusion. Response teams need training on tools, key concepts, and the overarching incident lifecycle. Realistic tabletop simulations should periodically test personnel on hypothetical but credible ransomware events, probing judgment, comprehension of roles, and effectiveness of response workflows [59]. Lessons from exercises identify knowledge gaps for correction through updated training.

Having incident response plans finessed by relevant training and testing allows rapid trustworthy activation when ransomware penetrates defenses rather than fumbling through ad-hoc reactions. Smooth response execution stems from breaches early before extensive damage when delays induced by confusion have severe impacts. Whether for initial containment, eradication of anchor footholds, or eventual recovery, rehearsed plans bolster resilience against incidents becoming catastrophes. Though ransomware prevention is ideal, infrastructure must withstand some attacks reaching mission-critical systems.

7.4.6 Adopt Innovative Safeguards

Ransomware continually evolves, requiring cybersecurity defenses to similarly progress with innovative capabilities attuned to agile adversarial threats aiming to evade traditional controls. Integrating backup into native software-as-a-service (SaaS) platforms provides inherent protection at scale while delighting users through transparent experiences meeting compliance and governance policies.[12] For example, through Microsoft Defender XDR, Microsoft 365 builds in layered security services spanning suspicious email filtering, data loss prevention, and backup/restoration for productivity workloads.[13]

AI-powered techniques such as machine learning (ML) and deep learning (DL) now surpass signature and rules-based cyber protections by discerning highly complex patterns that go unnoticed by static analysis [49, 60], [61]. Here, mathematical models are trained to autonomously learn environments autonomously, baselining normal vs. abnormal to uncover emerging attack permutations automatically without awaiting updates. Though difficult to fully trust as black boxes, the mathematical precision proves superior for detecting APTs [62]. Measures to provide interpretability of AI-powered models in ransomware threat mitigation have been undertaken, with the XRan technique proving a much better alternative than its counterparts [63]. Moreover, Blockchain's inherent resistance to tampering by recording transactions across decentralized nodes shows early promise for ransomware-resistant architectures struggling to gain enterprise trust and adoption [20, 64, 65]. The technology's decentralized ledger, focusing on ensuring the validity of sequenced data blocks, limits data destruction or manipulation attacks [66]. In healthcare, Blockchain has been applied to mitigate Ransomware attacks, effectively saving lives and protecting the reputation of healthcare service providers [67]. Embracing cloud-native security represents a paradigm shift in protecting critical infrastructure from ransomware attacks. Cloud platforms are increasingly prioritizing security natively, integrating features such as embedded backup, micro-segmentation, access controls, encryption, and analytics into their services [68, 69, 70]. This approach reduces the adoption barriers smaller entities face, allowing them to implement robust security measures without added complexity. Furthermore, using serverless architectures helps limit the blast radius of ransomware attacks, enhancing overall resilience [71, 72]. The future of ransomware defense involves leveraging automated infrastructure monitoring powered by tamper-resistant sensor networks and advanced machine learning algorithms. These technologies enable near real-time monitoring of infrastructure performance, allowing for the early detection of ransomware activities [73, 74]. Models capable of identifying abnormal operations, data mismatches, equipment downtimes, or chemistry changes contribute to the rapid identification of potential ransomware threats. This automated approach is significantly more efficient than manual monitoring, facilitating faster response times to mitigate potential risks to critical infrastructure.

While innovative capabilities hold promise, integration requires thoughtful IT policies, demand management, and cultural readiness as complementary runtime components to realize touted cybersecurity potential. Mature implementations leverage leading capabilities embedded inside refreshed services that already meet uptime, and experience benchmarks end users enjoy. Carefully incorporation of innovations with cloud services, trust in advanced mathematics through AI, and decentralization offset aggressive criminal extortion threatening critical infrastructure availability.

7.4.7 International Cooperation and Cybersecurity Diplomacy

Ransomware has rapidly emerged as a severe global threat, with attacks transcending borders and impacting critical infrastructure worldwide [12, 31, 32, 34]. International cooperation and cybersecurity diplomacy provide vital avenues for information sharing, joint operations, and norms of behavior to counter ransomware [31, 75, 76]. Accordingly, multilateral partnerships such as the annual United Nations Group of Governmental Experts provide platforms for major powers to find consensus on acceptable norms in cyberspace.[14] Key agreements declare that critical infrastructure should remain off-limits, along with calls for nations to take reasonable steps to ensure territory within their control is not used for internationally wrongful cyber activities. These cybersecurity tech accords foster collaboration on technical standards, capacity building, and sharing solutions [77]. Moreover, bilateral cyber dialogues allow the United States and its allies to coordinate joint diplomatic pressure against countries harboring ransomware attackers. Law enforcement partnerships through Interpol enable the pursuit of actors launching cross-border attacks by sharing digital forensics after significant incidents.[15]

While complex geostrategic realities limit some partnerships, ransomware presents universal threats to entire societies dependent on shared critical services. International cooperation can transcend traditional divides by framing cyberattacks on infrastructure as imperiling civilian safety. Technical working groups, multilateral accords, bilateral pressure on safe havens, and joint law enforcement actions combine to increase friction for ransomware groups to operate globally. Addressing this scourge requires a coordinated international front through cybersecurity diplomacy and collective pushback.

7.4.8 Public-Private Partnerships in Securing Critical Infrastructure

Public-private partnerships (PPPs) play an integral role in securing critical infrastructure by combining the resources and capabilities of both government and private sector organizations [78, 79].

Successful PPPs deliver improved information sharing, expanded technology development, joint training exercises, and coordinated incident response [80]. PPPs such as the Electricity Information Sharing and Analysis Center (E-ISAC) facilitate rapid information exchange on emerging ransomware tactics and vulnerabilities between utilities and the government [81].[16] Initiatives like the Cybersecurity Risk Information Sharing Program (CRISP) enable government threat intelligence pooling with vetted critical infrastructure companies across sectors.[17] Other partnerships focus on technology R&D tailored to industry needs, such as water treatment or emergency response networks. Additionally, joint simulation exercises between infrastructure owners and government cybersecurity agencies boost readiness and coordination. Public health preparedness drills involving tabletop simulations of coordinated contingency response to ransomware health sector crises strengthen regional resilience. International cross-sector drills like Locked Shields unite military, civilian government, and private teams to practice coordinated reactions.

While complex to establish across different missions and cultures, public-private collaboration has successfully thwarted numerous targeted intrusions through early warning systems. Information-sharing centers remain crucial for accelerating future ransomware response while averting potentially cascading national impacts. Sustained senior leadership buy-in, transparent participation incentives, and employing existing regulatory frameworks can overcome inherent PPP challenges.

7.4.9 Continuous Monitoring and Adaptation of Mitigation Strategies

Ransomware groups exhibit unprecedented innovation, seeking to evade and exploit defenses, requiring infrastructure owners to constantly monitor threat landscapes and refresh countermeasures [82]. Tactics rapidly shift from large-scale spam campaigns to highly targeted vulnerability research, enabling access to crucial systems. Continuously ingesting threat intelligence from information-sharing groups, researchers, and dark web sources provides visibility on emerging attack permutations like RaaS, empowering less sophisticated actors [83, 84, 85]. Tracking exploit kit code innovations, phishing lures copying trends, and malware obfuscation techniques ensures detection rules and analytics models align with current strategies [11]. Furthermore, upgrading essential controls like endpoint detection platforms yearly at minimum guarantees capabilities to keep pace with adversary innovation in evasion and exploitation.[18] Annual testing of incident response plans and crisis simulations ensures existing strategies match current adversarial sophistication and malware propagation speeds [86].

7.4.10 Cyber Insurance Reforms

The cyber insurance landscape is evolving in response to the increasing ransomware threat. As payouts for ransomware incidents prompt insurance companies to reassess their risks, policies are transforming to include specific controls for coverage. This includes multi-factor authentication (MFA), end-user education, viable backups, and response plans. Implementing these controls raises the baseline security requirements for asset owners to qualify for coverage, potentially leading to lower premiums. Additionally, government backstops may be introduced to support insurers in retaining infrastructure policies amid the rising uncertainty associated with ransomware threats [87, 88].

7.4.11 Threat Intelligence Sharing Expansion

Collaborative threat intelligence sharing is becoming an integral part of ransomware defense strategies. Member trust communities facilitate a two-way tangible exchange of threat intelligence, allowing organizations to continually adapt their defenses ahead of emerging innovations from ransomware adversaries. This collaborative approach goes beyond one-way information dissemination, evolving into real-time collective security efforts that accelerate incident response capabilities [84, 85, 89]. By fostering a community-driven response to ransomware threats, organizations can stay

TABLE 7.2
Summary of ransomware threat mitigation strategies

Mitigation Strategy	Summary
Prioritize cybersecurity basics	Ensure regular offline backups, multi-factor authentication, and continuous end-user education to recognize social engineering attempts.
Segment networks	Divide networks and strictly limit connectivity between environments to frustrate lateral movement using firewalls and micro-segmentation
Enable early threat detection	Employ behavioral analytics and centralized monitoring to recognize early ransomware indicators and contain attacks faster.
Secure communications channels	Scrutinize emails, texts, and calls using malware detection, authentication frameworks, and archiving to prevent infection vectors.
Test incident response plans	Develop playbooks documenting response protocols, train personnel through simulations on roles, and update plans with threat intelligence.
Adopt innovative safeguards	Integrate emerging capabilities like ML detection, immutable backup systems, cloud-native security, automated infrastructure monitoring, and Blockchain's tamper resistance to counter evolving threats.
International cooperation	Foster partnerships across governments and private industries to share intelligence, conduct joint operations, and establish cyber norms.
Public-private partnerships	Combine resources and capabilities across sectors through information-sharing programs, technology development, and coordinated incident response.
Continuous monitoring and adaptation	Ingest threat intelligence to stay abreast of shifting adversary tactics and upgrade defenses and response plans accordingly.
Cyber insurance reforms	Enact cyber insurance reforms using controls such as multi-factor authentication (MFA), end-user education, and viable backups, among others, to raise the baseline security requirements for asset owners to qualify for coverage.
Threat intelligence sharing expansion	Facilitate a two-way tangible exchange of threat intelligence among member trust communities to ensure collaborative threat intelligence sharing among them. This will allow organizations to continually adapt their defenses ahead of emerging innovations from ransomware adversaries.

ahead of developing attack techniques and strengthen their overall cybersecurity posture. Table 7.2 summarizes the ransomware threat mitigation strategies to protect critical infrastructures.

While foundational measures like segmentation, access controls, and backups provide lasting barriers, the fast evolution of tactics mandates continuous threat awareness. Establishing processes to rapidly incorporate new threat intelligence into security architectures prevents defenses from lagging years behind adversary capabilities. Though operationally burdensome, regularly reevaluating and refreshing countermeasures provides the only way to manage explosive ransomware innovation. With ransom payments skyrocketing into millions of US dollars, the criminal incentive for innovation shows no signs of abating. Only a commitment to continuous monitoring and adaptation of security programs can disrupt the exponential growth in attacks threatening infrastructure worldwide.

7.5 REAL-WORLD CASES OF RANSOMWARE ATTACKS ON CRITICAL INFRASTRUCTURE AND LESSONS LEARNED

As highlighted earlier, critical infrastructure, including energy grids, transportation systems, and healthcare facilities, plays a pivotal role in the functioning of societies. The increasing interconnectivity and reliance on digital technologies have made these sectors prime targets for malicious actors seeking financial gain or aiming to disrupt essential services. This section highlights real-world cases of ransomware attacks on critical infrastructure, exploring the tactics employed by cybercriminals and their profound impact on the affected organizations and the communities they serve. Examining these incidents, we aim to extract valuable lessons that can guide individuals, organizations, and policymakers in enhancing cybersecurity measures and resilience against future threats.

7.5.1 Colonial Pipeline Attack in 2021

The Colonial Pipeline ransomware attack in May 2021 represents one of the most disruptive cyber incidents to critical infrastructure [4]. The DarkSide affiliate adversary was motivated by financial gain when they exploited a compromised VPN password to traverse from the IT network into OT systems and encrypt nearly 100 GB of data. The crippling of pipeline operations prompted Colonial to pay a $4.4 million ransom to begin restoring systems, though they had backup capabilities. Key lessons learned indicate better segmentation between IT and industrial control networks and multi-factor authentications for privileged VPN access could have reduced the surface vulnerability.

7.5.2 Costa Rica Government Attack in 2022

The 2022 attack on Costa Rica's government by the Hive ransomware gang exhibited adversary motivations of financial gain and destabilization as multiple key agencies across transportation, education, and customs systems suffered total encryption.[19] The initial infection vector involved Trojan malware sent via phishing links, as adversaries displayed stealth by lurking undetected for weeks prior to launching ransom demands to decrypt 30 critical systems [90]. With backup stores also deleted in the precision strike, restoration has relied mainly on paper records as systems slowly return. More resilient offline backup postures and continued end-user security training could have bolstered defenses.

7.5.3 Norwegian Aluminum Producer Norsk Hydro Attack in 2019

When the LockerGoga malware compromised industrial aluminum producer Norsk Hydro in 2019, initial reconnaissance indicated motivations laser focused on extracting payment from large manufacturing firms through forced production halts.[20] Adversaries exploited on-premises exchange servers before timing encryption for maximum impact during European morning hours. With insurance covering much of the $35 million recovery costs, Norsk Hydro's response validated segmentation strategies that isolated plant floor impacts. The case highlights even air-gapped ICS networks warrant stronger protections. Table 7.3 summarizing details on real-world ransomware attacks impacting critical infrastructure.

7.5.4 Irish Health Service Executive (HSE) Ransomware Attack in 2021

The crippling 2021 attack on Ireland's Health Service Executive exemplifies the immense disruption ransomware poses to entire regions of critical infrastructure through single-point failures. Initial phishing emails infected accounting systems before Conti ransomware traversed across flat networks, encrypting systems and forcing hospitals to defer care and return to paper records. With lives jeopardized, restoring digital functionality relied on rebuilding networks from scratch rather than paying the $20 million ransom. Though recovery continues years later, the Irish aftermath cements the consequences from lacking segmentation controls and delayed incident response. As adversaries professionalize, the chemical toxicity and impaired care delivered during weeks of manual workarounds manifest in dangerous, lasting effects across communities reliant on the availability of digital infrastructure. The systemic impacts spur calls for better internal controls and rapid response protocols before single infections bind regional lifelines indefinitely.

TABLE 7.3
Summary of real-world ransomware attacks, motivations, tactics, patterns, lessons, and recovery mechanisms

Ransomware Attack	Adversary Motivations	Tactics	Attack Patterns	Key Lessons Learned	Recovery Mechanism
2021 Colonial Pipeline	Financial gain	Exploited VPN vulnerability	Encrypted systems via compromised access, extorted $4.4 million payment	Segment OT & IT networks, multi-factor VPN authentication	Paid ransom, began restoration with backups
2022 Costa Rica Government	Financial gain & social disruption	Phishing Trojan infection	Encrypted agencies' systems, deleted backups	Robust offline backups, end-user security training	Restoring from paper records
2019 Norsk Hydro	Financial gain from industrial firms	Exploited on-prem exchange server	Encrypted systems induced production halts	Network segmentation, cyber insurance	Restored the majority of systems from backups
2021 Irish Health Service Executive Attack	Financial gain and service disruption	Conti ransomware via a phishing link	Encrypted systems induced significant care delays	Robust network segmentation, rapid incident response	Rebuilding networks from backups
2021 New Jersey Hospital Chain	Financial gain	Ryuk ransomware via a phishing link	Encrypted systems forcing care delays	Pervasive security training, accessible reporting procedures	Restoring from backups
JBS USA (2021)	Financial gain	Sophisticated tactics, potential phishing, or compromised endpoints	Network breach, ransomware deployment across systems	Robust cybersecurity, proactive threat detection, comprehensive incident response	Paid $11 million ransom to restore systems
Travelex (2019)	Financial gain	Exploited VPN vulnerability, lateral movement	Initial foothold, ransomware encryption of data	Prompt patching, incident response planning, resilient backups, security awareness	Paid $2.3 million ransom, engaged cybersecurity professionals, rebuilt systems
Kyiv Power Grid (2016)	Suspected Russian state sponsorship	Spear-phishing, malware delivery	Reconnaissance, social engineering, lateral movement, privilege escalation	Robust security, incident response planning, supply chain security, collaboration	Switched to manual control, implemented contingency plans, system inspections, malware removal
Hollywood Presbyterian Medical Center (2016)	Financial gain	Likely phishing or software vulnerabilities	Unauthorized access, ransomware encryption of data	Cybersecurity measures, employee training, incident response plans, reliable backups	Paid $17,000 ransom, strengthened cybersecurity posture, invested in security solutions, data backup, and recovery strategies

7.5.5 New Jersey Hospital Chain Ransomware Attack

The coordinated Ryuk ransomware attack on the St. Lawrence Health Care chain highlights the healthcare sector's perpetual adversity from phishing vulnerabilities despite technical defenses.[21] A single employee clicking a malicious link prompted immediate critical system encryption and care delays for facilities across northern New Jersey until gradual restoration from backups. With phishing lures bypassing filters to exploit human susceptibility still causing over 90% of ransomware incidents, as highlighted earlier, the case cements that cultural transformation through pervasive workforce training and streamlined reporting mechanisms stands vital. To match robust backups, routine simulated scenarios must galvanize threat visibility and response instincts at all levels. Though arduous, organizations demonstrating phishing resilience thrive; those repeatedly falling demonstrate eroding community trust in the institutions most vital when adversity inevitably strikes.

7.5.6 JBS USA Ransomware Attack in 2021

In a significant blow to the global food supply chain, JBS USA, a prominent meat processor, was targeted in a ransomware attack by the Russian-linked REvil hacking group, shedding light on the critical vulnerability of essential infrastructure to cyber threats [91]. Motivated by financial gain, the attackers employed sophisticated tactics, potentially stemming from phishing emails or compromised endpoints, to breach JBS USA's network and unleash ransomware across its systems, causing widespread disruption. This event underscores the imperative for robust cybersecurity measures, proactive threat detection, and comprehensive incident response protocols to safeguard critical infrastructure. JBS paid $11 million to restore affected systems and gradually recover from the attack.[22] The huge payment underscores the dire situation companies find themselves in to resume operations.

7.5.7 Travelex Ransomware Attack in 2019

On 31 December 2019, the REvil ransomware syndicate struck gold by exploiting a vulnerability in Travelex's Pulse Secure VPN servers to breach the company's network defenses. This initial foothold paved the way for lateral movement throughout Travelex's systems, culminating in deploying the crew's malicious ransomware that encrypted swathes of critical data. Driven by unrelenting financial motivations, the cybercriminals issued a $6 million ransom demand in exchange for the decryption keys. While Travelex purportedly negotiated the fee down to $2.3 million (around £1.76 million) in Bitcoin, this represented merely the opening salvo in an escalating organizational crisis.[23] By the time this payment decision was reached, the company's internal systems had already endured a crippling two-week outage, forcing operations to grind to a near-halt, with staff resorting to archaic pen-and-paper processes. Despite initially rebuffing the ransom demands, the attack's devastating impacts persisted. Travelex shouldered estimated losses surpassing $32 million as it engaged cybersecurity professionals and law enforcement to spearhead the herculean efforts of rebuilding systems and restoring data from backups. However, the damages proved too severe, and seven months after the ransomware onslaught, the company collapsed into administration.

This incident served as a sobering reminder of the paramount importance of prompt vulnerability patching, robust incident response planning, maintaining resilient backup strategies, and fostering a pervasive culture of security awareness throughout an organization's ranks.

7.5.8 Kyiv Power Grid Ransomware Attack in 2016

The ransomware attack on Kyiv's power grid in 2016 was a significant cybersecurity incident believed to be sponsored or supported by Russia amid ongoing tensions with Ukraine [92]. The attackers employed spear-phishing emails to deliver malware, allowing them to gain a foothold in the network and deploy a variant of the KillDisk malware, corrupting critical system files and rendering the systems inoperable.[24] The attack followed a pattern of reconnaissance, social engineering, lateral movement, and privilege escalation, ultimately compromising the industrial control systems managing the power grid. While the systems were believed to be air-gapped, the attack underscored the need for robust security measures, incident response planning, supply chain security, and collaboration among critical infrastructure organizations. The power grid operators restored power relatively quickly by switching to manual control and implementing contingency plans. Still, the recovery process involved thorough system inspections, malware removal, and implementation of additional security measures.

7.5.9 Hollywood Presbyterian Medical Center Ransomware Attack in 2016

The ransomware attack on Hollywood Presbyterian Medical Center in February 2016 exposed the vulnerabilities of healthcare institutions to cyber threats [93]. Motivated by financial gain, the attackers gained unauthorized access to the hospital's systems, likely through phishing or software vulnerabilities, and deployed ransomware that encrypted critical data, including patient records. Faced with operational disruptions and the potential risk to patient care, the hospital ultimately paid a $17,000 ransom in Bitcoin to regain access to their encrypted files.[25] This incident served as a wake-up call, highlighting the urgent need for robust cybersecurity measures, employee training, incident response plans, and reliable backup systems in the healthcare sector to mitigate the risks posed by evolving cyber threats like ransomware. The attack prompted the hospital to strengthen its cybersecurity posture, invest in advanced security solutions, enhance employee awareness, and develop robust data backup and recovery strategies to better prepare for and respond to future cyber incidents. Table 7.3 summarizes the above cases, highlighting the adversary motivations, tactics, attack patterns, key lessons, and recovery mechanisms.

Collectively, these cases cement ransomware's dominance as the foremost threat to industrialized societies by jeopardizing the delivery of essential services. Whether financially or politically motivated, the attacks showcase poor segmentation, gaps in patching and training, and the necessity for resilient backup practices demanding ongoing attention across infrastructure sectors. As adversaries get bolder in targeting backup destruction itself, infrastructure owners need actionable intelligence on emerging tactics to adapt defenses before the next inevitable incident.

7.6 CONCLUSION

This study underscores the urgent need for robust defense mechanisms in the face of escalating ransomware threats within critical infrastructure sectors. The analysis of current threats, cybercriminal motivations, and attack patterns emphasizes the complexity and severity of the challenges. The exploration of mitigation strategies provides valuable insights into proactive measures that organizations can adopt to fortify their defenses. Real-world case studies shed light on the tangible impact of ransomware attacks, illustrating the ripple effects on affected organizations and the communities they serve. These cases serve as cautionary tales, emphasizing the importance of implementing comprehensive mitigation strategies. As we navigate the evolving landscape of cyber threats, stakeholders within critical infrastructure must collaborate, share intelligence, and invest in cutting-edge technologies. The collective effort to fortify defenses and a proactive stance on mitigation will be pivotal in safeguarding critical infrastructure assets from the ever-present menace of ransomware. Ultimately, a holistic and adaptive approach is essential to thwart current threats and stay ahead of emerging challenges in the ongoing battle against cybercriminals targeting our critical infrastructure.

NOTES

1 https://www.statista.com/statistics/494947/ransomware-attempts-per-year-worldwide/
2 https://www.statista.com/statistics/494947/ransomware-attempts-per-year-worldwide/
3 https://www.statista.com/statistics/1315826/ransomware-attacks-worldwide/
4 https://www.sangfor.com/blog/cybersecurity/healthcare-data-security-how-to-prevent-ransomware-in-healthcare
5 https://www.cbsnews.com/news/ireland-health-service-computer-systems-major-ransomware-attack/
6 https://www.nj.com/healthfit/2023/11/ransomware-attack-on-2-nj-hospitals-has-knocked-systems-offline-for-5-days.html
7 https://nurse.org/articles/hospital-overpays-employees/
8 https://securityintelligence.com/news/ransomware-attacks-agriculture/
9 https://www.connectwise.com/blog/cybersecurity/what-is-conti-ransomware-how-to-prepare
10 https://committees.parliament.uk/writtenevidence/114499/html/
11 https://www2.deloitte.com/my/en/pages/risk/articles/91-percent-of-all-cyber-attacks-begin-with-a-phishing-email-to-an-unexpected-victim.html
12 https://www.veritas.com/information-center/saas-backup-complete-guide
13 https://learn.microsoft.com/en-us/azure/architecture/solution-ideas/articles/microsoft-365-defender-build-second-layer-defense
14 https://ccdcoe.org/organisations/un/
15 https://www.interpol.int/en/Crimes/Cybercrime
16 https://www.nerc.com/pa/CI/ESISAC/Pages/default.aspx
17 https://www.eisac.com/s/crisp
18 https://www.gartner.com/reviews/market/endpoint-detection-and-response-solutions
19 https://cyberlaw.ccdcoe.org/wiki/Costa_Rica_ransomware_attack_(2022)
20 https://www.ft.com/content/7d93a6be-4a36–11e9-bbc9–6917dce3dc62
21 https://threatpost.com/hospitals-hit-by-ransomware/160695/
22 https://www.nytimes.com/2021/06/09/business/jbs-cyberattack-ransom.html
23 https://www.itgovernance.co.uk/blog/ransomware-victim-travelex-forced-into-administration
24 https://www.wired.com/2016/03/inside-cunning-unprecedented-hack-ukraines-power-grid/
25 https://www.latimes.com/business/technology/la-me-ln-hollywood-hospital-bitcoin-20160217-story.html

REFERENCES

1. H. Riggs *et al.*, "Impact, Vulnerabilities, and Mitigation Strategies for Cyber-Secure Critical Infrastructure," *Sensors*, vol. 23, no. 8, p. 4060, Apr. 2023, doi: 10.3390/S23084060.
2. W. Hurst and N. Shone, "Critical Infrastructure Security: Cyber-Threats, Legacy Systems and Weakening Segmentation," *Management and Engineering of Critical Infrastructures*, pp. 265–286, Jan. 2024, doi: 10.1016/B978-0-323-99330-2.00010-6.
3. M. Al-Hawawreh, M. Alazab, M. A. Ferrag, and M. S. Hossain, "Securing the Industrial Internet of Things against Ransomware Attacks: A Comprehensive Analysis of the Emerging Threat Landscape and Detection Mechanisms," *Journal of Network and Computer Applications*, vol. 223, p. 103809, Mar. 2024, doi: 10.1016/j.jnca.2023.103809.
4. J. Beerman, D. Berent, Z. Falter, and S. Bhunia, "A Review of Colonial Pipeline Ransomware Attack," *Proceedings – 23rd IEEE/ACM International Symposium on Cluster, Cloud and Internet Computing Workshops, CCGridW 2023*, pp. 8–15, 2023, doi: 10.1109/CCGRIDW59191.2023.00017.
5. L. S. van Boven *et al.*, "Hacking Acute Care: A Qualitative Study on the Health Care Impacts of Ransomware Attacks against Hospitals," *Annals of Emergency Medicine*, vol. 83, no. 1, pp. 46–56, Jan. 2024, doi: 10.1016/J.ANNEMERGMED.2023.04.025.
6. A. Alabdulatif, N. N. Thilakarathne, and K. Kalinaki, "A Novel Cloud Enabled Access Control Model for Preserving the Security and Privacy of Medical Big Data," *Electronics (Basel)*, vol. 12, no. 12, p. 2646, Jun. 2023, doi: 10.3390/electronics12122646.
7. K. Kalinaki, M. Fahadi, A. A. Alli, W. Shafik, M. Yasin, and N. Mutwalibi, "Artificial Intelligence of Internet of Medical Things (AIoMT) in Smart Cities: A Review of Cybersecurity for Smart Healthcare," in *Handbook of Security and Privacy of AI-Enabled Healthcare Systems and Internet of Medical Things*, 1st ed., CRC Press, 2023, pp. 271–292, doi: 10.1201/9781003370321-11.

8. K. E. Fahim, K. Kalinaki, and W. Shafik, "Electronic Devices in the Artificial Intelligence of the Internet of Medical Things (AIoMT)," in *Handbook of Security and Privacy of AI-Enabled Healthcare Systems and Internet of Medical Things*, 1st ed., CRC Press, 2023, pp. 41–62, doi: 10.1201/9781003370321-3.
9. M. Usama, U. Ullah, and A. Sajid, "Cyber Attacks Against Intelligent Transportation Systems," *Cyber Security for Next-Generation Computing Technologies*, pp. 190–230, Jan. 2024, doi: 10.1201/9781003404361-11.
10. M. M. Aslam, A. Tufail, K. H. Kim, R. A. A. H. M. Apong, and M. T. Raza, "A Comprehensive Study on Cyber Attacks in Communication Networks in Water Purification and Distribution Plants: Challenges, Vulnerabilities, and Future Prospects," *Sensors 2023*, vol. 23, no. 18, p. 7999, Sep. 2023, doi: 10.3390/S23187999.
11. M. Cen, F. Jiang, X. Qin, Q. Jiang, and R. Doss, "Ransomware Early Detection: A Survey," *Computer Networks*, vol. 239, p. 110138, Feb. 2024, doi: 10.1016/J.COMNET.2023.110138.
12. M. Ahmed, A. N. M. B. Rashid, and A.-S. K. Pathan, "Ransomware 3.0 – a Weapon for Next-Generation Information Warfare," pp. 397–405, 2024, doi: 10.1007/978-981-99-2229-1_33.
13. M. Benmalek, "Ransomware on Cyber-Physical Systems: Taxonomies, Case Studies, Security Gaps, and Open Challenges," *Internet of Things and Cyber-Physical Systems*, vol. 4, pp. 186–202, Jan. 2024, doi: 10.1016/J.IOTCPS.2023.12.001.
14. D. P. F. Möller, "Intrusion Detection and Prevention," *Advances in Information Security*, vol. 103, pp. 131–179, 2023, doi: 10.1007/978-3-031-26845-8_3.
15. P. S. Chauhan and N. Kshetri, "Ransomware as a Service Kit: A Novel Cybercrime Strategy to Monetize Victims' Data," *Computer (Long Beach Calif)*, vol. 56, no. 10, pp. 102–106, Oct. 2023, doi: 10.1109/MC.2023.3298072.
16. Z. Amos, "How Ransomware Gangs Automate Their Attacks." Accessed: Jan. 23, 2024. [Online]. Available: https://gca.isa.org/blog/how-ransomware-gangs-automate-their-attacks
17. S. J. Aquilina, F. Casino, M. Vella, J. Ellul, and C. Patsakis, "EtherClue: Digital Investigation of Attacks on Ethereum Smart Contracts," *Blockchain: Research and Applications*, vol. 2, no. 4, p. 100028, Dec. 2021, doi: 10.1016/J.BCRA.2021.100028.
18. M. Ryan, "Ransomware Revolution: The Rise of a Prodigious Cyber Threat," vol. 85, 2021, doi: 10.1007/978-3-030-66583-8.
19. M. Lang, L. Connolly, P. Taylor, and P. J. Corner, "The Evolving Menace of Ransomware: A Comparative Analysis of Pre-Pandemic and Mid-Pandemic Attacks," *Digital Threats: Research and Practice*, vol. 4, no. 4, pp. 1–22, Oct. 2023, doi: 10.1145/3558006.
20. K. Kalinaki, N. N. Thilakarathne, H. R. Mubarak, O. A. Malik, and M. Abdullatif, "Cybersafe Capabilities and Utilities for Smart Cities," in *Cybersecurity for Smart Cities*, Springer, Cham, 2023, pp. 71–86, doi: 10.1007/978-3-031-24946-4_6.
21. A. A. Alli, K. Kassim, N. Mutwalibi, H. Hamid, and L. Ibrahim, "Secure Fog-Cloud of Things: Architectures, Opportunities and Challenges," in *Secure Edge Computing*, 1st ed., M. Ahmed and P. Haskell-Dowland, Eds., CRC Press, 2021, pp. 3–20, doi: 10.1201/9781003028635-2.
22. E. Thron, S. Faily, H. Dogan, and M. Freer, "Human Factors and Cyber-Security Risks on the Railway – the Critical Role Played by Signalling Operations," *Information and Computer Security*, vol. ahead-of-print, no. ahead-of-print, 2024, doi: 10.1108/ICS-05-2023-0078.
23. M. S. Abbasi, "Automating Behavior-Based Ransomware Analysis, Detection, and Classification Using Machine Learning," Feb. 2023, doi: 10.26686/WGTN.22180858.
24. A. Mukhopadhyay and S. Jain, "A Framework for Cyber-Risk Insurance Against Ransomware: A Mixed-Method Approach," *International Journal of Information Management*, vol. 74, p. 102724, Feb. 2024, doi: 10.1016/J.IJINFOMGT.2023.102724.
25. K. E. Fahim, K. Kalinaki, L. C. De Silva, and H. Yassin, "The Role of Machine Learning in Improving Power Distribution Systems Resilience," *Future Modern Distribution Networks Resilience*, pp. 329–352, Jan. 2024, doi: 10.1016/B978-0-443-16086-8.00012-9.
26. S. R. Matthijsse, M. S. van 't Hoff-de Goede, and E. R. Leukfeldt, "Your Files Have Been Encrypted: A Crime Script Analysis of Ransomware Attacks," *Trends Organ Crime*, pp. 1–27, Apr. 2023, doi: 10.1007/S12117-023-09496-Z.
27. S. Yulianto, B. Soewito, F. L. Gaol, and A. Kurniawan, "Metrics and Red Teaming in Cyber Resilience and Effectiveness: A Systematic Literature Review," pp. 1–7, Dec. 2023, doi: 10.1109/ICT60153.2023.10374053.
28. T. Sherburne, M. M. Clifford, B. M. Horowitz, and P. A. Beling, "The Cyber Security Requirements Methodology and Meta-Model for Design of Cyber-Resilience," *Systems Engineering for the Digital Age: Practitioner Perspectives*, pp. 539–554, Sep. 2023, doi: 10.1002/9781394203314.CH26.

29. F. Teichmann, S. R. Boticiu, and B. S. Sergi, "The Evolution of Ransomware Attacks in Light of Recent Cyber Threats. How Can Geopolitical Conflicts Influence the Cyber Climate?" *International Cybersecurity Law Review*, vol. 4, no. 3, pp. 259–280, Jul. 2023, doi: 10.1365/S43439-023-00095-W.
30. G. M. Chiong and A. Capstone, "The Rise of Ransomware: Motivations, Contributing Factors, and Defenses," 2023.
31. J. Rees and C. J. Rees, "Cyber-Security and the Changing Landscape of Critical National Infrastructure: State and Non-state Cyber-Attacks on Organisations, Systems and Services," *Advanced Sciences and Technologies for Security Applications*, vol. Part F1417, pp. 67–89, 2023, doi: 10.1007/978-3-031-40118-3_5.
32. Z. A. El Houda, "Cyber Threat Actors Review: Examining the Tactics and Motivations of Adversaries in the Cyber Landscape," *Cyber Security for Next-Generation Computing Technologies*, pp. 84–101, Jan. 2024, doi: 10.1201/9781003404361-5.
33. N. Mahmudov, "Cyber Warfare: Understanding the Elements, Effects, and Future Trends of Cyber-Attacks and Defences," *Сигурност и отбрана*, no. 2, pp. 37–53, 2023.
34. K. A. Williams, "Conti Ransomware Gang: An Analysis of the Group's Motives and Methods – ProQuest," 2022. Accessed: Jan. 23, 2024. [Online]. Available: https://www.proquest.com/docview/2719083739?pq-origsite=gscholar&fromopenview=true&sourcetype=Dissertations%20&%20Theses
35. Z. Baig, H. Mekala, and S. Zeadally, "Ransomware Attacks of the COVID-19 Pandemic: Novel Strains, Victims, and Threat Actors," *IT Professional*, vol. 25, no. 5, pp. 37–44, Sep. 2023, doi: 10.1109/MITP.2023.3297085.
36. M. Chemisto *et al.*, "Artificial Intelligence for Improved Maternal Healthcare: A Systematic Literature Review," *2023 IEEE AFRICON*, pp. 1–6, Sep. 2023, doi: 10.1109/AFRICON55910.2023.10293674.
37. L. Axon, A. Erola, I. Agrafiotis, G. Uuganbayar, M. Goldsmith, and S. Creese, "Ransomware as a Predator: Modelling the Systemic Risk to Prey," *Digital Threats: Research and Practice*, vol. 4, no. 4, pp. 1–38, Dec. 2023, doi: 10.1145/3579648.
38. K. Begovic, A. Al-Ali, and Q. Malluhi, "Cryptographic Ransomware Encryption Detection: Survey," *Computer Security*, vol. 132, p. 103349, Sep. 2023, doi: 10.1016/J.COSE.2023.103349.
39. P. H. Chen, R. Bodak, and N. S. Gandhi, "Ransomware Recovery and Imaging Operations: Lessons Learned and Planning Considerations," *Journal of Digital Imaging*, vol. 34, no. 3, pp. 731–740, Jun. 2021, doi: 10.1007/S10278-021-00466-X/TABLES/2.
40. T. Suleski, M. Ahmed, W. Yang, and E. Wang, "A Review of Multi-Factor Authentication in the Internet of Healthcare Things," *Digital Health*, vol. 9, Jan. 2023, doi: 10.1177/20552076231177144.
41. W. Shafik and K. Kalinaki, "Smart City Ecosystem: An Exploration of Requirements, Architecture, Applications, Security, and Emerging Motivations," in *Handbook of Research on Network-Enabled IoT Applications for Smart City Services*, IGI Global, 2023, pp. 75–98, doi: 10.4018/979-8-3693-0744-1.CH005.
42. L. Pharris and B. Perez-Mira, "Preventing Social Engineering: A Phenomenological Inquiry," *Information and Computer Security*, vol. 31, no. 1, pp. 1–31, Feb. 2023, doi: 10.1108/ICS-09-2021-0137.
43. L. Hove, "Strategies Used to Mitigate Social Engineering Attacks – ProQuest." Accessed: Jan. 23, 2024. [Online]. Available: https://www.proquest.com/openview/eba1df4b1f40b33ff50b8cae48e4ea41/1?cbl=51922&diss=y&pq-origsite=gscholar&parentSessionId=PtrKSrKNfgx3SflFWeTdNBfhcERRSH65nZmN5ut4iI8%3D
44. C. Subbalakshmi, P. K. Pareek, and R. Sayal, "A Study on Social Engineering Attacks in Cybersecurity," *Lecture Notes in Networks and Systems*, vol. 385, pp. 59–71, 2022, doi: 10.1007/978-981-16-8987-1_7/COVER.
45. S. I. Ansarullah, M. M. Kirmani, Z. Mushtaq, and G. M. ud din Dar, "Cyber Security Future: Trends and Solutions," *Cyber Security for Next-Generation Computing Technologies*, pp. 1–15, Jan. 2024, doi: 10.1201/9781003404361-1.
46. P. Kumar, M. S. Obaidat, P. Pandey, M. Wazid, A. K. Das, and D. P. Singh, "Design of a Secure Machine Learning-Based Malware Detection and Analysis Scheme," *Proceedings of the 2023 IEEE International Conference on Communications, Computing, Cybersecurity and Informatics, CCCI 2023*, 2023, doi: 10.1109/CCCI58712.2023.10290761.
47. J. M. Kizza, "System Intrusion Detection and Prevention," pp. 295–323, 2024, doi: 10.1007/978-3-031-47549-8_13.
48. P. Sharma, S. Kapoor, and R. Sharma, "Ransomware Detection, Prevention and Protection in IoT Devices Using ML Techniques Based on Dynamic Analysis Approach," *International Journal of System Assurance Engineering and Management*, vol. 14, no. 1, pp. 287–296, Feb. 2023, doi: 10.1007/S13198-022-01793-0.

49. A. Djenna, A. Bouridane, S. Rubab, and I. M. Marou, "Artificial Intelligence-Based Malware Detection, Analysis, and Mitigation," *Symmetry*, vol. 15, no. 3, p. 677, Mar. 2023, doi: 10.3390/SYM15030677.
50. A. Alraizza and A. Algarni, "Ransomware Detection Using Machine Learning: A Survey," *Big Data and Cognitive Computing*, vol. 7, no. 3, p. 143, Aug. 2023, doi: 10.3390/BDCC7030143.
51. A. Patel, M. Taghavi, K. Bakhtiyari, and J. Celestino Júnior, "An Intrusion Detection and Prevention System in Cloud Computing: A Systematic Review," *Journal of Network and Computer Applications*, vol. 36, no. 1, pp. 25–41, Jan. 2013, doi: 10.1016/J.JNCA.2012.08.007.
52. B. Naqvi, K. Perova, A. Farooq, I. Makhdoom, S. Oyedeji, and J. Porras, "Mitigation Strategies against the Phishing Attacks: A Systematic Literature Review," *Computer Security*, vol. 132, p. 103387, Sep. 2023, doi: 10.1016/J.COSE.2023.103387.
53. T. Lam and H. Kettani, "Phattapp: A Phishing Attack Detection Application," *ACM International Conference Proceeding Series*, pp. 154–158, Apr. 2019, doi: 10.1145/3325917.3325927.
54. M. Kucherawy and E. Zwicky, "Domain-Based Message Authentication, Reporting, and Conformance (DMARC)," Mar. 2015, doi: 10.17487/RFC7489.
55. D. Arnaldy and R. P. Theyser, "Analysis of Apilogy.id Email Domain Security Status Using DMARC (Domain-Based Message Authentication, Reporting, and Conformance)," *2023 6th International Conference of Computer and Informatics Engineering (IC2IE)*, IEEE, Sep. 2023, pp. 125–130, doi: 10.1109/IC2IE60547.2023.10331296.
56. A. Y. Prasetya, K. I. Aini, and C. Lim, "Comparative Analysis of Attack Behavior Patterns in Petya, CryptInfinite, and Locky Ransomware Using Hybrid Analysis," *Proceedings – 2023 IEEE International Conference on Cryptography, Informatics, and Cybersecurity: Cryptography and Cybersecurity: Roles, Prospects, and Challenges, ICoCICs 2023*, pp. 29–34, 2023, doi: 10.1109/ICOCICS58778.2023.10276477.
57. A. Arabo, R. Dijoux, T. Poulain, and G. Chevalier, "Detecting Ransomware Using Process Behavior Analysis," *Procedia Computer Science*, vol. 168, pp. 289–296, Jan. 2020, doi: 10.1016/J.PROCS.2020.02.249.
58. P. Bajpai and R. Enbody, "Know Thy Ransomware Response: A Detailed Framework for Devising Effective Ransomware Response Strategies," *Digital Threats: Research and Practice*, vol. 4, no. 4, pp. 1–19, Dec. 2023, doi: 10.1145/3606022.
59. G. N. Angafor, I. Yevseyeva, and L. Maglaras, "Scenario-Based Incident Response Training: Lessons Learnt from Conducting an Experiential Learning Virtual Incident Response Tabletop Exercise," *Information and Computer Security*, vol. 31, no. 4, pp. 404–426, Oct. 2023, doi: 10.1108/ICS-05-2022-0085.
60. O. Dib, Z. Nan, and J. Liu, "Machine Learning-Based Ransomware Classification of Bitcoin Transactions," *Journal of King Saud University – Computer and Information Sciences*, vol. 36, no. 1, p. 101925, Jan. 2024, doi: 10.1016/J.JKSUCI.2024.101925.
61. M. J. Hossain Faruk *et al.*, "Malware Detection and Prevention Using Artificial Intelligence Techniques," *Proceedings – 2021 IEEE International Conference on Big Data, Big Data 2021*, pp. 5369–5377, 2021, doi: 10.1109/BIGDATA52589.2021.9671434.
62. N. Capuano, G. Fenza, V. Loia, and C. Stanzione, "Explainable Artificial Intelligence in CyberSecurity: A Survey," *IEEE Access*, vol. 10, pp. 93575–93600, 2022, doi: 10.1109/ACCESS.2022.3204171.
63. S. Gulmez, A. Gorgulu Kakisim, and I. Sogukpinar, "XRan: Explainable Deep Learning-Based Ransomware Detection Using Dynamic Analysis," *Computer Security*, vol. 139, p. 103703, Apr. 2024, doi: 10.1016/J.COSE.2024.103703.
64. S. S. Kirkman, S. Fulton, J. Hemmes, C. Garcia, and J. C. Wilson, "A Blockchain Architecture to Increase the Resilience of Industrial Control Systems from the Effects of a Ransomware Attack: A Proposal and Initial Results," *ACM Transactions on Cyber-Physical Systems*, Jan. 2024, doi: 10.1145/3637553.
65. W. Shafik, K. Kalinaki, and R. Y. Zakari, "Blockchain's Motivation for IoT-Enabled Smart City," *Secure and Intelligent IoT-Enabled Smart Cities*, pp. 195–221, Jan. 2024, doi: 10.4018/979-8-3693-2373-1.CH010.
66. A. Singh, Md. A. Ali, B. Balamurugan, and V. Sharma, "Blockchain: Tool for Controlling Ransomware Through Pre-Encryption and Post-Encryption Behavior," *2022 Fifth International Conference on Computational Intelligence and Communication Technologies (CCICT)*, IEEE, Jul. 2022, pp. 584–589, doi: 10.1109/CCiCT56684.2022.00107.
67. M. Wazid, A. Kumar Das, and S. Shetty, "BSFR-SH: Blockchain-Enabled Security Framework against Ransomware Attacks for Smart Healthcare," *IEEE Transactions on Consumer Electronics*, vol. 69, no. 1, pp. 18–28, Feb. 2023, doi: 10.1109/TCE.2022.3208795.

68. K. Kalinaki, W. Shafik, M. Masha, and A. A. Alli, "A Review of Artificial Intelligence Techniques for Improved Cloud and IoT Security," *Emerging Technologies for Securing the Cloud and IoT*, pp. 38–68, Jan. 2024, doi: 10.4018/979-8-3693-0766-3.CH002.
69. K. Kalinaki, U. Yahya, O. A. Malik, and D. T. C. Lai, "A Review of Big Data Analytics and Artificial Intelligence in Industry 5.0 for Smart Decision-Making," in *Human-Centered Approaches in Industry 5.0: Human-Machine Interaction, Virtual Reality Training, and Customer Sentiment Analysis*, 2024, pp. 24–47, doi: 10.4018/979-8-3693-2647-3.ch002.
70. K. Kalinaki, M. Abdullatif, S. A.-K. Nasser, R. Nsubuga, and J. Kugonza, "Paving the Path to a Sustainable Digital Future With Green Cloud Computing," *Emerging Trends in Cloud Computing Analytics, Scalability, and Service Models*, pp. 44–66, Jan. 2024, doi: 10.4018/979-8-3693-0900-1.CH002.
71. T. Theodoropoulos *et al.*, "Security in Cloud-Native Services: A Survey," *Journal of Cybersecurity and Privacy*, vol. 3, no. 4, pp. 758–793, Oct. 2023, doi: 10.3390/JCP3040034.
72. E. Russo, G. Longo, M. Guerar, and A. Merlo, "Cloud-Native Application Security Training and Testing with Cyber Ranges," *Lecture Notes in Networks and Systems*, vol. 841 LNNS, pp. 205–216, 2023, doi: 10.1007/978-3-031-48590-9_20.
73. A. Moawad, A. I. Ebada, A. A. El-Harby, and A. M. Al-Zoghby, "An Automatic Artificial Intelligence System for Malware Detection," *Automated Secure Computing for Next-Generation Systems*, pp. 115–138, Jan. 2024, doi: 10.1002/9781394213948.CH6.
74. B. Yamany, M. S. Elsayed, A. D. Jurcut, N. Abdelbaki, and M. A. Azer, "A Holistic Approach to Ransomware Classification: Leveraging Static and Dynamic Analysis with Visualization," *Information*, vol. 15, no. 1, p. 46, Jan. 2024, doi: 10.3390/INFO15010046.
75. M. Janovská, "Tackling Cybersecurity Threats to the EU Space Programme: Regional and International Cooperation," Jun. 2023, Accessed: Jan. 24, 2024. [Online]. Available: https://dspace.cuni.cz/handle/20.500.11956/182883
76. J. Billow, "No Country Is an Island: Embracing International Law Enforcement Cooperation to Reduce the Impact of Cybercrime," *Journal of Cyber Policy*, pp. 1–10, Aug. 2023, doi: 10.1080/23738871.2023.2245417.
77. T. Hitchens and N. Goren, "International Cybersecurity Information Sharing Agreements on JSTOR." Accessed: Jan. 24, 2024. [Online]. Available: https://www.jstor.org/stable/resrep20426?seq=1
78. A. D. Givens and N. E. Busch, "Realizing the Promise of Public-Private Partnerships in U.S. Critical Infrastructure Protection," *International Journal of Critical Infrastructure Protection*, vol. 6, no. 1, pp. 39–50, Mar. 2013, doi: 10.1016/J.IJCIP.2013.02.002.
79. G. Ampratwum, V. W. Y. Tam, and R. Osei-Kyei, "Critical Analysis of Risks Factors in Using Public-Private Partnership in Building Critical Infrastructure Resilience: A Systematic Review," *Construction Innovation*, vol. 23, no. 2, pp. 360–382, Feb. 2023, doi: 10.1108/CI-10-2021-0182.
80. E. Ilbiz and C. Kaunert, "Cybercrime, Public-Private Partnership and Europol," *Advanced Sciences and Technologies for Security Applications*, pp. 13–28, 2023, doi: 10.1007/978-3-031-20274-2_2.
81. R. Leszczyna, T. Wallis, and M. R. Wróbel, "Developing Novel Solutions to Realise the European Energy – Information Sharing & Analysis Centre," *Decision Support Systems*, vol. 122, p. 113067, Jul. 2019, doi: 10.1016/J.DSS.2019.05.007.
82. L. F. Ilca, O. P. Lucian, and T. C. Balan, "Enhancing Cyber-Resilience for Small and Medium-Sized Organizations with Prescriptive Malware Analysis, Detection and Response," *Sensors*, vol. 23, no. 15, p. 6757, Jul. 2023, doi: 10.3390/S23156757.
83. S. Saeed, S. A. Suayyid, M. S. Al-Ghamdi, H. Al-Muhaisen, and A. M. Almuhaideb, "A Systematic Literature Review on Cyber Threat Intelligence for Organizational Cybersecurity Resilience," *Sensors*, vol. 23, no. 16, p. 7273, Aug. 2023, doi: 10.3390/S23167273.
84. J. Dykstra, L. A. Gordon, M. P. Loeb, and L. Zhou, "Maximizing the Benefits from Sharing Cyber Threat Intelligence by Government Agencies and Departments," *Journal of Cybersecurity*, vol. 9, no. 1, Jan. 2023, doi: 10.1093/cybsec/tyad003.
85. N. Sun *et al.*, "Cyber Threat Intelligence Mining for Proactive Cybersecurity Defense: A Survey and New Perspectives," *IEEE Communications Surveys and Tutorials*, vol. 25, no. 3, pp. 1748–1774, 2023, doi: 10.1109/COMST.2023.3273282.
86. S. Bıçakcı and A. G. Evren, "Responding Cyber-Attacks and Managing Cyber Security Crises in Critical Infrastructures: A Sociotechnical Perspective," in *Management and Engineering of Critical Infrastructures*, Elsevier, 2024, pp. 125–151, doi: 10.1016/B978-0-323-99330-2.00006-4.

87. C. M. Rangu, L. Badea, M. C. Scheau, L. Găbudeanu, I. Panait, and V. Radu, "Cyber Insurance Risk Analysis Framework Considerations," *Journal of Risk Finance*, vol. ahead-of-print, no. ahead-of-print, 2024, doi: 10.1108/JRF-10-2023-0245.
88. R. Corbett-Wilkins *et al.*, "Cyber Risk and Insurance," *The Global Insurance Market and Change: Emerging Technologies, Risks and Legal Challenges*, pp. 286–332, Jan. 2023, doi: 10.4324/978100331 9054-11.
89. J. S. Shyam Mohan, M. Thirunavukkarasu, N. Kumaran, and D. Thamaraiselvi, "Deep Learning with Blockchain Based Cyber Security Threat Intelligence and Situational Awareness System for Intrusion Alert Prediction," *Sustainable Computing: Informatics and Systems*, p. 100955, Jan. 2024, doi: 10.1016/J. SUSCOM.2023.100955.
90. P. M. Datta and T. Acton, "Ransomware and Costa Rica's National Emergency: A Defense Framework and Teaching Case," *Journal of Information Technology Teaching Cases*, 2022, doi: 10.1177/ 20438869221149042.
91. J. Keary, "Rebuffing Russian Ransomware: How the United States Should Use the Colonial Pipeline and JBS USA Hackings as a Defense Guide for Ransomware," 2022.
92. P. M. Datta and T. Acton, "From Disruption to Ransomware: Lessons from Hackers," vol. 13, no. 2, pp. 182–192, Jun. 2022, doi: 10.1177/20438869221110246.
93. T. B. Slayton, "Ransomware: The Virus Attacking the Healthcare Industry," *Journal of Legal Medicine*, vol. 38, no. 2, pp. 287–311, Apr. 2018, doi: 10.1080/01947648.2018.1473186.

AUTHOR BIOGRAPHY

Kassim Kalinaki (MIEEE) is a computer science researcher, technologist, and educator with more than ten years of experience in the industry and academia. He received his diploma in computer engineering from Kyambogo University, BSc in computer science and engineering, and MSc in computer science and engineering from Bangladesh's Islamic University of Technology (IUT). Since 2014, He has lectured at the Islamic University in Uganda (IUIU), where he most recently served as the head of the Department of Computer Science (2019–2022). He's been pursuing his PhD in computer science at the School of Digital Science (SDS) at Universiti Brunei Darussalam (UBD) since January 2022. He is slated to complete it in December 2024 and graduate in August 2025. He's the founder and principal investigator of Borderline Research Laboratory (BRLab). His research areas include ecological informatics, data analytics, computer vision, ML/DL, digital image processing, cybersecurity, healthcare informatics, remote sensing, and educational technologies. He has authored and co-authored several published peer-reviewed articles in renowned journals and publishers, including Springer, Elsevier, Taylor & Francis, IGI Global, Emerald, and IEEE.

8 Ransomware Prevention Strategies

Building Robust Cyber Defenses

Taskeed Jabid, Mohammad Rifat Ahmmad Rashid, Md. Hasanul Ferdaus, Md. Sawkat Ali, Mohammad Manzurul Islam, Mahamudul Hasan, Rashedul Amin Tuhin, and Maheen Islam

8.1 INTRODUCTION

8.1.1 Overview of Ransomware Threat

In today's digital age, the increase in cyber threats significantly undermines the security of information systems across the globe. Ransomware stands out as a major concern. This malware encrypts the victim's files, making them unreachable unless a ransom is paid. Over time, ransomware has developed from simple screen blocking to complex, targeted assaults that use advanced encryption techniques [1]. Ransomware doesn't just encrypt data; it often involves a complex strategy that includes stealing sensitive information and threatening to expose it publicly, increasing its coercive power over the victims [2]. The impact of ransomware transcends mere financial losses; it destabilizes organizations, erodes public trust, and can potentially cripple critical infrastructure [3]. In recent years, ransomware campaigns have exhibited an alarming trend of precision and sophistication, with adversaries meticulously selecting their targets to maximize profit and impact. These cybercriminal syndicates operate with business-like efficiency, utilizing ransomware-as-a-service models and exploiting the dark web's anonymity to orchestrate their attacks [4].

Ransomware attacks are widespread, impacting everyone, from individual users to large businesses and government bodies. These attacks lead to various negative outcomes, including immediate financial loss, operational disruption, damage to reputation, and sometimes permanent data loss. The use of cryptocurrencies in these attacks provides attackers with a secure, anonymous way to receive payments, making it harder for authorities to track and stop them [5]. To counter the rising threat of ransomware, it's critical to adopt a comprehensive, multi-layered defense approach. This strategy should not only incorporate technological solutions but also focus heavily on promoting awareness, readiness, and resilience. Researchers, cybersecurity experts, and policymakers need to work together to create an environment inherently resilient to ransomware. This includes implementing advanced cybersecurity measures, fostering a culture of cybersecurity awareness, and establishing strict regulations to deter and reduce the effects of these cyber-attacks.

8.1.2 Significance of Robust Cyber Defenses

Robust cyber defenses stand not only as a technological necessity but also as a foundational element of organizational resilience and national security. The critical need for well-structured cyber defenses is especially pronounced against the backdrop of the evolving ransomware threat landscape, a realm where adversaries are relentlessly innovating to exploit information system vulnerabilities.

DOI: 10.1201/9781003469506-11

The importance of robust cyber defenses is multi-dimensional, showcasing a comprehensive strategy for mitigating the ransomware menace. Initially, strong defenses serve as a primary deterrent against ransomware attacks. Incorporating sophisticated threat detection and response systems enables organizations to spot potential threats early, reducing the likelihood of successful ransomware penetration [6]. The complexity of ransomware attacks, as detailed in extensive studies on their progression and counterstrategies, calls for a defense blueprint that not only protects traditional computing devices but also extends to mobile units and IoT/CPS frameworks [7].

Furthermore, cyber defenses play a crucial role in maintaining the integrity and accessibility of vital data. Characteristically, ransomware attacks aim to disrupt access to critical data, leading to operational standstills and financial demands. A defense strategy built on regular data backups, encryption, and stringent access controls can substantially mitigate the impact of these attacks, ensuring continuous business operations and the protection of sensitive data [1]. Beyond technical measures, the relevance of robust cyber defenses is far-reaching. In times where cyber threats pose significant risks to national security, economic stability, and public well-being, the role of cyber defenses in cultivating trust and assurance is paramount. Organizations fortified with robust cyber defenses are not only better shielded but also viewed as committed to cybersecurity, thereby boosting their reputation and earning stakeholder trust [8].

8.2 UNDERSTANDING RANSOMWARE

8.2.1 Fundamentals of Ransomware

Ransomware, a portmanteau of 'ransom' and 'software', represents a form of malicious software ingeniously crafted to restrict access to a computer system or encrypt files until a specified sum of money, termed 'ransom', is paid. This cyber threat has progressively evolved from basic lockout protocols to complex algorithms that utilize encryption to make data inaccessible, as highlighted by Kok et al. [9]. Grasping the essential principles of ransomware is fundamental for formulating effective strategies to combat this escalating menace. Intrinsically, ransomware capitalizes on vulnerabilities in software architectures or human psychology to penetrate systems, as discussed by Mansfield-Devine [10]. Once inside, it employs various tactics to fulfill its extortionate objectives. The two principal categories of ransomware, Crypto Ransomware and Locker Ransomware, are defined by their methods of operation, with Crypto Ransomware encrypting crucial system files and Locker Ransomware denying access to the operating system [11].

The lifecycle of a ransomware incursion [12] can be segmented into distinct phases:

- **Infection:** This initial phase involves the delivery of the ransomware to the target's system through several channels, such as phishing emails, malevolent advertisements, or exploitation of security loopholes.
- **Execution:** Following successful infiltration, the ransomware deploys its malicious payload. This stage may involve file encryption, alteration of file extensions, or complete system lockdown.
- **Demand:** Post-execution, the ransomware unveils a ransom note, typically outlining payment instructions and a stipulated deadline for the ransom payment.
- **Payment:** Victims may opt to pay the ransom, often in cryptocurrencies, in the hope of retrieving a decryption key.
- **Decryption:** In an ideal scenario, the victim, post-payment, acquires the decryption key and regains access to their data. However, this outcome is not guaranteed.

The trajectory of ransomware evolution has introduced more nuanced strategies, such as the double extortion scheme. In this approach, perpetrators not only encrypt the data but also threaten its public disclosure if the ransom demand is not met, thereby amplifying the pressure on the victim [13].

Furthermore, the scope of ransomware attacks has broadened, targeting not only individual users but also large-scale organizations and vital infrastructure. This expansion magnifies both the potential impact of attacks and the imperative to devise and implement robust defensive mechanisms against them [3].

8.2.2 Motivations of Ransomware Attacks

Ransomware is distinguished not only by its technical sophistication but also by the multifaceted and intricate motivations driving its perpetrators. Comprehending these motivations is pivotal in predicting potential targets and formulating robust countermeasures. While financial gain prominently stands out as the primary incentive, ransomware attacks are often motivated by a complex web of other factors.

Financial Gain: Undoubtedly, the most transparent motivation for ransomware attacks is financial profit. Cybercriminals are enticed by the significant monetary rewards from victims who are desperate to recover their critical data. The advent and anonymity of cryptocurrencies have intensified this trend, offering attackers a secure and hard-to-trace payment method, making ransomware an increasingly profitable venture for cybercriminals [14].

Data Exfiltration for Espionage or Sale: Beyond mere financial extortion, ransomware attacks serve as a mechanism for data exfiltration. Attackers covet sensitive data, from personal information to proprietary business secrets, which holds substantial value in the underground market. Such data can be exploited for espionage or sold to the highest bidder, providing attackers with an additional revenue source apart from the ransom [15].

Ideological or Political Motivation: Some ransomware attacks stem from ideological or political convictions. Perpetrators with allegiance to specific ideologies or political agendas may deploy ransomware to disrupt operations, garner attention for their cause, or compel targets into making concessions aligned with their beliefs [16].

Market Manipulation: In a sophisticated maneuver, ransomware can be used to manipulate market dynamics. Targeting key industry players can disrupt market operations, influencing stock values or creating advantageous conditions for competitors. This form of attack enables perpetrators to exploit the situation for financial or strategic benefits [17].

Disruption and Destruction: Unlike financially motivated attacks, some ransomware campaigns aim to disrupt, impair, or annihilate the target's data and infrastructure. These attacks, often orchestrated by state-sponsored entities or hacktivist groups, are designed to incapacitate critical systems, create turmoil, or camouflage more sinister cyber operations [18].

Reputation Damage: The menace of releasing sensitive data in the public domain is a potent tactic in ransomware attacks. Perpetrators may aim to damage the reputation of their targets by threatening data exposure, applying pressure not just for ransom payment but also to inflict reputational harm [10].

8.3 THE NEED FOR PREVENTION

8.3.1 Impact of Ransomware Attacks

The multifaceted impact of ransomware attacks underscores the crucial necessity for organizations to thoroughly comprehend potential repercussions and highlights the urgency for implementing preemptive defense measures. The following text explores the financial implications, reputational damage, and the legal and regulatory concerns associated with ransomware attacks.

Financial Implications:

- **Direct Costs:** The immediate financial impact of a ransomware attack not only includes the ransom payment, often demanded in cryptocurrencies, but also includes expenses related to crisis management, forensic investigation, data recovery, and system restoration. These direct costs can be substantial and pose a significant burden on the affected organization [14].
- **Indirect Costs:** Beyond the direct costs, ransomware attacks lead to operational downtime, lost productivity, deferred revenues, and the long-term costs associated with reconstructing lost or compromised data. The financial ramifications are further exacerbated by the need for organizations to invest in strengthening their cybersecurity infrastructure after the incident, to prevent future attacks [17].

Reputational Damage:

- **Loss of Trust:** Ransomware attacks can drastically diminish the trust and confidence that customers, partners, and stakeholders have in an organization. The perceived negligence or inadequacy in security measures can result in a loss of business, waning customer loyalty, and a damaged brand image, leading to long-term financial repercussions [10].
- **Public Exposure:** The risk or actual leaking of sensitive data in double extortion schemes introduces an additional layer of reputational risk. The exposure of confidential information can inflict severe damage to the organization's reputation and relationships with clients and partners, resulting in a loss of trust and potential legal consequences [12].

Legal and Regulatory Concerns:

- **Compliance Violations:** Organizations may face legal repercussions if a ransomware attack leads to a violation of data protection regulations, such as GDPR or HIPAA. Noncompliance can result in substantial fines and legal actions, adding to the financial and reputational damage [7].
- **Litigation Risks:** After a ransomware incident, organizations may face lawsuits from affected parties or shareholders, particularly if the attack is attributed to perceived negligence or a failure to comply with industry-standard cybersecurity practices. This can lead to lengthy and costly legal battles [8].
- **Regulatory Scrutiny:** Organizations often face increased scrutiny from regulators post-incident and may be required to adopt more stringent cybersecurity measures. This increased regulatory attention can add to the complexity and cost of maintaining compliance and ensuring robust cybersecurity measures are in place [19].

8.3.2 Importance of Proactive Defense Measures

The intricacy of ransomware threats underscores the need for a proactive and strategic approach to cybersecurity. By adopting comprehensive preventative measures, organizations can significantly reduce their vulnerability to these attacks and limit potential repercussions. In the following text we highlight the importance of a forward-thinking defense strategy to reinforce the digital safeguards protecting our invaluable data and systems.

Early Threat Detection:

- **Anticipatory Security Measures:** Implementing cutting-edge threat detection technologies and proactive monitoring is vital. These actions enable organizations to spot and neutralize threats early, reducing the chance for ransomware to establish itself [20].

- **Anomaly Detection:** Utilizing advanced algorithms for anomaly detection aids in spotting unusual patterns or behavior, which might indicate a brewing ransomware threat. Quick identification is key to stopping an attack in its early stages and preventing data encryption [21].

Regular System Updates and Patch Management:

- **Vulnerability Mitigation:** Consistently updating and patching software and systems closes off vulnerabilities that are frequently targeted by ransomware. Diligent patch management is essential for maintaining the security and integrity of IT ecosystems [22].
- **Continual Improvement:** As technology evolves, so do cyber threats. Cybersecurity measures must adapt accordingly. Routine updates and patches, informed by the latest in threat intelligence, ensure defenses remain robust against an ever-changing threat landscape [23].

Employee Education and Awareness:

- **Human Firewall:** Employees can serve as a formidable first line of defense. Regular training on identifying phishing attempts, safe browsing practices, and understanding how ransomware operates can transform staff into a vigilant, proactive force against threats [24].
- **Culture of Security:** Cultivating a security-focused culture ensures that cybersecurity is viewed as a collective responsibility, not just that of the IT department. A workforce attuned to security practices is an invaluable asset in preempting ransomware attacks [25].

Robust Backup and Recovery Strategy:

- **Data Resilience:** Regular, secure backups of essential data form a crucial component of a ransomware defense strategy. Access to clean backups can ensure business operations continue uninterrupted during an attack, diminishing the leverage attackers have via data encryption [26].
- **Disaster Recovery Planning:** A well-planned disaster recovery protocol not only offers a clear action plan for post-attack recovery but also instills stakeholder confidence, showcasing the organization's readiness to tackle adversities [27].

8.4 ASPECTS OF RANSOMWARE PREVENTION STRATEGIES

This section introduces the foundational elements of ransomware prevention, each serving as a vital part of the comprehensive strategy designed to counteract the ever-advancing ransomware threats. We explore the importance of user education and awareness, robust cybersecurity infrastructure, regular software updates and patch management, data backup and recovery planning, incident response planning, and testing and simulations, elucidating the critical role each plays in strengthening an organization's digital defenses. Figure 8.1 illustrates the aspects of ransomware prevention strategies. In the following sections we present a detailed overview of each of these components.

8.4.1 User Education and Awareness

8.4.1.1 Importance of Cybersecurity Training

The confrontation against ransomware encompasses not just the digital sphere but also the domain of human awareness and readiness. In the following we explore the critical importance of cybersecurity training, underlining its role in empowering individuals to recognize, resist, and effectively report potential threats, thereby converting potential weak links into pivotal bastions of the organization's cybersecurity strategy.

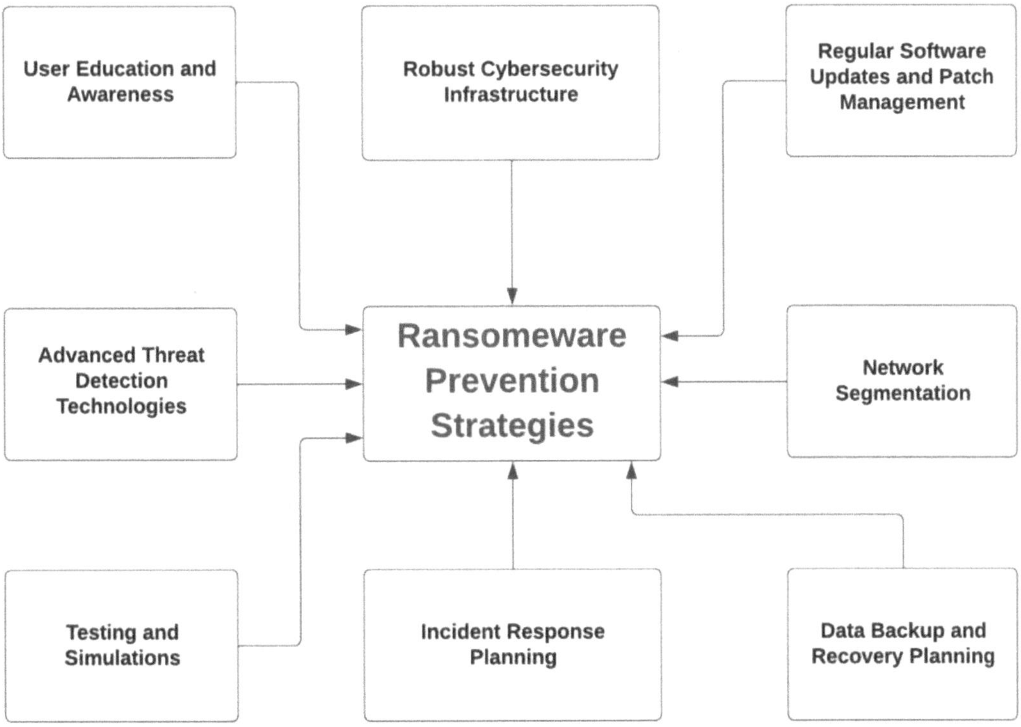

FIGURE 8.1 Aspects of ransomware prevention strategies.

Recognizing Phishing Attempts:

- **Vigilance as a Virtue:** Phishing, a preferred vector utilized by cyber adversaries to deploy ransomware, often capitalizes on human gullibility. Cybersecurity training arms individuals with the ability to identify and critically assess phishing attempts, whether manifesting as suspicious emails, dubious links, or deceptive requests for information [1].
- **Critical Evaluation:** Training nurtures a culture of critical scrutiny, prompting individuals to question the authenticity of unexpected requests or communications and verify the source's legitimacy before taking any action [3].

Secure Internet Browsing Practices:

- **Navigating Safely:** The internet, while an indispensable resource, is laden with potential hazards. Cybersecurity training instills best practices for secure browsing, encompassing the usage of HTTPS-encrypted websites, cautiousness regarding downloads from unknown sources, and judicious use of public Wi-Fi networks [11].
- **Data Protection:** Educating users about data protection principles such as utilizing robust, unique passwords, enabling two-factor authentication, and routinely updating privacy settings strengthens the defense against unauthorized access and potential data breaches [28].

Fostering a Security-Conscious Corporate Culture:

- **Collective Responsibility:** Cybersecurity transcends the IT department, representing a collective obligation. Training fosters a security-conscious culture wherein each member comprehends their role in protecting digital resources [10].

- **Proactive Reporting:** An informed workforce is more inclined to recognize and promptly report suspicious activities, facilitating swift response and containment of potential threats. Training instills a mindset of vigilance and a proactive stance toward cybersecurity within the organization [17].

8.4.1.2 Creating a Security-Conscious Culture

In the following we explore the strategies and methodologies businesses can implement to cultivate a security-conscious culture. This approach ingrains a shared sense of responsibility among all employees, reinforcing the organization's defensive fortifications against cyber threats.

Leadership Commitment and Advocacy:

- **Top-Down Approach:** The drive for a security-conscious culture should originate from the top. Leadership's visible commitment to and advocacy for cybersecurity set a precedent of seriousness and dedication, which permeate through the entire organization [1].
- **Resource Allocation:** This commitment is further exemplified by dedicating ample resources to cybersecurity initiatives, such as training programs, security tools, and recruitment of skilled personnel, accentuating the organizational dedication to a solid cybersecurity stance [3].

Continuous Education and Training:

- **Regular Training Sessions:** Given the rapid evolution of cyber threats, cybersecurity training cannot be sporadic. Ongoing, up-to-date training sessions are vital to keep the workforce informed about the latest threats, strategies, and protective measures [10].
- **Engaging Training Methods:** Training effectiveness hinges on employing engaging and interactive methods. Techniques like gamification, simulations, and real-life scenarios, especially those that align with the employees' roles, are crucial [17].

Open Communication Channels:

- **Encouraging Reporting:** It's essential for employees to feel comfortable reporting security issues or potential breaches. Establishing open, non-punitive communication channels is key for early detection and prompt action against security incidents [29].
- **Feedback Mechanism:** A feedback loop where employees can contribute ideas and voice concerns about cybersecurity practices promotes participation and continual refinement of security protocols [14].

Recognizing and Rewarding Secure Behavior:

- **Acknowledgment Programs:** Recognizing and rewarding employees for proactive security behaviors or for successfully spotting potential threats can significantly enhance morale and encourage a security-first mindset [7].
- **Security Champions:** Fostering a network of security champions across various departments can lead to peer-driven adherence to security practices, transforming cybersecurity into a collective and collaborative endeavor [1].

Policy Enforcement and Regular Audits:

- **Clear Security Policies:** Crafting clear, comprehensive, and enforceable security policies forms the bedrock of a security-conscious culture. Regularly reviewing and updating these policies ensures that they are in line with the evolving cyber threat landscape [8].

- **Regular Security Audits:** Periodic security audits and assessments are crucial for spotting potential vulnerabilities and confirming adherence to security policies [30].

8.4.2 Robust Cybersecurity Infrastructure

8.4.2.1 Network Security

It acts as the shield protecting an organization's precious digital resources from the myriad of threats that pervade the cyber landscape. In the following text, we delve into the crucial role of network security within an overarching cybersecurity strategy, emphasizing the essential roles of intrusion detection systems (IDS), firewalls, and secure network architectures in reinforcing an organization's digital defenses against unauthorized access and potential intrusions.

Intrusion Detection Systems (IDS):

- **Vigilant Monitoring:** IDS function as the vigilant guardians of network security, continuously monitoring and scrutinizing network traffic. They excel in spotting unusual patterns or anomalies that might signal a security compromise or a looming ransomware threat [21].
- **Proactive Alerting:** The potency of an IDS is not limited to detection; its real strength lies in its capacity to immediately alert network administrators of potential dangers. This proactive notification mechanism enables swift actions, ensuring that possible breaches are addressed before they evolve into significant incidents [22].

Firewalls:

- **Access Control:** Firewalls act as the custodians of network security, meticulously overseeing incoming and outgoing network traffic based on predefined security protocols. By managing access, firewalls are instrumental in deterring unauthorized entries and diminishing the risk of ransomware breaches [26].
- **Layered Defense:** Contemporary firewalls surpass conventional packet filtering by offering advanced functionalities such as stateful inspection, proxy services, and deep packet inspection. This multifaceted defense approach significantly enhances protection against the complex strategies used by cyber adversaries [27].

Secure Network Topologies:

- **Strategic Segmentation:** Adopting secure network architectures involves the thoughtful segmentation of the network into subnetworks. This not only boosts network performance but also localizes potential breaches to a specific segment, thus reducing the overall impact on the organization [24].
- **Resilience and Redundancy:** An optimally designed network architecture guarantees resilience and redundancy. It allows the network to sustain its operations amid attacks or system failures. By integrating redundancy and failover protocols, organizations can assure that their networks remain robust against disruptions, including ransomware attacks [25].

8.4.2.2 Endpoint Security

Endpoints are not just nodes in a network; they are crucial frontlines in the battle against cyber threats, especially ransomware. Securing these endpoints is vital as they often serve as the primary targets for attacks. In the following we explore the significance of endpoint security within a holistic cybersecurity strategy, emphasizing the deployment of antivirus solutions, the integration of Endpoint Detection and Response (EDR) systems, and the adoption of robust endpoint security practices to fortify defenses against pervasive cyber threats.

Antivirus Software:

- **Comprehensive Protection:** Antivirus software forms the fundamental layer of endpoint defense. It possesses the capability to detect, isolate, and eliminate malicious software, offering a broad spectrum of protection against various malware types, including ransomware [31].
- **Continuous Updates and Heuristics:** The effectiveness of antivirus solutions depends on their capacity to preempt emerging threats. Regular updates to virus signatures and heuristic analyses enable these solutions to identify novel and evolving malware forms, ensuring consistent endpoint protection against the latest threats [9].

Endpoint Detection and Response (EDR) Systems:

- **Real-time Monitoring and Response:** EDR systems mark a significant advancement in endpoint security, providing instant monitoring and automated response mechanisms. By continuously scrutinizing endpoint data, EDR systems can pinpoint suspicious activities that may signal a ransomware intrusion, initiating swift counteractions to mitigate the threat [18].
- **Forensic Capabilities:** EDR systems offer more than just prevention and reaction; they also afford extensive forensic capabilities. In the aftermath of a security incident, EDR systems yield critical insights into attack vectors, methodologies, and the extent of the impact, thereby guiding strategic decisions and enhancing subsequent defense measures [21].

Additional Endpoint Security Measures:

- **Regular Patching and Updates:** Consistently updating operating systems and applications is crucial. Routine patches and upgrades seal off security gaps and diminish the vulnerabilities that ransomware and other malicious entities might exploit [32].
- **Application Whitelisting:** By permitting only pre-authorized and verified applications to execute on endpoints, application whitelisting notably curtails the risk of ransomware and other malevolent programs infiltrating the system [22].
- **Privilege Management:** Limiting user privileges on endpoints to the bare minimum necessary can obstruct ransomware from obtaining the access it requires to encrypt files or disseminate across the network [33].

8.4.3 Regular Software Updates and Patch Management

8.4.3.1 Significance of Timely Updates

The importance of maintaining robust defenses through prompt software updates and diligent patch management is paramount. In the following text we shed the light on the crucial role that current software plays in blocking potential entry points for ransomware attacks. It discusses methods for detecting vulnerabilities and outlines best practices for effective patch implementation.

Closing the Window of Opportunity:

- **Mitigating Exploits:** Cyber adversaries tirelessly exploit software vulnerabilities to launch ransomware attacks. Timely updates and patches address these weak spots, significantly narrowing the window of opportunity for attackers to exploit known vulnerabilities [1].
- **Proactive Protection:** Regular updates not only fix known vulnerabilities but also often bolster the software's inherent security features, offering proactive defense against potential threats in the future [2].

Identification of Vulnerabilities:

- **Vulnerability Scanning:** Using vulnerability scanning tools is crucial in identifying unpatched software and potential security gaps. These tools provide comprehensive insights into the organization's security stance, spotlighting areas that require urgent attention [3].
- **Security Assessments:** Conducting consistent security assessments, including penetration tests and risk analyses, help gain a deeper understanding of the organization's vulnerabilities. This understanding aids in prioritizing and scheduling updates effectively [4].

Best Practices for Patch Deployment:

- **Prioritization and Testing:** Considering the wide range of software used within an organization, it's essential to prioritize patches for critical systems and test them before deployment to ensure stability and minimal disruption to business operations [5].
- **Automated Patch Management:** Deploying automated patch management systems streamlines the update process, ensuring consistent application of updates. Automation lessens the burden on IT staff and reduces human error, guaranteeing that no crucial system remains unpatched [34].
- **Patch Policy and Compliance:** Creating a clear patch policy that outlines responsibilities, timelines, and procedures for updates is crucial. Regular compliance checks ensure adherence to the patch policy, preserving the organization's security posture [11].

8.4.3.2 Automated Patching Solutions

The significance of automation in upholding robust cybersecurity measures cannot be overstated. Automated patching solutions stand out not just as tools but as strategic components in fortifying cybersecurity measures. In the following text, we explore the benefits of automated patching technologies, emphasizing their role in bolstering security and optimizing the patch management process, thereby reinforcing an organization's defense against the diverse threats presented by ransomware.

Streamlining Patch Management:

- **Efficiency and Consistency:** Automated patching solutions provide efficient and consistent delivery of updates across an organization's comprehensive software landscape. By reducing manual oversight for each update, these solutions ensure uniform protection across all systems, minimizing the chance of oversight or human error [2].
- **Timely Deployment:** The rapid deployment of patches is critical in reducing the risk of exploitation by cyber adversaries. Automated solutions guarantee that patches are applied promptly after release, drastically narrowing the window of vulnerability from the discovery of a security flaw to its resolution [5].

Scalability and Flexibility:

- **Adapting to Organizational Growth:** As organizations expand, the complexity of their software environments also grows. Automated patching solutions are inherently scalable, proficiently managing an increasing number of endpoints and software applications without compromising the speed or consistency of patch deployment [11].
- **Customizable Patching Policies:** Automated systems offer the capability to develop customizable patching policies that align with an organization's specific requirements, risk profile, and operational necessities, ensuring that critical systems are prioritized in patching schedules without interrupting key operations [15].

Reduced Operational Burden:

- **Resource Optimization:** Automation in routine patch deployment frees IT personnel from the labor-intensive process of manual patching. This liberation allows them to dedicate their skills to more strategic tasks that significantly contribute to the organization's cybersecurity stance [35].
- **Minimized Downtime:** Automated patching solutions can be set to deploy updates during non-business hours, minimizing downtime and ensuring that business operations are not interrupted by maintenance processes [10].

Compliance and Reporting:

- **Regulatory Compliance:** Numerous industries are subject to strict regulatory demands regarding data protection and cybersecurity. Automated patching solutions assist in meeting compliance by ensuring that all systems are updated with the latest security patches, a crucial requirement in many regulatory frameworks [14].
- **Comprehensive Reporting:** Automated systems provide detailed logs and reports of patching activities, delivering valuable insights into the organization's patching status and history. This not only is beneficial for audit trails but also aids informed decision-making in cybersecurity strategies [7].

8.4.4 Data Backup and Recovery

8.4.4.1 Implementing Regular Backup Protocols

Establishing regular backup protocols is fundamental, serving as a vital safeguard for data resilience. In the following we discuss the intricacies of implementing regular backup routines, emphasizing the importance of secure and current backups, and examine the considerations for offsite and cloud-based backup solutions. It highlights how a well-planned backup strategy enhances an organization's ability to recover swiftly and maintain continuity amid cyber challenges.

Establishing a Regular Backup Schedule:

- **Frequency and Regularity:** Setting up a consistent backup schedule is crucial. The backup frequency should correspond with the organization's data significance and operational requirements, ensuring recent data states are recoverable with minimal loss [34].
- **Automated Backup Processes:** Utilizing automated backup systems minimizes human error and guarantees regular backups. Automation ensures consistent adherence to the backup timetable, maintaining data resilience without burdening operational resources [35].

Diversification of Backup Solutions:

- **Offsite Backups:** Offsite backups add an extra security layer by storing data in a physically separate location. This geographical diversification reduces risks related to local calamities or security breaches, guaranteeing intact and retrievable data [10].
- **Cloud-Based Backups:** Cloud-based backup services provide scalability, adaptability, and accessibility. It's crucial to assess the cloud provider's security measures and compliance standards, ensuring data encryption during transfer and storage, and confirming the provider's adherence to sector-specific regulations [6].

Data Backup Integrity and Security:

- **Encryption and Access Control:** Encrypting backups and implementing strict access controls are vital for protecting backup data. These precautions prevent unauthorized access, ensuring data confidentiality and integrity, even in a breach scenario [1].
- **Regular Testing of Backups:** Testing backup integrity routinely is essential. This confirms backup system reliability and ensures the organization is ready for a quick and efficient recovery process. Regular tests help identify and address potential issues in the backup strategy promptly [30].

Backup Policy and Documentation:

- **Comprehensive Backup Policy:** Crafting an extensive backup policy that outlines procedures, schedules, responsibilities, and protocols is imperative. This policy should be periodically revisited and revised to stay in sync with changes in the IT infrastructure and organizational requirements [16].
- **Clear Documentation and Training:** Proper documentation of backup processes and protocols ensures consistency in execution. Training relevant staff in backup and recovery procedures cultivates a culture of readiness and equips the organization to respond adeptly post-ransomware attack [20].

8.4.4.2 Developing a Comprehensive Recovery Plan

Navigating the complexities of ransomware defense requires more than just strong backups; it necessitates a comprehensive recovery plan that orchestrates a swift, coordinated, and effective response to incidents. In the following we focus on developing a recovery plan that serves as a strategic blueprint, ensuring prompt recovery, minimizing downtime, and limiting data loss after a ransomware attack.

Identification of Critical Assets and Functions:

- **Asset Prioritization:** Identify and prioritize critical assets and business functions. Recognizing which systems, data, and services are vital for operational continuity is crucial for crafting a recovery plan that aligns with business priorities [2].
- **Impact Analysis:** Conduct a business impact analysis to understand the potential consequences of downtime. This analysis guides the recovery priorities and objectives [4].

Clear Recovery Objectives:

- **Recovery Time Objectives (RTO):** Define clear RTOs to determine the acceptable timeframe for restoring operations post-incident. Set these objectives based on each asset's and function's criticality, ensuring swift restoration of the most essential operations [34].
- **Recovery Point Objectives (RPOs):** Establish RPOs to dictate the maximum tolerable age of files that must be recovered from backups to resume operations. RPOs guide backup frequency and are key in minimizing data loss [28].

Recovery Team and Responsibilities:

- **Designated Recovery Team:** Assemble a dedicated recovery team with clear roles and responsibilities. Ensure each member knows their tasks during recovery, fostering a coordinated and efficient response [35].
- **Training and Simulations:** Regularly train and conduct simulation exercises to prepare the recovery team. Simulations help identify and rectify potential issues in the recovery plan [10].

Communication Plan:

- **Internal Communication:** Develop a communication plan to outline information dissemination among team members, stakeholders, and employees during and post a ransomware incident. Effective communication reduces confusion and streamlines the recovery process [6].
- **External Communication:** Prepare for external communication with clients, partners, and the media if necessary. Prompt and transparent communication can significantly lessen reputational damage [1].

Regular Review and Updates:

- **Plan Maintenance:** Continually review and update the recovery plan to align with the evolving IT landscape, organizational structure, and business goals. This ensures the plan's relevance and efficacy [30].
- **Lessons Learned:** Integrate lessons learned from recovery exercises and real incidents into the recovery plan. Emphasizing continuous improvement ensures that the recovery strategy adapts to new threats and organizational shifts [16].

8.4.5 Network Segmentation

8.4.5.1 Introduction to Network Segmentation

Transforming a unified network structure into smaller, rigorously isolated segments is called network segmentation. This intentional compartmentalization extends beyond structural reconfiguration; it embodies a proactive approach, a deliberate strategy aimed at bolstering security, refining control, and constructing formidable barriers against a multitude of cyber threats. In the following we introduce the concept of network segmentation, shedding light on its significance in strengthening cybersecurity defenses, reducing breach impacts, hindering lateral threat propagation, and preserving sensitive data from unauthorized access.

Principle of Least Privilege:

- **Minimized Access:** Network segmentation is underpinned by the principle of least privilege, ensuring that each segment and its components possess only the access essential for their operational roles. This approach substantially curtails the attack surface, limiting the potential ramifications of a breach [34].
- **Restricting Lateral Movement:** By dividing the network, organizations can effectively contain and isolate incidents, impeding attackers' lateral movements. This confinement is pivotal in curbing the proliferation of threats and associated damages [28].

Enhanced Security and Control:

- **Targeted Security Measures:** Network segmentation enables the implementation of customized security measures for individual segments. Areas housing sensitive data can be reinforced with extra security layers, guaranteeing that critical assets receive paramount protection [35].
- **Improved Monitoring and Detection:** Segmented networks facilitate more efficient monitoring and anomaly detection. By focusing surveillance on individual segments, security teams can more swiftly pinpoint and address suspicious activities [10].

Compliance and Data Protection:

- **Regulatory Compliance:** For entities bound by regulatory mandates, network segmentation aids in achieving compliance by ensuring sensitive information, like personal or financial data, is segregated and safeguarded as per the required standards [6].

- **Data Integrity and Confidentiality:** Segregating networks aids in protecting data integrity and confidentiality, diminishing the risk of unauthorized access and data breaches [1].

Operational Efficiency and Recovery:

- **Reduced Network Congestion:** Segmentation contributes to operational efficiencies by alleviating network congestion. Directing network traffic to pertinent segments ensures smoother operations and can boost the performance of critical systems [30].
- **Streamlined Recovery Efforts:** In instances of breaches or system failures, network segmentation simplifies the recovery process. Isolated segments can be individually addressed and reinstated, preventing an all-encompassing shutdown and enabling a more agile recovery [16].

8.4.5.2 Limiting Lateral Movement

Constraining the lateral progression of threats across an enterprise's network is a critical consideration. Network segmentation serves as a strategic fortification, a deliberate configuration that partitions the network, thereby curtailing the unrestrained proliferation of ransomware and other cyber threats. In the following text we explore the deployment of role-based access controls (RBAC) and micro-segmentation techniques, demonstrating their effectiveness in containing and mitigating threats, ensuring that the extent of any breach is limited, and preserving the security of the digital ecosystem.

Role-Based Access Control (RBAC):

- **Principle of Least Privilege:** RBAC operates on the principle of least privilege, guaranteeing that individuals or entities within the organization access only resources essential for their roles. This detailed control is crucial in minimizing the attack surface and decreasing the likelihood of unauthorized access or escalation [34].
- **Dynamic Access Management:** RBAC's dynamic management of access based on roles allows it to adjust to organizational shifts, ensuring that access rights consistently correspond with current roles and responsibilities. This flexibility is vital in upholding a secure and compliant access framework, particularly in the ever-changing environment of modern enterprises [28].

Micro-Segmentation:

- **Fine-Grained Isolation:** Micro-segmentation extends network segmentation to a more refined level, segregating workloads within the same network segment. This nuanced approach ensures that even if a segment is compromised, the breach is confined within a narrowly defined area, significantly reducing the impact range [35].
- **Context-Aware Security Policies:** Micro-segmentation facilitates the establishment of context-aware security policies specifically tailored to each workload or application's unique attributes. These policies, dynamically enforceable, offer robust security that adapts to the shifting context and threat landscape [10].

Containing and Mitigating Threats:

- **Rapid Response to Incidents:** The compartmentalized structure of a segmented network enables quick response and containment of incidents. In the case of a breach, security teams can immediately isolate affected segments, halting the lateral spread of the threat and allowing for concentrated remediation efforts [6].
- **Resilience against Attack Propagation:** By obstructing lateral movement, network segmentation and micro-segmentation not only localize the immediate threat but also enhance

the network's resilience against attack spread, ensuring the broader network's integrity remains uncompromised [1].

Best Practices for Implementation:

- **Continuous Monitoring and Adaptation:** Effective RBAC and micro-segmentation implementation demands ongoing monitoring and adaptation to ensure access controls and segmentation policies continue to counter new threats and resonate with the evolving business landscape [30].
- **Stakeholder Collaboration:** Successful deployment requires cooperation among various stakeholders, including IT, security, and business units. This collective approach ensures that segmentation strategies align with business goals and operational realities, promoting a security-aware organizational ethos [16].

8.4.5.3 Micro-Segmentation Strategies

Micro-segmentation strategic innovation plays a crucial role in establishing resilient digital strongholds within an organization's network infrastructure, each designed to robustly safeguard its domain against unauthorized access and diminish the impact of ransomware attacks. In the following text we explore the detailed process of crafting and deploying micro-segmentation strategies, focusing on creating isolated zones meticulously tailored to the specific needs and risk profiles of different network segments.

Defining Micro-Segmentation Boundaries:

- **Understanding Workload Characteristics:** The first step in micro-segmentation is a thorough analysis of network workloads. Comprehending the nature, needs, and interdependencies of these workloads is vital for determining effective segmentation strategies [28].
- **Risk-Based Segmentation:** Segment boundaries should be determined based on the risk profile of various workloads. Workloads that are highly sensitive or critical should be isolated in segments with stringent security protocols, thereby minimizing potential breach impacts [10].

Developing Segmentation Policies:

- **Context-Specific Policies:** Micro-segmentation enables the formulation of context-specific policies, carefully designed to meet the unique security demands of each segment. These policies manage aspects like access controls, communication protocols, and traffic flow, ensuring customized security measures [6].
- **Dynamic Policy Enforcement:** Policies within a micro-segmented network should be dynamic and adaptable to changes in the operational environment or threat landscape. This adaptability ensures ongoing robustness and relevance of security measures [1].

Implementing Security Controls:

- **Application of Granular Controls:** Micro-segmentation facilitates the application of granular security controls at the individual workload or application level. These controls, including firewall rules, intrusion detection systems, and access control lists, offer a layered defense approach [30].
- **Integration with Existing Security Infrastructure:** The micro-segmentation strategy should integrate seamlessly with the organization's prevailing security infrastructure.

This harmonization strengthens overall security and maximizes the effectiveness of the deployed controls [16].

Monitoring and Managing Segments:

- **Continuous Monitoring:** Persistent monitoring of micro-segments is crucial for the early detection of unusual activities or potential security breaches. Sophisticated monitoring tools can provide insights in real-time, allowing for rapid threat response [20].
- **Regular Policy Review and Updates:** Policies guiding micro-segments should be consistently reviewed and updated to align with the organization's evolving security requirements. Regular audits and assessments help pinpoint areas needing improvement or adjustment [9].

Training and Awareness:

- **Stakeholder Involvement:** Effective implementation of micro-segmentation necessitates the engagement and awareness of all stakeholders, including IT personnel, security teams, and end-users. Training initiatives should ensure everyone comprehends the significance of micro-segmentation and adheres to the established policies and guidelines [18].
- **Cultivating a Security-Centric Culture:** Micro-segmentation reaches its full potential when embedded in a broader security-centric culture within the organization. Promoting such a culture ensures that security considerations are integral to all operational activities and decisions [21].

8.5 ADVANCED THREAT DETECTION TECHNOLOGIES

8.5.1 Behavioral Analytics

Conventional detection methods often prove insufficient. Behavioral analytics, empowered by advancements in machine learning, stands as a pivotal tool in the cybersecurity arsenal. In the following text we delve into the transformative role of behavioral analytics in bolstering threat detection, emphasizing its proficiency in pinpointing anomalies in user behavior that could signal impending ransomware attacks.

Understanding Behavioral Analytics:

- **Pattern Recognition and Anomaly Detection:** Behavioral analytics involves examining data patterns to establish normal user behaviors and identify deviations. By setting a baseline of regular activities, the system can detect anomalies that might signal a security threat, including potential ransomware activities [6].
- **Leveraging Machine Learning:** Machine learning algorithms are central to behavioral analytics, allowing the system to learn from data, adapt to evolving patterns, and refine its accuracy. This continuous learning enhances the system's capability to identify subtle or emerging threats that traditional, signature-based detection systems may overlook [1].

Application in Threat Detection:

- **Early Detection of Ransomware:** Behavioral analytics can pinpoint early indicators of ransomware, such as unusual file access rates, atypical data encryption patterns, and irregular network traffic. Early detection enables the system to raise alerts and activate preemptive actions [30].

- **Reducing False Positives:** Behavioral analytics' precision in understanding user patterns and contexts helps diminish false positives, allowing security teams to concentrate on genuine threats without being inundated by false alarms [16].

Integration with Security Infrastructure:

- **Holistic Security Approach:** Behavioral analytics should integrate with the broader security infrastructure, synergizing with other security measures like firewalls, intrusion detection systems, and endpoint protection solutions. This comprehensive approach fortifies the overall security stance [20].
- **Actionable Insights for Response:** Beyond mere detection, behavioral analytics offers actionable insights that can guide an organization's response strategy. Detailed information about the anomaly can dictate the appropriate remediation steps, ensuring a quick and effective resolution [9].

Challenges and Considerations:

- **Data Privacy and Compliance:** Implementing behavioral analytics requires handling and analyzing sensitive user data. It's imperative to ensure compliance with data protection regulations and maintain user privacy [18].
- **Continuous Tuning and Oversight:** Although machine learning models in behavioral analytics adapt over time, they necessitate ongoing tuning and human supervision to stay effective and accurate. Regular reviews and updates are essential for the system to evolve in accordance with the shifting threat environment and organizational dynamics [21].

8.5.2 Threat Intelligence Integration

Threat intelligence stands as a linchpin in this context, offering insights that guide an organization through the complexities of cyber threats. Integrating threat intelligence into cybersecurity strategies transforms organizations from reactive entities to proactive defenders. In the following text we highlight the integration of threat intelligence, emphasizing its role in predicting and neutralizing emerging ransomware threats and strengthening an organization's cyber defenses.

Understanding Threat Intelligence:

- **Informed Cybersecurity Decisions:** Threat intelligence encompasses the gathering, analysis, and distribution of information about current and emerging threats. This knowledge enables organizations to make informed decisions, customize their defense mechanisms, and anticipate potential attack vectors [10].
- **Comprehensive Threat Landscape:** Effective threat intelligence provides an extensive overview of the threat environment, including adversaries' tactics, techniques, and procedures (TTPs), indicators of compromise (IoCs), and contextual insights into attackers' motives and capabilities [6].

Integration into Cybersecurity Strategies:

- **Dynamic Threat Feeds:** Integrating real-time threat feeds into security systems ensures that organizations remain updated with the latest threat intelligence. This timely information can activate alerts and empower automated defenses to counteract new threats swiftly [1].

- **Customized Security Measures:** Leveraging insights from threat intelligence allows organizations to tailor their security measures to confront specific threats or vulnerabilities. Adapting security controls to match the organization's distinct risk profile and threat landscape guarantees more effective protection [30].

Enhancing Predictive Capabilities:

- **Anticipating Attack Patterns**: Threat intelligence enables organizations to foresee potential attack patterns, including novel ransomware strategies. Understanding adversaries' methodologies allows organizations to proactively fine-tune their defense mechanisms, potentially thwarting attacks before they occur [16].
- **Behavioral Profiling of Adversaries:** Analyzing threat intelligence aids organizations in profiling cyber adversaries' behavior. This profiling assists in predicting likely targets, methods, and timings of attacks, fostering a preemptive security stance [20].

Collaboration and Information Sharing:

- **Collective Defense:** Collaboration and information sharing among organizations and cybersecurity communities are integral to threat intelligence. Exchanging insights and experiences regarding threats enhances collective defense, bolstering the security stance of all involved parties [9].
- **Participation in Threat Intelligence Platforms:** Active participation in threat intelligence platforms and communities grants organizations access to a wider array of knowledge and resources. These platforms act as hubs for sharing information, best practices, and strategies to counter emerging threats [21].

Continuous Learning and Adaptation:

- **Adaptive Security Infrastructure:** Incorporating threat intelligence calls for an adaptable security infrastructure that evolves with the shifting threat landscape. Continual learning from threat intelligence feeds should inform routine adjustments and refinements to security protocols [18].
- **Training and Awareness:** Embedding threat intelligence into training initiatives ensures that the organization's personnel stay informed about the latest threats and comprehend effective response strategies. A knowledgeable workforce is a vital component of the organization's proactive defense approach [21].

8.6 INCIDENT RESPONSE PLANNING

8.6.1 Developing an Incident Response Team

Establishing an incident response team (IRT) is a strategic necessity, arming organizations with specialized skills needed to tackle ransomware attacks effectively. Creating this team goes beyond merely assembling personnel; it involves orchestrating a blend of expertise, roles, and responsibilities to form a cohesive unit ready to deliver a coordinated and impactful response to cyber incidents. In the following text we outline the structure of the IRT, highlighting the composition, distinct roles, and the collective duties that characterize the team's operational framework.

Team Composition and Structure:

- **Cross-Functional Expertise:** A proficient IRT encompasses a spectrum of expertise, comprising members from IT, cybersecurity, legal, public relations, and human resources. This multidisciplinary approach ensures that the team is equipped to handle technical, legal, communicative, and personnel-related aspects of incident management [20].

- **Designated Leadership:** The team should be helmed by an incident response manager, charged with the activation and coordination of the team and the effective execution of the response plan [9].

Roles and Responsibilities:

- **Incident Response Manager:** This role entails overseeing the IRT, ensuring rapid activation, and ensuring seamless coordination. The manager is pivotal in decision-making, resource distribution, and liaising with upper management [18].
- **Technical Specialists:** These experts are tasked with identifying the breach, containing the threat, eradicating the ransomware, and reinstating systems. They bring profound knowledge in cybersecurity, forensics, and IT infrastructure [21].
- **Legal Advisor:** This individual provides guidance on legal proceedings during and post-incident, ensuring adherence to data protection regulations and advising on disclosure and reporting requirements [32].
- **Communications Coordinator:** Tasked with managing communications internally and externally, this coordinator ensures that all parties are informed promptly and accurately [22].
- **Human Resources Representative:** Focusing on the incident's human aspect, they address the impact on staff and ensure compliance with the organization's policies during the response phase [33].

Training and Preparedness:

- **Regular Training and Simulations:** IRT members should engage in consistent training and simulated cyber-attack scenarios. This ensures role proficiency and team cohesion in high-pressure situations [23].
- **Continuous Improvement:** Post-incident analyses are crucial in pinpointing lessons and enhancement opportunities. The insights gleaned should be integrated into the incident response plan, refining the team's strategies and protocols [36].

Collaboration and Communication:

- **Internal Collaboration:** Effective incident response demands fluid collaboration within the IRT and across the organization. Pre-established communication channels and protocols guarantee efficient information dissemination during crises [26].
- **External Coordination:** The IRT should be adept at liaising with external parties like law enforcement, cybersecurity agencies, and external forensic specialists when necessary. Pre-existing relationships with these entities can streamline response and recovery actions [37].

8.6.2 Post-Incident Analysis and Continuous Improvement

The post-incident phase offers invaluable insights, laying a foundation for enhancing the organization's resilience against future threats. In the following text we emphasize the criticality of thorough post-incident analysis following a ransomware attack. It focuses on the necessity of extracting lessons, compiling insights, and continuously refining incident response procedures to transform these experiences into a strategic asset for perpetual advancement.

Conducting a Post-Incident Review:

- **Comprehensive Analysis:** Once operations are stabilized and restored, a detailed review of the incident is imperative. This entails dissecting the sequence of events, pinpointing the breach's origin, evaluating the response's effectiveness, and assessing the organizational impact [21].
- **Cross-Departmental Involvement:** The analysis should involve input from all departments impacted by the incident. This inclusive approach ensures a comprehensive understanding of the incident's repercussions and the response's effectiveness across the entire organization [32].

Documenting Findings and Insights:

- **Detailed Incident Report:** Creating a comprehensive incident report is crucial. It should chronicle the event timeline, actions undertaken, response efficacy, lessons learned, and recommendations for future readiness [22].
- **Knowledge Repository:** Building a repository of incident reports and insights creates a valuable knowledge base. This resource can inform training initiatives and guide responses to similar future incidents [33].

Refining Incident Response Procedures:

- **Iterative Improvements:** Insights from the post-incident review should inform enhancements to existing incident response procedures. Modifications may include updates to response plans, role revisions, improved communication protocols, or strengthened defensive measures [23].
- **Adaptability to New Threats:** The cybersecurity landscape is in a state of constant flux. Incident response strategies should not just address current vulnerabilities but also be flexible enough to adapt to emerging threats and shifts within the organization [36].

Training and Awareness:

- **Incorporating Lessons into Training:** Insights from post-incident analyses should be woven into training curriculums. Real incident-based simulations offer profound experiential learning, ensuring better preparedness for future incidents among response teams and staff [26].
- **Cultivating a Culture of Continuous Learning:** Promoting an organizational culture that values ongoing learning and enhancement is vital. An environment where incident-derived insights are openly shared and integrated into practices encourages resilience and proactive cybersecurity measures [37].

Engaging with External Experts:

- **Independent Review:** Bringing in external cybersecurity experts for an unbiased review can offer fresh perspectives. These specialists can provide valuable insights, industry benchmarking, and recommendations to fortify the incident response approach [38].
- **Collaboration and Information Sharing:** Engaging with industry peers, cybersecurity groups, and law enforcement can yield broader insights. Sharing experiences and strategies fosters a collective defense approach, enhancing not only individual organizational resilience but also that of the broader community [27].

8.7 TESTING AND SIMULATIONS

8.7.1 Importance of Regular Cybersecurity Drills

Simulating ransomware attacks, these drills offer a proactive arena to assess, evaluate, and fine-tune an organization's response to cyber threats. In the following text we underscore the importance of conducting regular cybersecurity drills, spotlighting their role in validating preparedness, pinpointing vulnerabilities, and instilling a culture of ongoing vigilance and improvement.

Validating Defense Mechanisms:

- **Realistic Simulations:** Cybersecurity drills provide realistic scenarios to test the organization's defense mechanisms in a controlled setting. This enables an authentic assessment of how security measures hold up against potential ransomware attacks, revealing strengths and areas for improvement [10].
- **Response Coordination:** These drills are instrumental in testing the coordination and effectiveness of the incident response team, ensuring that roles, responsibilities, and communication protocols are not only well-defined but actionable and efficient during a cyber crisis [6].

Identifying and Addressing Vulnerabilities:

- **Exposing Weak Points:** Regular drills uncover vulnerabilities within the organization's cybersecurity framework, whether they are technical shortcomings, procedural flaws, or human errors. Recognizing these vulnerabilities is a critical step in bolstering defenses against actual ransomware threats [1].
- **Iterative Improvement:** Each drill provides valuable insights, which should be meticulously documented and analyzed. The knowledge gained serves as a basis for informed adjustments to security policies, procedures, and technologies, fostering a cycle of continuous refinement [30].

Training and Awareness:

- **Enhancing Staff Preparedness:** Drills act as practical training sessions, heightening staff awareness and comprehension of ransomware threats and the organization's response strategies. This hands-on experience is invaluable in creating a vigilant and knowledgeable workforce capable of effectively recognizing and reacting to threats [16].
- **Building a Security Culture:** The regular conduct of drills emphasizes the significance of cybersecurity throughout the organization. It cultivates a security-centric culture, where every member is an engaged defender against cyber threats [20].

Testing Recovery Procedures:

- **Assessing Recovery Capabilities:** Cybersecurity drills assess not just the detection and response capabilities but also the organization's recovery preparedness. They offer a practical evaluation of data backup systems, recovery protocols, and business continuity strategies [9].
- **Minimizing Downtime:** By consistently testing recovery procedures, organizations can ensure a rapid and efficient resumption of operations after an incident, thereby reducing downtime and mitigating the operational and financial impacts of a real ransomware attack [21].

Benchmarking and Compliance:

- **Meeting Industry Standards:** Conducting regular drills enables organizations to benchmark their cybersecurity readiness against industry standards and best practices, a crucial aspect for maintaining a competitive edge and instilling stakeholder confidence [32].

- **Ensuring Regulatory Compliance:** Many sectors are subject to regulations that necessitate regular cybersecurity testing. These drills assist organizations in adhering to these mandates, circumventing potential penalties and legal consequences [22].

8.7.2 Simulating Ransomware Attacks

The strategic enactment of ransomware attack simulations is a proactive and indispensable measure in fortifying cybersecurity resilience. These simulations are more than preparatory exercises; they immerse organizations in the simulated throes of a cyberattack, offering a profound testing ground for the organization's defensive capabilities. In the following text we discuss the meticulous orchestration of ransomware attack simulations, presenting a framework for scenario crafting, execution, and analytical review. These simulations act as a crucible to test, refine, and solidify an organization's cybersecurity mettle.

Designing Realistic Scenarios:

- **Tailored Attack Vectors:** Simulations should reflect the most probable attack vectors relevant to the organization. This requires an understanding of the organization's unique risk factors, industry-specific threats, and the latest tactics employed in ransomware attacks [10].
- **Comprehensive Scope:** Scenarios should include various phases of an attack, from initial penetration and lateral network movement to data encryption and ransom note delivery. Ensuring a holistic approach guarantees a rigorous evaluation of the entire response strategy of the organization [6].

Implementing the Simulation:

- **Controlled Environment:** Simulations must be executed in a controlled setting that closely mimics the organization's real network infrastructure. This fidelity ensures that the findings are relevant and directly applicable to the organization's actual environment [1].
- **Involvement of Key Stakeholders**: Essential stakeholders, including IT staff, security personnel, and decision-makers, should actively participate in the simulation. Their involvement is crucial to assess the efficiency of communication channels, decision-making processes, and overall coordination during the exercise [30].

Monitoring and Data Collection:

- **Real-Time Monitoring:** The simulation should be monitored live to observe the progression of the simulated attack and the organization's response. This vigilance ensures the simulation remains on track and yields valuable data for subsequent analysis [16].
- **Data Collection:** Detailed data collection during the simulation is paramount, encompassing logs, response timings, decisions made, and actions executed. This dataset is vital for post-simulation evaluation and for deriving actionable insights [20].

Post-Simulation Analysis and Feedback:

- **Debriefing and Analysis:** A thorough debriefing session should follow the simulation to dissect the organization's performance. This includes analyzing the response to the simulated attack, pinpointing strengths and weaknesses, and discussing enhancement avenues [9].

- **Actionable Insights:** The analysis should generate practical insights to bolster the organization's cybersecurity posture. This may involve revising response plans, improving security protocols, or rectifying specific vulnerabilities unveiled during the simulation [21].

Iterative Improvement:

- **Continuous Refinement:** Ransomware attack simulations should be a recurrent element in an ongoing process of iterative enhancement. Each simulation should leverage insights from preceding ones, continually augmenting the organization's preparedness and response acumen [32].
- **Adaptation to Evolving Threats:** The scenarios utilized in simulations should adapt to the shifting threat landscape. This ensures the organization is consistently prepared for the most current ransomware tactics and remains a step ahead of potential assailants [22].

8.8 CONCLUSIONS AND FUTURE DIRECTIONS

This chapter explored the various aspects of ransomware threats, meticulously analyzing a spectrum of strategies designed to reinforce organizational cyber defenses. In the following we summarize the prevention tactics discussed, offering a direction through the complexities of cybersecurity.

- **User Education and Awareness:** The chapter emphasizes the utmost importance of fostering a culture of security awareness within organizations. Regular cybersecurity education and awareness initiatives are crucial, transforming employees from potential weak points into vigilant guardians against ransomware threats.
- **Robust Cybersecurity Infrastructure:** A comprehensive, multi-layered defense system, integrating sophisticated threat detection, network segmentation, and endpoint security, constitutes the cornerstone of a formidable cybersecurity stance. When synergized and applied effectively, these technologies erect a robust bulwark against ransomware incursions.
- **Regular Software Updates and Patch Management:** The work explores the necessity of keeping software and systems up-to-date. Consistent updates and diligent patch management seal vulnerabilities, thwarting avenues ransomware might exploit and playing an essential role in preempting potential attacks.
- **Data Backup and Recovery Planning:** The critical importance of regular, secure data backups and a meticulously planned recovery strategy is paramount. These protocols ensure that organizations can promptly bounce back from ransomware attacks, significantly reducing downtime and operational interruptions.
- **Incident Response Planning:** Establishing a specialized Incident Response Team and crafting detailed incident response strategies guarantee that organizations are primed to address and recuperate from cyber incidents effectively and swiftly. Ongoing analysis post-incident and a commitment to continuous enhancement bolster the organization's resilience against future threats.
- **Advanced Threat Detection:** It highlights the significance of behavioral analytics in cybersecurity, utilizing machine learning for enhanced threat detection and anomaly identification, crucial in identifying potential ransomware activities. The integration of behavioral analytics into the broader security framework not only aids in early threat detection and minimizes false positives but also necessitates rigorous adherence to data privacy and continuous system refinement.

- **Robust Cybersecurity Infrastructure**: Intrusion detection system (IDS) and firewalls act as vigilant guardians and gatekeepers, providing continuous monitoring, proactive alerts, and layered defense mechanisms to detect and mitigate potential intrusions. Moreover, the strategic segmentation and resilient design of network topologies play a crucial role in enhancing performance, containing breaches, and ensuring network robustness against disruptions, including ransomware attacks.
- **Testing and Simulations:** Regular cybersecurity exercises and simulated ransomware attacks are indispensable practices. They not only test the organization's readiness but also yield essential insights, enabling a continuous refinement and strengthening of defense mechanisms.

8.8.1 Future Considerations in Ransomware Defense

It is critical to keenly scrutinize the horizon, anticipating the evolution of ransomware threats and gearing up to confront them with strategic foresight and innovation. It emphasizes the imperative of incessant evolution and agility in our defense strategies to maintain the upper hand in this unyielding cyber arms race.

Leveraging Artificial Intelligence and Machine Learning:

- **Predictive Threat Intelligence:** Employing AI and machine learning in cybersecurity heralds the advent of predictive threat intelligence. This advancement equips organizations to foresee and preempt threats before their actualization, morphing traditionally reactive defense tactics into proactive bulwarks.
- **Automated Response and Remediation:** AI-fueled systems offer the potential to automate certain facets of incident response and remediation, curtailing the interval from threat detection to containment and thereby mitigating the repercussions of ransomware invasions.

Adoption of Quantum-Resistant Cryptography:

- **Preparing for Quantum Computing:** The emergence of quantum computing poses significant challenges to prevailing encryption standards. It's incumbent upon organizations to pioneer quantum-resistant cryptographic techniques to defend their data against imminent threats empowered by quantum computing breakthroughs.

Enhancing Cybersecurity Frameworks with Blockchain Technology:

- **Decentralized Security Models:** Blockchain's intrinsic features – decentralization, transparency, and inalterability – herald innovative approaches in securing digital interactions and data integrity, potentially curtailing the pathways through which ransomware threats propagate.

Emphasizing Collaborative Defense Strategies:

- **Information Sharing and Collective Intelligence:** Fortifying alliances within the cybersecurity community, including public-private partnerships, can catalyze a united defense strategy. The exchange of threat intelligence and best practices can significantly elevate the collective defense stance against ransomware threats.
- **Global Cybersecurity Alliances:** In an era where cyber threats know no borders, establishing global cybersecurity coalitions is essential in devising and implementing cohesive defense strategies and regulatory frameworks.

Investing in Human Capital and Cybersecurity Education:

- **Building a Skilled Workforce:** Committing to education and training initiatives to cultivate a proficient cybersecurity workforce is paramount. A pool of talent adept in navigating and neutralizing emerging threats is an invaluable asset in combating the evolving tactics of ransomware.
- **Fostering a Culture of Continuous Learning:** Advocating for a culture that prizes continual learning, innovation, and adaptability within organizations can ensure that cybersecurity practices mature in lockstep with the dynamic threat landscape.

REFERENCES

1. I. Nadir and T. Bakhshi. "Contemporary cybercrime: A taxonomy of ransomware threats & mitigation techniques," in *2018 International Conference on Computing, Mathematics and Engineering Technologies (iCoMET)*, Sukkur, Pakistan: IEEE, Mar. 2018, pp. 1–7. doi: 10.1109/ICOMET.2018.8346329.
2. A. Adamov and A. Carlsson, "Reinforcement learning for anti-ransomware testing," in *2020 IEEE East-West Design & Test Symposium (EWDTS)*, IEEE, Sep. 2020, pp. 1–5. doi: 10.1109/EWDTS 50664.2020.9225141.
3. A. Pagan and K. Elleithy, "A multi-layered defense approach to safeguard against ransomware," in *2021 IEEE 11th Annual Computing and Communication Workshop and Conference (CCWC)*, IEEE, Jan. 2021, pp. 0942–0947. doi: 10.1109/CCWC51732.2021.9375988.
4. B. M. Khammas, "Ransomware detection using random forest technique," *ICT Express*, vol. 6, no. 4, pp. 325–331, Dec. 2020, doi: 10.1016/j.icte.2020.11.001.
5. D. W. Fernando, N. Komninos, and T. Chen, "A study on the evolution of ransomware detection using machine learning and deep learning techniques," *IoT*, vol. 1, no. 2, pp. 551–604, Dec. 2020, doi: 10.3390/iot1020030.
6. S. Mohurle and M. Patil, "A brief study of WannaCry threat: Ransomware attack 2017," *International Journal of Advanced Research in Computer Science*, vol. 8, no. 5, pp. 1938–1940, 2017.
7. C. M. Frenz and C. Diaz, "Anti-ransomware guide," *Open Web Application Security Project (OWASP)*, Mar. 12, 2017.
8. N. Aldaraani and Z. Begum, "Understanding the impact of ransomware: A survey on its evolution, mitigation and prevention techniques," in *2018 21st Saudi Computer Society National Computer Conference (NCC)*, IEEE, Apr. 2018, pp. 1–5. doi: 10.1109/NCG.2018.8593029.
9. J. S. Aidan, Zeenia, and U. Garg, "Advanced Petya ransomware and mitigation strategies," in *2018 First International Conference on Secure Cyber Computing and Communication (ICSCCC)*, IEEE, Dec. 2018, pp. 23–28. doi: 10.1109/ICSCCC.2018.8703323.
10. E. Kolodenker, W. Koch, G. Stringhini, and M. Egele, "PayBreak: Defense against cryptographic ransomware," in *Proceedings of the 2017 ACM on Asia Conference on Computer and Communications Security*, New York, NY: ACM, Apr. 2017, pp. 599–611. doi: 10.1145/3052973.3053035.
11. S. Aurangzeb, M. Aleem, M. A. Iqbal, and M. A. Islam, "Ransomware: A survey and trends," *Journal of Information Assurance & Security*, vol. 6, no. 2, pp. 48–58, 2017.
12. S. Mansfield-Devine, "Ransomware: Taking businesses hostage," *Network Security*, vol. 2016, no. 10, pp. 8–17, Oct. 2016. doi: 10.1016/S1353-4858(16)30096-4.
13. R. Brewer, "Ransomware attacks: Detection, prevention and cure," *Network Security*, vol. 2016, no. 9, pp. 5–9, Sep. 2016. doi: 10.1016/S1353-4858(16)30086-1.
14. R. Richardson and M. M. North, "Ransomware: Evolution, mitigation and prevention," *International Management Review*, vol. 13, no. 1, pp. 10–21, Jan. 2017.
15. M. Alam, S. Sinha, S. Bhattacharya, S. Dutta, D. Mukhopadhyay, and A. Chattopadhyay, "Rapper: Ransomware prevention via performance counters," *arXiv preprint arXiv:2004.01712*, 2020.
16. J. A. H. Silva, L. I. B. López, Á. L. V. Caraguay, and M. Hernández-Álvarez, "A survey on situational awareness of ransomware attacks – detection and prevention parameters," *Remote Sensing (Basel)*, vol. 11, no. 10, pp. 1–20, 2019.
17. R. Moussaileb, N. Cuppens, J.-L. Lanet, and H. Le Bouder, "A survey on windows-based ransomware taxonomy and detection mechanisms," *ACM Computing Surveys*, vol. 54, no. 6, pp. 1–36, Jul. 2022. doi: 10.1145/3453153.

18. A. Patel and J. Tailor, "A malicious activity monitoring mechanism to detect and prevent ransomware," *Computer Fraud & Security*, vol. 2020, no. 1, pp. 14–19, Jan. 2020. doi: 10.1016/S1361-3723(20)30009-9.
19. A. Arabo, R. Dijoux, T. Poulain, and G. Chevalier, "Detecting ransomware using process behavior analysis," *Procedia Computer Science*, vol. 168, pp. 289–296, 2020. doi: 10.1016/j.procs.2020.02.249.
20. H. Alshaikh, N. Ramadan, and H. Ahmed, "Ransomware prevention and mitigation techniques," *International Journal of Computer Applications*, vol. 177, no. 40, pp. 31–39, Feb. 2020. doi: 10.5120/ijca2020919899.
21. A. AlSabeh, H. Safa, E. Bou-Harb, and J. Crichigno, "Exploiting ransomware paranoia for execution prevention," in *ICC 2020–2020 IEEE International Conference on Communications (ICC)*, IEEE, Jun. 2020, pp. 1–6. doi: 10.1109/ICC40277.2020.9149005.
22. M. Ozer, S. Varlioglu, B. Gonen, and M. Bastug, "A prevention and a traction system for ransomware attacks," in *2019 International Conference on Computational Science and Computational Intelligence (CSCI)*, IEEE, Dec. 2019, pp. 150–154. doi: 10.1109/CSCI49370.2019.00032.
23. F. Malecki, "Best practices for preventing and recovering from a ransomware attack," *Computer Fraud & Security*, vol. 2019, no. 3, pp. 8–10, Jan. 2019. doi: 10.1016/S1361-3723(19)30028-4.
24. S. Kok, A. Abdullah, N. Jhanjhi, and M. Supramaniam, "Prevention of crypto-ransomware using a pre-encryption detection algorithm," *Computers*, vol. 8, no. 4, p. 79, Nov. 2019. doi: 10.3390/computers8040079.
25. S. Il Bae, G. Bin Lee, and E. G. Im, "Ransomware detection using machine learning algorithms," *Concurrency and Computation*, vol. 32, no. 18, Sep. 2020, doi: 10.1002/cpe.5422.
26. M. Patyal, S. Sampalli, Q. Ye, and M. Rahman, "Multi-layered defense architecture against ransomware," *International Journal of Business and Cyber Security*, vol. 1, no. 2, pp. 52–64, 2017.
27. Z. A. Genç, G. Lenzini, and P. Y. A. Ryan, "No random, no ransom: A key to stop cryptographic ransomware," pp. 234–255, 2018. doi: 10.1007/978-3-319-93411-2_11.
28. H. Turaev, P. Zavarsky, and B. Swar, "Prevention of ransomware execution in enterprise environment on Windows OS: Assessment of application whitelisting solutions," in *2018 1st International Conference on Data Intelligence and Security (ICDIS)*, IEEE, Apr. 2018, pp. 110–118. doi: 10.1109/ICDIS.2018.00024.
29. S. Saxena and H. K. Soni, "Strategies for ransomware removal and prevention," in *2018 Fourth International Conference on Advances in Electrical, Electronics, Information, Communication and Bio-Informatics (AEEICB)*, IEEE, Feb. 2018, pp. 1–4. doi: 10.1109/AEEICB.2018.8480941.
30. A. Ren, C. Liang, I. Hyug, S. Broh, and N. Jhanjhi, "A three-level ransomware detection and prevention mechanism," *EAI Endorsed Transactions on Energy Web*, vol. 0, no. 0, p. 162691, Jul. 2018. doi: 10.4108/eai.13-7-2018.162691.
31. D. Morato, E. Berrueta, E. Magaña, and M. Izal, "Ransomware early detection by the analysis of file sharing traffic," *Journal of Network and Computer Applications*, vol. 124, pp. 14–32, Dec. 2018. doi: 10.1016/J.JNCA.2018.09.013.
32. D. Y. Kim, G. Y. Choi, and J. H. Lee, "White list-based ransomware real-time detection and prevention for user device protection," *2018 IEEE International Conference on Consumer Electronics, ICCE 2018*, vol. 2018-January, pp. 1–5, Mar. 2018. doi: 10.1109/ICCE.2018.8326119.
33. A. El-Kosairy and M. A. Azer, "Intrusion and ransomware detection system," pp. 1–7, Sep. 2018. doi: 10.1109/CAIS.2018.8471688.
34. O. Ami, Y. Elovici, and D. Hendler, "Ransomware prevention using application authentication-based file access control," in *Proceedings of the ACM Symposium on Applied Computing*, pp. 1610–1619, Apr. 2018. doi: 10.1145/3167132.3167304.
35. K. Lee, K. Yim, and J. T. Seo, "Ransomware prevention technique using key backup," *Concurrency and Computation*, vol. 30, no. 3, Feb. 2018, doi: 10.1002/cpe.4337.
36. S. Song, B. Kim, and S. Lee, "The effective ransomware prevention technique using process monitoring on Android platform," *Mobile Information Systems*, vol. 2016, pp. 1–9, 2016. doi: 10.1155/2016/2946735.
37. J. K. Lee, S. Y. Moon, and J. H. Park, "CloudRPS: A cloud analysis based enhanced ransomware prevention system," *The Journal of Supercomputing*, vol. 73, no. 7, pp. 3065–3084, Jul. 2017. doi: 10.1007/s11227-016-1825-5.
38. T. Meurs, E. Cartwright, A. Cartwright, M. Junger, and A. Abhishta, "Deception in double extortion ransomware attacks: An analysis of profitability and credibility", *Computers & Security*, vol. 138, 2024, p. 103670. ISSN 0167–4048, https://doi.org/10.1016/j.cose.2023.103670.

AUTHOR BIOGRAPHY

Dr. Taskeed Jabid is an associate professor at East West University. Taskeed Jabid received his PhD in computer vision and image processing, Kyung Hee University, South Korea. He obtained his bachelor's degree in computer science and engineering from East West University (Bangladesh). His current research is in the fields of machine learning, deep learning, image processing, facial image analysis, texture analysis, bioinformatics, computer graphics, and algorithms.

Dr. Mohammad Rifat Ahmmad Rashid is an assistant professor in the Department of Computer Science and Engineering at East West University (EWU), Bangladesh. Before joining EWU, he worked as a researcher at the LINKS Foundation in the Pervasive Technologies Research Area, within the IoT Service Management Unit. Previously, he received his PhD degree in computer and control engineering from the Polytechnic University of Turin (Italy) and his master degree in computer engineering from the University of Pavia (Italy). His research is focused on social media data integration and event management for smart cities. Before that, he obtained his B.Eng. in computer science and engineering from Khulna University, Bangladesh.

Dr. Md. Hasanul Ferdaus has been working as an assistant professor in the Department of Computer Science and Engineering at East West University (Bangladesh) since September 2022. He obtained his PhD degree in computer science (cloud computing) from the Faculty of Information Technology at Monash University (Australia) in 2016, his M.Sc. Engg. degree in information and communication technologies from Karlsruhe Institute of Technology (Germany) and Polytechnic University of Turin (Italy) under the European Union-funded Erasmus Mundus scholarship program in 2009, and his BSc Engg. degree in computer science and engineering from Bangladesh University of Engineering and Technology (BUET) in 2004. Dr. Ferdaus has seven years of teaching experience at Australian universities, including Monash University, Central Queensland University, Southern Cross University, Melbourne Institute of Technology, and Victorian Institute of Technology. Moreover, he has five and a half years of research experience in Australia (CLOUDS Lab, Melbourne University, and Monash University) and Germany (Telematics Institute, KIT, and FZI Research Center for IT). Prior to this, he also worked as a system analyst for two years at Robi Axiata in Bangladesh. His current research interests include cloud computing, cybersecurity, internet of things (IoT), and software engineering.

Dr. Mohammad Manzurul Islam received M.Sc. degree in internetworking from the University of Technology Sydney, Australia, in 2013, and PhD degree in cybersecurity from Federation University, Australia, in 2021. He is an assistant professor at East West University Bangladesh. He served over 16+ years in many organizations, including universities (Monash University, Australia; Federation University, Australia; Canadian University, Bangladesh; Stamford University, Bangladesh) and IT industries (ZTE Corporation, Robi-Axiata Limited). His research interests include machine learning, data analysis, IoT, and cybersecurity.

Dr. Md. Sawkat Ali received his BSc in electrical and electronic engineering (EEE) from the Ahsanullah University of Science and Technology, Bangladesh. He completed M.Eng. (research) in electrical engineering from the University of New South Wales, Australia, and PhD in electrical engineering from Central Queensland University, Rockhampton, Australia. After completion of PhD, he worked as a post-doctoral research fellow at Central Queensland University and Deakin University, Australia. He is currently working as an assistant professor in the Department of Computer Science and Engineering, East West University, Bangladesh. His research interests include IoT, machine learning, power electronics, linear and nonlinear control theory and its applications, microgrids, and renewable energy.

Mahamudul Hasan received his MSc degree and BSc degree in computer science and engineering from the University of Dhaka, Bangladesh. He passed the H.S.C. examination from Dhaka College. He passed S.S.C. examination from Dhaka Collegiate School. He is now working as a senior lecturer in the Department of Computer Science and Engineering, East West University, Bangladesh. He also worked as a lecturer in the Department of CSE at United International University (2017). His research interests include recommender systems, deep learning, machine learning, mobile computing, data mining, bioinformatics, and artificial intelligence.

Rashedul Amin Tuhin is a senior lecturer at the Computer Science and Engineering Department of East West University, Dhaka. He has obtained his master's degree in network services and systems from KTH-Royal Institute of Technology, Stockholm, Sweden. His research interests include networked systems security, digital forensics, education technology, and global navigation satellite systems.

Dr. Maheen Islam received the BSc and MSc degrees from the University of Dhaka, Bangladesh in 1998 and 1999, respectively, and the PhD degree in wireless mesh networking from the Department of Computer Science and Engineering, University of Dhaka, in 2017. She is currently working as an associate professor in the Department of Computer Science and Engineering, East West University, Bangladesh. Her current research interests include wireless mesh networks, wireless sensor networks, cognitive radio networks, and software defined networks. She is a member of the Green Networking Research Group (GNR), IEEE, and BWIT.

Section IV

Human Factors and Futuristic Challenges

9 Malicious Minds

Psychological Profiling of Ransomware Attackers and Policing Challenges

Oliver Guidetti and Scott Mather

9.1 INTRODUCTION

The Australian Signals Directorate's [1] Cyber Threat Report has identified a drastic increase in cybercrime's scale, frequency, and profitability. For example, between 2022 and 2023, the average cost of cybercrime to Australia has increased by 14 percent, and the volume of calls answered by the Australian Cyber Security Hotline has grown by 32 percent. Additionally, purchasable cybercrime services have broadened the demographic of cybercriminals. For example, ransomware attacks are now easy to perform as ransomware-as-a-service (RaaS) can be purchased by inexperienced attackers on the dark web [1, 2]. Out of the long list of cybercrimes, ransomware is the most dangerous cybercrime threat that Australians face and is becoming more prevalent, with a 7.2 percent increase in ransomware-like incidents seen in 2022–2023 when compared to the year prior, accounting for 10 percent of the year's total recorded cybersecurity breaches [1].

Attackers use ransomware software to encrypt systems and data, which is held hostage until the victim pays for a decryption key that allows them to regain access [1]. Ransomware attacks are defined by two essential criteria [1]. First, the attack uses malware to control a system or data set. Second, the attackers demand ransom payments to restore compromised systems or data access. For example, in 2022, up to 9.8 million Optus customers' personal and identifying information was encrypted by malicious actors threatening to release the information on the dark web unless a $1 million ransom was paid. Despite fitting both of the ASD's [1] criteria, the Federal Department of Home Affairs [3] stated that there was no reason to suspect that the attack was a ransomware attack. The disparity between the Federal Department of Home Affairs [3] and the ASD's [1] classification of the Optus incident as ransomware may be the result of differences in the technical aspects of the attack; there may have been strategic reasons for the disparity, or at the very least, a difference in definition. Regardless of where this classification disparity comes from, the Optus incident underscores gaps in understanding the complex and evolving nature of this form of virtual threat. Classification discrepancies like this might be avoided by viewing ransomware as a broader form of cybercrime that reflects an understanding of the criminal psychology that drives perpetrators. Therefore, the primary focus of this chapter is to shed light on the criminal psychology behind ransomware attacks.

Ransomware attacks target two essential human vulnerabilities. The primary method of delivering ransomware attacks is phishing emails containing links to malicious software that incautious or unaware employees click on [4]. The human stress response is the second human vulnerability ransomware leverage [5]. The human stress response is a natural reaction to threats, whereby higher-order thinking is paralysed in place of instinctive reactions, including fighting, fleeing, freezing, or appeasing [5]. These hardwired responses have developed over hundreds of thousands

DOI: 10.1201/9781003469506-13

of years of evolution and protect humans and other mammals from physical threats in the real world, but actively advantage ransomware attackers in cyberspace. For example, fighting a ransomware attack is generally not an option for victims. Likewise, victims cannot simply take flight from the ransomware threat because it exists outside the physical realm in cyberspace. Freezing is also generally not an option for victims, as most ransomware attacks come with a countdown timer, after which precious data can be leaked online or deleted out of existence. The only option this leaves for a ransomware victim is to appease the threat by paying the ransom. However, even this is not advisable, as there is no guarantee that payment will stop the attack, and the ASD [1] actively advises against paying attackers the ransom.

When the human stress response fails to protect from a threat, it can cause profound psychological trauma [6]. Trauma itself can be characterised by a range of symptoms that vary in severity, from persistent emotions like anger and anxiety to severe symptoms like paranoia, depression, and insomnia [7]. Ransomware victims are known to experience anger and anxiety, paranoia, depression, and insomnia, which suggests the experience is psychologically traumatising [4]. For example, Yilmaz et al. [4] reported that in certain situations, these psychological effects of ransomware victimisation can sufficiently impair and necessitate clinical intervention. These human vulnerabilities that ransomware threats take advantage of may help explain why this method of cybercrime is so effective and rising in popularity.

The psychological underpinnings of ransomware attackers are not as well understood as those of their victims. However, a better understanding of the ransomware attackers' psychology may provide new avenues by which to reduce the prevalence of this form of crime, identify suspects, and better support victims [8, 9]. By analogy, consider the evolution of strategies used to combat car theft. Initial efforts focused on deterrents and legal penalties. However, once thrill-seeking and peer influence were motivators for car theft beyond just simple economic gain, better strategies evolved to combat the prevalence of that type of crime. For example, this included interventions that targeted demographics most likely to commit car theft, such as at-risk youth community programs that address the underlying psychosocial factors that made thrill-seeking and peer pressures influence car theft motivators. The psychological motivators of ransomware attackers could similarly go beyond economic gain, providing yet-to-be-explored avenues to combat the problem [8, 10]. For example, ransomware may be motivated by ideological reasons, a desire to be recognised within certain circles, or the thrill of the challenge alone. Likewise, understanding the psychological factors that motivate ransomware attackers could lead to strategies for preventing and rehabilitating them, potentially reducing their prevalence and recidivism [10].

9.2 PSYCHOLOGICAL DIMENSIONS OF CYBERCRIMINALS

9.2.1 Personality and Eysenck's Theory of Crime

Regardless of the purpose for which technology is invented, its ultimate use is determined by the ethics, motives, and objectives of human users, which can include originally unintended criminal ends [10, 11, 12]. Personal psychological attributes like personality, intelligence, and autistic spectrum disorder (ASD) can influence the likelihood of someone engaging in cybercrime. Certain personality traits and higher intelligence might predispose individuals to cybercrime. At the same time, people with ASD might have skills that can be useful in fields like computer programming and cybersecurity, yet the literature also suggests this may also contribute to the propensity for cybercrime [8, 13–17].

Personality is the stable and long-lasting product of interactions between biological predispositions and environment, which describe one's behavioural, thought, and affective inclinations, including those of a criminal nature [15, 18–21]. The Five-Factor Model proposes that personality is a heritable construct that is universally composed of five underlying factors, known as the Big Five: openness to experience, conscientiousness, extraversion, agreeableness, and neuroticism [15, 18, 19, 21, 22]. Openness to experience highlights an appreciation for art, emotion, and various experiences, emphasising creativity and curiosity. Conscientiousness is characterised by self-discipline, dutiful action, and achievement orientation. Extraversion involves energy, positive emotions, and sociability, focusing on seeking stimulation in social settings. Agreeableness points to a preference for compassion and cooperation over suspicion and antagonism. Neuroticism reflects a propensity to experience negative emotions like anger, anxiety, and depression.

Eysenck and Eysenck's [20] Theory of Criminal Personality asserts that criminals commonly possess the personality trait combination of high extraversion, neuroticism, and psychoticism, which is referred to as their three-factor model. Eysenck and Eysenck [20] even suggested that their theory may not fully explain the complex relationship between genetic and environmental factors, which they regarded as limiting its scope in explaining crime as a function of personality. For example, Eysenck and Eysenck [20] developed his theory well before the emergence of criminal activities in cyberspace in the late 1980s, and hence may not effectively distinguish between online and offline offenders because it was formulated at a time when society did not have attitudes towards digital deviance [23].

Despite this limitation, Eysenck and Eysenck's (1970) theory of crime has provided a foundation for discussing correlations between personality traits and cybercriminal behaviour [24]. However, Eysenck and Eysenck's [20] theory of crime may not adequately describe the drivers of cybercriminals. For example, Matulessy and Humaira [15] demonstrated that cybercriminals, also known as black hat hackers, report higher levels of openness to experience than neuroticism and extraversion [15]. This is in opposition to Eysenck and Eysenck's [20] theory of crime, which associates criminality with higher levels of extraversion and neuroticism.

Indeed, Matulessy and Humaira's [15] modern exploration of cybercriminal personality characteristics differs drastically from Eysenck and Eysenck's [20] theory of crime. Matulessy and Humaira [15] explored the connection between the Big Five personality traits and the hacker types individuals identify with. They categorised hackers according to the three types that Prasad [25] defined, which included ethical and non-malicious white hats, unethical and malicious black hats, and grey hats, which display a mix of white and black hat traits. Matulessy and Humaira [15] conducted a between-subjects study of 30 participants, each of whom completed a Big Five personality inventory and an interview. Matulessy and Humaira [15] found that grey-hat-identified hackers reported high-range scores for the trait neuroticism and that white-hat hackers reported higher levels of the trait agreeableness. However, black-hat-identified hackers reported higher openness to experience than white- and grey-hat-identified hackers (Figure 9.1). Matulessy and Humaira [15] further demonstrated mid-range scores for the traits conscientiousness and extraversion across all groups.

Black hat hackers are of predominant interest in this chapter due to ransomware attacks' unethical and malicious nature [25]. Matulessy and Humaira [15] characterised black-hat-identified participants as highly open to experience, creative, intellectual, curious, original, fixated on current activities, adventurous, and open to unconventional ideas and behaviours [18, 19, 21].

Furthermore, Matulessy and Humaira [15] proposed that the high openness to experience characteristic of black hats could account for their propensity towards digital deviance. Contrary to this, however, Rieger [21] asserted that openness to experience is the only factor out of the Big Five that is not correlated with personality disorders. However, pathological openness to experience has also been associated with social and occupational dysfunctions; for example, Chiesa et al. [26] discovered that self-identified hackers frequently reported experiencing insomnia, anxiety, paranoia, panic attacks, and hallucinations. Indeed, these symptoms are associated with Cluster A personality

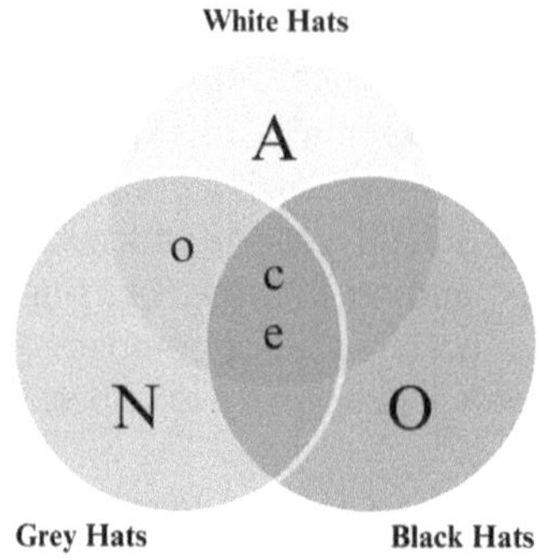

FIGURE 9.1 Big Five personality trait scores by hacker type.

Source: Adapted from Matulessy and Humaira [15].
Note: Uppercase letters represent high-range scores, and lowercase letters represent mid-range scores.

disorders in the American Psychiatric Association's [27] Diagnostic and Statistics Manual, further emphasising the connection between high openness to experience and black-hat-identified hackers' digital deviance tendencies.

The Big Five that Matulessy and Humaira [15] used is not regarded as comprehensive a model of personality as the HEXACO model [28, 29]. The HEXACO model is an extension of the Big Five and is comprised of Honesty-Humility, Emotionality, Extraversion, Agreeableness, Conscientiousness, and Openness to Experience [29, 30]. Honesty-Humility is unique to the HEXACO model and describes individuals' propensity to be sincere, fair, and averse to exploitative or corrupt activities for personal gain, aspects that the original Big Five model did not capture [29, 30]. Emotionality, akin to Neuroticism, includes emotional attachment and anxiety, with high scorers often being empathetic and sensitive to fear. Extraversion encompasses sociability and liveliness, describing energetic and outgoing individuals. Agreeableness in HEXACO emphasises patience, gentleness, and forgiveness over mere compassion. Conscientiousness involves organisation and diligence, denoting thorough, careful, and dependable people. Lastly, Openness to Experience focuses on creativity and inquisitiveness, similar to its Big Five counterpart but with a unique emphasis on creativity and unconventional thinking. Each dimension collectively represents varied aspects of human behaviour, thoughts, and emotions.

Additional distinctions exist between the Big Five and HEXACO models beyond Honesty-humility [31]. For instance, extraversion, conscientiousness, and openness to experience are mostly comparable between the HEXACO and Big Five models. However, content that refers to irritability and anger under the neuroticism factor of the Big Five model is instead included under the HEXACO agreeableness dimension. Second, where sentimentality was included under the Big Five agreeableness trait, the HEXACO was included under emotionality. The HEXACO model has been demonstrated to explain better psychological elements of crime, such as Machiavellianism, pretentiousness, psychopathy, immorality, egoism, and integrity [32–35]. For example, the honesty-humility scores of non-cybercriminals are lower than the general population [36, 37]. Moreover, Kranenbarg et al. [13] examined the HEXACO personality traits of 261 cybercrime suspects, 260 non-cybercrime suspects, and 512 general population members. Kranenbarg et al. [13] reported that the HEXACO conscientiousness and openness to experience of cybercrime suspects were significantly higher than that of non-cyber offenders and the general population. Moreover, Kranenbarg et al. [13] reported that non-cyber offenders and the general population scored significantly higher than cybercrime suspects on the HEXACO trait extraversion.

Kranenbarg et al.'s [13] study also extended to the subcomponents of each HEXACO trait. For example, Kranenbarg et al. [13] reported that cybercrime suspects scored higher diligence scores than the general population. Moreover, both non-cybercrime offenders and cybercrime suspects exhibit similar traits that could support criminal behaviour, such as higher levels of inflexibility and lower levels of fearfulness and modesty. However, traits that would align with the tendency to commit crime, such as patience, prudence, and perfectionism, were similarly high in both cyber suspects and the general population.

9.2.2 Intelligence

It is often assumed that a hacker generally has high intelligence, due to the necessity to understand and update the technical knowledge required for hacking [8, 15]. Although a lower Intelligence Quotient (IQ) has reportedly correlated with criminals more than non-criminals, the NCA (2022) suggests that high IQ is a risk factor for becoming a cybercriminal. Moreover, Schiks et al. [8] pointed out that such a belief may be distorted via the ability of someone of a lower IQ to purchase hacking services developed by experts [1, 8]. This appears to complicate further the process of psychologically profiling ransomware attackers. That is, how much can we rely on high intelligence and technical knowledge as a criterion for psychologically profiling a ransomware attacker if we are not sure whether the attacker used technology developed by a third party? For example, Schiks et al. [8] investigated the correlation between adolescent cybercriminal suspects and intelligence measured by the CITO. They found that although adolescent cybercriminal suspects generally score higher than traditional adolescent criminals, they also generally score lower than adolescent non-criminals. However, several methodological limitations may constrain the generalisability of Schiks et al.'s [8] conclusions. First, Schiks et al. [8] investigated only adolescents who were approximately 12 years old when they took the test. Second, it is unclear if their sample of adolescents was convicted of a cybercrime. Finally, there was no way to be sure that the non-criminal group indeed consisted of non-criminals and did not include criminals who had not been caught yet.

9.2.3 Autistic Quotient (AQ)

There is a commonly held belief that individuals with ASD are overrepresented in the population of cybercriminals. However, this belief does not align with the literature, which shows that individuals with ASD are typically law-abiding [16]. The American Psychiatric Association [27] describes ASD as an early childhood-onset neurodevelopmental disorder marked by persistent social communication challenges and limited and repetitive behaviours and interests, which causes dysfunctions in daily living. Interestingly, over a decade of conflicting evidence exists of a relationship between ASD and cybercrimes like ransomware attacks [14, 16, 17].

For example, Seigfried-Spellar et al. [17] examined the relationship between cybercrime engagement, or 'cyber deviancy' as measured by the Computer Crime Index-Revised (CCI-R) questionnaire and autistic-like traits, as measured by the Autism Spectrum Quotient (AQ-50), a widely used 50-item questionnaire for screening autistic-like traits [16, 38]. Through analysing 275 participants' scores on the CCI-R and AQ-50, Seigfried-Spellar et al. [17] found that participants who self-reported engaging in all four of the measured cyber deviant behaviours (hacking, identity theft, cyberbullying, and virus writing) scored significantly higher on the AQ-50. However, they found no significant correlations between those above the AQ-50 clinical cut-off and cyber deviancy. This means that participants were less likely to engage in cyber-deviant behaviours when they passed the proposed threshold of clinical levels of autistic-like traits. The latter could be because only a small sample of participants (two) scored over the suggested clinical cut-off of 32/50 on the AQ-50. However, Seigfried-Spellar et al. [17] also analysed the effects of moving the clinical cut-off to the recently proposed level of 26/50, where 18 out of 275 participants scored over the threshold (10 out of 161 cyber deviants and 8 out of 114 non-cyber deviants), and there were still no significant correlations between clinical levels of autistic-like traits and cyber deviancy.

Second, Payne et al. [16] aimed to build upon Seigfried-Spellar et al.'s [17] study by investigating diagnosed autism and autistic-like traits' correlations with self-reported engagement in *cyber-dependent* crime, specifically, to separately analyse the effect of this subcomponent of the previously studied 'cyber deviancy'. Participants completed Payne et al.'s [16] eight-question self-report Cyber-Dependent Crime Questionnaire (CDCQ) and the AQ-50. Payne et al. [16] demonstrated that high levels of autistic-like traits were more inclined to engage in cyber-dependent crimes, which supported Seigfried-Spellar et al.'s [17] similar conclusions. However, Payne et al. [16] also reported that advanced digital proficiencies accounted for 40 percent of this link. Intriguingly, individuals with a clinical diagnosis of autism were less likely to report having committed a cyber-dependent crime compared to their counterparts without an autism diagnosis. Payne et al.'s [16] results therefore do appear to indicate that people diagnosed with autism are less likely to commit, or at least self-report committing, a cyber-dependent crime than people without autism.

Finally, Lim et al. [14] conducted a similar study to that of Payne et al. [16] to investigate the correlations between autism and autistic-like traits and cybercrime. Unlike Payne et al. [16], who solely focused on correlations with cyber-dependent crime, Lim et al. [14] similarly investigated correlations with cyber-dependent crime using the CDCQ but also investigated cybercrime in general with the CCI-R, akin to Seigfried-Spellar et al. [17]. As opposed to the 50-item AQ used by Seigfried-Spellar et al. [17] and Payne et al. [16], Lim et al. [14] measured autistic-like traits with a 12-item version of the AQ (AQ-12), claiming that it seemingly measures autistic traits more appropriately than the AQ-50. No significant correlations were found between cyber-dependent crime and autistic-like traits or with an autism diagnosis. The prior findings from Lim et al. [14] do not align with Payne et al. [16], but the latter does. However, Lim et al. [14] did report a significant correlation between participation in cybercrime in general and diagnosed autism but not autistic-like traits. The latter does not correspond with the findings of Seigfried-Spellar et al. [17]. Lim et al. [14] proposed that a possible reason for the correlation found between people with autism and self-reporting participation in cybercrime, in general, could be due to people with autism being more willing to follow requests, whereas people without autism may be more hesitant to self-disclose this information.

9.3 PSYCHOLOGICAL PROFILING OF RANSOMWARE ATTACKERS

While law enforcement has historically relied on digital efforts to combat cybercrimes, more recent efforts have begun recognising the need to psychologically profile cyber offenders [39]. However, much of the early literature on cybercrime's human component is scattered, and conclusions are derived from limited empirical evidence [24, 40, 41]. For example, Dowden et al. [40] reviewed over three decades of cybercriminal profiling research and found most conclusions limited by a scarcity of primary data. In the decade following Dowden et al.'s [40] study, Fox and Farrington [41] found an improvement in the scientific rigour of cybercriminal profiling research but also noted a decline in ecological validity. More specifically, Fox and Farrington [41] noted a problematic lack of research exploring the actual performance of cybercriminal profiling methods in actual investigations.

Given that threats in the virtual threat landscape have evolved in sophistication, diversity, and accessibility, it is unclear how well cybercriminal profiling methods derived from Dowden et al.'s [40] thirty- to forty-year-old information may have served in an actual criminal investigation. For example, it is notoriously difficult to sample actual criminal hackers for the purposes of scientific research [17]. This sampling limitation has meant that many of the conclusions drawn from the literature reviewed in Dowden et al. [40] and Fox and Farrington [41] are based on outdated data, small individual case studies, or data from fields outside of cybercrime [24].

The review by Bada and Nurse [24] marked a shift beyond Dowden et al. [40] and Fox and Farrington [41] towards a more precise understanding of cybercrime, categorising it as situations where a computer becomes the target of an attack initiated by another computer. Although the approach enhanced ecological validity, Bada and Nurse [24] found that the cybercriminal profiling literature was still limited due to small-scale case studies with limited examples of primary data derived from actual cybercriminals. The fundamental limitations of Dowden et al. [40], Fox and Farrington [41], and Bada and Nurse [24] identified in their reviews underscore the need for more comprehensive, empirically grounded, and practically evaluated research in cybercriminal profiling.

The best attempt to address the gaps Dowden et al. [40], Fox and Farrington [41], and Bada and Nurse [24] identified came from Martineau et al. [10], who provided a focused qualitative meta-synthesis of cybercrime profiling literature. Martineau et al. [10] then used their review to inform their Cyber Behavioural Analysis (CBA). Martineau et al.'s [10] CBA integrated behavioural analysis with cybercrime data to provide a more effective and empirically supported approach to cybercrime profiling.

Martineau et al.'s [10] introduced the CBA as an adaptation of the Behavioural Evidence Analysis (BEA), traditionally used in other contexts, to the realm of cyber-dependent crimes [12, 42, 43]. The CBA is a comprehensive framework incorporating various typologies, motivations, demographic characteristics, and psychological traits specific to cybercriminals.

Martineau et al. [10] identified twenty distinct typologies of cybercriminals, ranging from traditional hackers to nation-state actors, each with unique characteristics and motivations [9, 26, 43–62]. These typologies provide the CBA with a nuanced understanding of the diverse profiles within the cybercriminal world. Martineau et al. [10] also integrated twenty-four distinct motivational factors into the CBA from their review of cybercriminal profiling. These motivational factors range from non-specific malice and revenge to more complex drivers like ideological motives and the pursuit of notoriety. Additionally, Martineau et al. [10] integrated analysis of psychological traits and demographic characteristics into the CBA, offering a deeper insight into the personal attributes of cybercriminals. Their review indicated a wide range of traits, including narcissism, aggressiveness, and a propensity for certain mood disorders, as well as diverse demographic backgrounds. Martineau et al.'s [10] comprehensive approach not only aids in understanding the current landscape of cybercrime but also assists in making the CBA a functional framework for profiling cybercriminals.

9.3.1 Cyber Behaviour Analysis

Three methods are used to profile criminals: deductive, inductive, or a combination of the two [63]. Profiles created by theories derived at the scene of a crime are deductive methods [63]. Inductive methods involve statistical data comparisons that lead to inferences about the traits or characteristics a cybercriminal may share with others who commit the same type of offence [63]. Hybrid methods also attempt to profile cybercriminals by combining deductive and inductive approaches [64]. Martineau et al.'s [10] CBA takes a deductive approach to profiling that first involves collating the total set of evidence associated with the cybercrime under investigation, including digital forensics and victimology [65]. Martineau et al.'s [10] CBA integrates victimology into profiling cybercriminals. This involves exploring why individuals may have been victimised, the characteristics of both victims and prospective offenders, and situational antecedents to the crime [65]. This also includes considering factors such as the victim's identity, their level of cybersecurity, and any relationship they may have with an attacker to understand if they were specifically targeted or randomly chosen. CBA profiles are opinions about cybercriminals based on observed behavioural patterns in case evidence. Analysts use digital forensic information, victimology, and public information to deduce likely characteristics. An inductive process is then followed to consider any additional information that might support these opinions.

The lack of a universally accepted taxonomy for cybercrime and profiling and the need for more empirical, ecologically valid data were limitations Dowden et al. [40], Fox and Farrington [41], and Bada and Nurse [24] identified in the cybercrime profiling literature that Martineau et al. (2023) attempted to overcome with the CBA.

Dowden et al. [40], Fox and Farrington [41], and Bada and Nurse [24] identified limitations in the cybercrime profiling literature, including the lack of a universally accepted taxonomy for cybercrime and profiling, and the need for more empirical, ecologically valid data. The extent to which Martineau et al.'s [10] CBA overcame these limitations is unclear. For example, Martineau et al. [10] did not empirically validate the CBA using data derived from real-world cybercrimes, making its practical utility in an actual cybercrime investigation unclear. Hence, while Martineau et al.'s [10] CBA represents a crucial development in the field of cybercrime profiling, amalgamating insights from decades of research, their framework is not without its limitations [24, 40, 41]. One significant shortcoming of the CBA is the inability to profile criminals who utilise computers as a tool to attack victims effectively. For example, a DDOS attack is designed to prevent legitimate users from accessing websites and online services by flooding these with traffic, whereas ransomware involves the targeted encryption of a victim's data. Each type of attack constitutes a different type of victim, offender, and computerised weapon. However, because Martineau et al. [10] designed their CBA to profile cybercriminals that treat computers, not people, as the target, their approach may not be sufficient to profile crimes like ransomware, where the human is targeted through a computer.

Overcoming this limitation of Martineau et al.'s [10] CBA may require profiling cybercriminals according to how computers target victims [17, 24]. For example, ransomware is responsible for most cyber-attacks against businesses, with attacks occurring approximately every 11 seconds [66]. Furthermore, the rising popularity of ransomware as an attack vector has fuelled the growth of online marketplaces, where cybercrime vendors offer services to offenders [67]. There are three layers of internet crime. The first layer occurs on the open web, while the second layer sits beneath it on the deep web. The third layer, a subset of the deep web, is known as the dark web and is where ransomware markets can be found [68]. The open web component of the internet is indexed by search engines and accessible to all users. The deep web is the internet component that search engines have not indexed and does not necessarily encompass illegal content [69]. The dark web is a subset of the deep web where criminals hide illegal activity [68]. Dark web servers are accessed only by criminals and law enforcement through specialised Tor software. Tor is not only used by criminals; law enforcement can also use the technology to scour the dark web for information [69]. The mere existence of ransomware marketplaces suggests a new typology of ransomware criminals that neither Dowden et al. [40], Fox and Farrington [41], Bada and Nurse [24] nor Martineau et al. [10] identified, namely, cybercrime customers and cybercrime merchants.

The evolution of cybercrime into a marketplace model, where merchants and customers engage in transactions, underscores the need to study the profile of cybercriminals according to their attack vectors [70]. For example, a criminal capable of deploying a DDOS attack differs markedly from those who deploy a ransomware attack that can be purchased from dark web merchants. However, profiling cybercriminals according to the method of attack they leverage may be challenging for many reasons. First, accessing cybercriminals to derive data that reflects their driving psychology is a complex challenge [24].

Second, much of the available data on cybercriminals is nonrepresentative of the general population of cybercriminals; rather, it predominately represents those who have been detected [8, 9]. For example, Matulessy and Humaira [16] reported that beginner and advanced hackers differ in personality trait scores, and it could be that the latter is arrested less often through practice avoiding detection. Furthermore, criminals with a lower IQ are more likely to be caught than those with a higher IQ, further exacerbating the nonrepresentative nature of the available data [8]. Therefore, if the characteristics of the caught cybercriminals differ significantly from those undetected, any conclusions drawn from data collected from this group may not apply to the broader population of cybercriminals [8].

It may not be helpful to rely on the research of caught cybercriminals through self-report measures such as questionnaires and interviews to determine their level of involvement in cybercrime for practical cybercrime investigations. These methods may not always produce conclusions that generalise well, as participants' bias influences self-report measures to provide socially desirable answers rather than their actual answers to questions [8, 14, 16, 17]. For example, Van Dam et al. [71] demonstrated that the correlation between personality traits and criminal recidivism differed depending on whether the results were based on police reports or self-reports.

These limitations make narrowing the scope of cybercrime profiling to an individual category, such as ransomware, challenging but not impossible. Acknowledging these limitations and advancing cybercrime profiling, especially within specialised categories like ransomware, necessitates innovative research methodologies that extend traditional approaches beyond the lab and into the real world.

9.4 AVENUES TOWARDS ADVANCING CYBERCRIME PROFILING

9.4.1 Empirical Research in Cybercriminal Communities

A range of consistent limitations across the cybercrime profiling literature was cited by Dowden et al. [40], Fox and Farrington [41], Bada and Nurse [24], as well as Martineau et al. (2023). Due to the significant challenges in accessing cybercriminals in real-world settings, much of the profiling literature was based on limited empirical data, which in turn could not be subsequently validated in real-world investigations [24, 40, 41, 57]. This reliance on constrained empirical data in profiling literature, without the possibility of practical validation, highlights a critical concern in the field. These limitations suggest that methods employed in cybercriminal research and the samples used may have lacked ecological validity. While primates inhabit the jungle, cybercriminals reside in the dark web [68, 72]. Therefore, undertaking research in real-world settings, like ransomware marketplaces on the dark web, is essential to understanding ransomware criminals' true nature and complexity, which cannot be accurately reflected in controlled environments [70].

9.4.2 Dark Web Research Methods

Research methods must evolve to study real-world cybercriminals effectively within their essential habitat: dark web marketplaces where services like ransomware attacks are traded. Researchers must engage with these communities to achieve ecologically valid insights through various research methods. By immersing themselves in these enclaves, researchers can gain a deeper understanding of cybercriminal behaviour and the dynamics that drive it. Adopting this approach would provide the cybercrime profiling literature with ecologically valid data, thereby addressing and overcoming the traditional limitations identified by Dowden et al. [40], Fox and Farrington [41], Bada and Nurse [24], and Martineau et al. [10]. These traditional limitations stem from the significant challenges in accessing cybercriminals in real-world settings, where much of the profiling literature has historically relied on limited empirical data, data that often could not be validated in real-world investigations.

Psychological researchers interested in studying ransomware customers and merchants could attempt to recruit participants from dark web forums. However, this approach might require modifying traditional research methods to engage with a sceptical and distrustful participant group. For example, dark web users might be motivated to participate in research in return for financial compensation. Unlike traditional research, however, remunerating dark web users to participate in research might be more effective in the form of cryptocurrency. Moreover, getting dark web participants to trust and interact with standard research platforms, like Qualtrics, may be challenging to complete surveys, questionnaires, or interviews. Therefore, these tools must be adapted to work within dark web environments that ransomware criminals already trust. The risk of exposure to traumatising content within these spaces could be mitigated by implementing content filtering mechanisms to protect researchers from such material while working in these areas.

Cyber ranges are helpful for researchers to access cybercriminals for research purposes. A cyber range is an isolated computing environment designed to simulate any victim an offender might target [73]. By creating a controlled environment, cyber ranges can potentially lure dark web cybercriminals into unwittingly participating in criminal profiling research. This research could provide valuable insights into cybercrime victimology and cybercriminal profiling.

This research method is derived from the work of Donato [74] and Frumento et al. [65]. Donato used Behavioral Evidence Analysis (BEA) to examine digital forensic data from cyber-attacks on honeypot networks, revealing a techno-signature of the human elements of cybercrime. Moreover, Furmento et al.'s Victim Communication Stack (VCS) provided a framework for understanding the victimology of cybercrime targets, which could be reversed in a cyber range to better understand the characteristics of victims that attract ransomware attackers.

On the one hand, using cyber ranges as a tool for researching cybercriminals presents one of the first empirically valid approaches to studying cybercrime. By simulating various potential victim networks and profiles, these controlled environments could entice dark web cybercriminals into engaging with what they perceive as legitimate targets, thereby unwittingly participating in criminal profiling research. This method, drawing on Donato's [74] Behavioral Evidence Analysis (BEA) and Frumento et al.'s [65] Victim Communication Stack (VCS), offers a way to gather data directly from the actions of cybercriminals – something that has not yet been done before. It promises to yield invaluable insights into the nature of cybercrime victimology and the profiling of cybercriminals, particularly in understanding the characteristics that make specific profiles more attractive to ransomware attackers.

On the other hand, this research method raises significant ethical concerns. First and foremost is the question of consent. The cybercriminals lured into these cyber ranges are unaware that they are part of a research study, violating the principle of informed consent, a cornerstone of ethical research practices. Furthermore, there is the moral dilemma of deceiving participants, even if they are engaging in criminal activities. This approach could also be entrapment, leading to legal and ethical complications. There is also the risk of these simulations inadvertently causing actual harm, as cybercriminals might redirect their efforts towards real targets in response to the study's interventions. Lastly, the researchers may face ethical conflicts in balancing the pursuit of knowledge against the tactics used to obtain it and the potential consequences of their actions on the wider digital community.

While enticing cybercriminals to attack a cyber range for research purposes may raise ethical concerns, these may be justifiable considering the broader context and potential benefits. While fundamental in most research contexts, the principle of informed consent faces unique challenges in cybercrime research. Gaining consent from individuals knowingly engaging in illegal activities is impractical and could compromise the integrity and effectiveness of the study. In this case, the ethical dilemma is offset by the significant value of the insights gained, which could be instrumental in enhancing cybersecurity measures and protecting legitimate users. Moreover, the controlled environment of a cyber range ensures that no real harm is inflicted on actual victims, redirecting potential criminal activities to a harmless simulation. This approach also avoids legal entrapment concerns, as it merely observes and analyses the behaviour of cybercriminals in a simulated environment without inciting them to commit crimes they would not otherwise commit. The ethical conflicts researchers face are mitigated by the potential for substantial contributions to public safety and cybersecurity, outweighing the ethical breaches regarding deceit and lack of consent. Ultimately, this method serves a greater good, aiming to understand and mitigate cyber threats more effectively, benefiting the wider digital community.

Using honeypot networks to profile hackers is nothing particularly new; for example, Li and Parsioan [75] demonstrated the use of honeypot networks to attract malicious operators into a trap where their activities can be comprehensively monitored. The information left behind by hackers can be categorised into two main groups. The first group includes network activity, which covers all traffic exchanged with the honeypot. The second group includes system and file information, including system logs and tools the infiltrator uses. These two data sets can be used to create separate timelines, which can be combined later to create a comprehensive picture of the attack. This can provide insights into the tools and tactics used in the invasion and potentially identify the perpetrator. In addition, this collected data can also be used to build an attacker profile, an analytical approach that has gained popularity in recent years. An attacker profile is a composite of features of the event, its consequences, the hacker's characteristics, and the target's features. These event components, such as motive or modus operandi, can provide valuable insights into the hacker's intentions and psyche. As a result, this profiling can significantly enhance pre-emptive measures and the system's overall security.

Jayakrishnan and Vasanthi [76] also demonstrated that simulated honeypot targets can inform the cybercriminal profiling process by trapping and recording offenders. However, they also highlighted the fact that the effectiveness of a honeypot could be compromised if attackers are aware of its existence. However, a core element of the participant researcher approach would be infiltrating ransomware markets, not merely as an observer but as an active participant, posing convincingly as a ransomware customer. This participant researcher approach would circumvent the limitations Jayakrishnan and Vasanthi [76] identified, as it eliminates the attacker's awareness of being monitored within a honeypot environment.

The primary goal of the participant researcher approach would be to overcome traditional limitations in the cybercriminal profiling space that Dowden et al. [40], Fox and Farrington [41], Bada and Nurse [24], and Martineau et al. [10] identified. By integrating into these communities, researchers could derive empirical data from ecologically valid investigations of actual ransomware attackers, which have traditionally been difficult for researchers to access. This approach could lead to a deeper understanding of ransomware attackers' motivations, decision-making processes, negotiation techniques, and interaction patterns. In addition, a deeper understanding of the financial motivations of ransomware attackers might be derived by performing a market analysis of ransomware services. This participant researcher approach could provide real-world empirical insights into the psychological drivers of ransomware criminals.

The participant researcher approach would first involve a meticulous planning phase in which the cyber range is set up. This would also involve deriving a fictitious range of victim users, which researchers could compose to understand better how offenders choose targets within a network. The setup phase involves installing honeypots and attack activity monitors to monitor network traffic and capture ransomware behaviour closely.

Regarding security measures, the cyber range would need to be meticulously isolated and safeguarded to ensure that the attacks do not extend beyond the controlled environment, thus preventing any real-world harm or unintentional data leakage. After configuring the range to emulate a high-value corporate network with simulated sensitive data, decoy servers, databases, and honeypots would come to an engagement phase. The engagement phase would then involve crafting a dark web persona for the researcher to use in contracting a ransomware attacker to target the cyber range. The researchers' dark web persona must be plausible enough to be accepted and trusted within dark web communities. This may include creating a fabricated digital history with manufactured organisational affiliations and credentials. The detail and depth of this backstory are crucial in establishing the persona as a legitimate and exciting party to ransomware merchants.

The approach for engaging ransomware merchants would be a critical factor in understanding the ransomware ecosystem and the psychology of its operators. This strategy must be carefully designed to build rapport and trust with potential ransomware providers. The researchers' dark web persona must skilfully navigate conversations and express a keen interest in ransomware services, discussing specific needs related to ransomware to elicit detailed responses from the merchants to derive valuable insights into their operations and psychology.

This engagement would amount to an unstructured, open-ended interview of sorts. For example, the researcher must actively engage in dark web forums and interact with ransomware merchants. The researcher could even use the cyber range to generate fake evidence of previously successful ransomware attacks that could be used to ingratiate within these dark web communities.

The engagement phase would provide crucial intelligence and split into two primary activities: participating in forums and acquiring ransomware. The researcher would need to immerse themselves in these dark web communities and engage in open-format discussions to understand current ransomware trends, merchant responsiveness, reputations, and communication styles. Simultaneously, the researcher would need to focus on gathering specific information on ransomware variants, pricing models, and merchant services. Soliciting the ransomware services of a merchant would involve direct negotiations and service evaluations, aiming to understand merchant flexibility, pricing strategies, and capabilities.

Following the engagement phase, the experiment would move into execution, where the ransomware merchant deploys the ransomware attack against the controlled cyber range. This phase would allow for observing the ransomware lifecycle, from infiltration to encryption and, potentially, the ransom negotiation process. The researcher could use the cyber range's monitoring tools to track the attacker's movements, tactics, and techniques while conducting a comprehensive communications analysis, focusing on linguistic patterns and decision-making processes. The participant researcher approach could, therefore, overcome the limitations of traditional cybercriminal profiling by deriving conclusions from empirical data gathered through ecologically valid investigations of actual ransomware criminals [10, 24, 40, 41].

This participant researcher approach could also expand the study of ransomware victimology by moving beyond theoretical models and anecdotal evidence to a more nuanced understanding of the dynamics between attackers and victims based on empirical evidence. Not only could this help in profiling ransomware attackers, insights derived through this approach could also lead to more effective prevention strategies and support for victims of these types of cybercrimes.

To better understand how ransomware attackers select their targets, one possible approach is to create a simulated cyber range with a diverse set of fictitious victims. The cyber range could include fictitious victims representing various potential users, such as those with different levels of security, industry types, organizational sizes, and positions within the organization. This could help researchers gain insights into the patterns and strategies ransomware attackers use when selecting their targets, such as those with varying levels of security, industry type, organisation size, and organisational position. This would enable the researcher to study the effect of these variables on the likelihood of being targeted. To do this, the researcher would engage with a ransomware merchant to contract their services in attacking the simulated environment. By monitoring which entities the attacker targets first or most aggressively, the researcher could observe patterns in their selection criteria, such as a preference for attacking less secure or financially lucrative targets. This information might help understand the victimology used in profiling ransomware attackers and help organisations develop more effective protective measures against ransomware attacks.

Additionally, allowing ransomware attackers to operate within a controlled environment would allow a researcher to observe its entire lifecycle and the impacts from the victims' perspective. This includes understanding the extent of data encryption, the disruption of services, and the psychological forces that drive victims' responses to ransomware attacks. Furthermore, by observing and participating in ransom negotiations, a researcher could gain insights into the psychological and financial pressures placed on victims and the tactics used by attackers to coerce payment.

Linguistic analyses of conversations between dark web attackers and simulated victims could also help understand the language, persuasion tactics, and psychological strategies attackers use. This approach to cybercrime research could help understand how attackers manipulate victims through language to achieve their goals. Additionally, this approach could help understand how attackers react to different victim reactions and how different reactions might affect the attackers' decision-making process.

This method of broadening the study of ransomware victimology has the potential to contribute significantly to cybercriminals' profiling. Gathering factual evidence on the communication and interaction between attackers and victims in the context of cybercrime could help uncover the underlying dynamics of victimisation in the crime process.

Profiling ransomware criminals can yield valuable insights that can influence policymakers and cybersecurity professionals in developing better strategies to protect potential victims and mitigate the impacts of ransomware attacks. This approach can help build a more comprehensive understanding of ransomware victimisation, which can inform more than just cybercriminal profiling.

REFERENCES

1. ASD. (2023). *ASD cyber threat report 2022–2023*. https://www.cyber.gov.au/sites/default/files/2023-11/asd-cyber-threat-report-2023.pdf
2. Hull, G., John, H., & Arief, B. (2019). Ransomware deployment methods and analysis: views from a predictive model and human responses. *Crime Science*, *8*, 1–22. https://doi.org/10.1186/s40163-019-0097-9
3. The Department of Home Affairs. (2022). *Question time brief – data security breaches (QB22–000255)*. https://www.homeaffairs.gov.au/foi/files/2022/fa-221001083-document-released.PDF
4. Yilmaz, Y., Cetin, O., Grigore, C., Arief, B., & Hernandez-Castro, J. (2023). Personality types and ransomware victimisation. *Digital Threats: Research and Practice*, *4*(4), 1–25. https://doi.org/10.1145/3568994
5. Glaser, J. E., & Tartell, R. (2014). Conversational intelligence at work. *OD Practitioner*, *46*(3), 62–67. https://doi.org/10.4324/9781315230443-11
6. Baldwin, D. V. (2013). Primitive mechanisms of trauma response: An evolutionary perspective on trauma-related disorders. *Neuroscience & Biobehavioral Reviews*, *37*(8), 1549–1566. https://doi.org/10.1016/j.neubiorev.2013.06.004
7. Suman, L. (2018). Cyber trauma: An overview. *Indian Journal of Clinical Psychology*, *45*(1), 7–17. https://ijcp.co.in/wp-content/uploads/2022/01/2018fa.pdf#page=14
8. Schiks, J. A., van de Weijer, S. G., & Leukfeldt, E. R. (2022). High tech crime, high intellectual crime? Comparing the intellectual capabilities of cybercriminals, traditional criminals and non-criminals. *Computers in Human Behavior*, *126*, 106985. https://doi.org/10.1016/j.chb.2021.106985
9. Warikoo, A. (2014). Proposed methodology for cyber criminal profiling. *Information Security Journal: A Global Perspective*, *23*(4–6), 172–178. https://doi.org/10.1080/19393555.2014.931491
10. Martineau, M., Spiridon, E., & Aiken, M. (2023). A comprehensive framework for cyber behavioral analysis based on a systematic review of cyber profiling literature. *Forensic Sciences*, *3*(3), 452–477. https://doi.org/10.1016/b978-0-12-382165-2.00026-x
11. Aiken, M., Farr, R., & Witschi, D. (2022). Cyberchondria, coronavirus, and cybercrime: A perfect storm. In *Handbook of research on cyberchondria, health literacy, and the role of media in society's perception of medical information* (pp. 16–34). IGI Global. https://doi.org/10.4018/978-1-7998-8630-3.ch002
12. Turvey, B. E. (2011). *Criminal profiling: An introduction to behavioral evidence analysis*. Academic Press. https://doi.org/10.1016/b978-0-12-385243-4.00005-8
13. Kranenbarg, M. W., Van Gelder, J.-L., Barends, A. J., & de Vries, R. E. (2023). Is there a cybercriminal personality? Comparing cyber offenders and offline offenders on HEXACO personality domains and their underlying facets. *Computers in Human Behavior*, *140*, 107576. https://doi.org/10.1016/j.chb.2022.107576
14. Lim, A., Brewer, N., & Young, R. L. (2023). Revisiting the relationship between cybercrime, autistic traits, and autism. *Journal of Autism and Developmental Disorders*, *53*(4), 1319–1330. https://doi.org/10.1007/s10803-021-05207-1
15. Matulessy, A., & Humaira, N. H. (2016). Hacker personality profiles reviewed in terms of the Big Five personality traits. *Psychology and Behavioral Sciences*, *5*(6), 137–142. https://doi.org/10.11648/j.pbs.20160506.12
16. Payne, K.-L., Russell, A., Mills, R., Maras, K., Rai, D., & Brosnan, M. (2019). Is there a relationship between cyber-dependent crime, autistic-like traits and autism? *Journal of Autism and Developmental Disorders*, *49*, 4159–4169. https://doi.org/10.1007/s10803-019-04119-5
17. Seigfried-Spellar, K. C., O'Quinn, C. L., & Treadway, K. N. (2015). Assessing the relationship between autistic traits and cyberdeviancy in a sample of college students. *Behaviour & Information Technology*, *34*(5), 533–542. https://doi.org/10.1080/0144929x.2014.978377

18. Costa, P. T., & McCrae, R. R. (1992). The five-factor model of personality and its relevance to personality disorders. *Journal of Personality Disorders, 6*(4), 343–359. https://doi.org/10.1521/pedi.1992.6.4.343
19. Costa, P. T., & McCrae, R. R. (2010). The five-factor model, five-factor theory, and interpersonal psychology. In *Handbook of interpersonal psychology: Theory, research, assessment, and therapeutic interventions* (pp. 91–104). https://doi.org/10.1002/9781118001868.ch6
20. Eysenck, S. B., & Eysenck, H. J. (1970). Crime and personality: An empirical study of the three-factor theory. *The British Journal of Criminology*, *10*(3), 225–239. https://api.semanticscholar.org/CorpusID:147686502
21. Rieger. (2017). *Abnormal psychology: Leading researcher perspectives*. McGraw Hill.
22. Barańczuk, U. (2019). The five factor model of personality and emotion regulation: A meta-analysis. *Personality and Individual Differences*, *139*, 217–227. https://doi.org/10.1016/j.paid.2018.11.025
23. Schjolberg, S. (2014). *The history of cybercrime: 1976–2014*. BoD–Books on Demand.
24. Bada, M., & Nurse, J. R. (2021). Profiling the cybercriminal: A systematic review of research. *2021 International Conference on Cyber Situational Awareness, Data Analytics and Assessment (CyberSA)*.
25. Prasad, S. T. (2014). Ethical hacking and types of hackers. *International Journal of Emerging Technology in Computer Science & Electronics (IJETCSE)*, *11*(2), 24–27.
26. Chiesa, R., Ducci, S., & Ciappi, S. (2008). *Profiling hackers: The science of criminal profiling as applied to the world of hacking (Vol. 49)*. CRC Press. https://doi.org/10.1201/9781420086942
27. American Psychiatric Association (2013). *Diagnostic and statistical manual of mental disorders: DSM-5 (Vol. 5)*. American Psychiatric Association, Washington, DC. https://doi.org/10.1176/appi.books.9780890425787
28. De Vries, R. E., Tybur, J. M., Pollet, T. V., & Van Vugt, M. (2016). Evolution, situational affordances, and the HEXACO model of personality. *Evolution and Human Behavior*, *37*(5), 407–421. https://doi.org/10.1016/j.evolhumbehav.2016.04.001
29. Lee, K., & Ashton, M. C. (2004). Psychometric properties of the HEXACO personality inventory. *Multivariate Behavioral Research*, *39*(2), 329–358. https://doi.org/10.1177/1088868314523838
30. Paunonen, S. V., & Jackson, D. N. (2000). What is beyond the big five? Plenty! *Journal of Personality*, *68*(5), 821–835. https://doi.org/10.1111/1467-6494.00117
31. Ashton, M. C., Lee, K., Perugini, M., Szarota, P., De Vries, R. E., Di Blas, L., Boies, K., & De Raad, B. (2004). A six-factor structure of personality-descriptive adjectives: Solutions from psycholexical studies in seven languages. *Journal of Personality and Social Psychology*, *86*(2), 356. https://doi.org/10.1037/0022-3514.86.2.356
32. Ashton, M. C., & Lee, K. (2008). The prediction of honesty–humility-related criteria by the HEXACO and five-factor models of personality. *Journal of Research in Personality*, *42*(5), 1216–1228. https://doi.org/10.1016/j.jrp.2008.03.006
33. De Vries, R. E., & van Kampen, D. (2010). The HEXACO and 5DPT models of personality: A comparison and their relationships with psychopathy, egoism, pretentiousness, immorality, and Machiavellianism. *Journal of Personality Disorders*, *24*(2), 244–257. https://doi.org/10.1521/pedi.2010.24.2.244
34. Gaughan, E. T., Miller, J. D., & Lynam, D. R. (2012). Examining the utility of general models of personality in the study of psychopathy: A comparison of the HEXACO-PI-R and NEO PI-R. *Journal of Personality Disorders*, *26*(4), 513–523. https://doi.org/10.1521/pedi.2012.26.4.513
35. Lee, K., & Ashton, M. C. (2005). Psychopathy, Machiavellianism, and narcissism in the five-factor model and the HEXACO model of personality structure. *Personality and Individual Differences*, *38*(7), 1571–1582. https://doi.org/10.1016/j.paid.2004.09.016
36. Rolison, J. J., Hanoch, Y., & Gummerum, M. (2013). Characteristics of offenders: The HEXACO model of personality as a framework for studying offenders' personality. *The Journal of Forensic Psychiatry & Psychology*, *24*(1), 71–82. https://doi.org/10.1080/14789949.2012.752024
37. Ścigała, K. A., Ruhara, N., Nitschke, J., & Pfattheicher, S. (2022). Honesty-humility and criminal behavior among imprisoned criminal offenders. *Journal of Research in Personality*, *101*, 104289. https://doi.org/10.31234/osf.io/t9r3b
38. Lundqvist, L.-O., & Lindner, H. (2017). Is the Autism-Spectrum Quotient a valid measure of traits associated with the autism spectrum? A Rasch validation in adults with and without autism spectrum disorders. *Journal of Autism and Developmental Disorders*, *47*, 2080–2091. https://doi.org/10.1007/s10803-017-3128-y
39. Chng, S., Lu, H. Y., Kumar, A., & Yau, D. (2022). Hacker types, motivations and strategies: A comprehensive framework. *Computers in Human Behavior Reports*, *5*, 100167. https://doi.org/10.1016/j.chbr.2022.100167

40. Dowden, C., Bennell, C., & Bloomfield, S. (2007). Advances in offender profiling: A systematic review of the profiling literature published over the past three decades. *Journal of Police and Criminal Psychology, 22*, 44–56. https://doi.org/10.1007/s11896-007-9000-9
41. Fox, B., & Farrington, D. P. (2018). What have we learned from offender profiling? A systematic review and meta-analysis of 40 years of research. Psychological Bulletin, 144(12), 1247. https://doi.org/10.1037/bul0000170
42. Bachmann, M. (2010). The risk propensity and rationality of computer hackers. *International Journal of Cyber Criminology, 4*(1/2), 643. https://doi.org/10.1016/j.clsr.2005.07.001
43. Kirwan, G., & Power, A. (2013). *Cybercrime: The psychology of online offenders*. Cambridge University Press. https://doi.org/10.1017/cbo9780511843846
44. Al-Mhiqani, M. N., Ahmad, R., Zainal Abidin, Z., Yassin, W., Hassan, A., Abdulkareem, K. H., Ali, N. S., & Yunos, Z. (2020). A review of insider threat detection: Classification, machine learning techniques, datasets, open challenges, and recommendations. *Applied Sciences, 10*(15), 5208. https://doi.org/10.3390/app10155208
45. Back, S., LaPrade, J., Shehadeh, L., & Kim, M. (2019). Youth hackers and adult hackers in South Korea: An application of cybercriminal profiling. *2019 IEEE European Symposium on Security and Privacy Workshops (EuroS&PW).*
46. Barber, R. (2001). Hackers profiled – who are they and what are their motivations? *Computer Fraud & Security, 2001*(2), 14–17. https://doi.org/10.1016/s1361-3723(01)02017-6
47. Becker, J. (1982). Who are the computer criminals? *ACM SIGCAS Computers and Society, 12*(1), 18–20. https://doi.org/10.1145/957893.957898
48. Bissett, A., & Shipton, G. (2000). Some human dimensions of computer virus creation and infection. International Journal of Human-Computer Studies, 52(5), 899–913. https://doi.org/10.1006/ijhc.1999.0361
49. Cayubit, R. F. O., Rebolledo, K. M., Kintanar, R. G. A., Pastores, A. G., Santiago, A. J. A., & Valles, P. B. V. (2017). A cyber phenomenon: A Q-analysis on the motivation of computer hackers. *Psychological Studies, 62*, 386–394. https://doi.org/10.1007/s12646-017-0423-9
50. Chiu, S. M. (2013). *Self-reported criminal computer behavior among university students in Hong Kong: A study of Big-Five personality traits, moral choice, exploitive manipulative behavior, and addictive tendencies.* Alliant International University, California School of Professional Psychology, Hong Kong.
51. Loper, D. K. (2000). *The criminology of computer hackers: A qualitative and quantitative analysis* [Doctoral Dissertation, Michigan State University]. East Lansing, MI.
52. Madarie, R. (2017). Hackers' motivations: Testing Schwartz's theory of motivational types of values in a sample of hackers. *International Journal of Cyber Criminology, 11*(1). https://doi.org/10.5281/zenodo.495773
53. McBrayer, J. (2014). *Exploiting the digital frontier: Hacker typology and motivation* [Masters Dissertation, The University of Alabama]. Tuscaloosa, AL. Retrieved April 24, 2023 from https://www.proquest.com/dissertations-theses/exploiting-digital-frontier-hacker-typology/docview/1562270477/se-2?accountid=44888.
54. Palmieri, M. J. (2022). *Decrypting personality: The effects of motivation, social power, and anonymity on cybercrime* [Doctoral Dissertation, University of Massachusetts Lowell]. Lowell, MA. https://www.proquest.com/dissertations-theses/decrypting-personality-effects-motivation-social/docview/2724700785/se-2?accountid=44888
55. Preuß, J., Furnell, S. M., & Papadaki, M. (2007). Considering the potential of criminal profiling to combat hacking. *Journal in Computer Virology, 3*, 135–141. https://doi.org/10.1007/s11416-007-0042-4
56. Rogers, M. K. (2006). A two-dimensional circumplex approach to the development of a hacker taxonomy. *Digital Investigation, 3*(2), 97–102. https://doi.org/10.1016/j.diin.2006.03.001
57. Seigfried-Spellar, K. C., Villacís-Vukadinović, N., & Lynam, D. R. (2017). Computer criminal behavior is related to psychopathy and other antisocial behavior. *Journal of Criminal Justice, 51*, 67–73. https://doi.org/10.1016/j.jcrimjus.2017.06.003
58. Shaw, E. D. (2006). The role of behavioral research and profiling in malicious cyber insider investigations. *Digital Investigation, 3*(1), 20–31. https://doi.org/10.1016/j.diin.2006.01.006
59. Virgara, J. L., & Whitten, T. (2023). A systematic literature review of the longitudinal risk factors associated with juvenile cyber-deviance. *Computers in Human Behavior, 141*, 107613. https://doi.org/10.1016/j.chb.2022.107613
60. Withers, K. L. (2019). *A psychosocial behavioral attribution model: Examining the relationship between the" Dark Triad" and cyber-criminal behaviors impacting social networking sites.* Nova Southeastern

University. https://www.proquest.com/dissertations-theses/psychosocial-behavioral-attribution-model/docview/2208411493/se-2?accountid=44888

61. Woo, H.-J. (2003). *The hacker mentality: Exploring the relationship between psychological variables and hacking activities* [Doctoral Dissertation, University of Georgia Athens]. Athens, GA. https://esploro.libs.uga.edu/esploro/outputs/doctoral/The-hacker-mentality{-}{-}-exploring/9949334952002959
62. Zhang, X., Tsang, A., Yue, W. T., & Chau, M. (2015). The classification of hackers by knowledge exchange behaviors. *Information Systems Frontiers*, *17*, 1239–1251. https://doi.org/10.1007/s10796-015-9567-0
63. Möller, D. P. (2023). Cyberattacker profiles, cyberattack models and scenarios, and cybersecurity ontology. In *Guide to cybersecurity in digital transformation: Trends, methods, technologies, applications and best practices* (pp. 181–229). Springer. https://doi.org/10.1007/978-3-031-26845-8_4
64. Pahi, T., & Skopik, F. (2019). Cyber attribution 2.0: Capture the false flag. *Proceedings of the 18th European Conference on Cyber Warfare and Security (ECCWS 2019).*
65. Frumento, E., Freschi, F., Andreoletti, D., & Consoli, A. (2017). Victim communication stack (VCS) a flexible model to select the human attack vector. *Proceedings of the 12th International Conference on Availability, Reliability and Security.*
66. McLean, M. (2024). *2024 Must-know cyber attack statistics and trends.* Retrieved January 19, 2024 from https://www.embroker.com/blog/cyber-attack-statistics/
67. Nazah, S., Huda, S., Abawajy, J., & Hassan, M. M. (2020). Evolution of dark web threat analysis and detection: A systematic approach. *IEEE Access*, *8*, 171796–171819. https://doi.org/10.1109/access.2020.3024198
68. Horan, C., & Saiedian, H. (2021). Cyber crime investigation: Landscape, challenges, and future research directions. *Journal of Cybersecurity and Privacy*, *1*(4), 580–596. https://doi.org/10.3390/jcp1040029
69. Tavabi, N., Bartley, N., Abeliuk, A., Soni, S., Ferrara, E., & Lerman, K. (2019). Characterizing activity on the deep and dark web. *Companion Proceedings of the 2019 World Wide Web Conference.*
70. Macanovic, A., & Przepiorka, W. (2023). The moral embeddedness of cryptomarkets: Text mining feedback on economic exchanges on the dark web. *Socio-Economic Review*, mwad069. https://doi.org/10.1093/ser/mwad069
71. Van Dam, C., Janssens, J. M., & De Bruyn, E. E. (2005). PEN, Big Five, juvenile delinquency and criminal recidivism. *Personality and Individual Differences*, *39*(1), 7–19. https://doi.org/10.1016/j.paid.2004.06.016
72. Domdouzis, K. (2019). *Detecting psycho-anomalies on the world-wide web: Current tools and challenges.* https://shura.shu.ac.uk/id/eprint/24406
73. Neville, S. W., & Li, K. F. (2009). The rational for developing larger-scale 1000+ machine emulation-based research test beds. *2009 International Conference on Advanced Information Networking and Applications Workshops.*
74. Donato, L. M. (2021). *Computer criminal profiling applied to digital investigations.* De Montfort University. https://www.proquest.com/dissertations-theses/computer-criminal-profiling-applied-digital/docview/2685242618/se-2?accountid=44888
75. Li, C., & Parsioan, T. (2005). Profiling honeynet attackers. *Proceedings of the Class of 2006 Senior Conference on Natural Language Processing.*
76. Jayakrishnan, A., & Vasanthi, V. (2018). Empirical survey on advances of network forensics in the emerging networks. *International Journal of Cyber-Security and Digital Forensics*, *7*(1), 38–46. https://doi.org/10.17781/p002320

AUTHOR BIOGRAPHY

Dr Oliver Guidetti is a post-doctoral researcher, specialising in the human factors of cyber security. He has an extensive background working on applied socio-technical projects that examine the interplay between the human brain and technology. His PhD research focused on measuring and mitigating vigilance decrement in cyber network defence tasks. Oliver has published numerous research papers on topics such as cyber vigilance tasks, the neuropsychology of network defence operators, human resource policy in relation to neurotechnology, and the effects of cognitive load on the performance of cyber first responders.

Mr Scott Mather is a dedicated Honours psychology student at Notre Dame University and an experienced mental health professional. Skilled in AUSLAN, mental health advocacy, and holistic care, Scott excels in creating supportive environments for clients. He has a strong background in psychology and security operations, holding several qualifications from North Metropolitan TAFE. Scott is the inventor of the SOMA Brain Computer Interface system, which he developed by leveraging his exceptional neuropsychology knowledge. Known for his innovation, wisdom, compassion, and commitment, Scott has been praised by both clients and colleagues alike.

10 The Human Firewall
Mitigating Ransomware Risks in Critical Infrastructures through Human-Centric Approaches

Avisen Moonsamy, Mohiuddin Ahmed, Oliver Guidetti, and Bazlur Rashid

10.1 INTRODUCTION

10.1.1 Understanding the Human Factor in Cybersecurity

In the rapidly evolving landscape of cyber threats, ransomware attacks have become a significant threat to global critical infrastructures. Despite the advancements in cybersecurity technologies, the human element within cybersecurity often remains the most vulnerable link in the chain, presenting a persistent challenge and serving as an entry point for cyber adversaries [1]. The problem, therefore, is not confined to the technological infrastructure alone but extends to the human interactions with these systems, highlighting a crucial vulnerability often overlooked by organisations confident in their state-of-the-art cybersecurity technologies [2]. The evidence supporting the critical role of human error in cybersecurity breaches is overwhelming, with various instances where lapses in security protocols, often due to human error, have led to significant breaches [3]. Moreover, evaluating and enhancing human capabilities have been paramount in securing critical infrastructures against sophisticated cyber-attacks [4, 5]. This underscores the necessity for a shift towards a human-centric approach in cybersecurity strategies, an argument gaining traction among cybersecurity professionals and researchers alike. On this end, Chamkar, Maleh, and Gherabi (2022) highlight the significance of understanding human factor capabilities within security operation centres (SOCs), suggesting that such an understanding can significantly mitigate cyber threats [4]. This perspective is grounded in the realisation that technology alone cannot fully protect against threats exploiting human psychology and behaviour. Thus, incorporating a human-centric approach into cybersecurity strategies addresses a critical vulnerability and enhances the overall resilience of critical infrastructures against cyber-attacks.

Many cybersecurity professionals feel overwhelmed by the technical complexities of defending against ransomware attacks, often overlooking the simpler yet profound impact of human vulnerabilities. Researchers and practitioners alike have felt the repercussions of this oversight, as evidenced by the increasing number of breaches facilitated by human error despite advances in cybersecurity technologies. Upon closer examination, it has been found that integrating human-centric approaches into cybersecurity measures significantly enhances defence mechanisms, turning potential human liabilities into proactive assets in combating ransomware threats. While technological defences are indispensable, addressing the human factor in cybersecurity is equally crucial. The problem of ransomware and other cyber threats cannot be effectively tackled without acknowledging and fortifying the human element. The paramount importance of the human factor in cybersecurity is evident, advocating for a balanced approach that values human-centric strategies alongside technological solutions. By addressing human vulnerabilities through education, awareness, and

 DOI: 10.1201/9781003469506-14

behavioural changes, organisations can create a more comprehensive and effective defence against the ever-evolving landscape of cyber threats.

10.1.2 The Intersection of Human Behavior and Ransomware

The intersection of human behaviour and ransomware constitutes a critical nexus at which the sophisticated tactics of cybercriminals meet the often-underestimated human element of cybersecurity. Ransomware attacks do not operate in a technological vacuum; instead, they frequently exploit human psychology and behavioural patterns to gain access to secure systems. Abomhara and Køien's (2015) exploration of cybersecurity vulnerabilities emphasises the complexity of the cyber threat landscape, particularly highlighting how the human factor can become a significant security gap [1]. The importance of human vulnerabilities is further echoed by Bates (2017), who notes that despite advances in cybersecurity technologies, the oversight of human factors often leads to breaches, illustrating that human error or manipulation can significantly undermine even the most sophisticated technical defences [2]. Brebbia, Garzia, and Lombardi (2018) provide a broader perspective on safety and security engineering, suggesting that understanding the human dimension is crucial for developing effective security strategies [3]. This underscores the necessity of a holistic cybersecurity approach incorporating human operators' psychological and behavioural aspects within critical infrastructures. Similarly, Chamkar, Maleh, and Gherabi (2022) discuss the role of human factor capabilities in SOCs, indicating that recognising and enhancing these capabilities can significantly reduce the risk of cyber threats, including ransomware [4].

The methods employed by ransomware attackers often rely on social engineering tactics, such as phishing, which directly target human vulnerabilities. Daniel Ani, He, and Tiwari (2016) highlight the importance of evaluating human capabilities in critical industrial infrastructure, suggesting that a deeper understanding of human behaviour can inform more effective defences against cyber-attacks [5]. This evaluation is critical in ransomware, where attackers leverage psychological manipulation to deceive individuals into compromising their or their organisation's security. The intersection of human behaviour and ransomware is further complicated by the evolving nature of ransomware attacks. The rise of Ransomware 2.0 and 3.0 further illustrates an increasing sophistication in how attackers exploit human psychology and organisational behaviour patterns to orchestrate successful attacks [6–28]. These versions of ransomware encrypt data and employ tactics such as double extortion, where attackers will threaten to release sensitive data in a public forum if the ransom is not paid, leveraging fear and urgency to coerce victims into complying with their demands. The intersection of human behaviour and ransomware highlights the critical role that human vulnerabilities play in the success of ransomware attacks. It underscores the need for a cybersecurity strategy beyond technological defences to include a deep understanding of human psychology and behaviour.

10.2 LITERATURE REVIEW

The literature review investigates the intricate relationship between human vulnerabilities and cyber threats, focusing on social engineering and the psychological factors contributing to security breaches. This section synthesises findings from various studies, highlighting the critical role that human behaviour plays in the cybersecurity landscape. The literature review is broken down into the following sections:

10.2.1 Studies on Human Vulnerabilities and Cyber Threats

Human vulnerabilities are a significant catalyst in the success of cyber threats, particularly ransomware attacks. The human component of cybersecurity is not just a peripheral concern but a central factor that influences organisations' overall security posture. Integrating human factors into cybersecurity strategies is not merely a recommendation but a necessity, as underscored by the breadth of research in this field [1–28].

Abomhara and Køien (2015) provide a foundational understanding of how cyber adversaries can exploit human vulnerabilities, emphasising the need for a comprehensive approach that includes technological and human-centric solutions [1]. This dual approach is essential because while technology can filter out many threats, it cannot address human behaviour's complex and dynamic nature that often leads to security breaches. Bates (2017) further argues that the reliance on technology alone is insufficient to safeguard against cyber threats, particularly ransomware attacks, which have become increasingly sophisticated in exploiting human vulnerabilities [2]. This highlights a gap in many cybersecurity defences focusing primarily on technological solutions without adequately addressing the human element.

On the other hand, Brebbia, Garzia, and Lombardi (2018) suggest that integrating safety and security engineering principles with an understanding of human behaviour can significantly enhance the effectiveness of cybersecurity measures [3]. This approach recognises that human errors or misjudgements are often the result of inadequate training, lack of awareness, or the complex interplay of psychological factors that influence decision-making processes. Chamkar, Maleh, and Gherabi (2022) underscore the importance of developing capabilities within SOCs that go beyond technical skills, including behavioural insights and psychological profiling [4]. This perspective is crucial in identifying and mitigating threats that exploit human tendencies, such as the susceptibility to phishing attacks or the inclination to bypass security protocols for convenience.

The literature further indicates that the challenges posed by human vulnerabilities are not insurmountable. Strategies such as continuous awareness programs, simulated phishing exercises, and incorporating behavioural analytics into security protocols can significantly reduce the risk of cyber threats [5–28]. These strategies emphasise the need for a proactive and comprehensive approach to cybersecurity that addresses both the technological and human aspects. Moreover, the evolution of ransomware and the sophistication of cyber threats necessitate an ongoing reassessment of human vulnerabilities and the development of innovative solutions to mitigate these risks. Incorporating human-centric approaches into cybersecurity frameworks strengthens the defences against current threats and prepares organisations for future challenges in the cyber landscape.

10.2.2 Social Engineering and Its Impact

Ransomware is a form of cyber attack that is becoming one of the most dangerous methods of exploiting human vulnerabilities. Social engineering techniques, which range from phishing emails to pretexting and baiting, rely on psychological manipulation, exploiting the innately human traits of trust and curiosity. The effectiveness of these tactics in bypassing sophisticated technological defences underscores the need for a more nuanced approach to cybersecurity that encompasses both technological solutions and human behaviour understanding. Daniel Ani, He, and Tiwari (2016) emphasise the critical role of evaluating and reinforcing human defences against social engineering, suggesting that a deep understanding of human psychology is essential in crafting robust defences against such attacks [5]. This approach acknowledges that while technology can filter and block many threats, it cannot fully compensate for the complexity and unpredictability of human behaviour, especially when manipulated by skilled adversaries.

The work of Furnell and Emm (2017) on the ABC of ransomware protection, such as awareness, behaviour, and control, further highlights the foundational elements necessary to defend against social engineering [7]. Awareness involves educating users about the nature of these threats and how they manifest. Behaviour focuses on fostering a security-conscious culture where safe practices become second nature. Control encompasses the policies and technologies that support these efforts. This triad forms a comprehensive strategy against social engineering by addressing the threat and transforming the organisational culture into one that values and practices cybersecurity vigilance. Gazzan, Alqahtani, and Sheldon (2021) also highlight the increasing prevalence of ransomware attacks that leverage social engineering tactics to target industrial control systems, illustrating these threats' broad scope and high stakes [8]. The fact that critical infrastructure, which is essential for national security and public safety, can be compromised through social engineering underscores the urgency of addressing this issue.

The literature further suggests that the impact of social engineering extends beyond the immediate security breach. It can have profound psychological effects on the victims, including a loss of trust in digital communications and a sense of vulnerability, which can undermine the overall morale and productivity of an organisation [9–28]. Additionally, successful social engineering attacks can lead to significant financial losses, reputational damage, and legal liabilities, emphasising the need for a comprehensive approach to mitigating these threats. To counteract the threat posed by social engineering, organisations must implement multifaceted strategies that include regular and engaging security awareness training, simulation exercises to test employee responses to phishing attempts, and behavioural analytics to identify unusual patterns of behaviour that may indicate a security breach. Moreover, fostering an organisational culture encouraging scepticism and information verification can be a powerful deterrent against social engineering tactics.

10.2.3 Psychological Factors in Security Breaches

The psychological dimensions of security breaches represent a critical yet often underexplored facet of cybersecurity. The interplay between human psychology and cyber threats underscores organisations' nuanced challenge in safeguarding against these incursions. Ghafir et al. (2018) delve into how attackers exploit psychological tactics to facilitate security breaches, revealing that a profound understanding of human behaviour is pivotal in pre-empting these threats [9]. This acknowledgement of the human psyche as a battleground in cybersecurity necessitates a more sophisticated approach to defence mechanisms that transcends traditional technical safeguards.

The literature advocates implementing psychological profiling and behavioural analytics to fortify defences against security breaches. Franchina et al. (2021) distinguish themselves in this discourse by proposing passive and active training methods that leverage psychological insights to bolster the security posture of critical infrastructures [6]. This approach not only educates individuals on the potential threats but also actively engages them in scenarios that test and enhance their psychological resilience to social engineering and other psychologically manipulative tactics. Further exploration reveals that the impact of psychological factors extends beyond the individual to influence organisational culture and security practices. For instance, the work of Furnell and Emm (2017) on the ABC of ransomware protection emphasises the role of awareness, behaviour, and control in creating a cybersecurity-aware culture within organisations [7]. This framework suggests that psychological resilience against cyber threats can be cultivated through consistent and comprehensive training programs that inform and empower individuals to act decisively against potential breaches.

Moreover, the rise of ransomware attacks targeting human vulnerabilities highlights the urgent need for cybersecurity strategies integrating psychological defences. Gazzan, Alqahtani, and Sheldon (2021) illustrate how ransomware campaigns have evolved to exploit the psychological tendencies of individuals, thereby necessitating a shift in defence strategies to address these evolving threats [8]. This evolution points to the importance of adaptive security measures capable of countering the dynamic nature of cyber threats. The application of behavioural analytics emerges as a particularly promising strategy in this context. By monitoring and analysing user behaviour, organisations can identify anomalous activities that may indicate a breach or an attempted attack, allowing for swift and effective responses. This proactive approach to cybersecurity, grounded in psychological principles, represents a significant advancement in the field, moving towards a more holistic understanding of security that encompasses both the technological and human elements.

We see a complex relationship between human vulnerabilities, social engineering tactics, and psychological factors in cybersecurity threats. The collective findings underscore the necessity of a paradigm shift towards a more human-centric approach to cybersecurity, where psychological resilience, awareness, and behaviour modification are considered integral components of a comprehensive defence strategy. This approach advocates for enhancing human capabilities alongside technological defences, aiming to create a more robust and effective cybersecurity posture that can adapt to the ever-evolving nature of cyber threats.

10.2.4 Ransomware Evolution and Human Targets

The evolution of ransomware and its strategic pivot towards exploiting human vulnerabilities underscores a dynamic cyber threat landscape where technological advancements and human factors intersect. As Abomhara and Køien (2015) highlight, the progression of ransomware tactics necessitates a deeper understanding of both the technical mechanisms and the psychological tactics employed by attackers [1]. This evolution is not merely a testament to the adaptability of cybercriminals but also a call to action for cybersecurity professionals to integrate a more nuanced understanding of human behaviour into their defence strategies.

In the early stages of ransomware, the primary method of attack was straightforward – encrypt the victim's data and demand a ransom for the decryption key. However, as users and organisations became more adept at securing their data and backups, attackers recognised the need to evolve their strategies. This realisation led to a more sophisticated approach, focusing not just on the technological vulnerabilities but also the human ones. The shift towards targeting human behaviours through phishing and social engineering represents a strategic exploitation of the intrinsic human tendencies to trust and seek information.

This deeper exploitation of the human factor is evident in the design and dissemination of phishing emails, which have become increasingly sophisticated, mimicking legitimate communications from trusted entities. The psychological manipulation involved in these tactics is based on a detailed understanding of human psychology, including the principles of urgency, authority, and familiarity. By creating a sense of urgency, attackers compel the victim to act hastily, often bypassing rational judgement and security protocols. The invocation of authority, such as impersonating a company executive or a well-known institution, exploits the human tendency to comply with requests from perceived authority figures. Similarly, using familiar logos and language patterns leverages the trust associated with recognised entities to deceive the victim into engaging with malicious content.

The transition to more human-centric attack vectors is further exemplified in the evolution to Ransomware 2.0 and 3.0, which incorporate techniques such as double extortion and the targeting of backups. These tactics aim to encrypt data and threaten to leak sensitive information unless additional ransoms are paid, exploiting the fear of public exposure and reputational damage. This evolution highlights the attackers' reliance on psychological manipulation to achieve their goals, emphasising the importance of psychological resilience alongside technical defences. In response to this evolving threat, cybersecurity strategies must also evolve, integrating a comprehensive understanding of human vulnerabilities into their frameworks. Developing effective defences against ransomware requires technological solutions and a focus on educating users about social engineering and phishing risks. This educational aspect is crucial in building a culture of cybersecurity awareness that empowers individuals to recognise and resist manipulation attempts.

The evolution of ransomware from a primarily technical threat to one that exploits human vulnerabilities underscores the complex interplay between technology and psychology in cybersecurity. As ransomware tactics become increasingly sophisticated, leveraging human trust, curiosity, and fear, the need for a multidimensional approach to cybersecurity becomes evident. This approach must blend technological defences with an in-depth understanding of human behaviour, emphasising the critical role of education, awareness, and psychological resilience in combating the ever-evolving ransomware threat.

10.2.5 Rise of Ransomware 2.0 and 3.0

The advent of Ransomware 2.0 and 3.0 marks a significant evolution in the threat landscape, characterised by increasingly sophisticated tactics that leverage technological advancements and deep insights into human psychology. Ransomware 2.0 introduced the concept of double extortion, where attackers demand a ransom to decrypt the victim's data and threaten to release sensitive information publicly if their demands are not met [7]. This tactic exploits the victim's fear of reputational damage and the potential legal ramifications of data breaches, adding psychological pressure to the already daunting challenge of dealing with encrypted data. Ransomware 3.0 further escalates the threat by incorporating more advanced technologies, such as using machine learning to identify and target specific data types or individuals within an organisation and automating attacks to increase the number of potential victims [7]. Targeting backups, a key recovery strategy for many organisations, represents another layer of sophistication in these ransomware variants. By eliminating the possibility of recovery from backups, attackers leave victims with fewer options other than paying the ransom, thereby increasing the efficacy of the attack. Gazzan, Alqahtani, and Sheldon (2021) discuss the rise of ransomware attacks on industrial control systems, illustrating the extent to which cybercriminals are willing to go to ensure the success of their campaigns [8]. This shift demonstrates the technical prowess of attackers and their understanding of organisational dependencies on digital infrastructures.

A strategic shift in the selection of targets has accompanied the rise of Ransomware 2.0 and 3.0. Cybercriminals have increasingly focused on sectors where the urgency for access to encrypted data is paramount, such as healthcare, finance, and critical infrastructure. These sectors are often willing to pay ransoms quickly to restore access to vital data and services, making them attractive targets for ransomware attacks. This strategic targeting is informed by a thorough understanding of market dynamics and the critical nature of the targeted sectors' operations, highlighting the need for sector-specific cybersecurity strategies.

10.2.6 Behavioural Patterns in Ransomware Attacks

The relationship between ransomware attackers and their targets is heavily influenced by the behavioural patterns of the latter. As cybercriminals refine their strategies, understanding and addressing the human behaviours predisposing organisations to ransomware attacks become paramount. Gazzan, Alqahtani, and Sheldon (2021) delve into the mechanics of social engineering, a cornerstone of modern ransomware campaigns, which meticulously exploit human tendencies to trust and seek convenience and conclude that this exploitation is not random but a calculated manipulation of routine behaviours and psychological vulnerabilities [8].

10.2.6.1 Exploitation of Routine Behaviours

Routine behaviours, such as checking emails and clicking on links without due diligence, serve as the primary vector for ransomware attacks. The familiarity and frequency of these actions make them ripe for exploitation, as attackers disguise malicious intent within the guise of legitimacy. This manipulation influences human cognitive bias towards patterns and routines, making deviations harder to detect. The effectiveness of these tactics underscores the need for a vigilant and informed user base trained to scrutinise even the most routine activities for signs of wrongdoing.

10.2.6.2 Behavioural Analytics as a Countermeasure

The deployment of behavioural analytics emerges as a crucial defence mechanism against ransomware attacks. Ghafir et al. (2018) advocate for this technology, highlighting its potential to identify and mitigate threats by monitoring for deviations from established norms of user behaviour [9]. This approach is predicated on the understanding that ransomware attacks, despite their sophistication, often induce abnormal behaviour patterns in infected systems or individuals. By establishing a "normal" behaviour baseline, cybersecurity systems can swiftly identify, alert, and sometimes auto-remediate suspicious activities indicative of a ransomware attack in progress. Franchina et al.'s (2021) discussion on passive and active training methods reflects the importance of ongoing education and awareness programs in altering user behaviour to reduce susceptibility to these attacks [6].

10.3 ANATOMY OF RANSOMWARE AND HUMAN ERROR

In the evolving landscape of cybersecurity threats, ransomware stands out for its insidious ability to exploit the most unpredictable element of any security system: human behaviour. The anatomy of a ransomware attack reveals a strategic exploitation of human error, which remains a constant vulnerability despite advancements in cybersecurity technologies. The assertion that human error is often the weakest link in the security chain is supported by a wealth of evidence [1, 2, 4, 5, 7, 8, 9]. In their research, Abomhara and Køien (2015) elucidate how simple mistakes, such as clicking on a malicious link or downloading an infected attachment, can be the initial vector for devastating ransomware attacks [1]. This reliance on human fallibility underscores the attackers' understanding that the most sophisticated cybersecurity measures can be bypassed with relative ease through social engineering tactics. The premise that understanding and mitigating human error is crucial for defending against ransomware is further highlighted by examining real-world incidents where human error led to significant security breaches. For example, Ghafir et al. (2018) present a case where a seemingly innocuous action by an employee – opening a phishing email – facilitated a ransomware attack, demonstrating the outsized role of human error in security breaches [9]. These incidents highlight a critical vulnerability in cybersecurity defences: attackers often do not need to overcome security systems directly; they can simply persuade or trick users into granting access. This analysis underlines the urgent need for organisations to prioritise human factors in their cybersecurity strategies, emphasising that technological defences, while necessary, are insufficient. A significant aspect of ransomware incidents involves the targeting of industrial control systems. This tactic poses a financial threat and a potential hazard to critical infrastructure and public safety. The sophistication of these attacks, as discussed by Gazzan, Alqahtani, and Sheldon (2021), often involves initial entry points that exploit routine user interactions with digital systems, such as the clicking of a link or the opening of an attachment [8]. These actions, benign in isolation, become vectors for significant breaches when manipulated by malicious actors.

Building on the necessity to address human vulnerabilities, psychological profiling is another effective tool for strengthening organisational defences against ransomware. Furnell and Emm (2017) discuss the importance of psychological resilience against social engineering, noting that certain psychological traits may make individuals more susceptible to manipulation [7]. By identifying and understanding these traits, organisations can tailor their training programs to address specific vulnerabilities, significantly reducing the risk of successful ransomware attacks. This approach suggests that psychological profiling is not merely an academic exercise but a practical strategy that can inform more effective, targeted cybersecurity training. Integrating psychological insights into cybersecurity education highlights a paradigm shift towards a more holistic approach to defence that incorporates an understanding of human psychology alongside technological solutions. Organisations that recognise the multifaceted nature of ransomware threats often find greater success in mitigating their impact. They understand that fostering a culture of vigilance and continuous education is crucial in combating the ever-evolving tactics of ransomware attackers. These organisations often report a decrease in successful attacks, attributing their resilience to enhanced user training programs that emphasise awareness, behaviour modification, and psychological resilience as key components of their cybersecurity posture.

The battle against ransomware is as much about understanding human psychology as it is about deploying technological defences. The strategic exploitation of human error by ransomware attackers necessitates a comprehensive response addressing technological vulnerabilities and human factors. By analysing the anatomy of ransomware attacks, learning from past breaches, and applying

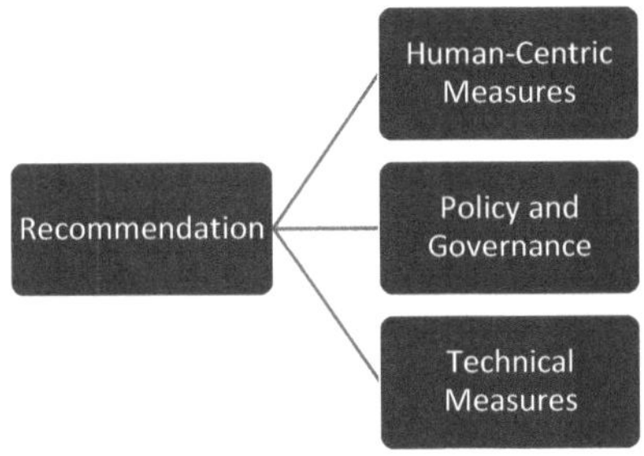

FIGURE 10.1 Categories of Recommendations.

psychological insights, organisations can enhance their defences against these malicious threats. This comprehensive approach, which includes regular, targeted training and a commitment to fostering a security-conscious culture, is essential for building resilience against ransomware attacks. It underscores the importance of reacting to cyber threats and proactively preparing for them by understanding and mitigating the human errors that often pave the way for these attacks.

10.4 RECOMMENDATIONS

The literature review and the analysis of ransomware incidents underscore the need to strengthen cybersecurity frameworks by focusing on the human element, refining policy recommendations, enhancing technical defences, and integrating human factors into security protocols. Drawing insights from the literature, including key studies and expert analyses, this section outlines comprehensive recommendations for bolstering cyber defences against ransomware threats. The recommendations are categorised into three primary groups: human-centric measures, policy and governance, and technical defences, as illustrated in Figure 10.1.

This categorisation helps highlight the multifaceted approach necessary for effective cybersecurity strategy, emphasising the balance between human elements, policy frameworks, and technological solutions.

10.4.1 Human-Centric Measures (HCM)

10.4.1.1 HCM-1: Strengthening the Human Element in Cyber Defense

The human element in cybersecurity, often considered the weakest link, can be transformed into a formidable first line of defence with the right strategies. Furnell and Emm (2017) emphasise the critical role of continuous awareness and training programs in instilling a proactive security culture within organisations [7]. Training programs should be dynamic, engaging, and reflective of the latest cyber threat trends, ensuring employees are aware of the risks and equipped to respond effectively. Incorporating psychological insights into these programs, as Ghafir et al. (2018) suggest, can further enhance their effectiveness by addressing the underlying behaviours and motivations that make individuals susceptible to social engineering tactics [9]. These programs serve as the cornerstone of a robust cybersecurity strategy, aiming not only to inform but also to engage and empower employees to act as vigilant guardians of their digital domains.

10.4.1.2 HCM-2: Dynamic and Engaging Training Programs

For training programs to be effective, they must transcend traditional, often tedious formats that fail to capture the attention or interest of employees. Organisations can significantly increase engagement and retention of critical cybersecurity principles by adopting dynamic and engaging methodologies, such as gamified learning experiences, interactive workshops, and real-world simulations.

These innovative approaches make learning more accessible and enjoyable, encouraging active participation and ongoing engagement with cybersecurity practices.

10.4.1.3 HCM-3: Reflecting the Latest Cyber Threat Trends

Cybersecurity is an ever-evolving field, with threat actors continually adapting and refining their tactics. As such, training programs must be equally adaptive, incorporating the latest intelligence on cyber threat trends and emerging vulnerabilities. This ensures that employees are aware of traditional threats and prepared to recognise and respond to new and sophisticated attacks. Regular updates to training content, informed by the latest research and incident analyses, will keep the organisation at the forefront of cyber defence.

10.4.1.4 HCM-4: Incorporating Psychological Insights

Incorporating psychological insights into cybersecurity training represents a critical advancement in designing and implementing these programs [9]. Understanding the psychological tactics employed by attackers, such as the exploitation of trust, the manipulation of authority, and the creation of urgency, can arm employees with the knowledge to critically evaluate and respond to potential threats. Training that addresses these psychological aspects can help demystify the strategies used by cybercriminals, reducing the likelihood of employees falling prey to social engineering tactics.

10.4.1.5 HCM-5: Addressing Underlying Behaviours and Motivations

A key component of strengthening the human element in cyber defence lies in addressing the underlying behaviours and motivations predisposing individuals to cybersecurity risks. This involves educating employees about the mechanics of cyber threats and fostering an environment where security-minded behaviours are recognised and rewarded. Creating a culture that values security as a collective responsibility can motivate individuals to adopt safer practices and encourage their peers to do the same. Moreover, understanding individual motivations and barriers to secure behaviour can inform the development of targeted interventions that address specific vulnerabilities within the organisation.

10.4.1.6 HCM-6: Psychological and Behavioural Considerations

Understanding the psychological and behavioural aspects of cybersecurity is another crucial method in developing security protocols that are effective and embraced by users. Incorporating principles from behavioural science, such as using nudges to encourage secure behaviours or understanding cognitive biases that might lead to security oversights, can enhance the design of security measures. For instance, reminders or alerts timed to occur when users are most receptive can increase compliance with security protocols.

10.4.1.7 HCM-7: Integrating Human Factors in Security Protocols

Integrating human factors into security protocols involves a holistic approach that considers cybersecurity's psychological, behavioural, and emotional aspects. This integration can be achieved by designing security interfaces and protocols that are intuitive and user-friendly, reducing the likelihood of user error. Furthermore, engaging employees in developing and reviewing security protocols can provide valuable insights into potential vulnerabilities and foster a sense of ownership and responsibility towards cybersecurity. Encouraging an open dialogue about cyber threats and security concerns within the organisation can also demystify cybersecurity, making it more accessible and understandable to all employees.

10.4.1.8 HCM-8: Fostering an Open Dialogue

Encouraging an open dialogue about cyber threats and security concerns within an organisation is essential for demystifying cybersecurity. Organisations can enhance their collective understanding and awareness of cybersecurity issues by creating a culture where discussions about cyber risks are encouraged and valued. This openness not only aids in educating employees but also helps identify and address concerns that could lead to potential breaches. Regular cybersecurity forums, newsletters, and awareness campaigns can serve as platforms for this dialogue, ensuring that cybersecurity remains a central focus of the organisational culture.

10.4.1.9 HCM-9: Training and Awareness

Complementing policies with regular training and awareness programs enhances their effectiveness. Employees should be educated on the rationale behind policies, non-compliance risks, and their role in maintaining the organisation's cybersecurity defences. Interactive training sessions, simulations, and assessments can reinforce policy principles and encourage proactive security behaviours.

10.4.1.10 HCM-10: Engaging Employees in Development and Review

Involving employees in developing and reviewing security protocols is a strategy that improves the effectiveness of these measures and fosters a deeper sense of ownership and responsibility among staff. This participatory approach identifies potential vulnerabilities that might not be evident to IT, cyber, and security teams alone. As employees interact with different facets of an organisation's digital environment, their insights can be invaluable in creating more secure and practical security protocols. This engagement can be facilitated through regular feedback sessions, workshops, and inclusion in security task forces.

10.4.1.11 HCM-11: Designing Intuitive Security Interfaces and Protocols

The design of security interfaces and protocols that are intuitive and user-friendly is paramount in minimising the risk of human error, a significant factor in cybersecurity breaches. By simplifying complex processes and ensuring that security measures are accessible and understandable, organisations can significantly reduce the likelihood of mistakes that could lead to exploited vulnerabilities. For example, password policies that require complex combinations can be complemented with password managers that assist users in creating and storing secure passwords, thus balancing security with usability.

10.4.2 Policy and Governance (PG)

10.4.2.1 PG-1: Comprehensive Coverage

Effective cybersecurity policies must encapsulate the entirety of an organisation's digital and physical interactions with data. Beyond the basics of email usage and password management, policies should address the use of portable devices, remote work protocols, social media guidelines, and the handling of sensitive information. This comprehensive coverage ensures that employees know the expectations in all aspects of their work and provides a clear reference point for acceptable behaviour.

10.4.2.2 PG-2: Feedback Mechanisms

Incorporating feedback mechanisms into policy development and enforcement processes allows for continuously improving cybersecurity measures. As the end-users of these policies, employees can provide valuable insights into their practicality and areas for enhancement. An open-door policy for feedback encourages a culture of security-mindedness and collective responsibility, making it easier to identify and address potential vulnerabilities before they are exploited.

10.4.2.3 PG-3: Regular Review and Updates

The dynamic nature of the cyber threat landscape necessitates that policies are not static documents but living frameworks that evolve alongside new threats and organisational changes. Regular reviews, ideally annually or following significant technological updates, ensure that policies remain relevant and effective. This process should involve stakeholders from various departments to ensure that policies are practical and reflect the organisation's operational reality, thus fostering broader ownership and adherence.

10.4.2.4 PG-4: Consistent Enforcement and Consequences

The effectiveness of policies is contingent upon their consistent enforcement across all levels of the organisation. Clear consequences for non-compliance, communicated transparently to all employees, underscore the seriousness with which the organisation views cybersecurity. This enforcement mechanism should be fair and impartial, with procedures in place for investigating breaches and determining appropriate responses. Such consistency reinforces the importance of cybersecurity and ensures that policies are more than mere suggestions – they are integral to the organisation's operational integrity.

10.4.2.5 PG-5: Policy Recommendations for Employee Security Practices

Policies and procedures play a crucial role in governing employee behaviour and establishing clear guidelines for cybersecurity. Abomhara and Køien (2015) advocate for developing comprehensive policies covering all cybersecurity aspects, from email usage to data access and password management [1]. These policies should be regularly reviewed and updated to reflect the evolving threat landscape and organisational changes. Moreover, they should be enforced consistently across all levels of the organisation, with clear consequences for non-compliance, to underscore their importance and ensure adherence. These policies serve as the blueprint for expected behaviour, delineating the boundaries within which employees operate and interact with organisational and customer data.

10.4.3 Technical Defences (TD)

10.4.3.1 TD-1: Zero-Trust Architecture

Adopting a zero-trust architecture represents a paradigm shift in cybersecurity, moving away from the traditional perimeter-based defence model. In a zero-trust framework, no entity is automatically trusted, whether inside or outside the network. Instead, every access request is rigorously verified, and the principle of least privilege is applied to minimise the access rights of users and devices. This approach significantly reduces the attack surface, limiting the opportunities for ransomware and other cyber threats to exploit vulnerabilities within the network.

10.4.3.2 TD-2: Regular Security Audits

Conducting regular security audits is essential for maintaining a robust cybersecurity posture. These audits provide a comprehensive assessment of an organisation's security infrastructure, identifying vulnerabilities and areas for improvement. By systematically evaluating the effectiveness of existing security measures, organisations can adapt their strategies to address emerging threats, ensuring their defences remain resilient over time.

10.4.3.3 TD-3: Technical Recommendations Supporting Human Defences

While human-centric approaches are vital, they must be complemented by robust technical defences that provide a safety net for when human errors occur. Implementing advanced threat detection systems, encryption technologies, and regular security audits can significantly enhance an organisation's resilience to ransomware attacks. As highlighted by Ghafir et al. (2018), behavioural analytics offer a proactive means of detecting unusual activities that may signify a breach, allowing for swift containment and response [9]. Adopting a zero-trust architecture, where no entity within or outside the network is automatically trusted, can further secure organisational assets against ransomware threats.

10.4.3.4 TD-4: Advanced Threat Detection Systems

Deploying advanced threat detection systems is paramount in identifying potential threats before they can cause significant damage. These systems utilise a combination of signature-based detection, heuristic analysis, and behaviour monitoring to identify malicious activities indicative of ransomware or other cyber threats. The continuous evolution of these systems ensures they remain effective against the latest threats, providing organisations with the tools necessary to respond to attacks swiftly and decisively.

10.4.3.5 TD-5: Encryption Technologies

Encryption technologies play a crucial role in protecting sensitive data, ensuring that the information remains inaccessible to unauthorised users even in the event of a breach. Organisations can significantly reduce the risk of data theft and ransomware attacks by encrypting data at rest and in transit. This layer of protection is especially critical in sectors where the confidentiality and integrity of data are paramount, such as healthcare, finance, and government.

10.4.3.6 TD-6: Behavioural Analytics

As Ghafir et al. (2018) emphasised, behavioural analytics offers a proactive approach to cybersecurity, enabling organisations to detect and respond to unusual activities that may indicate a breach [9]. By analysing user behaviour patterns, these systems can identify deviations from the norm, such as unusual login attempts or the unexpected movement of data, that may signify an attack in progress. This capability allows for swift containment and response, minimising the potential impact of a breach.

These technical defences complement human-centric measures and policy and governance approaches, forming a comprehensive barrier against the multifaceted threats of ransomware and other cyber-attacks. The integration of advanced technical measures fortifies an organisation's defence mechanisms. It acts as a critical safety net, mitigating the impact of human errors, an inevitable aspect of any security system.

10.5 ACTION PLAN

In addressing the multifaceted challenge of ransomware and other cyber threats, organisations must deploy a blend of immediate and strategic actions tailored to fortify their human firewall. It advocates for the incorporation of tabletop exercises, the development of a comprehensive response plan, and the utilisation of workbooks to enhance employees' cybersecurity education and preparedness.

10.5.1 Short-Term Actions for Immediate Improvement

1. **Immediate Cybersecurity Awareness Evaluation:** Initiate a baseline assessment to gauge the current cybersecurity awareness levels within the organisation. Use tailored quizzes and simulated phishing exercises to mimic recent cyber threats, identifying knowledge gaps and areas for immediate reinforcement.
2. **Launch Interactive Cybersecurity Training Sessions:** Roll out an immersive training program focusing on urgent vulnerabilities. Incorporate the use of workbooks that offer practical exercises and real-world scenarios, encouraging active learning and retention. Make these sessions mandatory to ensure organization-wide participation and awareness.
3. **Develop and Communicate Clear Cybersecurity Policies:** Based on Abomhara and Køien's (2015) advice, craft comprehensive and understandable cybersecurity policies that are readily accessible to all employees. These should be communicated effectively, ensuring everyone understands their role in safeguarding the organisation's digital assets [1].
4. **Conduct Initial Security Audits and Tabletop Exercises:** Conduct an exhaustive security audit to pinpoint vulnerabilities. Following the audit, organise tabletop exercises that simulate ransomware attack scenarios, involving various teams to walk through the response plan. This will test the organisation's preparedness and identify areas for improvement in the response strategy.

10.5.2 Long-Term Strategies for Sustainable Security Culture

1. **Cultivate a Continuous Learning Environment:** Implement a structured program for ongoing cybersecurity education that adapts to emerging threats. Regularly update training materials, including workbooks and scenario-based exercises, to keep the content relevant and engaging. Encourage feedback from employees to tailor the education materials to their needs and experiences.
2. **Integrate Advanced Behavioural Analytics:** Leverage behavioural analytics to monitor for deviations from normal activity patterns, as highlighted by Ghafir et al. (2018) [9]. This proactive surveillance enables early detection of potential threats, facilitating a swift and informed response.
3. **Engage Employees with Regular Tabletop Exercises:** Regularly scheduled tabletop exercises should become a staple in the organisation's cybersecurity regimen. These exercises simulate various cyberattack scenarios, including ransomware, allowing teams to practice their response in a controlled environment. This practice reinforces the response plan and builds employee confidence in responding to real incidents.
4. **Continually Update the Cybersecurity Response Plan:** Develop a dynamic response plan that evolves with the cybersecurity landscape. This plan should outline specific roles and responsibilities, communication protocols, and recovery processes in the event of an attack. Regular reviews and updates of the plan are essential to incorporate lessons learned from tabletop exercises and actual incidents.
5. **Promote a Culture of Security Ownership:** Foster an organisational culture where every employee feels responsible for cybersecurity. Encourage the reporting of suspicious activities and offer regular opportunities for employees to contribute to the security dialogue. Recognising and rewarding proactive security behaviours can significantly enhance this culture of ownership.

Enhancing the human firewall against cyber threats requires a comprehensive, proactive approach integrating technical and human-centric strategies. Organisations can quickly bolster their defences by undertaking immediate actions such as conducting baseline assessments, launching interactive training, and organising tabletop exercises. For long-term resilience, fostering a culture of continuous learning, regularly engaging in exercises that test the response plan, and ensuring cybersecurity policies and practices evolve in tandem with emerging threats are crucial. This action plan, enriched with practical tools like workbooks and behavioural analytics, equips organisations to counter current cyber threats and build a sustainable security culture capable of facing future challenges.

10.6 CONCLUSION

Transforming the human element from the weakest link into a formidable line of defence against cyber threats requires a comprehensive and adaptive approach. Organisations can significantly enhance their cybersecurity posture by developing dynamic and engaging training programs, keeping abreast of the latest cyber threat trends, incorporating psychological insights, and addressing underlying behaviours and motivations. This human-centric approach to cyber defence mitigates the risk of successful attacks. It fosters a resilient and proactive security culture that empowers employees to act as key defenders in the ongoing battle against cyber threats.

The analysis of ransomware defence mechanisms underscores the indispensable role of the human element in fortifying cybersecurity infrastructures. The discussions emphasise that while technical defences provide a necessary barrier against cyber threats, integrating human-centric security measures is pivotal in creating a resilient and robust defence system against the sophisticated landscape of ransomware attacks. The pivotal role of the human element in ransomware defence cannot be overstated. The effectiveness of cybersecurity strategies significantly hinges on the awareness, behaviour, and control exerted by the organisation's human resources. The discussions around integrating human factors into security protocols, coupled with the emphasis on designing intuitive security interfaces and engaging employees in developing security measures, highlight the necessity of considering cybersecurity's psychological, behavioural, and emotional aspects. This approach mitigates the risk of human error and fosters a culture of security-mindedness that is crucial in anticipating and countering ransomware threats.

Recapping the need for human-centric security measures, it is clear that addressing the human element in cybersecurity strategies is not merely an option but a requirement. By adopting a multi-layered approach that combines advanced technical defences with comprehensive human-centric strategies, organisations can significantly enhance their resilience to ransomware attacks. Furthermore, adopting policies that reflect a deep understanding of human behaviour and establishing a culture that prioritises cybersecurity awareness across all levels of the organisation are critical in mitigating the risks associated with ransomware, as well as developing comprehensive policies that cover all aspects of cybersecurity is essential in governing employee behaviour and ensuring adherence to security protocols.

In conclusion, the fight against ransomware demands a holistic approach that recognises the critical role of the human element. The discussions drawn from the literature advocate for a balanced strategy that integrates technical and human-centric measures, emphasising the need for continuous innovation and adaptation in cybersecurity practices. By prioritising the human element and fostering a culture of proactive cybersecurity awareness, organisations can build a more effective defence mechanism against the ever-evolving threat of ransomware, ensuring the security and integrity of their digital assets.

REFERENCES

1. Abomhara, M., & Køien, G. M. (2015). Cyber security and the internet of things: Vulnerabilities, threats, intruders and attacks. *Journal of Cyber Security and Mobility*, 4(1), 65–88. https://doi.org/10.13052/JCSM2245-1439.414
2. Bates, S. (2017). Managing human factors. *62nd Annual Business Aviation Safety Summit, BASS 2017*, May 2017, 105–110. https://doi.org/10.1007/978-3-319-77492-3_11
3. Brebbia, C. A., Garzia, F., & Lombardi, M. (2018). *Safety and security engineering VII*. Vol. 174. WIT Press. ISBN: 9781784662127, 1784662127
4. Chamkar, S. A., Maleh, Y., & Gherabi, N. (2022). *The human factor capabilities in Security Operation Center (SOC)*. Lecture Notes in Networks and Systems, 357 LNNS, 579–590. https://doi.org/10.1007/978-3-030-91738-8_53
5. Daniel Ani, U. P., He, H. M., & Tiwari, A. (2016). Human capability evaluation approach for cyber security in critical industrial infrastructure. *Advances in Intelligent Systems and Computing*, 501, 169–182. https://doi.org/10.1007/978-3-319-41932-9_14
6. Franchina, L., Inzerilli, G., Scatto, E., Calabrese, A., Lucariello, A., Brutti, G., & Roscioli, P. (2021). Passive and active training approaches for critical infrastructure protection. *International Journal of Disaster Risk Reduction*, 63, 102461. https://doi.org/10.1016/J.IJDRR.2021.102461
7. Furnell, S., & Emm, D. (2017). The ABC of ransomware protection. *Computer Fraud and Security*, 2017(10), 5–11. https://doi.org/10.1016/S1361-3723(17)30089-1
8. Gazzan, M., Alqahtani, A., & Sheldon, F. T. (2021). Key factors influencing the rise of current ransomware attacks on industrial control systems. *2021 IEEE 11th Annual Computing and Communication Workshop and Conference, CCWC 2021*, 1417–1422. https://doi.org/10.1109/CCWC51732.2021.9376179
9. Ghafir, I., Saleem, J., Hammoudeh, M., Faour, H., Prenosil, V., Jaf, S., Jabbar, S., & Baker, T. (2018). Security threats to critical infrastructure: The human factor. *Journal of Supercomputing*, 74(10), 4986–5002. https://doi.org/10.1007/S11227-018-2337-2/TABLES/1
10. Hassanzadeh, A., Rasekh, A., Galelli, S., Aghashahi, M., Taormina, R., Ostfeld, A., & Banks, M. K. (2020). A review of cybersecurity incidents in the water sector. *Journal of Environmental Engineering*, 146(5). https://doi.org/10.1061/(ASCE)EE.1943-7870.0001686
11. Kovacevic, A., & Nikolic, D. (2015). Cyber attacks on critical infrastructure. 1–18. https://doi.org/10.4018/978-1-4666-6324-4.CH001

12. Lazányi, K., & Danaj, A. (2022). Critical threat of critical infrastructures: The human factor. *NATO Science for Peace and Security Series C: Environmental Security*, 1–11. https://doi.org/10.1007/978-94-024-2174-3_1
13. Le Blanc, K. (2021). Human factors challenges in developing cyber-informed risk assessment for critical infrastructure. *Advances in Intelligent Systems and Computing*, 1213 AISC, 536–541. https://doi.org/10.1007/978-3-030-51328-3_73
14. Lehto, M. (2020). Cyber security in aviation, maritime and automotive. *Computational Methods in Applied Sciences*, 54, 19–32. https://doi.org/10.1007/978-3-030-37752-6_2
15. Lehto, M. (2022a). Cyber-attacks against critical infrastructure. *Computational Methods in Applied Sciences*, 56, 3–42. https://doi.org/10.1007/978-3-030-91293-2_1
16. Lehto, M. (2022b). Cyber-attacks against critical infrastructure BT – cyber security: Critical infrastructure protection. 3–42. https://doi.org/10.1007/978-3-030-91293-2_1
17. Loukas, G., Gan, D., & Vuong, T. (2013). A review of cyber threats and defence approaches in emergency management. *Future Internet*, 5(2), 205–236. https://doi.org/10.3390/FI5020205
18. Luiijf, E., & Klaver, M. (2019). Resilience approach to critical information infrastructures. *Advanced Sciences and Technologies for Security Applications*, 3–16. https://doi.org/10.1007/978-3-030-00024-0_1
19. Maglaras, L., Janicke, H., & Ferrag, M. A. (2022). Cybersecurity of critical infrastructures: Challenges and solutions. *Sensors*, 22(14), 5105. https://doi.org/10.3390/S22145105
20. Makrakis, G. M., Kolias, C., Kambourakis, G., Rieger, C., & Benjamin, J. (2021). Industrial and critical infrastructure security: Technical analysis of real-life security incidents. *IEEE Access*, 9, 165295–165325. https://doi.org/10.1109/ACCESS.2021.3133348
21. Plachkinova, M., & Vo, A. (2022). A taxonomy of cyberattacks against critical infrastructure. *Journal of Cybersecurity Education, Research and Practice*, 2021(2).
22. Pollini, A., Callari, T. C., Tedeschi, A., Ruscio, D., Save, L., Chiarugi, F., & Guerri, D. (2022). Leveraging human factors in cybersecurity: An integrated methodological approach. *Cognition, Technology and Work*, 24(2), 371–390. https://doi.org/10.1007/S10111-021-00683-Y
23. Rass, S., Schauer, S., König, S., & Zhu, Q. (2020). Cyber-security in critical infrastructures. https://doi.org/10.1007/978-3-030-46908-5
24. Reshmi, T. R. (2021). Information security breaches due to ransomware attacks – a systematic literature review. *International Journal of Information Management Data Insights*, 1(2), 100013. https://doi.org/10.1016/J.JJIMEI.2021.100013
25. Soldatos, J., Philpot, J., & Giunta, G. (2020). Cyber-physical threat intelligence for critical infrastructures security a guide to integrated cyber-physical protection of modern critical infrastructures. https://doi.org/10.1561/9781680836875
26. Stellios, I., Kotzanikolaou, P., Psarakis, M., Alcaraz, C., & Lopez, J. (2018). A survey of IoT-enabled cyberattacks: Assessing attack paths to critical infrastructures and services. *IEEE Communications Surveys and Tutorials*, 20(4), 3453–3495. https://doi.org/10.1109/COMST.2018.2855563
27. Walker-Roberts, S., Hammoudeh, M., & Dehghantanha, A. (2018). A systematic review of the availability and efficacy of countermeasures to internal threats in healthcare critical infrastructure. *IEEE Access*, 6, 25167–25177. https://doi.org/10.1109/ACCESS.2018.2817560
28. Warren, M., Pye, G., & Hutchinson, W. (2010). Australian critical infrastructure protection: A case of two tales. *Australian Information Warfare and Security Conference*, 30. https://doi.org/10.4225/75/57a8366fbefa5

AUTHOR BIOGRAPHY

Avisen Moonsamy is a seasoned professional in the field of cybersecurity, with a robust experience spanning over 18 years. He has concentrated the past eight years of his career on the protection and resilience of critical infrastructures. His expertise has been instrumental for numerous large mining and utility companies in Australia and around the globe. His approach to cybersecurity is holistic and wide-ranging, with deep industry experience in other domains such as networking, infrastructure, cloud, virtualisation, and telephony. This multidisciplinary expertise allows him to provide comprehensive solutions to these critical sectors' complex cyber challenges. Avisen is currently pursuing a PhD in cybersecurity, specialising in risk and cyber insurance. Simultaneously, he is undertaking a Juris Doctor in Law, expanding his competencies and understanding of legal and regulatory aspects related to the field. Through his blend of practical experience, academic pursuits, and leadership roles, Avis continues to shape the field of cybersecurity, demonstrating his deep commitment to enhancing security across critical infrastructures.

EDITOR BIOGRAPHY

Mohiuddin Ahmed attained his PhD in computer science from the University of New South Wales (UNSW Australia). He has been educating the next generation of cyber leaders and researching to disrupt the cybercrime ecosystem. His research is focused on ensuring national security and safeguarding critical infrastructures from cyber terrorists. Mohiuddin has edited several books and contributed articles to The Conversation. His research publications in reputed venues attracted more than 3,700 citations and have been listed in the world's top 2% of scientists for the 2020–2022 citation impact. Mohiuddin secured several external and internal grants worth more than $1.5 million and has been collaborating with academia and industry. He has been regularly invited to speak at international conferences and public organisations and interviewed by the media for expert opinion.

Oliver Guidetti's research focuses on applied human factors of cyber security, socio-technical systems, and human–computer interaction. Oliver's career in research began in 2018 with a project that demonstrated the ability to extract the score of a cyber security training exercise from the Galvanic Skin Response (GSR) of its participants. His PhD was supported by a scholarship provided by the Cyber Security Research Cooperative and industry-led placement in the Western Australian Department of the Premier and Cabinet's Office of Digital Government. He developed the Western Australian Cyber Defence Task (WACDT) during his PhD, which was used as a test bed for human factors experiments in network defence. He used the WACDT to show that changes in the way command and control consoles are composed affect the blood flow in the brain and result in either improved performance or decreased performance.

Bazlur Rashid received his PhD in Big Data analytics and cyber security from Edith Cowan University (ECU). He is an adjunct lecturer and a casual academic at ECU and coordinated, tutored, and facilitated a range of computing and cyber security courses. He has 14 years of academic teaching-learning and research experience in overseas and Australian tertiary-level institutions. He facilitated both on-campus and online learning and teaching using various platforms. He also worked in the industry for about five years before joining as an academic. He published several research papers in top-ranked journals, including *ACM Transactions on Management Information Systems*, *Digital Communications and Networks*, *Journal of Big Data*, and *IEEE Access*. He is also actively collaborating in research works across the universities within Australia and overseas. His research interests include cyber security, data science, machine learning, ransomware, feature engineering, and evolutionary computation.

11 Space Systems and Malware
Potential Threats

Abebe Diro

11.1 INTRODUCTION

The journey into space, a realm once confined to the dreams of visionaries and storytellers, has unfolded into an extraordinary voyage of discovery and innovation. From the early days of exploratory missions, this journey has evolved into the establishment of enduring space stations, marking a significant milestone in humanity's quest to conquer the final frontier [1]. This remarkable expansion has been fuelled by a synergistic collaboration between governmental space agencies and visionary private enterprises, together driving the vibrant and ever-expanding space industry forward [2]. The history of space technology is a narrative of human ambition and ingenuity. The launch of Sputnik 1 by the Soviet Union in 1957 marked the dawn of the space age, showcasing humanity's ability to send objects into orbit [3]. This milestone was followed by a series of significant advancements, including the American Apollo moon landings, the deployment of the Hubble Space Telescope, and the construction of the International Space Station [4]. Each of these achievements not only expanded our understanding of space but also spurred technological developments that have had wide-ranging applications on Earth [5]. The evolution of space technology has been driven by both competition and collaboration, with nations and private entities alike contributing to its growth. Today, space information systems are more sophisticated and integral to global infrastructure than ever before, reflecting decades of research, investment, and innovation [6, 7].

Space information systems are a pivotal component of modern technological infrastructure, encompassing a broad range of technologies and applications. At their core, these systems are designed to facilitate the collection, transmission, and processing of data from space to Earth and vice versa. They typically include satellites, ground control stations, and the necessary communication links that form the backbone of this intricate network [8, 9]. Satellites, varying in size and function, orbit Earth and are instrumental in gathering and relaying data. Ground control stations serve as the crucial terrestrial hubs where data is received, processed, and dispatched [10]. The communication links, meanwhile, ensure a seamless flow of information between the satellites and ground stations, using sophisticated transmission technologies [11, 12]. At the heart of this evolution is space technology, with satellite systems standing as its most prominent element. These technological marvels have intricately woven themselves into the fabric of our daily lives on Earth. The importance of space information systems transcends a multitude of sectors, driving advancements and providing essential services [13, 14]. In the realm of navigation, these systems are the cornerstone of the Global Positioning System (GPS), enabling precise location tracking and navigation services vital for everything from personal smartphones to commercial aviation and military operations [15]. In telecommunications, satellites are indispensable for long-distance communication, broadcasting, and internet services, particularly crucial in remote or underserved areas [16]. Meteorological satellites play a critical role in weather forecasting and monitoring, providing data that is essential for predicting weather patterns, natural disasters, and climate change [17]. Furthermore, space information systems are fundamental to a range of scientific research endeavors, offering unique perspectives on Earth's atmosphere, oceans, and land, as well as deep-space exploration [18, 19].

 DOI: 10.1201/9781003469506-15

The commercialization and utilization of space have been greatly accelerated by the convergence of multiple technological advancements [20]. The digital revolution, characterized by the rapid progress in digital technologies and data processing capabilities, has been a cornerstone in this transformation. This era is defined not just by the digitalization of information but by the profound impact it has had on space operations and exploration. Key to this advancement has been the development in hardware, particularly the miniaturization of components and a significant increase in computing power. This progress has given rise to a new generation of small, yet highly capable satellites [21, 22]. These compact satellites, when combined with the strategic use of Commercial Off-the-Shelf (COTS) components, have drastically reduced the costs associated with satellite manufacturing and deployment. This cost-effectiveness has revolutionized the space industry, making it more accessible and opening up new horizons for exploration and utilization [23, 24]. Moreover, the reduced expense of launching payloads into orbit has catalyzed the deployment of constellations of small satellites. This strategy has vastly improved our capabilities in terms of global coverage, frequency of revisits, and the quality of data collection and communication [25]. The result is a more connected and informed world, with applications ranging from detailed Earth observation to comprehensive global internet coverage, and enhanced communication networks. Together, these advancements have nurtured a flourishing commercial space sector, characterized by innovation and opportunity. This sector is not only transforming space into a domain ripe for commercial ventures but also elevating it as a pivotal arena for scientific exploration and discovery. The integration of space technology into various aspects of our lives is not just a testament to human ingenuity but a beacon of the limitless potential that space exploration and utilization hold for the future [26].

11.2 SPACE SECURITY CHALLENGES

As we venture further into the realm of space exploration and increasingly rely on sophisticated space systems, a shadow of vulnerability looms large in the form of cyber threats. This emerging concern highlights a critical weakness in our interconnected space infrastructure. The intricate network of systems, which are the bedrock of satellite operations, is becoming progressively susceptible to cyber intrusions [27]. This vulnerability is further exacerbated by the integration of space technologies with terrestrial networks, amplifying the risks and extending the potential for far-reaching consequences. These vulnerabilities pose significant threats to a range of vital services that depend heavily on satellite operations [28]. Telecommunications, weather monitoring, and even national defense systems, all integral to the functioning of modern society, stand at risk. The possibility of compromised space assets extends beyond mere service disruption; it poses a grave threat to national security, potentially laying bare critical vulnerabilities to nefarious actors. The economic implications of such cyber incidents are profound and far-reaching. Both government and commercial entities, which rely on these space-based systems for their daily operations, could face severe repercussions. The impact stretches across various sectors, underlining the critical nature of safeguarding space-based technologies.

There has been multifaceted and evolving threat landscape and their attack methodologies in space evolution. Earlier incidents were often straightforward, but recent events have evolved into complex cyber operations, reflecting advances in both offensive and defensive cybersecurity measures. This trend indicates a growing sophistication in the nature of threats faced by satellite and communication systems. This landscape is characterized by a variety of attack types, diverse targets, a range of perpetrators, and evolving techniques, all of which have significant implications for global security and communication infrastructure. The categorization of attacks reveals a spectrum of methods, including hijacking, jamming, control, cyber network exploitation (CNE), denial of service, phishing/CNE, and spoofing [28]. Initially, hijacking was prevalent, where unauthorized control of communication channels led to the replacement of intended content, often with political propaganda or warnings. As technology advanced, methods became more sophisticated, as seen in CNE attacks involving intricate hacking techniques to infiltrate networks and extract or manipulate data. Jamming and spoofing, involving intentional signal interference and data falsification, respectively, highlight the tactical manipulation of communication systems [29]. These evolving techniques underscore a shift from direct, overt actions to more clandestine and technologically advanced operations. The targets of these attacks encompass commercial entities, government and military infrastructure, and civilian systems. Commercial targets, often broadcasting networks, are chosen for their broad impact, reflecting motives from political to criminal. Government and military targets center around espionage, data theft, or operational disruption, highlighting the strategic value of communication systems in national security [30]. Civilian incidents, though frequently accidental, sometimes serve personal or research objectives, demonstrating the pervasiveness of satellite and communication technology in everyday life. Perpetrators range from state-sponsored entities and organized hacking groups to individual actors. This diversity underscores the myriad motivations behind such attacks, including political activism, espionage, criminal intent, and personal use [31]. This range of actors and motives reflects the broad appeal and utility of satellite and communication systems as targets for various agendas. Moreover, the global impact of these attacks cannot be overstated. They have far-reaching effects across multiple countries and sectors, highlighting the interconnected nature of modern communication systems and the widespread consequences of disruptions in this domain [27, 30, 31].

In the spectrum of cyber threats, malware emerges as a particularly insidious and formidable adversary [32]. Crafted with precision, these malicious software programs are designed to infiltrate and disrupt the smooth functioning of space-based systems. Their nature presents a complex threat, capable of exploiting the vulnerabilities inherent in interconnected space networks. Malware has the potential not only to compromise satellite systems but also to impair vital communication channels and penetrate critical data repositories. One of the most alarming aspects of these malware threats is their stealthy nature [33, 34]. Often, their presence goes undetected until they have inflicted significant damage, making the potential for devastation even more acute. This underscores the urgency for robust cybersecurity measures in the space sector. As we continue to explore and expand our presence in space, the imperative to bolster our defenses against these cyber threats becomes increasingly critical, not just for the protection of space assets but for the security and continuity of the myriad services they support.

The potential fallout from a successful malware intrusion into space infrastructure cannot be overstated [35]. Such an event could severely disrupt satellite services, leading to dire outcomes. This disruption risks more than routine operations; it imperils essential services including emergency communication systems, weather forecasting, and the pivotal global navigation networks. The consequences of such an attack ripple out, not just affecting the functionality of these services but also posing severe risks to economic stability, national security, and the overall safety of our globally connected society [36]. As our reliance on space technologies deepens, interweaving with the very fabric of our daily existence and the broader global infrastructure, the urgency to reinforce our cybersecurity defenses escalates. Therefore, ensuring robust cybersecurity in space systems requires not only drawing lessons from terrestrial sectors but also addressing the unique challenges of the space environment. This includes developing advanced encryption techniques, ensuring regular software updates, and implementing rigorous security protocols during the design and development stages of space systems. Collaboration between space agencies and cybersecurity experts is crucial to develop defenses against sophisticated malware threats, ensuring the security and continuity of vital space-based operations [37].

11.3 SPACE SEGMENTS AND CYBER VULNERABILITIES

11.3.1 Space Segment

The "space segment" embodies a marvel of engineering, a symphony of sophisticated components harmoniously designed to operate in the vast, uncharted realms of space. This ensemble is anchored by satellites or spacecraft, marvels of modern technology, each outfitted with a variety of complex subsystems tailored to fulfill specific roles. At the heart of these spacecraft lies the power system, an essential lifeline, often deriving energy from advanced solar panels or batteries. This power system is the pulse that drives all onboard operations, ensuring uninterrupted functionality in the harsh environment of space [38].

Communication is the lifeline of these celestial voyagers, with payloads comprising advanced antennas and transponders. These elements are pivotal in establishing and maintaining a lifeline of signals, facilitating critical communication with Earth stations and enabling intricate inter-satellite dialogues. Beyond this, satellites are adorned with a diverse spectrum of sensors and instruments. From high-resolution cameras to sophisticated radars and specialized scientific equipment, these tools are meticulously designed for an array of tasks. They enable a multitude of functions such as detailed Earth observation, comprehensive climate monitoring, remote sensing, and groundbreaking scientific research, making satellites invaluable observers and explorers of our planet and beyond. Propulsion systems integrated into these satellites are feats of engineering, granting them the ability to perform vital maneuvers. These systems facilitate precise orbit adjustments and station-keeping, ensuring that satellites maintain their designated paths and positions within the vastness of space [27, 28].

In terms of data and communication flows, satellites are indispensable intermediaries, bridging space and Earth. Ground-based Earth stations transmit uplink signals, conveying commands and essential data for the satellites' operational needs and mission objectives. In response, satellites serve as diligent messengers, relaying a wealth of critical data back to Earth through downlink transmissions. This data can include real-time telemetry, vivid imagery, and invaluable scientific measurements. Furthermore, the establishment of cross-links between satellites in orbit fosters a seamless network of communication and coordination. This interconnectivity is vital for collaborative operations within constellations or satellite networks, enhancing the efficiency and scope of data relay among multiple spacecraft. Central to their functionality, satellites are equipped with robust onboard data storage systems [29]. These digital repositories are the memory of the spacecraft, housing mission-critical information such as telemetry data for health monitoring; payload outputs from onboard instruments; and operational logs that record system activities, command histories, and communication exchanges. These advanced storage systems are crucial, endowing satellites with the autonomy to independently manage, retain, and dispatch a diverse array of data, pivotal for their multifaceted missions and scientific investigations in the vast expanse of space [30, 39].

The vulnerabilities of space information systems, particularly in the space segment, encompass several critical aspects:

1. **Onboard Computer Systems and Software Vulnerability:** The central computer systems that manage satellite operations are potentially susceptible to malware attacks. These systems, running complex software for command and control, data processing, and other critical functions, could be compromised. Malware could disrupt operational software, leading to the malfunction of satellite systems or, in extreme cases, complete satellite failure. Given the sophistication and customization of this software, it might lack the frequent updates and patches typical in more conventional computer systems, leaving it vulnerable to newer forms of cyber threats.
2. **Communication Systems Risks:** Satellites rely heavily on communication systems to transmit and receive data from Earth. These systems, including antennas and transponders, are vital for the control and operation of the satellite. If malware were to infiltrate these systems, it could lead to a range of issues, from the interception and manipulation of sensitive data to the disruption of control signals. Such vulnerabilities could compromise not just the satellite's functionality but also the integrity and confidentiality of the data being transmitted.

3. **Power System Vulnerabilities:** Satellites operate with finite power resources, typically derived from solar panels or batteries. Malware that targets the power management systems could disrupt the delicate balance of power allocation onboard. This could result in insufficient power for critical systems or, conversely, the overuse of power resources, leading to premature depletion. The consequences of such attacks could range from reduced operational capabilities to a total loss of the satellite.
4. **Propulsion and Navigation System Weaknesses:** The systems responsible for maintaining a satellite's orbit and position are also at risk. Malware could potentially interfere with the propulsion system, affecting the satellite's ability to make necessary adjustments to its orbit or perform avoidance maneuvers. This could endanger the satellite itself and other nearby satellites or space debris, raising the risk of collisions.
5. **Sensor and Payload Compromise:** The various sensors and instruments aboard satellites, designed for specific tasks such as Earth observation or scientific experimentation, could be compromised by malware. This could lead to corrupted data, impacting everything from weather prediction accuracy to scientific research validity. In scenarios where satellites are used for critical national security purposes, such compromises could have significant strategic implications.
6. **Data Storage and Processing Threats:** The onboard data storage and processing systems are repositories of valuable information gathered during the satellite's mission. Malware attacks targeting these systems could lead to data theft, loss, or corruption. Such incidents could compromise the mission's objectives and the value of the satellite's long-term operations.
7. **Inter-Satellite Link Vulnerabilities:** For satellite constellations, inter-satellite links are essential for efficient operation. Malware that exploits these links could spread across the constellation, magnifying the impact of the attack and potentially leading to a cascading failure across multiple satellites.
8. **Vulnerability due to Ground Segment Interaction:** While technically external to the space segment, the interaction with ground systems is a crucial point of vulnerability. The satellite could be compromised during software updates, data transmission, or command and control operations initiated from ground stations. This necessitates stringent cybersecurity measures not only in space but also in the supporting ground infrastructure.

Hence, the vulnerabilities in the space segment are diverse and complex, reflecting the intricate nature of these advanced systems. Addressing these vulnerabilities requires a comprehensive approach to cybersecurity, combining robust technological solutions with vigilant operational practices.

11.3.2 Ground Segment

The "ground segment" is an integral and indispensable part of satellite communication systems, acting as the terrestrial counterpart to the orbiting "space segment." It is composed of a network of essential components and sophisticated infrastructure that plays a critical role in managing, controlling, and processing the data relayed by satellites. This segment encompasses various vital elements such as ground stations, tracking antennas, control centers, and a suite of associated hardware and software, forming the pivotal bridge that connects terrestrial operations with space-based assets [31].

Spread strategically across the globe, ground stations function as the nerve centers of satellite communication. These stations are equipped with advanced equipment like high-precision tracking antennas and state-of-the-art hardware systems. They stand as the primary interface for communication with satellites, facilitating the vital exchange of information between Earth and the orbiting machines [32, 33]. The communication within the ground segment is characterized by a bidirectional data flow. Ground stations adeptly capture telemetry data sent from satellites through downlink transmissions. This data, rich in detail, provides insights into the satellite's health, its exact position, and a range of performance metrics. In response, these stations also send critical commands and instructions (uplink) back to the satellites. These commands are crucial for various operational aspects, including orbit adjustments, activation of payloads, and configuration of satellite systems. Moreover, ground stations are the first receivers of payload data such as images, sensor readings, or scientific data, undertaking the initial stages of data processing before its further analysis or dissemination. The ground segment's effectiveness hinges on a sophisticated data storage infrastructure. Ground-based servers, expansive databases, and archival systems act as the primary repositories for the enormous volumes of data received from satellites. These facilities not only store the immediate telemetry information and command logs but also maintain extensive archives of historical data. This repository enables in-depth trend analysis, performance evaluation, and troubleshooting. Furthermore, detailed logs of command sequences, satellite responses, and operational activities are systematically recorded and preserved. This meticulous record-keeping is vital for comprehensive system analysis, diagnostics, and strategic mission planning, ensuring the seamless and efficient operation of satellite missions [34, 35].

The ground segment of satellite communication systems, specifically in the context of malware vulnerabilities, faces several unique challenges:

1. **Infiltration through Software Systems:** The ground stations' software, responsible for processing satellite data and controlling operations, is a primary target for malware. Malware can infiltrate these systems through various means, such as email phishing, compromised software updates, or insecure network connections. Once inside, it could disrupt operations, corrupt data, or even take control of satellite communications.
2. **Malware Spread via Network Connections:** The interconnected nature of ground station networks can facilitate the spread of malware. If one part of the network is compromised, the malware can potentially propagate to other parts of the network, affecting multiple systems and potentially disrupting communication with multiple satellites.
3. **Data Storage and Processing Vulnerability:** Ground segment's data storage and processing infrastructure, handling vast amounts of satellite data, is susceptible to malware attacks. Malware can corrupt, delete, or encrypt critical data, including telemetry and payload data, leading to loss of vital information and potential mission failure.
4. **Malware in Command and Control Systems:** The systems used for sending commands to satellites are particularly sensitive. Malware in these systems could lead to unauthorized commands being sent to satellites, potentially causing them to malfunction, change orbits, or deactivate payloads.
5. **Supply Chain Attacks:** The ground segment is also vulnerable to supply chain attacks, where malware is introduced into systems through third-party providers of software or hardware components. These attacks can be challenging to detect and can compromise the integrity of ground station operations.
6. **Insider Threats and Human Error:** Malware can be introduced unintentionally by employees or contractors through actions such as using infected USB drives or downloading compromised software. Insider threats can also involve deliberate introduction of malware into the ground systems.
7. **External Services Dependency:** Ground stations often depend on external services for various functionalities, such as internet access or cloud computing services. Malware attacks on these external services can indirectly compromise the security of the ground segment.
8. **Remote Access Vulnerabilities:** The need for remote access to ground systems, especially prevalent in large operations spanning multiple locations, opens up additional vulnerabilities. Remote access points can be exploited by attackers to introduce malware into the ground systems.

To mitigate these vulnerabilities, it's crucial to implement robust cybersecurity measures, including regular software updates, network monitoring, employee training on cyber hygiene, strict access controls, and the use of advanced malware detection and prevention tools. Additionally, a comprehensive incident response plan should be in place to quickly address any malware intrusion in the ground segment of satellite communication systems.

11.3.3 Link Segment

The "link segment" is the vital communication artery in satellite systems, forming a complex and intricate network that bridges the expanse between the satellites in orbit and ground stations on Earth. This segment's infrastructure is a technological tapestry that extends beyond mere transmitters and receivers. It encompasses a suite of sophisticated components like signal amplifiers, modems, multiplexers, and frequency converters. These diverse elements work in concert to master the art of transmitting, receiving, modulating, and demodulating signals across various frequencies and bands, ensuring a robust and seamless flow of data [40].

In link segment, the communication dynamics are bifurcated into distinct channels. The uplink path is dedicated to sending a spectrum of data from Earth's ground stations to the orbiting satellites. This crucial data stream includes essential commands for satellite control, pivotal software updates, critical configuration changes, and other operational directives [41]. These inputs are key to the efficient management and regulation of satellite functions. On the flip side, the downlink channel is a conduit for the wealth of information flowing from satellites back to ground stations. This stream includes telemetry data, which sheds light on the satellites' health, status, and performance, as well as a rich payload of data comprising images, sensor readings, and scientific data garnered by the spacecraft. An innovative feature of the link segment is the incorporation of cross-links. These sophisticated inter-satellite links create interconnected networks or constellations in the orbit. They enable a dynamic exchange of data, commands, and synchronization signals among the various satellites within these constellations, enhancing the capabilities and efficiency of the entire network. At the operational core of the link segment, stringent data management and log storage mechanisms are paramount. This involves implementing and adhering to standardized communication protocols such as TCP/IP, CCSDS protocols, and specialized space communication frameworks. These protocols are the governing principles for all data transmission and reception activities across the segments. Furthermore, detailed logs that capture every nuance of the communication protocols, signal processing operations, and the status of the links are meticulously maintained. These comprehensive records are invaluable for validation, troubleshooting, and auditing purposes [42, 43]. They play a crucial role in ensuring the communication pathways between the space and ground segments operate with the highest levels of reliability, quality, and security. The link segment thus stands as a cornerstone in the architecture of satellite systems, embodying the precision and sophistication required for managing the critical flow of data and commands between space and terrestrial infrastructures. Its meticulous approach to managing communication pathways and thorough documentation of processes is essential for the efficiency, reliability, and security of the entire satellite communication network.

The link segment, serving as the crucial communication conduit in satellite systems, is particularly vulnerable to malware threats due to its complex and integral role in data transmission:

1. **Malware in Signal Processing Systems:** The link segment's infrastructure includes signal amplifiers, modems, multiplexers, and frequency converters, all of which are involved in the critical process of transmitting and receiving data. Malware infiltrating these systems could disrupt signal processing, leading to the corruption or loss of data during transmission. This could severely impact the reliability and integrity of the communication between satellites and ground stations.

2. **Uplink Channel Vulnerabilities:** The uplink path, responsible for sending commands and software updates from ground stations to satellites, is a prime target for malware. Malware introduced into this channel could corrupt the commands and software updates, potentially leading to compromised satellite functionality. This could range from minor disruptions to complete loss of control over the satellite.
3. **Downlink Data Corruption:** In the downlink channel, malware could corrupt the data being sent from the satellites to the ground stations. This includes telemetry data, which is crucial for monitoring the health and status of the satellite, as well as payload data like images and sensor readings. The integrity of this data is essential for various applications, and its corruption could lead to significant operational and strategic setbacks.
4. **Inter-Satellite Link Security Risks:** The innovative use of cross-links in the link segment, facilitating communication between satellites, adds another layer of vulnerability. If malware were to infiltrate these inter-satellite links, it could spread across the satellite network or constellation, causing widespread disruption and data corruption.
5. **Exploitation of Communication Protocols:** The link segment relies on standardized communication protocols, such as TCP/IP and CCSDS protocols, for data transmission. Malware specifically designed to exploit vulnerabilities in these protocols could disrupt or intercept communications, posing a significant security risk.
6. **Log Storage and Management Threats:** Detailed logs are crucial for the validation, troubleshooting, and auditing of communication processes. Malware targeting these log storage systems could alter or delete logs, hindering the ability to monitor and diagnose issues in the link segment, and potentially covering up malicious activities.
7. **Risk of Malware Transmission via Data Streams:** Given the bidirectional nature of the link segment's communication, there's a risk of malware being transmitted along with data streams, either from the ground to the satellite or vice versa. This could lead to cross-contamination between the space and ground segments.

The vulnerabilities in the link segment to malware highlight the need for robust cybersecurity measures, including advanced malware detection systems, secure communication protocols, and continuous monitoring of the communication channels. Given the critical role of the link segment in satellite operations, ensuring its security against malware threats is paramount for the reliability and integrity of the entire satellite communication network.

11.3.4 User Segment

The user segment in satellite communication systems is a diverse and dynamic domain, encompassing a wide array of sophisticated components and systems essential for harnessing the capabilities of space-based technologies [44]. This segment includes an array of specialized end-user devices, applications, and systems designed for specific functionalities. Within this array are GPS receivers, which are critical for precise location determination, time synchronization, and navigation, utilizing signals from navigation satellites. Additionally, satellite phones emerge as vital communication tools, especially in remote areas beyond the reach of conventional network coverage, enabling voice and data communication. Equally important are weather monitoring devices, which are adept at receiving and interpreting satellite-derived imagery and atmospheric data for meteorological analysis, forecasting, and disaster preparedness. Remote sensing instruments also play a key role, gathering data from satellites for environmental monitoring, agricultural analysis, and scientific research [45].

The interaction between users and satellite services is facilitated through a multitude of devices and systems, each tailored to specific applications. GPS receivers decode signals from navigation satellites to provide essential navigational and timing information, crucial for various sectors. Satellite TV dishes harness broadcasting signals from orbiting satellites, offering a diverse range of television and radio content globally. Weather monitoring devices leverage satellite imagery and data to provide vital insights for weather analysis and decision-making across numerous fields. Remote sensing instruments, on the other hand, are invaluable for capturing and analyzing satellite data for environmental assessments, agricultural monitoring, and scientific explorations. Data management and storage in the user segment vary depending on the application or service rendered by the satellite systems [46]. Devices may store data locally, such as GPS location histories or weather forecasts, or transmit it to centralized servers or cloud systems for broader storage and analysis. GPS receivers, for instance, might maintain location logs and waypoints on the device or utilize cloud-based systems for enhanced navigation and tracking functionalities. Satellite phones typically store call logs, messages, and user data either internally or on network servers, mainly for purposes like billing, record-keeping, and regulatory compliance. Weather monitoring devices often archive historical weather data and satellite imagery for ongoing analysis, forecasting, and comparative studies over time. Furthermore, remote sensing instruments collect and store data for scientific research, environmental modeling, and analysis, within either local databases or specialized servers. The logging of user interactions with satellite-based services is multifaceted, serving functions ranging from troubleshooting technical issues to enhancing service quality, ensuring billing accuracy, adhering to regulatory requirements, and enriching overall user experiences. These logs include a diverse range of information, such as communication session records, usage patterns, and diagnostic data, which are vital for maintaining system integrity and continuously improving the quality of satellite services [47, 48].

The user segment of satellite communication systems, encompassing various end-user devices and applications, faces distinct malware vulnerabilities:

1. **End-User Devices Compromise:** Devices like GPS receivers, satellite phones, and weather monitoring equipment are susceptible to malware. Malware can disrupt their functionalities, leading to incorrect location data, compromised communication, or false weather predictions. This could have significant repercussions, from misguiding navigation to impacting disaster response efforts.
2. **Data Transmission and Reception Vulnerability:** As these devices transmit and receive data to and from satellites, they are at risk of intercepting malware-infected data streams. This could occur through compromised satellite transmissions or through the devices' interaction with infected ground-based systems.
3. **Malware in Remote Sensing Instruments:** Remote sensing instruments, which collect environmental and scientific data, are vulnerable to malware that can corrupt the data they gather and store. This could lead to inaccurate environmental assessments or flawed scientific research findings.
4. **Local Data Storage Threats:** Many user segment devices store data locally, such as GPS location histories or weather forecasts. Malware could target this data for corruption, theft, or encryption (as in ransomware attacks). This not only would affect the individual user but could also compromise broader data analysis and research efforts that rely on this information.
5. **Network and Cloud-Based System Vulnerabilities:** For devices that rely on network or cloud-based systems for additional functionalities, such as enhanced navigation or data analysis, there is a risk of malware infiltrating these systems. This could lead to broader data breaches, compromising the privacy and security of user data.
6. **Malware Affecting Satellite TV and Communication Services:** Devices like satellite TV dishes are also part of the user segment. Malware could disrupt the reception of broadcasting signals, affecting a wide range of users and services globally.
7. **User Interaction Logs Manipulation:** Logs that record user interactions with satellite services could be targeted by malware. Altering or deleting these logs can hinder troubleshooting efforts, regulatory compliance, and service quality analysis, and can cover up evidence of a malware attack.

8. **Insider Threats and Human Error:** User segment devices can be compromised through human error or insider threats, such as downloading infected applications or using compromised USB devices. This could introduce malware into otherwise secure systems.

To mitigate these vulnerabilities, it's essential to implement robust security measures across the user segment. This includes ensuring secure data transmission, regularly updating and patching software, employing advanced malware detection tools, and educating users about potential security risks and best practices. Given the diverse and widespread use of user segment devices, maintaining their security is critical to the overall integrity and reliability of satellite communication systems.

11.4 MALWARE AND SPACE SYSTEMS

Malware attacks in space information systems are a serious threat to the security and functionality of satellites and other space-based assets, as well as the critical infrastructure that depends on them. Malware can infect systems on the ground, such as satellite control centers, or interfere with the communication links between the ground and the spacecraft.

11.4.1 Overview of Malware

In cybersecurity, malware stands as one of the most formidable threats, constantly evolving and adapting in a digital arms race. Malware, a portmanteau of "malicious software," encompasses any software intentionally designed to cause harm to a computer system, network, or server. Its forms are as diverse as the intentions behind them, ranging from viruses, which are self-replicating programs designed to spread from host to host, disrupting systems and corrupting files, to worms, which are similar in nature but can spread across networks without human interaction. Then there are trojans, deceptively benign-looking software that, once executed, can give attackers unauthorized access to affected systems. Ransomware, a particularly nefarious type, encrypts the victim's data and demands payment for its release. Each type of malware has its unique characteristics and methods of infection, but they all share the common goal of exploiting vulnerabilities for various malicious purposes [32].

The operation of malware is a complex, multi-stage process that often begins with infiltration. This can occur through seemingly innocuous means: an email attachment, a download from an untrusted website, or exploitation of a network vulnerability. Once inside the system, the malware can execute its programmed task, which might be to steal sensitive information, encrypt data for ransom, or simply disrupt operations. Sophisticated malware can even remain dormant, avoiding detection while it spreads across the network, only activating under certain conditions or when it has reached a critical target. Historical examples of significant malware attacks highlight the evolving nature of these threats. The "ILOVEYOU" virus, unleashed in 2000, used social engineering to trick people into opening a malicious email attachment, leading to widespread damage estimated in billions of dollars. In 2003, the "Slammer" worm exploited a vulnerability in Microsoft SQL Server, causing significant internet disruptions. More recently, the "WannaCry" ransomware attack in 2017 affected hundreds of thousands of computers across the globe, encrypting data and demanding Bitcoin payments, impacting healthcare systems, government agencies, and private organizations alike. These examples underscore the continual threat posed by malware, demonstrating the necessity for vigilant cybersecurity measures and the ongoing challenge of defending against increasingly sophisticated attacks [38].

The types of malware that target space systems, such as ransomware, are similar to those in other sectors like telecommunications, defense, and finance. These malware typically aim to disrupt operations, steal sensitive information, or gain unauthorized access. For instance, a malware in the financial sector can disrupt transaction processing, akin to how it might disrupt communication in a satellite system. Similarly, ransomware attacks in healthcare, which lock out vital patient data, mirror potential attacks on space systems that could encrypt critical operational data. The vulnerabilities exploited by malware often stem from common issues like outdated software, unpatched security holes, and insufficiently secured networks. In space systems, these vulnerabilities might include outdated onboard computer systems or unencrypted communication links, similar to vulnerabilities in terrestrial IT infrastructures. The interconnected nature of modern systems, both in space and on Earth, magnifies these vulnerabilities, as a breach in one part of the network can lead to widespread compromise [35]. The impacts of malware in different sectors can be devastating and far-reaching. In the defense sector, a malware attack can compromise national security, just as an attack on space systems can threaten global communication networks or satellite-based navigation. In the financial sector, a malware attack can lead to economic instability, similar to how an attack on space systems can disrupt critical satellite operations, leading to significant financial and operational losses. While there are similarities, the space sector faces unique challenges due to the remote and harsh operating environment of space. Malware in space systems must be managed remotely, and there's often no way to physically repair or update infected satellites. This aspect demands more robust pre-launch cybersecurity measures in space systems compared to terrestrial sectors. Additionally, the long lifespans of satellites mean that they might operate with outdated technology, increasing their vulnerability to new types of malware attacks.

11.4.2 Historical Perspective of Malware in Space

The historical trajectory of malware's interaction with space systems provides a compelling narrative of the evolving cybersecurity landscape and its implications for space-based technologies. This journey maps the transition from an era where cybersecurity in space missions was a peripheral concern to one where it has become a central focus, reflecting the changing dynamics and increased vulnerabilities of these critical systems. In the nascent stages of space exploration, the emphasis was predominantly on exploration and scientific discovery. Cybersecurity threats were minimal, largely because space missions operated in a vacuum, insulated from the cyber vulnerabilities associated with terrestrial networks. However, as space missions evolved to include commercial and civilian applications, the landscape began to shift. The integration of space infrastructure with ground-based systems and the proliferation of interconnected networks marked a turning point, significantly heightening the susceptibility of space systems to cyber intrusions [32].

The chronology of malware attacks on space systems dates back to notable incidents starting in 1997. One of the earliest recorded instances was at NASA's Goddard Space Flight Centre, where malware facilitated unauthorized control over computers crucial in designing and testing command and control codes, leading to a breach of sensitive information. Following this, in 2005, key NASA centers, including Kennedy Space Center and Johnson Space Center, suffered malware attacks that compromised data and propagated through their networks. In 2008, Germany's space research center experienced a malware attack, impacting computers used by researchers and administrators [27]. The hacking of NASA's Terra satellite in 2007 and 2008, the CosmicDuke malware that targeted European space agencies and aerospace companies in 2014, and the Chinese hackers that attempted to steal trade secrets from a U.S. satellite communications company in 2018 are some examples of malware-related satellite breaches. A more orchestrated cyber intrusion occurred in 2015, when NASA faced an attack by the hacking group Anonsec, leading to the unauthorized release of substantial amounts of data. The landscape of cyber threats continued to evolve, with ransomware attacks becoming more prominent in recent years. In 2022, amid the Russia-Ukraine crisis, Network Battalion 65 (NB65), associated with the Anonymous hacktivist group, claimed responsibility for a cyber attack on ROSCOSMOS, Russia's primary space agency. This incident disrupted the agency's control center operations. In a similar vein, 2023 saw the ransomware group "LockBit" breach Maximum Industries, a third-party manufacturer for SpaceX [28, 29]. This attack resulted in the exfiltration of confidential schematics, with LockBit demanding a ransom from SpaceX to prevent the release of this sensitive information [30].

These incidents highlight an alarming trend: as satellite networks become more integrated into our daily lives, the threat landscape expands, paving the way for increasingly sophisticated malware. This malware is specifically designed to infiltrate and disrupt space systems, targeting vital components such as satellite communication, navigation, and control systems. The potential damage ranges from severe operational disruptions to compromising mission-critical operations. The historical analysis of malware in space systems underscores the escalating importance of cybersecurity in space missions. It illustrates the critical need for proactive measures, continuous vigilance, and the development of robust cybersecurity protocols. This historical perspective serves as a stark reminder of the ever-evolving nature of cyber threats and the imperative to continually enhance the security measures protecting our space-based technologies. This evolution calls for an adaptive and forward-thinking approach to cybersecurity, ensuring the protection and resilience of space systems against the dynamic and ever-advancing landscape of malware threats.

11.4.3 Malware and Space Supply Chains

The accelerated integration of cutting-edge technologies within space systems has undoubtedly propelled scientific discovery and space exploration to new heights. Nonetheless, this technological progression simultaneously magnifies the susceptibility of space supply chains to malware, a form of malicious software designed to infiltrate and compromise system integrity. Within the intricate ecosystem of space systems, various components, from satellite software and communication networks to ground stations and data transfer protocols, are at risk of malware attacks [39].

Malware infiltrates space supply chains through a myriad of avenues. These include compromised third-party software, infected firmware during the manufacturing process, and vulnerabilities in network connections used for system updates. The points of vulnerability are dispersed across the entire supply chain, encompassing stages such as development, assembly, testing, deployment, and ongoing maintenance. Even components that appear innocuous, when sourced from compromised suppliers or introduced at any point in the supply chain, can act as conduits for malware, posing significant risks to the operational integrity and security of space systems. The components most vulnerable to malware include onboard control systems of satellites, communication modules, software used in ground stations, and networks responsible for data transmission. Malware can exploit weaknesses in these components to cause system failures, corrupt data, or disrupt communications. Furthermore, as space systems increasingly interlink with terrestrial networks for updates and maintenance, these connections become potential gateways for malware, escalating the overall risk within the supply chain [38].

To effectively safeguard space supply chains against malware threats, a comprehensive and multilayered approach is essential. This includes meticulous vetting of software components, the implementation of robust cybersecurity protocols, continuous system monitoring, and thorough testing at all stages of the supply chain. Key strategies involve rigorous supplier scrutiny, secure coding practices, regular cybersecurity audits, and the establishment of secure communication channels and firewalls. In an era where technological dependency is escalating, the protection of space supply chains from malware infiltration requires unwavering vigilance, innovative cybersecurity methodologies, and cooperative efforts among various stakeholders. These include space agencies, manufacturers, contractors, and cybersecurity experts. The collective commitment to reinforce these supply chains against malware is critical in maintaining the resilience and security of space systems, which are pivotal not only for scientific and exploratory missions but also for the wide array of communications and services that underpin modern society.

11.4.4 Malware and COTS

In the rapidly advancing arena of space technology, the adoption of Commercial Off-the-Shelf (COTS) components has become increasingly prevalent. This strategy offers a cost-efficient and time-effective approach to developing space systems. However, the incorporation of COTS components brings with it distinct vulnerabilities, particularly a heightened susceptibility to malware threats within the space supply chains [38].

COTS components, while instrumental in fostering innovation and reducing costs, inherently carry the risk of malware infiltration. This risk stems from their broad availability and varied manufacturing sources. These components, procured from a multitude of manufacturers and suppliers, may possess intrinsic vulnerabilities or inadvertently contain malware, a result of compromised systems at their point of origin. When integrated into space systems, any malware lurking undetected within these components can pose a significant threat to the security and operational integrity of the entire space infrastructure. The risk of malware penetration through COTS components spans various stages of the space supply chain, including procurement, integration, and maintenance. A malware-compromised COTS component, if not identified and mitigated, has the potential to undermine the performance and reliability of crucial space systems. This can lead to severe consequences such as operational failures, data security breaches, and disruptions in communication [34, 36].

To counteract the vulnerabilities introduced by COTS components, it is imperative to establish and maintain rigorous supplier vetting processes, thorough testing and validation protocols, and comprehensive cybersecurity measures throughout the lifecycle of these components. This approach should encompass detailed risk assessments and strict adherence to security standards during the procurement process. Additionally, continuous monitoring and secure coding practices are vital to mitigate the risks associated with COTS components in space systems. The integration of COTS components into space supply chains highlights the urgent need for proactive and robust cybersecurity strategies. These strategies should include stringent vetting procedures and collaborative efforts among various stakeholders in the space industry. Ensuring the security and integrity of space infrastructure against evolving cyber threats is crucial. Vigilant and adaptive cybersecurity measures are essential in safeguarding the functionality and reliability of space systems, which are indispensable for scientific exploration, global communication, and the advancement of society at large.

11.5 THREAT MODEL

Creating a threat model for malware within space systems using the STRIDE model involves assessing distinct threat categories and their potential impacts. The application of the STRIDE model to space systems provides a structured approach to identify and mitigate potential security threats in a highly specialized and technologically advanced domain. Each category of STRIDE highlights unique challenges and necessitates specific countermeasures to protect space assets and their associated infrastructure. The STRIDE model encompasses Spoofing, Tampering, Repudiation, Information Disclosure, Denial of Service (DoS), and Elevation of Privilege as fundamental threat categories [49].

Spoofing threats in space systems are a significant security concern, involving unauthorized impersonation of legitimate entities and potentially leading to dire consequences. This type of threat can manifest in various ways, from attackers mimicking satellite signals or ground station communications to more sophisticated methods enabled by malware [50]. Malware-induced spoofing presents a particularly severe risk, as it allows malicious actors to compromise the integrity of data and command systems. For instance, if malware infiltrates a satellite's communication system, it could enable attackers to spoof the satellite's identity, transmitting false telemetry or positional data to ground control. Such deception can lead to erroneous commands being issued, unauthorized access being granted, or even disruption of the satellite's intended trajectory, thereby compromising mission-critical operations and communication reliability [51, 52].

These spoofing attacks can also manipulate communication protocols, allowing attackers to mimic authentic spacecraft identifiers [27]. This results in potential unauthorized access and misleading commands to ground control, posing substantial risks to the operational integrity of space systems. To mitigate these risks, a combination of strategies is required. Implementing robust authentication protocols is crucial to validate the identity of communication sources and prevent unauthorized access. Encrypting communication channels adds an additional layer of security, safeguarding data and command transmissions. Regular verification processes are also essential to confirm the authenticity of signals and data sources, thereby ensuring the integrity of received information. Furthermore, comprehensive measures must be taken to safeguard against malware infiltration. This includes rigorous software testing, secure coding practices, and constant vigilance for vulnerabilities within the system. By combining these strategies – enhanced authentication, encryption, verification, and malware protection – space systems can be better protected against the multifaceted threats posed by spoofing, ensuring the security and reliability of their critical operations.

Tampering threats, particularly those induced by malware, pose a profound risk to space systems by enabling unauthorized modifications to critical software, hardware, or mission-critical data [53]. Malware infiltrating these systems can compromise the integrity of key components, leading to potentially catastrophic consequences. For instance, malware might target command and control software responsible for satellite trajectory, causing unauthorized manipulations in guidance systems. This could result in erroneous adjustments in satellite orbits or misdirected commands during pivotal operations, severely risking the spacecraft's functionality and the success of its mission. The remote and often inaccessible nature of space assets makes them especially vulnerable to such tampering. Attackers could, for example, introduce malware through software updates or firmware modifications [43, 44]. This threat is illustrated by a scenario where malware-infected software within a satellite's navigation system alters the telemetry data sent to ground control. The compromised software manipulates the satellite's reported coordinates, providing falsified positional information to the ground station. Consequently, ground operators, relying on these altered telemetry readings, may execute miscalculated positioning or incorrect orbit adjustments. Such manipulations not only compromise the accuracy of navigation systems but also risk erroneous orbital maneuvers or inaccurate data being relayed to ground control, endangering the satellite's functionality and the broader mission objectives. To counter these significant tampering risks, a multi-faceted approach to cybersecurity is imperative. Employing cryptographic signatures for all software and data ensures the authenticity and integrity of these components. End-to-end encryption of transmitted data provides an additional security layer, protecting against unauthorized interception and alteration. Rigorous testing and validation of all updates, patches, and transmitted commands are also crucial in identifying and mitigating potential vulnerabilities. In essence, understanding and addressing the risks associated with tampering threats, particularly those induced by malware, are critical for the security of space systems. Vigilant cybersecurity measures, encompassing system integrity checks and continuous monitoring, are essential to safeguard against unauthorized modifications. These measures ensure the reliability, safety, and success of mission-critical operations in the uniquely challenging environment of space.

Repudiation threats within space systems, especially when facilitated by malware, pose a significant risk due to their potential to create untraceable instances, thereby complicating incident investigations and obscuring the identification of malicious activities [28]. Malware can compromise essential systems such as onboard logging and monitoring, allowing unauthorized parties to manipulate data or perform actions without leaving detectable traces. For instance, consider a scenario where malware infiltrates the onboard systems of a space probe, enabling intruders to tamper with sensor data surreptitiously. When anomalies occur or malfunctions are detected, investigators are challenged in tracing the source or origin of these issues due to the absence of reliable evidence. This lack of traceability not only hinders the investigation of incidents but also makes it difficult to determine the causes of malfunctions or identify parties responsible for malicious actions within space systems. Furthermore, repudiation threats can manifest as operators or systems denying the issuance of commands leading to unintended consequences, like an inadvertent change in a satellite's trajectory. The absence of accountability in such scenarios is a critical concern, as it can lead to operational hazards and compromised mission integrity. To effectively mitigate these threats, it is essential for space systems to implement robust logging and monitoring mechanisms. These systems must be designed to create secure and immutable audit trails, ensuring that every action, command, or event within the space system is traceable and accountable. Hence, addressing repudiation threats in space systems requires a two-pronged approach. First, there needs to be a strong defense against malware that could compromise logging and monitoring systems, thereby preventing the manipulation of data and ensuring the integrity of recorded information. Second, comprehensive and tamper-proof logging mechanisms must be in place to maintain a transparent and accountable record of all operations. This combination of cybersecurity measures and accountable logging is crucial in ensuring the reliability, security, and operational success of space missions, safeguarding them against the risks posed by repudiation threats.

Information Disclosure threats in space systems represent a substantial risk, particularly when malware facilitates unauthorized access to sensitive and mission-critical data. One potential scenario is malware compromising a satellite's data storage, allowing unauthorized access to crucial mission information. For instance, a breach in a spacecraft's data storage by malicious software could expose sensitive telemetry data, operational codes, or even encryption keys. This leaked information might include technological specifications or confidential mission plans, the disclosure of which could be detrimental to national security interests, intellectual property, or reveal critical details to adversaries. Another concern is malware targeting ground-based communication systems responsible for transmitting mission-related data. Such an infiltration could lead to the exposure of proprietary communication protocols, encryption algorithms, or operational schedules. Access to this sensitive information could enable adversaries to intercept or decode communication transmissions, thereby compromising mission confidentiality or manipulating mission operations. The risk of Information Disclosure extends further if malware infiltrates mission control systems, potentially exposing key information about spacecraft functionalities, orbital parameters, or mission objectives. Unauthorized access to such data could severely undermine mission confidentiality, compromise operational security, or aid in cyber espionage activities. To guard against these Information Disclosure threats, it is essential to encrypt sensitive data, both during transmission and while stored. This ensures that even if data is accessed unauthorizedly, its contents remain secure and indecipherable. Additionally, implementing stringent access controls is vital to prevent unauthorized access to confidential information. These measures are crucial in protecting against the risks of espionage or data theft, maintaining the integrity and confidentiality of mission-critical information within space systems. This approach to cybersecurity combines proactive defenses against malware infiltration with robust data protection strategies, ensuring the security and confidentiality of sensitive information in the highly vulnerable and strategically critical environment of space operations.

Denial of Service (DoS) threats, particularly those induced by malware, represent a significant risk to the functionality and reliability of space systems [46, 48]. Malware-initiated DoS attacks are designed to overwhelm or disrupt the normal operations of these systems, either rendering them completely unavailable or substantially degrading their performance. In the context of space operations, the consequences of DoS attacks can be especially severe, potentially leading to service interruptions, blockages of communication channels, or complete system unavailability, especially during critical mission phases. A specific instance of this threat could be a sophisticated malware-induced DoS attack targeting a spacecraft responsible for relaying communication signals. In such a scenario, the malware might be subtly injected into the spacecraft's communication systems, initiating an overwhelming flood of data requests and overloading the spacecraft's processing capabilities. Consequently, this can lead to the saturation of communication channels, making them ineffective for transmitting essential data or commands. The resulting temporary unavailability or disruption of communication services can severely impede ongoing missions, causing delays or interruptions in data transmission and compromising the successful execution of operations. If executed successfully, such DoS attacks could incapacitate the vital components of the space infrastructure, affecting data transmission, communication channels, and operational control. To protect space systems against the threat of DoS attacks, robust cybersecurity measures are essential. This includes continuous monitoring of systems to detect and respond to potential threats promptly. Proactive strategies should also be in place to mitigate the impact of DoS attacks, ensuring the operational reliability and functionality of space systems. Additionally, building system resilience is crucial, which involves implementing redundancy and failover mechanisms to maintain service continuity even under attack. Traffic filtering and rate limiting are also effective techniques to prevent or minimize the impact of DoS attacks. These measures collectively enhance the defense against DoS threats, safeguarding critical space system services like communications and navigation, and ensuring they remain functional and secure against these potentially debilitating attacks [32, 35].

Elevation of Privilege threats in space systems represent a significant security risk, particularly when unauthorized entities gain access levels beyond their initial authorization, potentially leading to control over critical system components with catastrophic consequences [34, 35]. This threat becomes more pronounced when malware exploits vulnerabilities to escalate user privileges unauthorizedly. Such unauthorized escalation allows attackers to access system functionalities beyond their authorized levels, potentially compromising system integrity and control. Consider a scenario where malware exploits a vulnerability in a satellite's command and control infrastructure's authentication system. This breach could enable unauthorized users to elevate their privileges, gaining access to critical system controls or functionalities not initially within their purview. With such elevated access, attackers could manipulate critical commands, alter telemetry data, or compromise the spacecraft's control mechanisms. This kind of unauthorized control over a spacecraft's operations can lead to severe disruptions, compromise mission objectives, and enable detrimental maneuvers that endanger the spacecraft's safety. Another potential situation could involve malware infiltrating a space station's onboard software and exploiting a flaw in the access control mechanisms. This breach might allow unauthorized personnel to gain elevated privileges, accessing sensitive systems or confidential data beyond their initial clearance. Such escalated privileges could enable these users to bypass critical safety protocols or tamper with vital systems, jeopardizing the station's functionality, crew safety, and the overall success of the mission. To prevent such scenarios, it is crucial to enforce the principle of least privilege in space systems, ensuring that individuals and entities have only the access necessary for their roles. Regular system audits are vital for identifying and addressing vulnerabilities that could be exploited for privilege escalation. Promptly addressing known vulnerabilities is also crucial to prevent exploitation by malicious actors. This comprehensive approach, combining strict access control, regular audits, and rapid vulnerability management, is essential to safeguard against Elevation of Privilege threats, ensuring the integrity, security, and success of space missions [54].

11.6 MALWARE AND IMPACTS IN SPACE

Malware attacks targeting space systems represent a grave threat with extensive repercussions. Among the most pressing impacts is the imminent disruption of satellite communication and navigation. These attacks have the potential to induce communication blackouts, resulting in the unavailability of essential telecommunication services, data transmission, and broadcasting capabilities. Furthermore, tampering with satellite-based navigation systems, including GPS, poses a serious risk by causing substantial disruptions in crucial sectors such as transportation, logistics, and emergency services. These industries rely heavily on precise positioning information provided by satellites, making them vulnerable to malfunctions triggered by such attacks. The implications encompass not only inconvenience but also severe hindrances to daily operations and emergency responses that rely on uninterrupted and accurate satellite-based services [32, 38].

The compromise of spacecraft operations due to space systems malware is a critical and concerning outcome. Malicious software infiltrating control systems can severely jeopardize satellite functionalities, posing a significant threat to essential operations. Manipulation of sensors, alterations in data, or unauthorized manipulation of commands can disrupt scientific observations, compromise imaging processes, or interfere with vital spacecraft functions. The potential consequences range from mission failures to the extreme risk of losing the satellite itself. This interference not only undermines the reliability and accuracy of data gathered by the spacecraft but also endangers the success and longevity of the entire mission. The potential loss or incapacitation of a satellite due to these compromised operations highlights the gravity of space systems malware, emphasizing the need for robust cybersecurity measures to safeguard against such risks [37].

The economic implications resulting from disruptions caused by space systems malware are profound and wide-ranging. Industries reliant on satellite technology, encompassing telecommunications, banking, agriculture, and transportation, face the prospect of substantial financial losses due to service interruptions. These disruptions can directly impact the operations and revenue streams of these sectors, leading to decreased efficiency and potential economic setbacks. Moreover, the interconnected nature of global commerce and trade means that disruptions in satellite-based logistics and communication can have cascading effects on international supply chains. Interruptions in these critical systems can impede the smooth functioning of global supply chains, causing delays, increased costs, and logistical challenges across various industries. The repercussions extend to international trade and commerce, potentially affecting markets and economies on a significant scale. The reliance of multinational companies and trade networks on timely and accurate satellite-based information underscores the susceptibility of global economic systems to these disruptions, highlighting the far-reaching economic consequences of space systems malware incidents [55].

The impact of space systems malware extends beyond economic concerns, significantly affecting societal functions and daily life [56]. During emergencies such as natural disasters or humanitarian crises, impaired communication and navigation systems can significantly hinder the effectiveness and timeliness of emergency response operations. These disruptions exacerbate the challenges faced during such critical situations, potentially delaying rescue efforts, hampering coordination among response teams, and ultimately intensifying the impact of the event on affected communities. Furthermore, various routine activities crucial for societal functioning rely heavily on satellite services. Weather forecasting, an essential tool for disaster preparedness and agricultural planning, could suffer disruptions, affecting the ability to predict and mitigate the effects of adverse weather conditions. Precise time synchronization, fundamental for a multitude of sectors including finance, transportation, and telecommunications, may face inconsistencies due to compromised satellite systems. Moreover, internet access in remote or underserved areas often depends on satellite-based services, and any interruption could isolate these regions, limiting access to vital information, communication, and services. The potential disruption of these essential services highlights the vulnerability of societal functions to space systems malware. Beyond immediate emergencies, the cumulative impact on daily life underscores the critical role satellite services play in supporting various aspects of modern society and the challenges posed by their compromised functionality [57].

The national security implications stemming from space systems malware are indeed significant and multifaceted. Military satellites, critical components of defense and intelligence operations, represent attractive targets for malicious actors seeking to compromise national security [58]. Any successful infiltration or compromise of these systems could have severe repercussions, potentially undermining the effectiveness and confidentiality of defense strategies, intelligence gathering, and communication within the armed forces. Moreover, exploiting vulnerabilities in space systems can extend beyond mere disruption and espionage. It could serve as a precursor to cyber warfare between nations. Malicious activities aimed at space infrastructure may not only disrupt services but also escalate geopolitical tensions and conflicts. By targeting these crucial systems, malicious actors could aim to disrupt a nation's ability to respond during conflicts or even cause significant damage to its military capabilities, thereby increasing the potential for conflicts or exacerbating existing ones. The interconnectedness between space systems and national security emphasizes the strategic importance of securing these assets against cyber threats. Safeguarding military satellites and space-based defense and intelligence capabilities is vital to maintaining a nation's security posture and preventing potential vulnerabilities that could be exploited to undermine national defense mechanisms or escalate global tensions. Therefore, ensuring the resilience and security of space systems becomes an integral aspect of preserving national security interests in an increasingly interconnected and technology-dependent world [59].

The long-term consequences resulting from persistent cyber threats against space infrastructure extend beyond immediate disruptions, profoundly impacting trust, cooperation, and the future development of space-based technologies [60]. The continuous presence of cyber threats targeting space systems has the potential to erode public trust and confidence in the reliability and security of these technologies. Such erosion could deter widespread adoption and slow down the pace of future advancements in the field of space exploration and satellite ventures. Moreover, these incidents of space systems malware have the capacity to strain diplomatic relations and hinder collaborative efforts among nations involved in space-related activities. Collaborations and partnerships in space exploration and satellite ventures often require a high degree of trust and cooperation among nations. Persistent cyber threats may sow seeds of suspicion and distrust, potentially leading to strained diplomatic relations and a decrease in collaborative efforts aimed at advancing scientific discoveries or mutually beneficial space projects. The erosion of trust and strained international relations could impede the exchange of knowledge, resources, and expertise necessary for the progress and innovation in space technologies. It may impinge upon the collective efforts of nations to explore new frontiers, conduct scientific research, and utilize space-based assets for societal and economic benefits [54, 61].

Hence, safeguarding space infrastructure against cyber threats becomes not only a matter of technological security but also a critical factor in maintaining trust, fostering international collaboration, and facilitating future advancements in the field of space exploration and satellite technologies. Collaborative efforts to enhance cybersecurity measures are essential to mitigate these long-term consequences and sustain the progress and trust necessary for the continued development of space-based technologies.

11.7 DETECTION AND DEFENCE MECHANISMS, AND CHALLENGES

Recognizing the distinctive operational environment of space systems, including their isolation, the criticality of their mission, and the limited opportunity for physical intervention, the approach to ransomware defense is multifaceted.

Pre-Deployment Phase: Secure by Design [36, 62]:

- **Incorporating Ransomware-Resilient Features:** From the outset, space systems should integrate ransomware-resilient architectures. This includes the use of hardware and software that can withstand encryption attempts and allow for rapid recovery. Techniques like immutable backups, which cannot be altered or deleted by ransomware, are crucial.
- **Advanced Encryption and Authentication Protocols:** Emphasize the implementation of cutting-edge encryption techniques that are quantum-resistant, foreseeing the potential future threat landscape. Enhanced authentication protocols are essential to prevent unauthorized access, a common vector for ransomware attacks.
- **Supply Chain Risk Management:** Implement strict security protocols and continuous monitoring for all suppliers and third-party components integrated into space systems. This includes conducting regular security assessments and requiring adherence to stringent cybersecurity standards.

Operational Phase: Detection and Response [63, 64]

- **Global Threat Intelligence Sharing**: Establish and participate in global cybersecurity alliances specific to the space sector, facilitating real-time sharing of threat intelligence. This includes details about new malware variants, threat actor tactics, and vulnerability advisories, enabling proactive defense postures.

- **Behavioral Analytics for Anomaly Detection:** Utilize advanced machine learning algorithms to monitor system behavior for anomalies that could indicate a ransomware attack, such as unusual encryption activity or significant changes in data access patterns.
- **Segmentation and Isolation:** Strategically design space systems to compartmentalize operations. If one segment is compromised by ransomware, this containment strategy prevents the spread, protecting critical functionalities from being encrypted.
- **Rapid Response and Recovery Protocols**: Develop and simulate rapid response strategies for ransomware incidents. These protocols should include steps for isolating affected systems, eradicating the ransomware, and restoring operations from backups without succumbing to ransom demands.

Continuous Vigilance and Updates [35, 65, 66]:

- **Automated Patch Management:** Implement systems for the automated deployment of security patches, designed to work within the limited bandwidth and unique operational constraints of space systems, ensuring timely updates against vulnerabilities exploited by ransomware.
- **Real-Time Monitoring and Incident Response:** Maintain constant vigilance through real-time monitoring of all satellite systems. Equip operations teams with the tools and protocols necessary to quickly identify and respond to ransomware incidents, minimizing operational disruption.
- **Automated Malware Removal and System Recovery:** Develop automated systems capable of isolating infected components, eradicating malware, and restoring systems to a secure state without significant human intervention. This is crucial for space systems where immediate physical access for remediation is not feasible.

Regulatory Compliance and International Cooperation [30, 67]:

- **Adherence to International Cybersecurity Standards:** Ensure that all space systems comply with relevant international cybersecurity standards and best practices. Engage in the development of new standards that address the unique challenges of space systems.
- **International Collaboration on Cybersecurity Defense:** Foster international cooperation to enhance collective defense capabilities against cyber threats targeting space systems. This includes joint exercises, shared cybersecurity services, and mutual assistance in incident response.

Challenges and Innovative Solutions [28–30, 67]:

- **Overcoming Technical Constraints:** Address the challenges posed by limited computing resources and the space environment by developing lightweight, efficient security software tailored for space systems. Research and leverage novel technologies that provide robust security without imposing significant computational overhead.
- **Regulatory and Cooperative Frameworks:** Advocate for and participate in the development of international cybersecurity standards specific to space operations, fostering a collaborative approach to ransomware defense. Encourage the establishment of space-focused cyber threat intelligence sharing platforms to enhance collective security postures.
- **Future-Proofing against Emerging Threats:** Invest in research to stay ahead of evolving ransomware techniques, including those potentially leveraging artificial intelligence (AI) and quantum computing. Explore innovative defenses, such as blockchain for data integrity and next-generation encryption algorithms resilient against future decryption methods.

11.8 FUTURE THREAT LANDSCAPE AND RECOMMENDATIONS

As we look toward the future of spaceborne malware and cyber threats, a landscape emerges that is characterized by increasingly sophisticated capabilities and intricate attack strategies. One of the most notable advancements anticipated is the integration of AI into spaceborne malware. This development is expected to bring forth a new generation of threats that are adaptable, able to dynamically evolve, and capable of circumventing traditional cybersecurity countermeasures. The potential application of AI in malware presents a formidable challenge, as it could lead to the creation of self-learning and autonomously evolving threats that are more difficult to predict and counter. Another significant concern is the advent of quantum computing, which poses potential vulnerabilities for the encryption methods currently employed within space systems. Quantum computing's immense processing power could enable the decryption of complex cryptographic protections, making encrypted data and communication channels within space systems vulnerable to interception and exploitation.

The increasing proliferation of Internet of Things (IoT) devices in space missions also presents a new avenue for exploitation. These interconnected devices, if not adequately secured, could be exploited for unauthorized access or become targets for disruptive actions by cyber attackers. The complexity and diversity of IoT devices within space systems add another layer of vulnerability that needs to be addressed proactively. An emerging trend in space cybersecurity is the potential for space-based ransomware attacks. These attacks could target critical mission data or system functionalities, holding them at ransom and potentially causing severe disruptions to ongoing space operations. Additionally, the development of autonomous or self-propagating malware poses significant risks. Such malware, capable of independent propagation across interconnected space networks, could lead to rapid and widespread disruption if not promptly identified and contained. To prepare for and address these anticipated threats, several proactive measures are necessary. Embracing advanced threat modeling techniques and conducting comprehensive risk assessments are crucial steps in proactively identifying vulnerabilities within space systems. Regular security updates and patching are essential in strengthening defenses against evolving threats. Exploring the integration of blockchain technology in space systems could enhance security by ensuring tamper-proof records and fortifying communication channels.

Advancements in anomaly detection systems, particularly those leveraging machine learning and AI algorithms, could play a vital role in swiftly identifying and responding to abnormal activities or potential threats within space networks. These technologies offer the promise of early detection and rapid response, which are critical in the dynamic environment of space operations. Given the global nature of space activities, international cooperation is fundamental in effectively addressing space cybersecurity challenges. Establishing universally accepted cybersecurity standards and protocols specifically tailored for space missions is pivotal for a unified defense strategy. Mutual defense agreements among spacefaring nations, information-sharing initiatives, and joint cybersecurity exercises can foster collective defense strategies and preparedness against potential cyber attacks. Dedicated platforms for sharing threat intelligence and best practices create a collective defense mechanism, enabling a more robust and coordinated response to emerging spaceborne cyber threats. Therefore, the future threat landscape in space cybersecurity is marked by advanced, evolving threats that require equally sophisticated and collaborative defense strategies. By combining technological innovation with international cooperation and proactive preparedness, the space community can effectively safeguard space systems against the evolving spectrum of cyber threats.

The exploration and understanding of malware threats in space have illuminated profound vulnerabilities within our space systems, painting a complex landscape where satellites and interconnected technologies are highly susceptible to sophisticated cyber threats. The historical precedence of malware incidents in space emphasizes the criticality of enhanced cybersecurity measures for safeguarding space missions. To ensure the security and operational integrity of these missions, a robust and comprehensive approach to cybersecurity is paramount.

Key Recommendations:

1. **Advanced Security Integration:** Cybersecurity must be integrated into the space systems from the ground up, by adopting a security-by-design approach. This involves the incorporation of advanced encryption, multi-factor authentication, and intrusion detection systems that are tailored to the unique requirements of space operations.
2. **Stringent Access Controls and Regular Audits:** Implementing strict access controls and conducting regular security audits are vital. These controls should include both physical and digital access limitations, ensuring that only authorized personnel and systems interact with critical space infrastructure. Regular audits help in identifying potential vulnerabilities and addressing them proactively.
3. **Development of Space-Specific Intrusion Detection Systems:** Given the unique operational environment of space systems, developing intrusion detection systems that are specifically designed for space operations is crucial. These systems should be capable of detecting anomalies and potential threats in the high-latency, high-radiation environment of space.
4. **Collaborative Frameworks and Standardization:** Establishing collaborative frameworks involving space agencies, commercial space entities, cybersecurity experts, and international regulatory bodies is essential. These collaborations can lead to the development of standardized security protocols and coordinated responses to threats. Shared databases for threat intelligence and best practices can significantly enhance collective defensive capabilities.
5. **Continual Adaptation to Emerging Threats:** The space cybersecurity landscape is dynamic, with threats continuously evolving. It is essential to adopt an agile approach in cybersecurity measures, continuously updating and adapting to new threats. This includes staying abreast of advancements in AI, quantum computing, and other technologies that could potentially be exploited in cyberattacks.
6. **Integration of Blockchain for Enhanced Security:** Exploring the integration of blockchain technology can offer new ways to secure communications and data transmissions in space. Blockchain's inherent characteristics of decentralization, transparency, and immutability make it a promising tool for enhancing the integrity and security of data in space systems.
7. **Global Cooperation and Regulatory Frameworks:** Cybersecurity in space is a global issue that requires international cooperation. Developing comprehensive regulatory frameworks and international agreements on cybersecurity standards in space is imperative. These frameworks should address aspects like responsible behavior in space, sharing of threat intelligence, and collaborative responses to incidents.
8. **Simulated Cyberattack Drills and Preparedness:** Regularly conducting simulated cyberattack drills can prepare space agencies and companies for potential cybersecurity incidents. These simulations should include various scenarios, ranging from minor breaches to full-scale attacks, to test the resilience and response strategies of space systems.
9. **Research and Development in Space Cybersecurity:** Investing in research and development dedicated to space cybersecurity is crucial. This includes funding initiatives that explore new security technologies, study potential threat vectors in space, and develop innovative solutions to safeguard against malware and other cyber threats.
10. **Public-Private Partnerships:** Encouraging public-private partnerships in space cybersecurity can leverage the strengths of both sectors. The agility and innovation of private companies combined with the regulatory and strategic capabilities of public entities can create a powerful alliance against cyber threats in space.

Hence, addressing malware threats in space requires a comprehensive, multi-layered strategy that encompasses technological innovation, regulatory coherence, international collaboration, and continuous adaptation to the evolving threat landscape. By implementing these recommendations, we can fortify our space systems against current and future cyber threats, ensuring the continued advancement and safety of space exploration and utilization.

11.9 CONCLUSION

The exploration of cybersecurity in space systems has unraveled the intricate challenges of protecting our celestial assets against the pervasive threat of malware. From the marvels of engineering in the space segment to the diverse applications in the user segment, this journey highlights a spectrum of vulnerabilities ripe for exploitation by malicious software. In the space segment, the susceptibility of onboard systems to malware underscores the fragility of these technologies. The ground segment, vital for data processing and commands, faces similar risks of cyber infiltration. The link segment, crucial for space-Earth communication, is vulnerable to malware that could distort and obstruct data flow. Likewise, the user segment, integral to daily operations on Earth, confronts the constant threat of disruption. Historically, the evolution of malware in space systems reflects a shift from peripheral concern to a central focus on cybersecurity. The integration of Commercial Off-the-Shelf components and expanding space supply chains introduce new vulnerabilities. The future landscape anticipates advanced threats, including AI-driven malware and challenges from quantum computing and IoT devices. The response to these threats requires sophisticated defence strategies. Blockchain technology, enhanced anomaly detection systems, and global cooperation are pivotal in this battle against space cyber threats. Continuous adaptation and resilience in cybersecurity strategies are critical for maintaining the integrity and reliability of space missions.

In summary, the realm of space cybersecurity transcends technological challenges, embodying our resilience in the face of evolving cyber threats. As we advance in space exploration, our unwavering commitment to securing these ventures against cyber threats is paramount. This relentless pursuit of security ensures the safe and prosperous continuation of humanity's journey into space, safeguarding our celestial endeavors for the future.

REFERENCES

1. G. Falco, "Cybersecurity principles for space systems," *J. Aerosp. Comput. Inf. Commun.*, vol. 16, no. 2, pp. 61–70, 2019.
2. A. Martin, "Cybersecurity regulations for space activities," *J. Air L. Com.*, vol. 88, no. 1, pp. 1–26, 2023. doi: 10.1080/14777622.2023.2195101.
3. G. Falco, "The vacuum of space cyber security," in *2018 AIAA SPACE and Astronautics Forum and Exposition*, 2018.
4. C. Van Camp and W. Peeters, "A world without satellite data as a result of a global cyber-attack," *Space Pol.*, vol. 59, no. 101458, p. 101458, 2022.
5. J. J. Plotnek and J. Slay, "Space systems security: A definition and knowledge domain for the contemporary context," *J. Inf. Warf.*, vol. 21, no. 3, pp. 103–119, Summer 2022.
6. T. Ellis, B. Hitaj, U. Lindqvist, D. Shands, L. Tinnel, and B. DeBruhl, "Critical infrastructure security goes to space: Leveraging lessons learned on the ground," 2023. doi: 10.48550/arXiv.2309.15232.
7. K. Thangavel, J. J. Plotnek, A. Gardi, and R. Sabatini, "Understanding and investigating adversary threats and countermeasures in the context of space cybersecurity," in *Proceedings of the 41st Digital Avionics Systems Conference (DASC)*, 2022. doi: 10.1109/DASC55683.2022.9925759.
8. S. Zatti, "Space and cyber threats," in *Handbook of Space Security*. Cham: Springer International Publishing, 2020, pp. 245–263.
9. O. Kodheli et al., "Satellite communications in the new space era: A survey and future challenges," *IEEE Commun. Surv. Tutor.*, vol. 23, no. 1, pp. 70–109, 2021.
10. Z. Jia, M. Sheng, J. Li, and Z. Han, "Toward data collection and transmission in 6G space–air–ground integrated networks: Cooperative HAP and LEO satellite schemes," *IEEE Internet Things J.*, vol. 9, no. 13, pp. 10516–10528, 2022.

11. G. Maral, M. Bousquet, and Z. Sun, *Satellite communications systems: Systems, techniques and technology*, 6th ed. Nashville, TN: John Wiley & Sons, 2020.
12. Y. Su, Y. Liu, Y. Zhou, J. Yuan, H. Cao, and J. Shi, "Broadband LEO satellite communications: Architectures and key technologies," *IEEE Wirel. Commun.*, vol. 26, no. 2, pp. 55–61, 2019.
13. J. Kua, S. W. Loke, C. Arora, N. Fernando, and C. Ranaweera, "Internet of Things in space: A review of opportunities and challenges from satellite-aided computing to digitally-enhanced space living," *Sensors (Basel)*, vol. 21, no. 23, p. 8117, 2021.
14. J. Guyot, A. Rao, and S. Rouillon, "Oligopoly competition between satellite constellations will reduce economic welfare from orbit use," *Proc. Natl. Acad. Sci. U. S. A.*, vol. 120, no. 43, 2023.
15. U. Uhongora, R. Mulinde, Y. W. Law, and J. Slay, "Deep-learning-based intrusion detection for software-defined networking space systems," *Proc. Eur. Conf. Inf. Warf. Secur.*, vol. 22, no. 1, pp. 639–647, 2023.
16. M. Guerster, J. Dingley, E. Crawley, and B. Cameron, "Contract structures for SatCom: How will competition from low earth orbit mega constellations change how communications services are purchased?" *New Space*, vol. 11, no. 3, pp. 168–181, 2023.
17. K. Kauristie et al., "Space weather services for civil aviation – challenges and solutions," *Remote Sens. (Basel)*, vol. 13, no. 18, p. 3685, 2021.
18. V. Demyanov and J. Becedas, Eds., *Satellites missions and technologies for geosciences*. London: IntechOpen, 2020.
19. A. C. Fassoni-Andrade et al., "Amazon hydrology from space: Scientific advances and future challenges," *Rev. Geophys.*, vol. 59, no. 4, 2021.
20. L. Zhao, C. Wang, K. Zhao, D. Tarchi, S. Wan, and N. Kumar, "INTERLINK: A digital twin-assisted storage strategy for satellite-terrestrial networks," *IEEE Trans. Aerosp. Electron. Syst.*, vol. 58, no. 5, pp. 3746–3759, 2022.
21. G. Pan, H. Zhang, R. Zhang, S. Wang, J. An, and M.-S. Alouini, "Space simultaneous information and power transfer: An enhanced technology for miniaturized satellite systems," *IEEE Wirel. Commun.*, vol. 30, no. 2, pp. 122–129, 2023.
22. F. Aguirre, "Miniaturized and reconfigurable RF electronics architecture for SmallSat applications," in *2020 IEEE Aerospace Conference*, 2020.
23. J. Budroweit and H. Patscheider, "Risk assessment for the use of COTS devices in space systems under consideration of radiation effects," *Electronics (Basel)*, vol. 10, no. 9, p. 1008, 2021.
24. A. Olejnik, Ł. Kiszkowiak, P. Zalewski, and A. Dziubiński, "Low-cost satellite launch system – aerodynamic feasibility study," *Aerospace*, vol. 9, no. 6, p. 284, 2022.
25. G. Bertolucci, F. Barato, E. Toson, and D. Pavarin, "Impact of propulsion system characteristics on the potential for cost reduction of earth observation missions at very low altitudes," *Acta Astronaut.*, vol. 176, pp. 173–191, 2020.
26. J. D. Liddle, A. P. Holt, S. J. Jason, K. A. O'Donnell, and E. J. Stevens, "Space science with CubeSats and nanosatellites," *Nat. Astron.*, vol. 4, no. 11, pp. 1026–1030, 2020.
27. A. Diro, S. Kaisar, A. V. Vasilakos, A. Anwar, A. Nasirian, and G. Olani, "Anomaly detection for space information networks: A survey of challenges, techniques, and future directions," *Comput. Secur.*, vol. 139, no. 103705, p. 103705, 2024.
28. J. Pavur and I. Martinovic, "Building a launchpad for satellite cyber-security research: lessons from 60 years of spaceflight," *J. Cybersecur.*, vol. 8, no. 1, 2022.
29. G. Falco, "When satellites attack: Satellite-to-satellite cyber attack, defense and resilience," in *ASCEND 2020*, 2020.
30. J. Pavur and I. Martinovic, "The cyber-ASAT: On the impact of cyber weapons in outer space," in *2019 11th International Conference on Cyber Conflict (CyCon)*, 2019.
31. V. Varadharajan and N. Suri, "Security challenges when space merges with cyberspace," *Space Pol.*, no. 101600, p. 101600, 2023.
32. G. Falco, R. Thummala, and A. Kubadia, "WannaFly: An approach to satellite ransomware," in *2023 IEEE 9th International Conference on Space Mission Challenges for Information Technology (SMC-IT)*, 2023.
33. J. Hamilton, "Cybersecurity in space: New threats for new frontiers," *ITNOW*, vol. 62, no. 2, pp. 42–43, Jun. 2020. doi: 10.1093/itnow/bwaa057.
34. G. Falco and N. Boschetti, "A security risk taxonomy for commercial space missions," in *ASCEND 2021*, 2021.
35. N. Koroniotis, N. Moustafa, and J. Slay, "A new intelligent satellite deep learning network forensic framework for smart satellite networks," *Comput. Electr. Eng.*, vol. 99, no. 107745, p. 107745, 2022.
36. M. Zhuo, L. Liu, S. Zhou, and Z. Tian, "Survey on security issues of routing and anomaly detection for space information networks," *Sci. Rep.*, vol. 11, no. 1, pp. 1–18, 2021.

37. M. Al-Hawawreh, N. Moustafa, and J. Slay, "A threat intelligence framework for protecting smart satellite-based healthcare networks," *Neural Comput. Appl.*, vol. 36, no. 1, pp. 15–35, 2024.
38. B. Nussbaum and G. Berg, "Cybersecurity implications of commercial off the shelf (COTS) equipment in space infrastructure," in *Space Infrastructures: From Risk to Resilience Governance*. IOS Press, 2020, pp. 91–99.
39. K. Murbach, T. Morris, F. Wiersig, and J. Golden, "Small satellite system modeling for vulnerability analysis," in *2023 IEEE International Conference on Cyber Security and Resilience (CSR)*, 2023.
40. S. E. O'Connor, "Managing the cyber-related risks to space activities," in *Risk Management in Outer Space Activities*. Singapore: Springer Nature Singapore, 2022, pp. 151–175.
41. J. Finke, R. Thummala, R. Elbasheer, P. Hansen, W. Henry, D. Mamula, A. M. Noor, T. York, K. Zheng, and G. Falco, "Satellite cybersecurity testbed to improve commercial space security," in *Proceedings of the AIAA Scitech 2023 Forum*, 2023. doi: 10.2514/6.2023-4768.
42. A. Costin, S. Khandker, H. Turtiainen, and T. Hämäläinen, "Hacking space: A study of cybersecurity threats to COSPAS-SARSAT space-/satellite-based systems," 2023. doi: 10.48550/arXiv.2302.08361.
43. C. Fleming, M. Reith, and W. Henry, "Space cyber supply chain framework," in *Proceeding of the 18th International Conference on Cyber Warfare and Security*, 2023. doi: 10.34190/iccws.18.1.1062.
44. B. Lin, W. Henry, and R. Dill, "Defending small satellites from malicious cybersecurity threats," in *Proceedings of the 17th International Conference on Cyber Warfare and Security*, 2022. doi: 10.34190/iccws.17.1.60.
45. R. Peled, E. Aizikovich, E. Habler, Y. Elovici, and A. Shabtai, "SATACK: A satellite cybersecurity taxonomy and attack classification," 2023. doi: 10.48550/arXiv.2312.01330.
46. A. K. Alharam et al., "Revised onboard cybersecurity architecture for small satellites," in *Proceeding of the 4th International Conference on Computing and Information Technology (ICCIT-2022)*, 2022. doi: 10.1109/3ICT56508.2022.9990704.
47. L. Vessels, K. Heffner, and D. P. Johnson, "Cybersecurity risk assessment for space systems," in *Proceedings of the 2019 Space Computing Conference*, 2019, pp. 1–8. doi: 10.1109/SpaceComp.2019.00006.
48. I. Ashraf, M. Narra, M. Umer, R. Majeed, S. Sadiq, F. Javaid, and N. Rasool, "RFMLP: A novel deep learning-based framework for cybersecurity threat detection," *Electronics*, vol. 11, no. 4, p. 667, Feb. 2022. doi: 10.3390/electronics11040667.
49. Z. Abuabed, A. Alsadeh, and A. Taweel, "STRIDE threat model-based framework for assessing the vulnerabilities of modern vehicles," *Comput. Secur.*, vol. 133, no. 103391, p. 103391, 2023.
50. B. Cyr, Y. Long, T. Sugawara, and K. Fu, "Position paper: Space system threat models must account for satellite sensor spoofing," in *Proceedings 2023 Workshop on Security of Space and Satellite Systems*, 2023.
51. H. Wen, P. Huang, A. John, and J. Fagan, "Countermeasures for GPS signal spoofing," in *Proceedings of the 18th International Technical Meeting of the Satellite Division of The Institute of Navigation (ION GNSS 2005)*, Long Beach, CA, 2005, pp. 1285–1290.
52. J. Pavur and I. Martinovic, "Threat models for future space missions: A survey of attacks and defenses," *J. Cybersecur.*, vol. 8, no. 1, 2022. doi: 10.1093/cybsec/tyac008.
53. H. Caudill, "Big risks in small satellites: The need for secure infrastructure as a service," in *ASCEND 2020*, 2020.
54. A. Geetha, V. Keerthika, and D. M. Deepak Raj, "Cybersecurity kill chain in outer space and cyberspace security," in *Cyber Space and Outer Space Security*, River Publishers, 2024, pp. 81-95.
55. J. Smailes, S. Köhler, S. Birnbach, M. Strohmeier, and I. Martinovic, "Watch this space: Securing satellite communication through resilient transmitter fingerprinting," in *Proceedings of the 2023 ACM SIGSAC Conference on Computer and Communications Security*, 2023. doi: 10.1145/3576915.3623135.
56. P. Hansen, W. C. Henry, M. G. Reith, R. Thummala, and G. Falco, "Guarding the galaxy: Satellite ransomware and countermeasures," in *2024 IEEE Aerospace Conference*, 2024, pp. 1–6.
57. N. Tieby, J. Khoury, and E. Bou-Harb, "Characterizing and analyzing LEO satellite cyber landscape: A Starlink case study," in *ICC 2024 – IEEE International Conference on Communications*, 2024, pp. 1352–1357.
58. S. Salim, N. Moustafa, and M. Reisslein, "Cybersecurity of satellite communications systems: A comprehensive survey of the space, ground, and links segments," in *IEEE Communications Surveys & Tutorials*, 2024.
59. R. Kesavamoorthy and P. Karthikeyan, "Cyberspace and outer space security and mitigation strategies," in *Cyber Space and Outer Space Security*, River Publishers, 2024, pp. 1–15.
60. B. Bace, Y. Gökce, and U. Tatar, "Law in orbit: International legal perspectives on cyberattacks targeting space systems," *Telecom. Policy*, vol. 48, no. 4, p. 102739, 2024.

61. R. Mahalakshmi and M. Gautam, "Navigating the boundless: Security in cyberspace and outer space," in *Cyber Space and Outer Space Security*, River Publishers, 2024, pp. 239-260.
62. Y. Shin et al., "ITAD: Integrative tensor-based anomaly detection system for reducing false positives of satellite systems," in *Proceedings of the 29th ACM International Conference on Information & Knowledge Management*, 2020.
63. C.-C. Tsai, C.-Y. Sun, and S.-H. Yang, "Note on 'RAKS: Robust authentication and key agreement scheme for satellite infrastructure'," in *2023 International Conference on Consumer Electronics – Taiwan (ICCE-Taiwan)*, 2023.
64. M. H. Abdulmonem, A. K. Ismail, and H. Mostafa, "Design and implementation of authenticated encryption co-processors for satellite hardware security," in *2021 International Conference on Microelectronics (ICM)*, 2021.
65. C. OMeara, L. Schlag, L. Faltenbacher, and M. Wickler, "ATHMoS: Automated telemetry health monitoring system at GSOC using outlier detection and supervised machine learning," in *SpaceOps 2016 Conference*, 2016.
66. K. Lang, B. Xu, M. Simon, and B. Seibert, "Automated satellite fault detection using machine learning," in *ASCEND 2022*, 2022.
67. R. Popova, "Space technology and cybersecurity: Challenges and technical approaches for the regulation of large constellations," in *Space Law in a Networked World*. Brill I Nijhoff, 2023, pp. 102–128.

AUTHOR BIOGRAPHY

Dr Abebe Diro is a lecturer at RMIT University's School of Accounting, Information Systems and Supply Chain. He is a cyber security scientist with interests in machine learning-based cyber security, and cryptography. He has made outstanding contributions to these fields with publications in high-quality journals. The research outputs include pioneering work on distributed machine learning for intrusion detection in the Internet of Things. Further, Dr Diro has proven his ability to establish relevant research collaborations with industry through various projects, which is supported by RMIT University's emphasis on aligning research with areas of national interest. He has also established collaborations with academics in Europe, Australia, South Korea, Indonesia, and Turkey, where he has co-published journal articles with researchers. His high-quality research in cyber security and his extensive research networks in cyber security and cryptography mark him as a leading researcher at RMIT.

Index

Kolibri 360 GmbH
Ferdinand-Jühlke-Straße 7
99095 Erfurt, Deutschland
produktsicherheit@kolibri360.de